Complementary Themes for Painting Techniques

THE COMPLETE COURSE ON PAINTING AND DRAWING

Complementary Themes for Painting Techniques

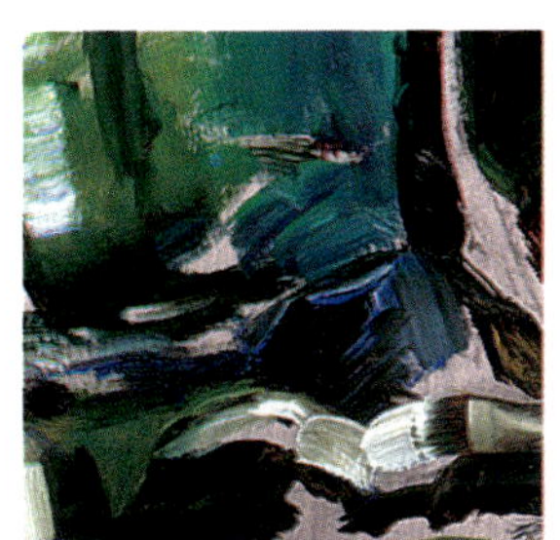

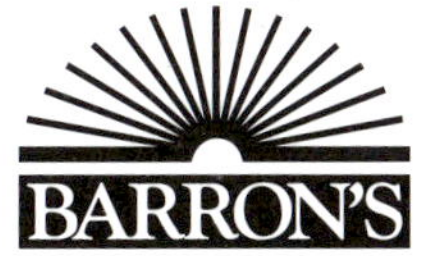

Original title of the book in Spanish is "Técnica y práctica en Dibujo y Pintura: Temas Complementarios de Técnicas de Pintura"

Published by Parramón Ediciones, S.A., Barcelona, Spain.

Author: Parramón Ediciones Editorial Team
Illustrators: Parramón Ediciones Editorial Team

All inquiries should be addressed to:
Barron's Educational Series, Inc.
250 Wireless Boulevard
Hauppauge, NY 11788

Library of Congress Catalog Card No. 97-72658

International Standard Book No. 0-7641-0266-4

Printed in Spain
9 8 7 6 5 4 3 2 1

Contents

Introduction

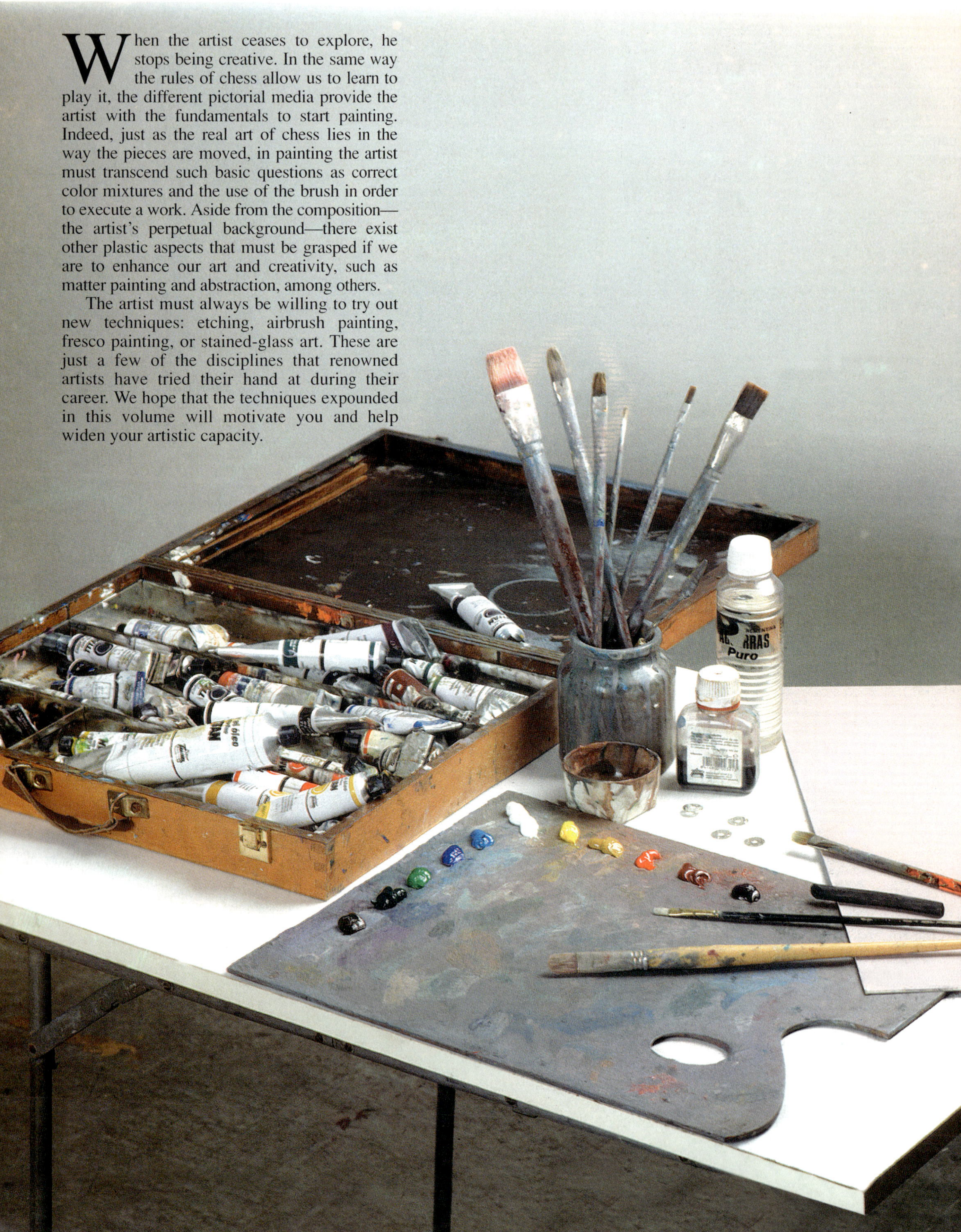

When the artist ceases to explore, he stops being creative. In the same way the rules of chess allow us to learn to play it, the different pictorial media provide the artist with the fundamentals to start painting. Indeed, just as the real art of chess lies in the way the pieces are moved, in painting the artist must transcend such basic questions as correct color mixtures and the use of the brush in order to execute a work. Aside from the composition—the artist's perpetual background—there exist other plastic aspects that must be grasped if we are to enhance our art and creativity, such as matter painting and abstraction, among others.

The artist must always be willing to try out new techniques: etching, airbrush painting, fresco painting, or stained-glass art. These are just a few of the disciplines that renowned artists have tried their hand at during their career. We hope that the techniques expounded in this volume will motivate you and help widen your artistic capacity.

Composition and the human figure

When composing a work in which the human figure is the center of attention, our first priority is to create a simple design scheme showing the model within a determined space. To do this, the artist must visually interpret the forms that compose the figure, without going into details.

The models' clothes and surroundings also can be reflected in this initial design. One important decision when composing a figure is whether or not to include the entire body in the portrait. Diagonal design schemes used in half-length portraits are very common; by choosing an appropriate point of view, you can perfectly adapt this type of scheme to the model's pose. In the examples shown on this page, the diagonal scheme repeatedly appears in works done in widely diverse styles.

Diagonal and triangular schemes are only two of the many compositional possibilities available to painters. It is important that the composition fits your chosen model, and that your design scheme contributes to the clarity of the painting as a whole, as well as of the forms within it.

This section will be devoted to the importance of creating a solid design scheme and its impact on the final product—the painting itself.

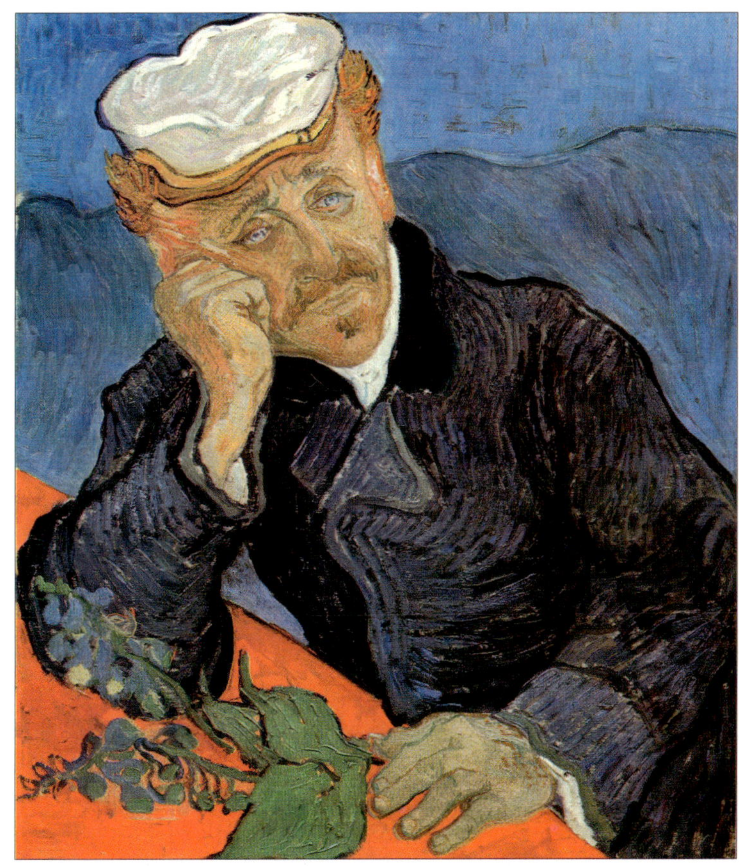

Vincent van Gogh, Portrait of Doctor Gachet. *By placing the table diagonally, the artist enhanced the diagonal design scheme of this portrait.*

Edouard Manet, The Fife Player. *The simplicity of this vertically designed piece is misleading; an intense analysis of forms and their articulation went into the creation and placement of the central figure.*

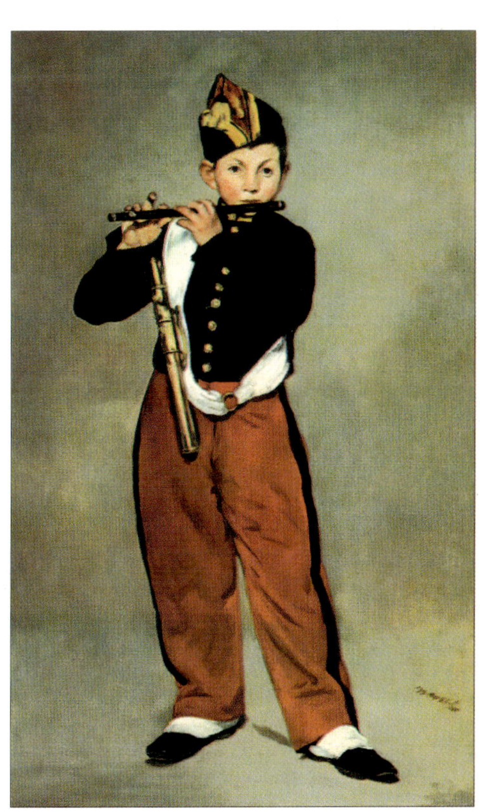

Paul Gauguin, Vairumati. *The reclining body and vertical arm create a clear compositional triangle that controls and conditions the whole painting. The artist has shifted it to one side to break the symmetry.*

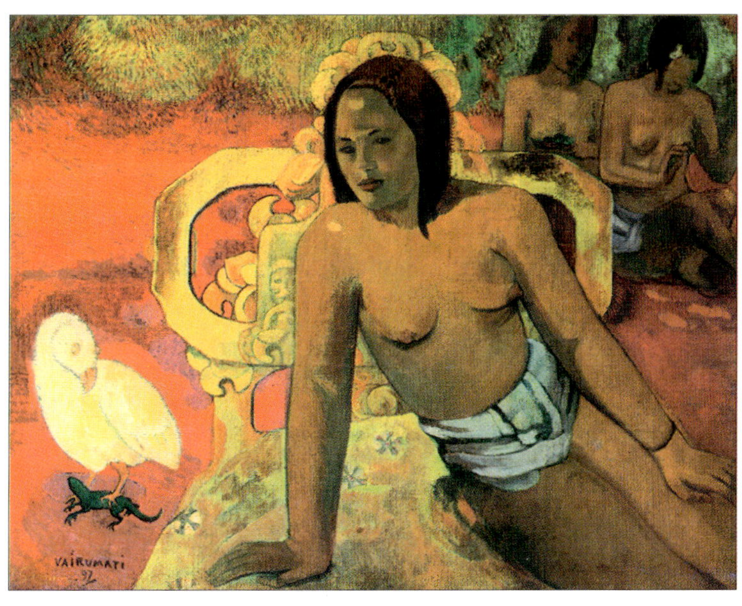

Composition according to the model's age and sex

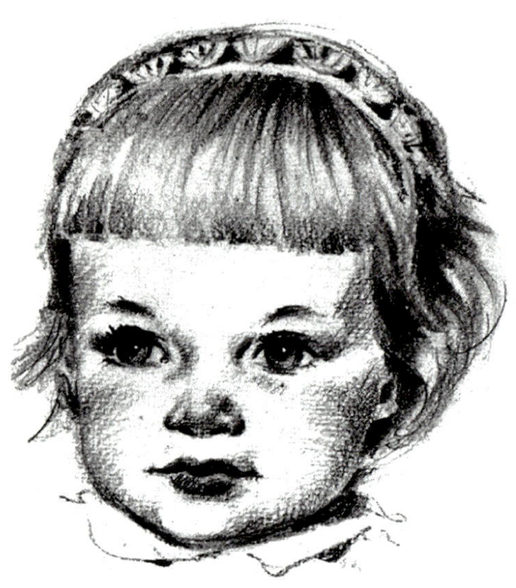

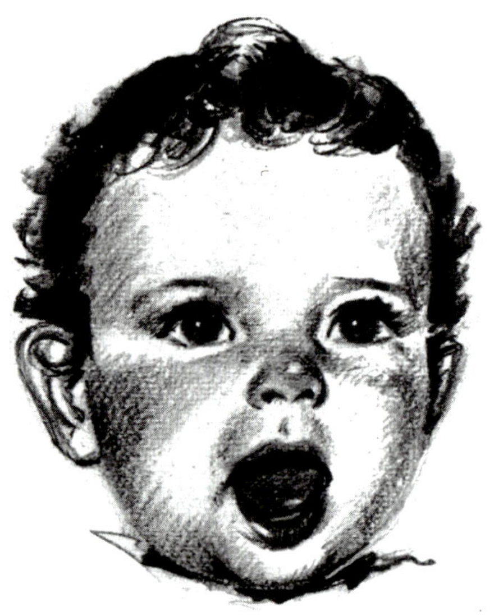

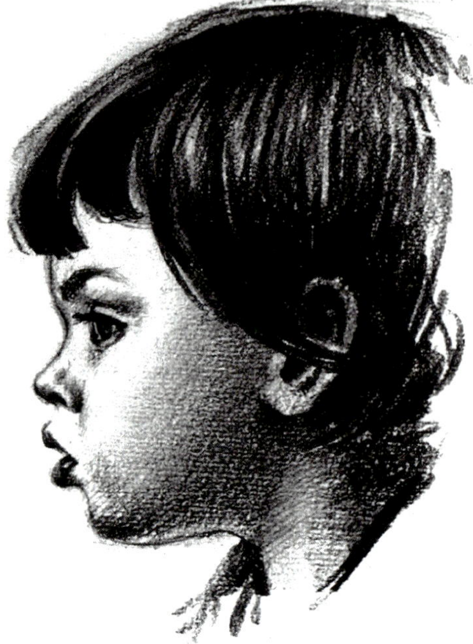

The head of a child under five has several unique characteristics, apart from each child's specific facial features. Keep this in mind when you begin a child's portrait.

There are multiple factors that contribute to a portrait's composition. One of the most important is to adapt your work to the age, sex, and personality of the model. To do this you must observe the model and look for the poses, the gestures, and attitudes that best define his or her personality.

Portraits of children

When doing portraits of children, take note of how soft their faces are. This requires you to use soft lighting without exaggerated contrasts. Also, you must pay close attention to proportions, especially with small children; their heads and eyes are proportionally larger than the rest of their bodies. Conversely, their noses are smaller and often turned up. Older children resemble adults, but their eyes are still wider apart, their chins are smaller, and their faces are still soft and undefined. Painting children is hard work, not only because they cannot keep still for very long but also because they lack prominent facial features. The painter must paint carefully, delicately unveiling the subtle individual qualities of each child.

Portraits of women

When painting a woman's portrait, it is important to bear in mind that, generally, her features will be less bold than those of a man. For instance, her chin may be smaller and curved. Her mouth and nose also may be smaller and must not be exaggerated. Make-up and hairstyles are often important factors in female portraits.

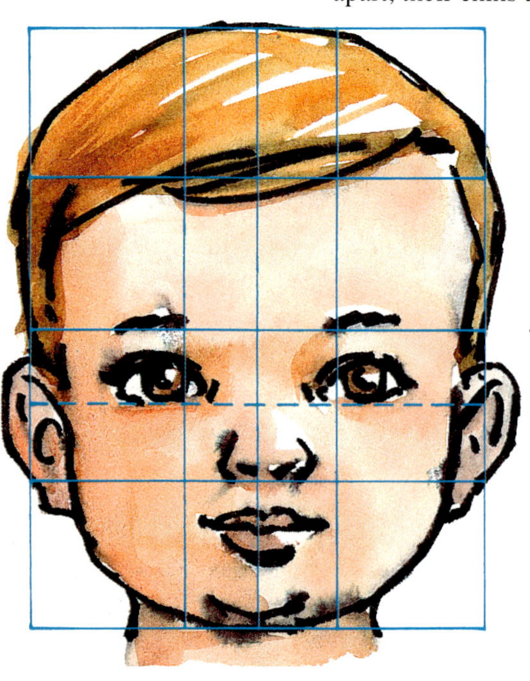

Generally, a child's countenance is characterized by a clear, high forehead, large eyes and ears, and, often, a turned-up nose. Other features include puffy cheeks, and a slightly underdeveloped jaw. The illustrations to the left and right show the proportions and characteristics of this early age better than any words.

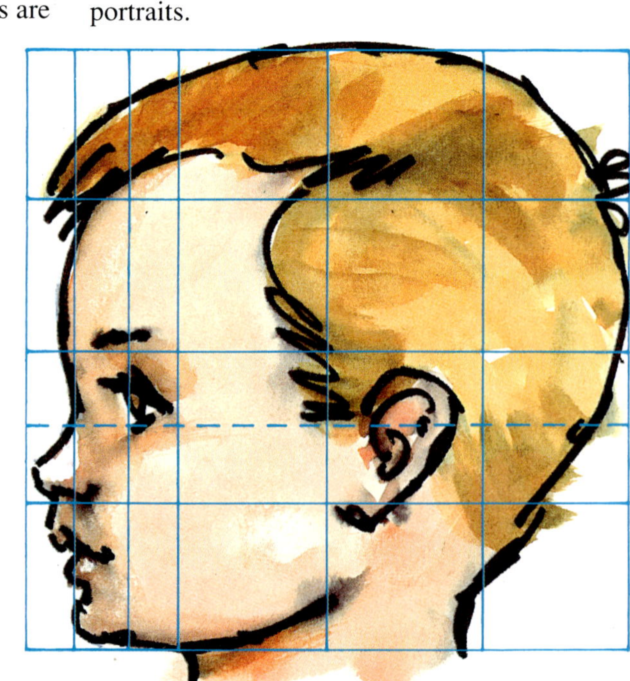

Here are some examples of women's portraits drawn with different media. Obviously, the facial structure is more delicate than that of men, a crucial factor you must always keep in mind.

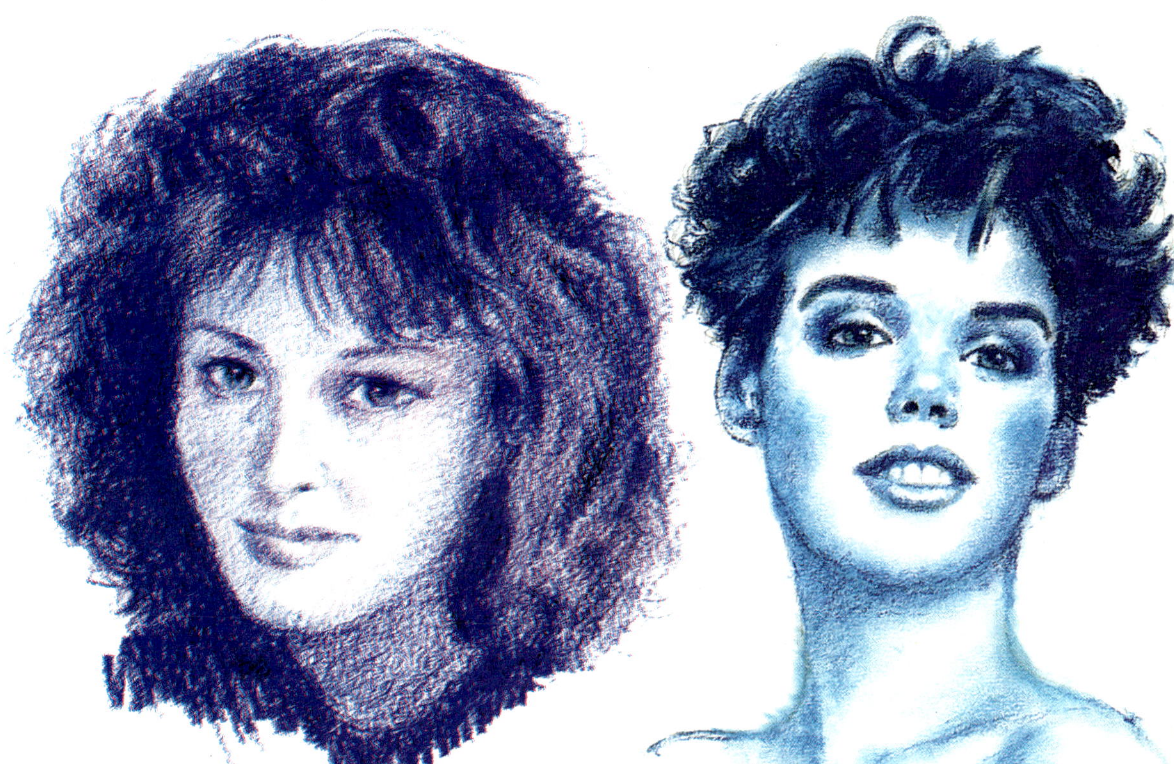

Similarly, shadows should not be exaggerated so as not to deform the face.

Portraits of older people

The features of older people show changes produced by aging. For example, fat disappears and the skin becomes thin and dry, revealing the bone structure. Men may tend to be bald. The forehead, apart from wrinkles, reveals the bones clearly, as do the eye sockets; the eyes appear deeper, exaggerating the surrounding structures. Generally, the nose and cheekbones have more volume; the lack of fat results in an exaggeration of the features. Other common characteristics are bags under the eyes, jowls, and double chins. Painting the portrait of an older person is a beautiful artistic exercise because, instead of painting physical beauty, you are capturing the accumulated life of a human being.

In terms of features and character, the head of an older person offers more artistic possibilities than any other model and fewer difficulties, because they have more points of reference.

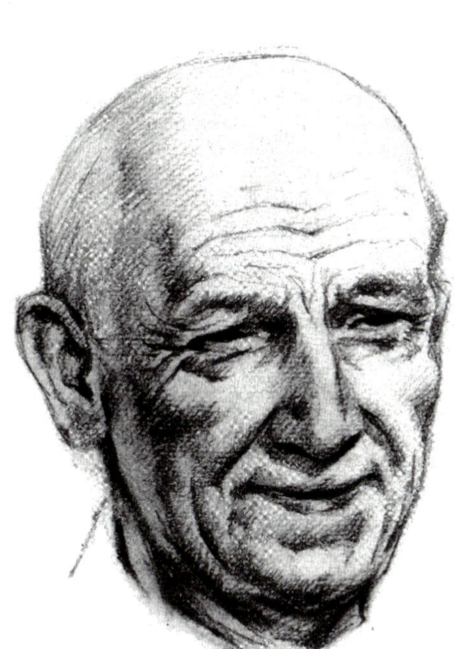

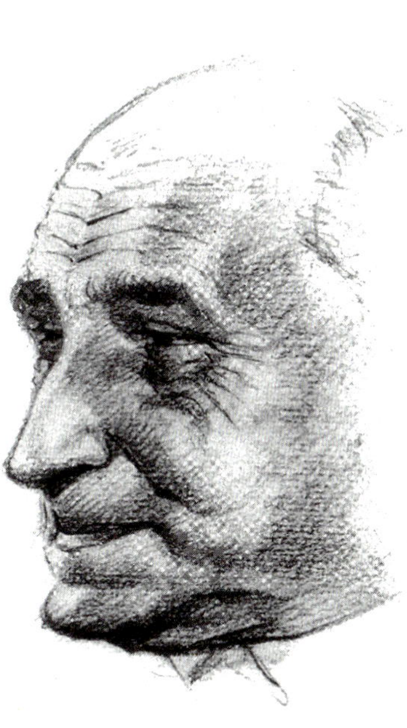

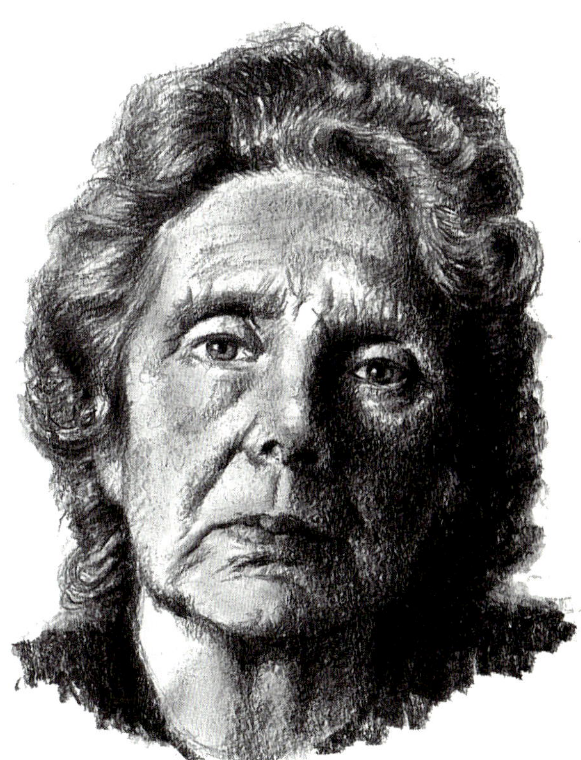

Understanding the model

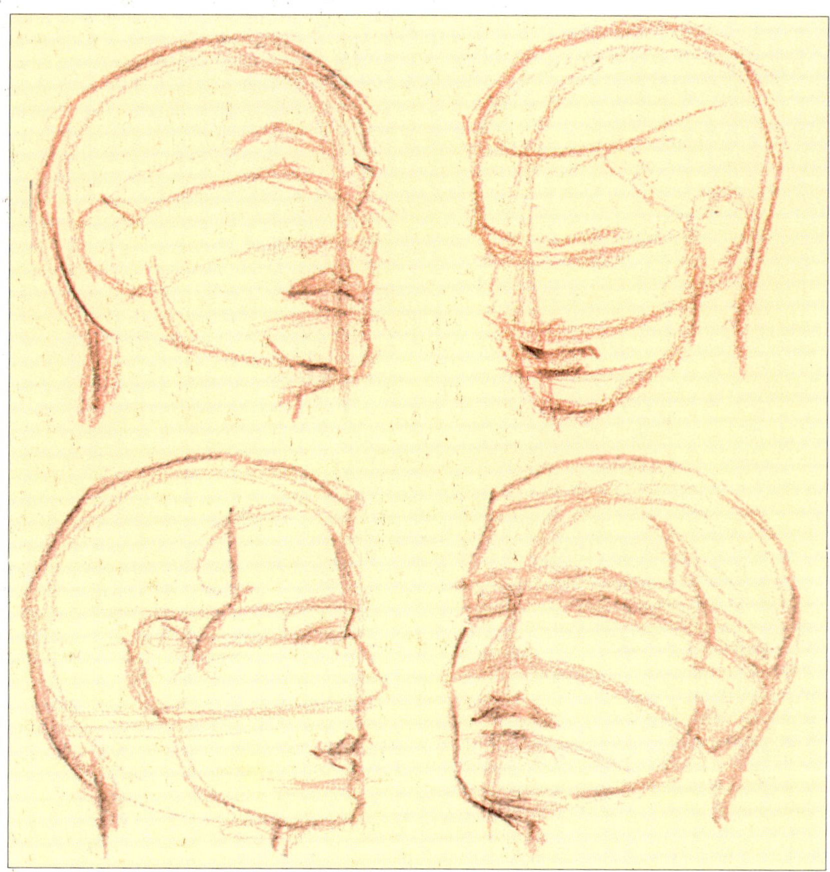

In this section we will study the development of several entirely different portraits—different in style, technique, and results—but all good examples to follow. To begin, you must ask yourself: What do I need to do to create a good portrait? We will show you that although capturing your model's physical appearance is important, there are other elements that deserve more attention. They are what we will call "the inner portrait"—the subject's personality as reflected by multiple physical facets. A sparkle in the eyes, for instance, the skin's texture, the position of the head in relation to the body, or the arch of the eyebrows. Each one of these details tells us a lot about the model. Capturing them will enhance the quality of your portrait.

Before you even begin to sketch, there are several things that you must keep in mind; among the most important is choosing a setting. This will determine your psychological attitude toward the model. Lighting is another important element to bear in mind. Obviously, this will determine many other things, such as the roughness of the features, the length of the face, and of course, the general color scheme of the scene. You must pay close attention to all the factors that may influence the outcome of your work.

Once you've identified the model's most salient characteristics, as explained above, then you will be ready to begin your portrait.

Finally, it is essential to get to know your model before embarking on a definitive picture. For instance, draw as many outlines and sketches of the model as necessary. These preliminary drawings don't require much preparation; they can be done at any time.

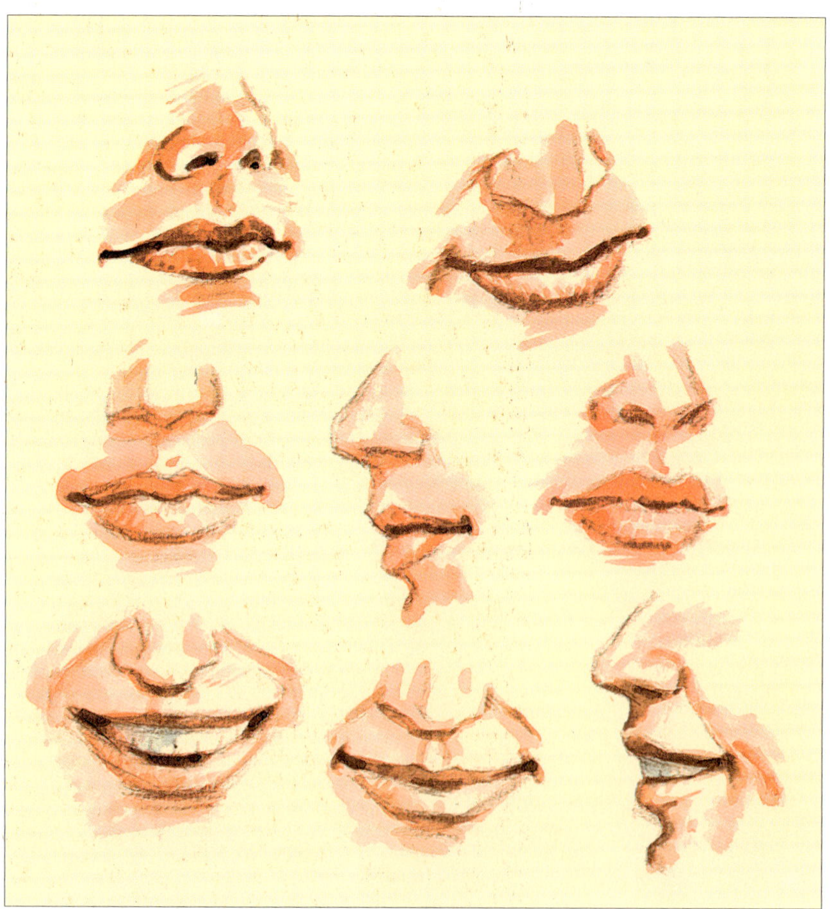

Look at the schematic drawings shown on this page. Observe and remember where the mouth is situated on the skull's sphere, and notice its volume.

When you begin a portrait, you must first draw all of the features or essential geometric forms that will be developed in the drawing later on. A mouth is not a straight line; rather, it is divided into curves and reverse curves. Its size will depend on personal characteristics. How do you approach mouths in distinct positions, male or female, serious or smiling? When drawing, pay attention to the undulating line between the lips (an excellent clue about how to continue) and remember its likely foreshortening.

Before you take the plunge as a portrait painter, consider several technical matters regarding the eyes, nose, and mouth.

First, observe the eyebrows. They are not all the same; they can be thin, bushy, or more or less full, and are almost never symmetrical. They are situated, as are the eyes, on a curved surface; therefore, viewing them in perspective will be indicative of the head's position.

You should concentrate first on the model's gaze. The gaze is probably one of the most important elements of a portrait as the eyes reveal the inner self. After you have practiced this, reflect on the shape of the eyes and the arch of the brows. Pay close attention to the eye sockets, since their shadow will determine not only their depth but the width of the nose.

The tendency to give the same curve to the upper eyelid as the lower is a common mistake made by beginners. In fact, the eyelids are not totally symmetrical. The upper eyelid always has a greater curve than the lower.

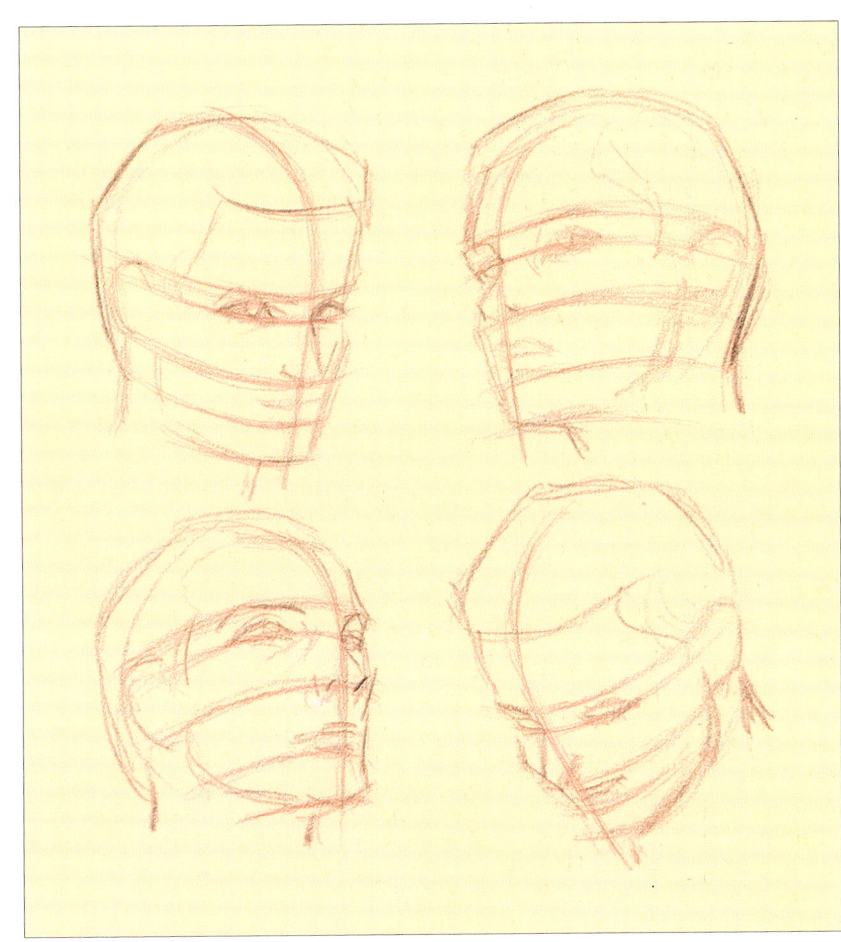

In these schematic drawings, notice the placement of the eyes on the skull, as well as their volume.

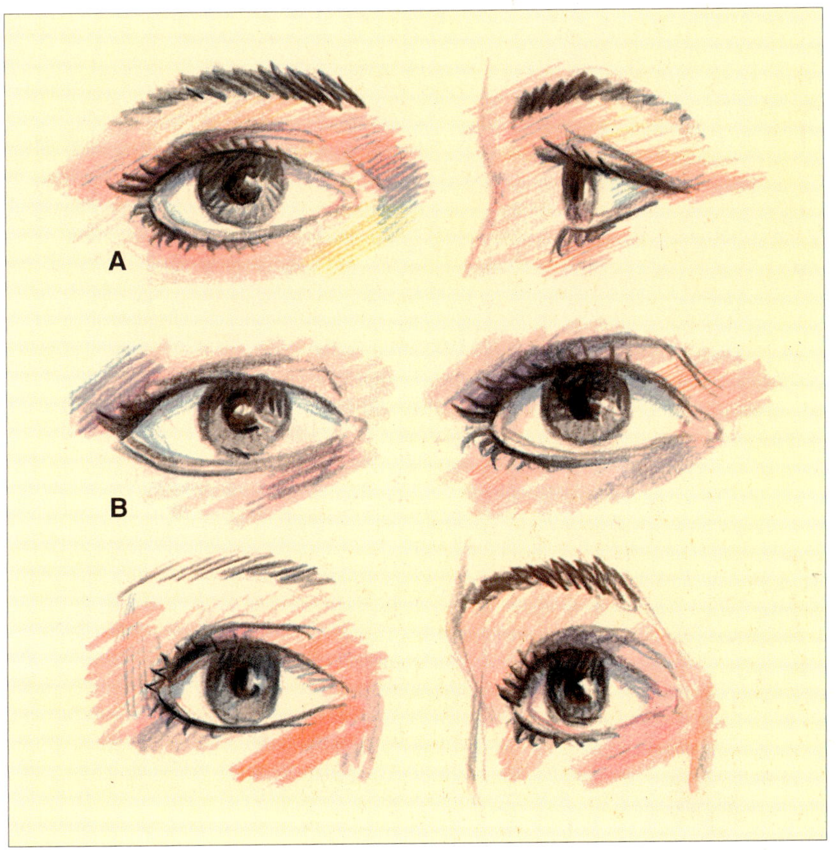

*This is the correct way to draw the eyelashes and eyelids; sometimes, the eyelids may make a crease that hides their shape. Drawing **A** contains a common error: The lower eyelid's curve must be more open than the upper one, as in drawing **B**. Another error in drawing **A**: Since the eyes are placed on a sphere (the skull), when the model is in the three-quarter position, they should never be drawn as symmetrical.*

A fragment of a self-portrait by Rembrandt. Notice how he has managed to capture his own gaze by depicting the position of his eyebrows in relation to his eyes.

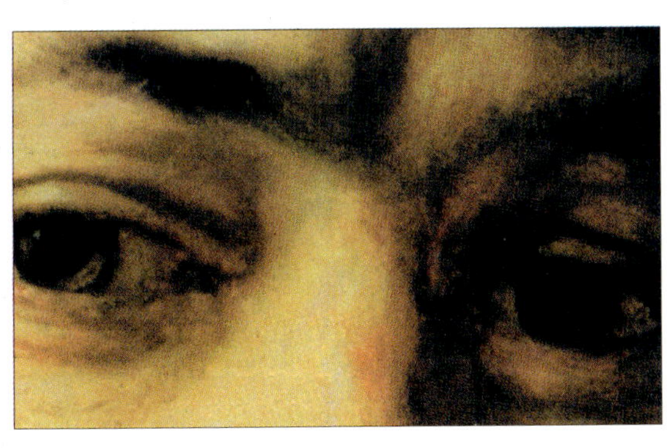

Understanding the model

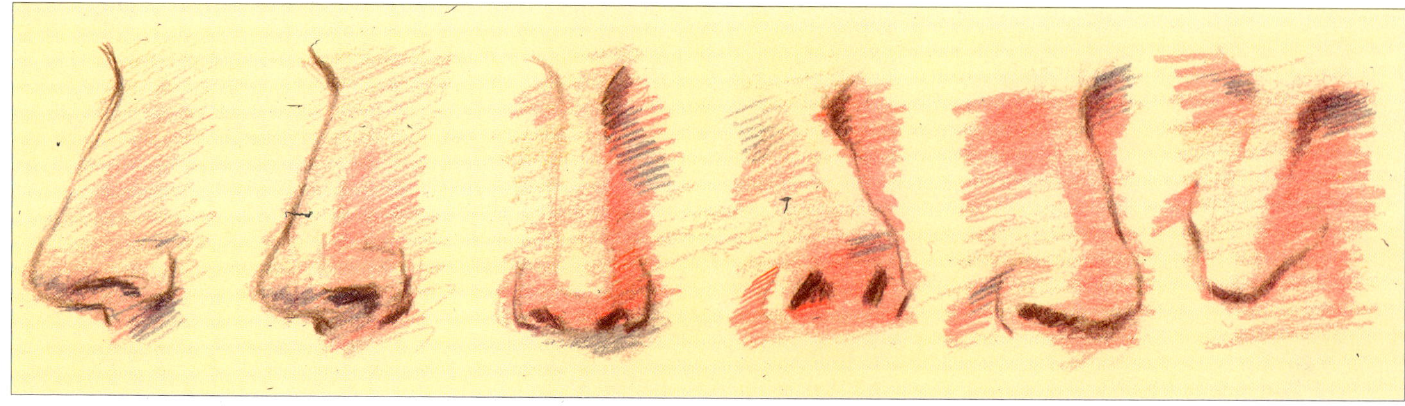

When drawing volume, you will learn that the nose, as seen from above, almost hides the mouth, whereas when seen from below, you can see into the nostrils.

When drawing the nose, forget that it is a nose and even forget it has volume. Look at yourself and do some sketches—a light smudge here, a darker one there. Your nose will practically draw itself!

Like the eyes and the eyebrows, the nose, defines, to a great extent, the character of the face. This feature, like the others, must abide by the laws of perspective. Depending on the position of the head, it may be foreshortened. With the head bowed, the perspective impedes the view of the nostrils. While in a frontal pose, the nostrils may or may not be visible, depending on the type of nose. You must also pay attention to the shape of the nose. Is it thin or thick, straight or curved? First and foremost, however, you must keep in mind the harmony of the features and the need to maintain the right proportions among them.

The lips often appear foreshortened when they are on the curved plane of the face. This requires great care on your part, since mentally, you have to place the mouth in the skull. Shape and fullness are what make lips individual features. You will notice that the lower lip is larger than the upper lip and that the corners of the mouth tend to bend upward, in a more or less pronounced manner.

As you will see, each facial feature must be approached by the painter in a unique way; however, they all have to be done in relation to each other according to the rules of perspective. You will also see that each person has his or her own set of unique facial characteristics. That includes you; look carefully in the mirror and you will learn more than you think.

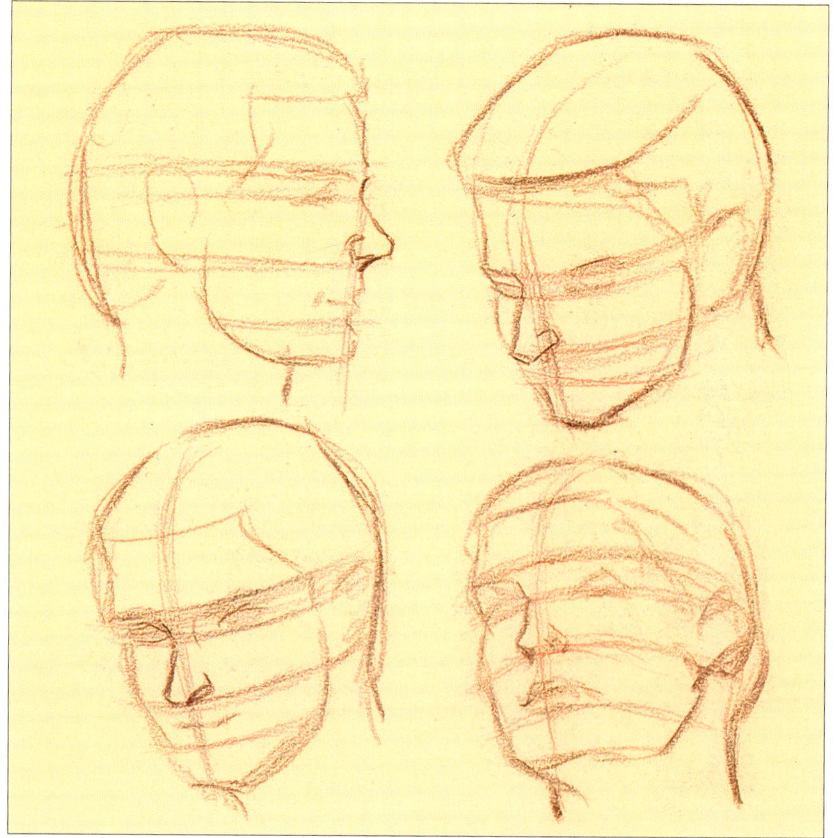

In this fragment of a self-portrait by Meléndez you can see how the upper part differs from the lower and how there is a shadow in the corners of the mouth.

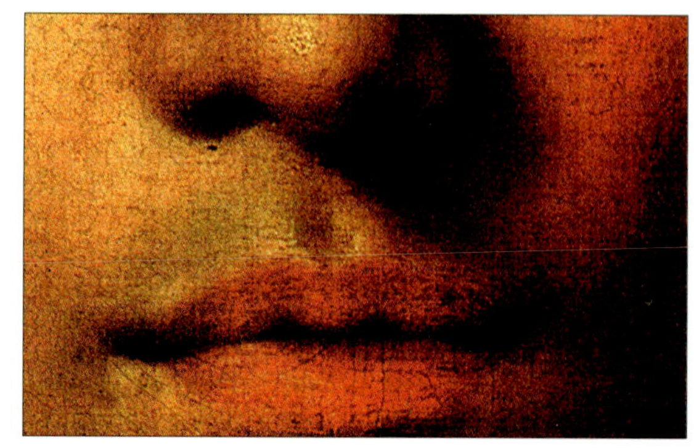

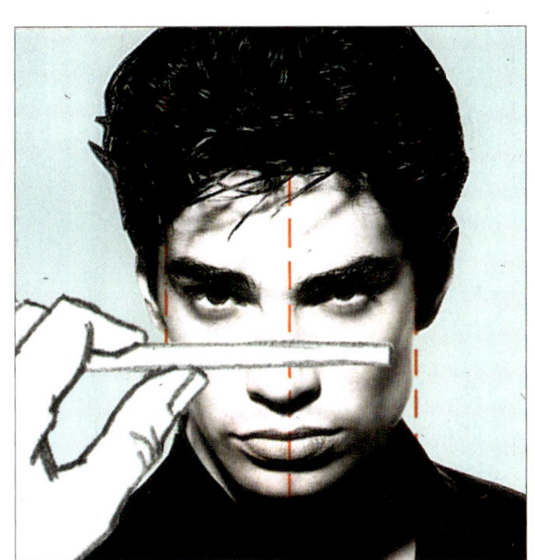

"Mathematic" drawing starts when we compare the distance between features using a pencil or charcoal stick.

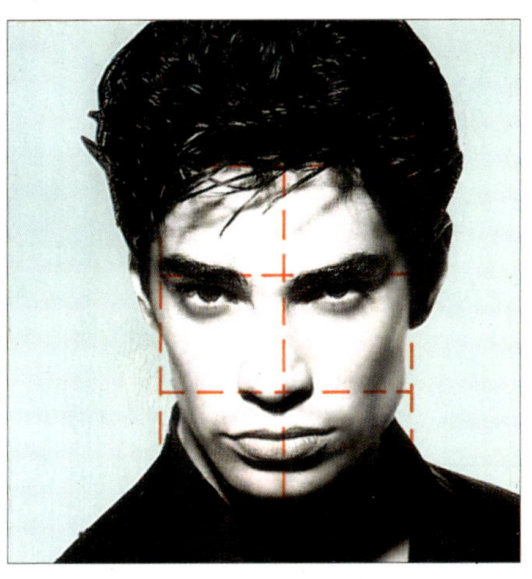

The most common comparative measurements are the distance between the eyebrows and the nose, the relation between the height of the ears and the eyes, and the width of the temple and the neck.

The successful creation on canvas of a likeness of the model has always obsessed almost every artist. With other types of subject matter, likeness has little relative importance. Portrait painting, however, is another story. You can paint with whatever medium you like, and in the style best suited for the portrait, and yet your work may still lack a likeness to the subject. How can it be achieved?

One of the best ways is to use the "mathematic sketch" approach. In this approach, the different parts of the head are accurately traced on a grid, with all distances, dimensions, and proportions exactly calculated, and all light and shadow values precisely analyzed.

The standard way of drawing a portrait using this method is to guess the model's proportions or to use a pencil. It all comes down to comparing distances, checking if, for instance, the height of the nose is equal to that of the forehead, if the eye is one and one-half times the mouth, if the space of the cheeks is equal to the space between the eyebrows and the hairline, etc., then, transferring all these calculations onto paper so they can be drawn in more detail.

There is a good way to test if this formula has worked for you: Place a mirror in front of your drawing; as if by magic, the reflection will reveal any mistakes.

Taking photographs of the model will allow you to continue drawing when the model is not around. It also might help you to compare the dimensions within the photo itself. Finally, when superimposed onto photos or sketches, grids allow total accuracy.

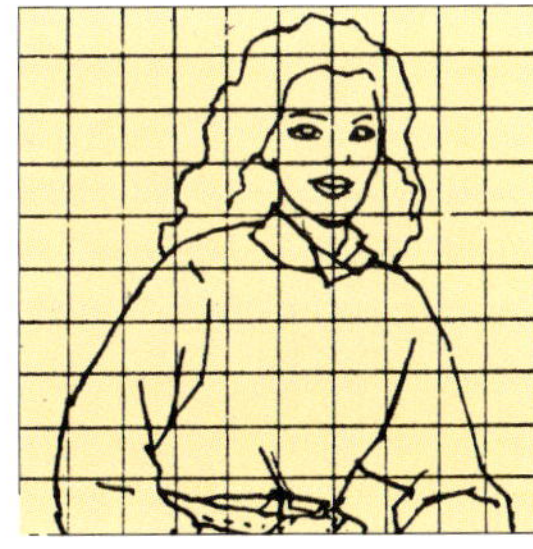

Using a grid to take measurements of a photograph or sketch is a good way to reproduce the pose accurately and guarantee a likeness.

The measurements taken are translated into a geometric scheme, where it will be easy to insert the facial features.

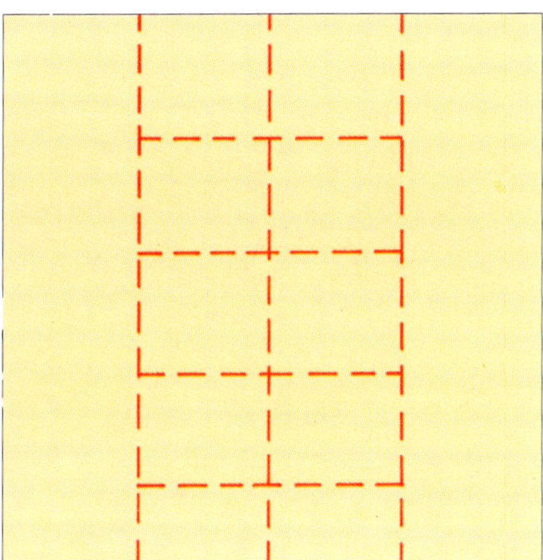

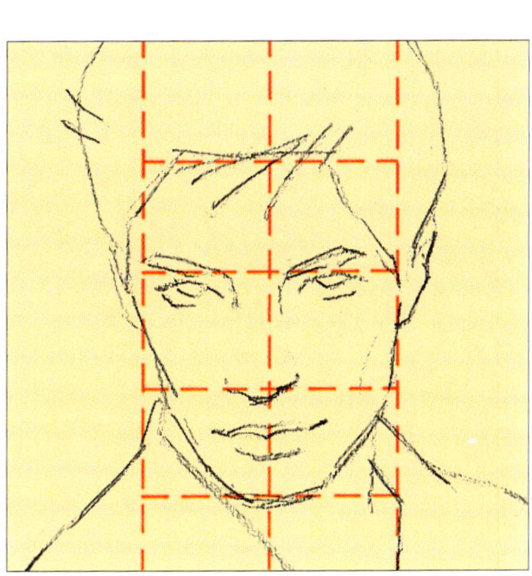

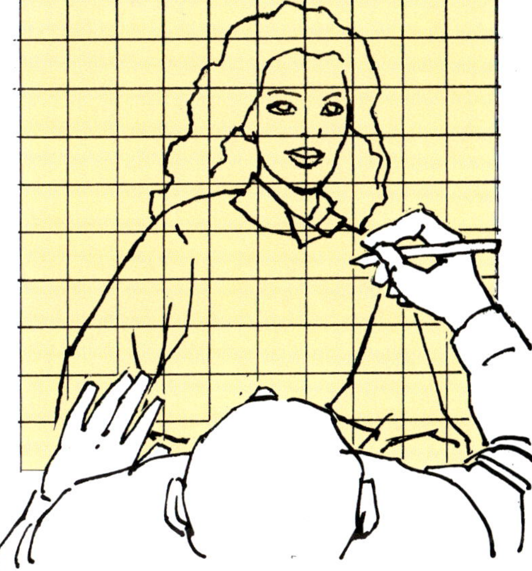

The importance of sketches

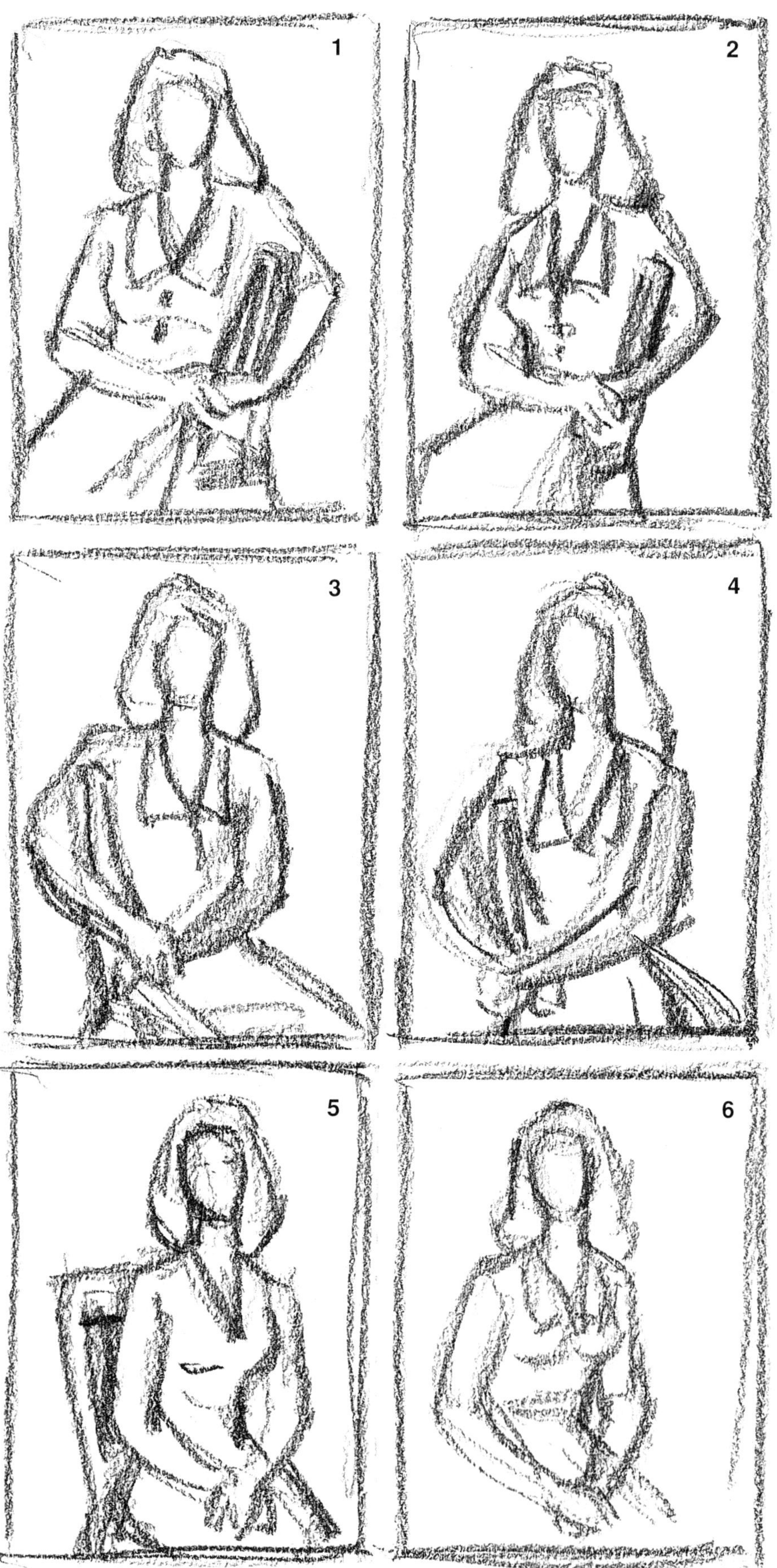

All artists draw sketches or studies of the portraits they are going to paint. Sketching can be very helpful in achieving a number of objectives, such as getting to know the model, trying out different poses, planning the composition, trying different lighting, and searching for the right color harmony. Achieving these objectives, in turn, will lead to a pleasing result. The painter must reflect on the theme. This must be done with the standard tools: pencils, paper, paintbrush, or pastels. This kind of reflection by sketching or drawing is extremely positive and constructive for the painter.

There are many different types of possible studies: more or less detailed or schematic, focusing on proportions on the distribution of shadows and light, or on color. The artist must keep these variables in mind, testing them in his or her sketches before committing them to the canvas.

Many artists even make a series of drawings before using a model, imagining different poses and sketching them schematically. In these simple forms, the artist focuses on different positions of the head, body, or extremities, and leaves details aside.

Discovery through drawings

Keeping all this in mind, try to find a pose that will yield the best results from an artistic point of view.

Draw several sketches, slightly changing your point of view, so you see more or less of the model. Change the pose of the model as well.

1. *In the first sketch, notice how the model is supported by her left arm while the chair remains clearly visible.*

2. *The same pose as before, with only a slight change: The model is seated further back and her figure is more visible.*

3. *The model's body and arms are now leaning to the right.*

4. *In this outline the model is in a more erect position, the chair more to one side. The right arm stays closer to the body.*

5. *The pose has visibly changed: The model has her head slightly to one side and the back of the chair is visible.*

6. *This is the definitive pose; the chair and part of the skirt are omitted. The model's shoulder and left arm fall back in line with the neck.*

You must draw at least five or six sketches, even if the first one comes out just as you wanted, because there is always room for improvement. Do these drawings in a small sketchbook or on loose sheets of paper cut into quarters. In the series of sketches on the previous page there is a sequence of pose studies to follow.

Problems with composition

When you try to find the best position for the model you are trying to solve a two-tiered compositional problem: the problem of what pose to put the model in while calculating the ideal proportions between the mass constituted by the model and the space you have on paper.

Composition of the head

First of all, you must keep in mind the kind of composition you wish to create and the character you wish to produce in your portrait. You must decide whether to do a frontal pose, a three-quarter view, or a profile. Remember, the frontal position and three-quarter positions are the most common. Don't forget, the picture appears more harmonious when the head is facing away from the body. Finally, you must practice drawing with the model's head slightly raised or lowered, tilted to one side or the other, etc. Always stay focused on the characteristic pose that will best serve your initial goal.

Concerning the placement of the model's mass in an available space, there are three classic formulas that you can select or play around with.

a) When the model is facing front, place the head in the center.

b) When the head is in a three-quarter position, place it a little off center. Leave more space in front of the face than behind it.

c) When drawing a profile, again place the head off center. This time, leave even more space in front of the face than behind it.

Composition of half-body portraits

With a sitting model, consider placing the hands on the lap. Place them more or less crossed on either the left thigh or the right. With the body facing forward, have the head turned slightly to one side. Another possibility is to place the body almost in profile, and have the model face forward. You may also consider having the model lean slightly forward, separating the back from the chair, sitting up straight, or leaning to one side.

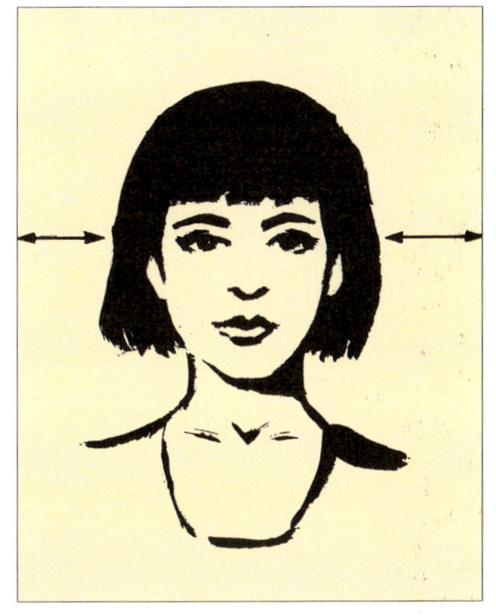

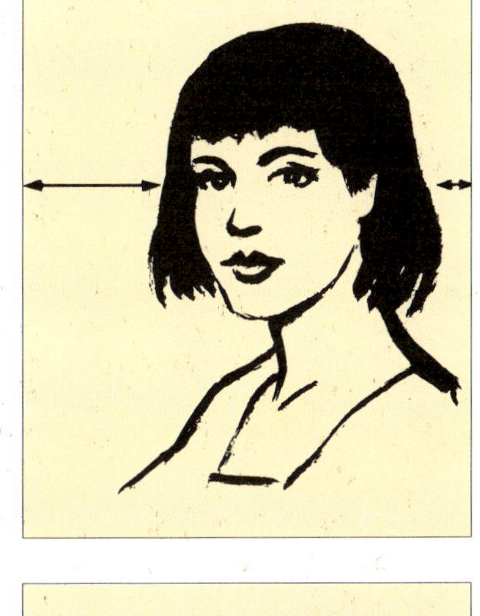

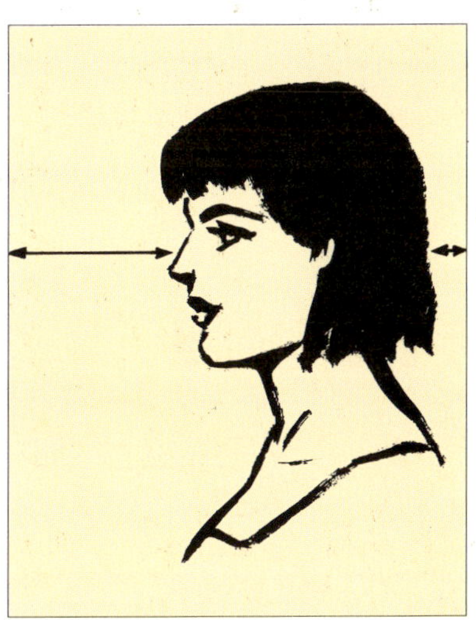

Placement of the head will be determined by the pose you choose: frontal, three-quarter, or profile. In a frontal pose, the head is centered on the canvas. In a three-quarter position, leave more space in front of the face than behind it. Leave even more space in front of the face when doing a profile. While you must feel free to organize your picture as you see it, it's advisable not to deviate too much from this formula.

The success of your portrait will be determined in part by the pose you choose. As a result, many professional artists devote long sketching sessions to the study of poses.

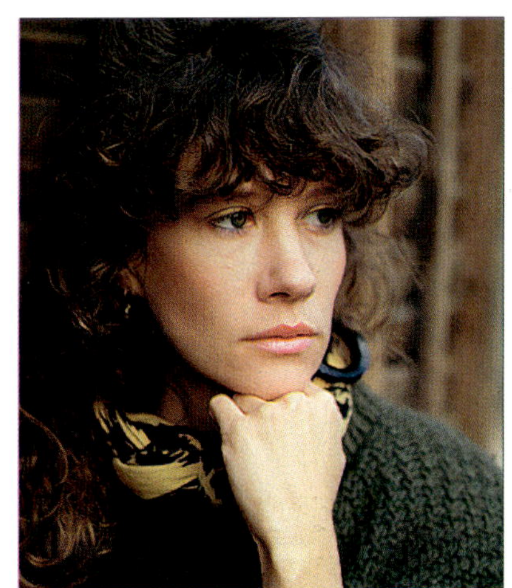

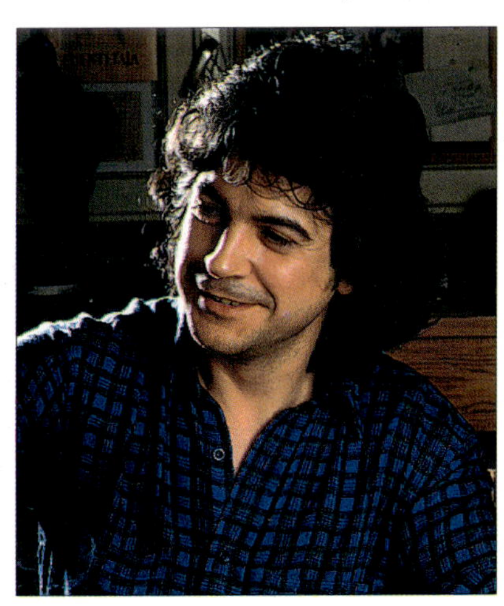

The study of poses

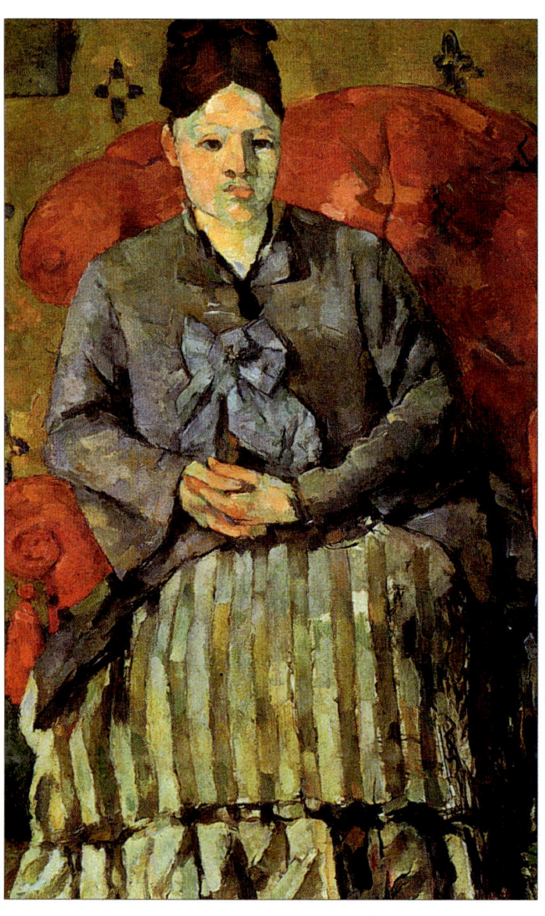

Paul Cézanne, Madame Cézanne in a Red Chair. *Although the pose chosen for this portrait is static (or perhaps because of it), it illustrates the formal and serious character of the model.*

The pose is an essential factor in portrait painting. It's important from an aesthetic (pictorial) point of view, as much as from a psychological viewpoint (what the pose expresses about the person in the portrait).

When painting the human figure in works that are not portraits, the pose should be subordinate to drawing and color possibilities. In such cases, the pose is a thematic excuse to develop your sense of drawing, your ideas of anatomy, and your perception of form. In art schools, nude painting always has been an essential educational tool precisely for these reasons.

However, in portrait painting, the essential idea is to keep in mind the naturalness of the person you are painting. The model should be seated comfortably, so that he or she can remain motionless for the required period of time. The model's clothes should look natural, matching the context in which the model is placed. Of course, if the shirt is too wrinkled, you can always get rid of some of the creases when you paint your subject. Retain the essential elements, the most favorable and harmonious. You may take any liberties you find necessary to achieve an artistic result. Remember, painting is not photography: It is interpretation.

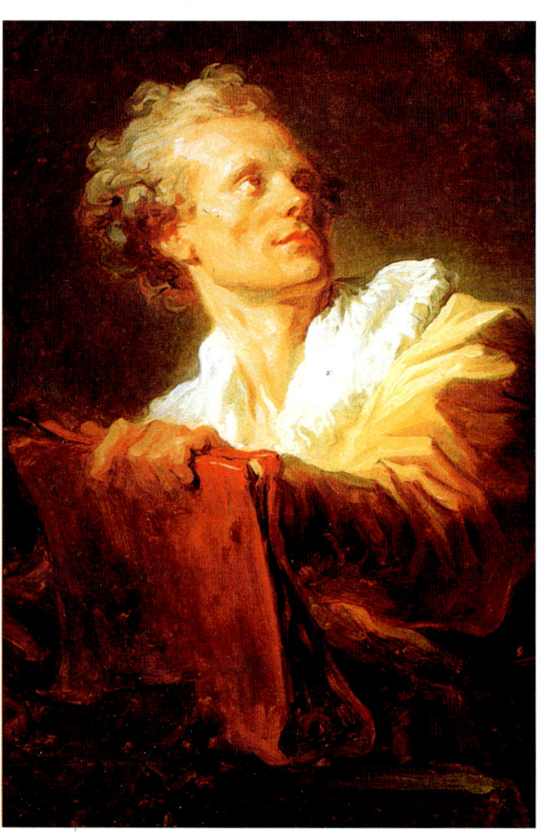

J.H. Fragonard, Portrait of a Young Artist. *In this example, the pose contributes to a heightened psychological expression. The young artist seems preoccupied by something more than meets the eye. His idealism and spirituality are evident.*

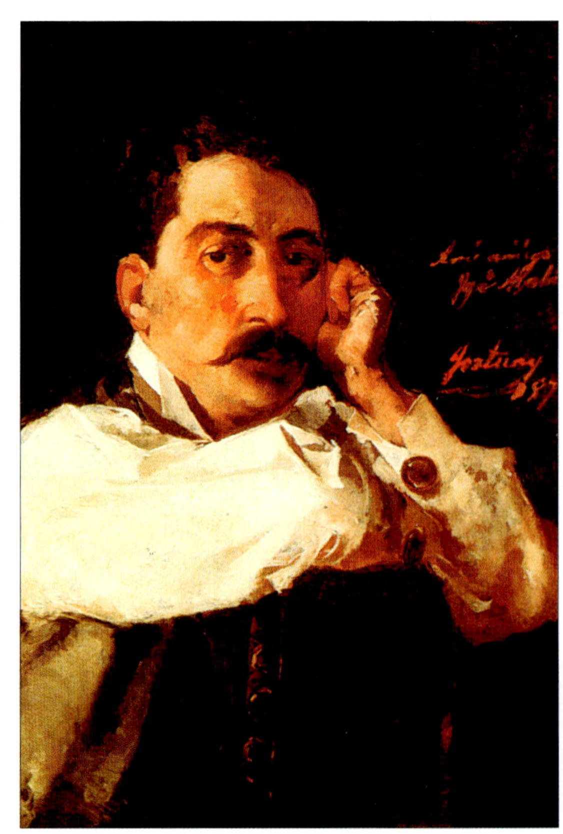

Mariano Fortuny, Portrait of Ignasi Aixelà i Font. *The informal posture suggests a cordial relationship between painter and model. This work radiates naturalness. With the relaxed pose and the model's dreamy gaze, the painter conveys the complete personality of his subject.*

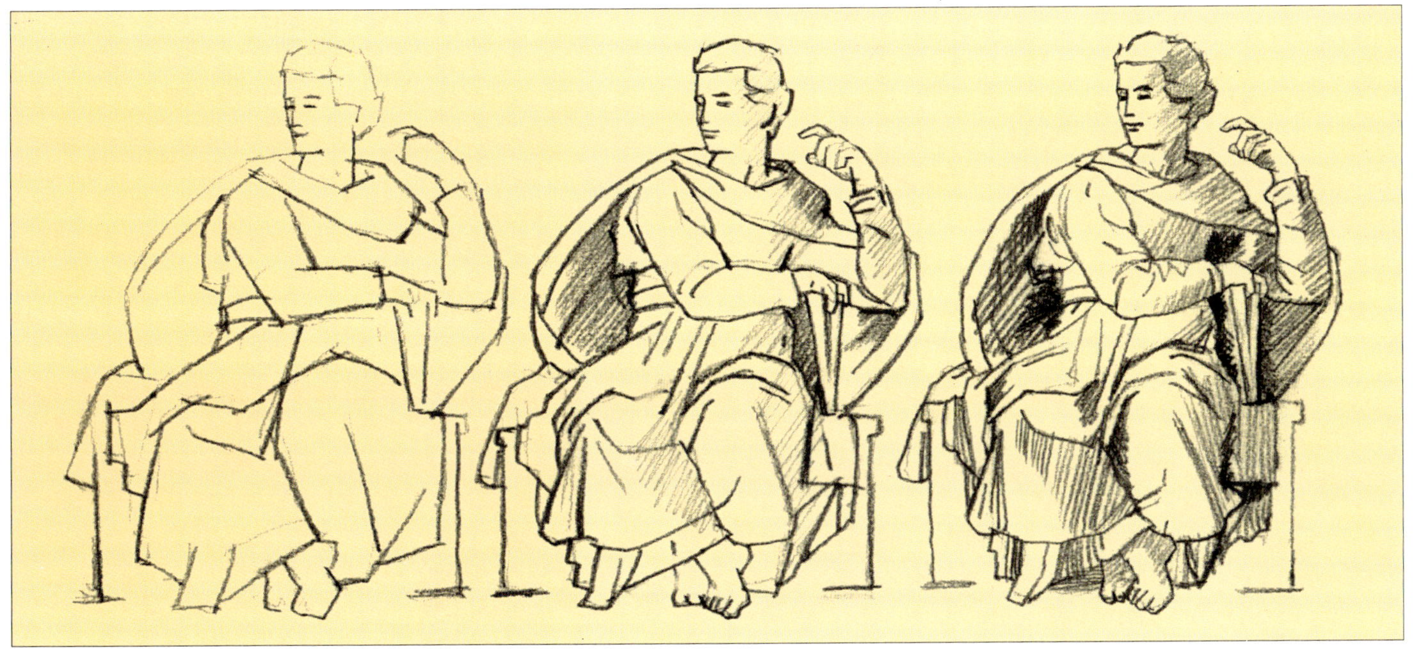

Whether the portrait is made in one or several sessions, shifts in the model's pose are almost inevitable. Small movements or variations of the pose will change the appearance of the model's clothes; some wrinkles will be more obvious, a sleeve will seem shorter, a hat more to one side, etc. Artists must not let such superficial variations interfere with their main objective. On the contrary, the painting is your creation and its outcome depends on you, not the other way around. In light of this, the following suggestions should be helpful. First, pay close attention to the pose as soon as you begin your preliminary drawings. Second, learn how to draw clothes so you won't be at the mercy of superficial variations.

The key, as always, is to see the clothed model as a whole, defining the directions of creases and folds without going into detail. Be sure to articulate the shadows and light to show relief.

Once you have practiced the study of clothes, remember that clothes should not hide or confuse the model's anatomy or gestures. They should help you to understand the model. An excess of creases or attention to minor points can make you forget what is underneath. To reiterate: Draw the body that is below the surface, enclose the forms correctly, and synthesize the clothes even when they seem too wrinkled. How, then, do we go about synthesizing? By closely observing the points that best describe the body's shape, the gesture of the arms, the bend of the knee, etc. Remember, the wrinkles and folds have a reason for being, as can be seen in the illustrations on this page. A quick preliminary sketch that brings together the most important details can be of great help.

To study any type of drape, robes, or clothes, you can follow the simple steps shown here: First, fill in the principal volume; next, gradually define the areas of light and shadow until you have clarified each of the folds with their appropriate intensity.

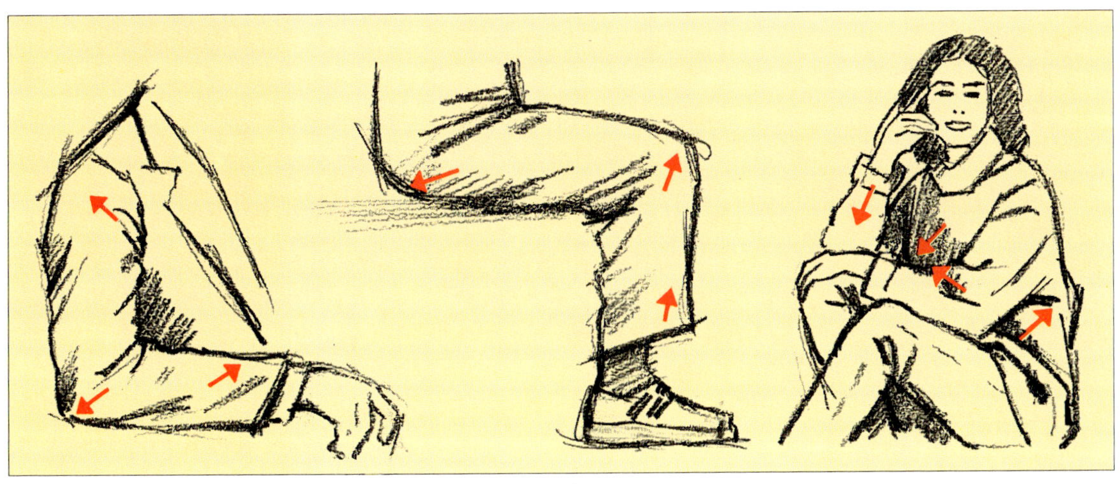

Pay attention to the logical tensions on your clothes. When you bend an arm or a leg, the sleeves shrink or double up in different places. The red arrows in the illustration indicate the different tensions they create.

Poses and the distance from the model

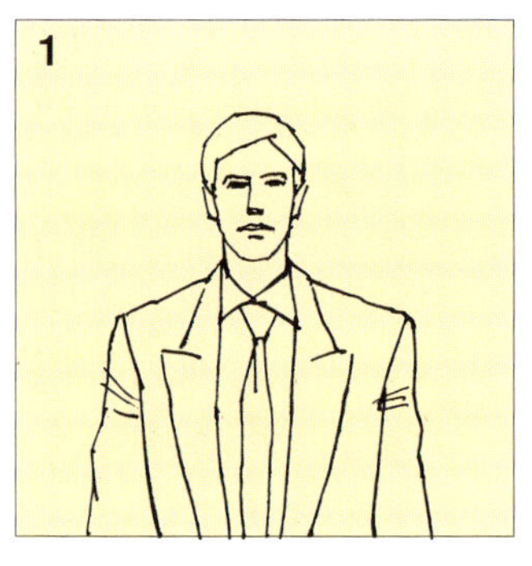

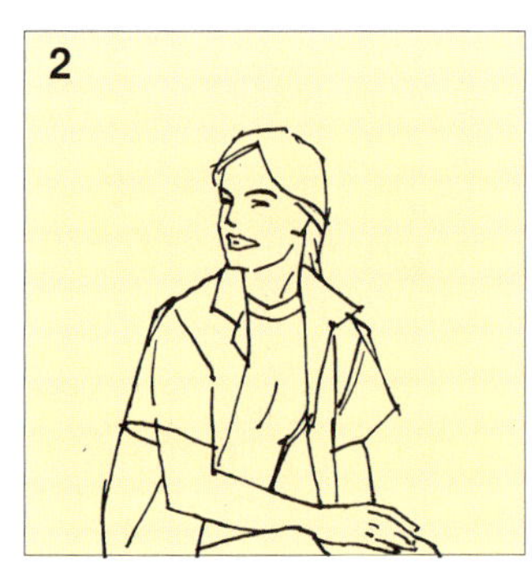

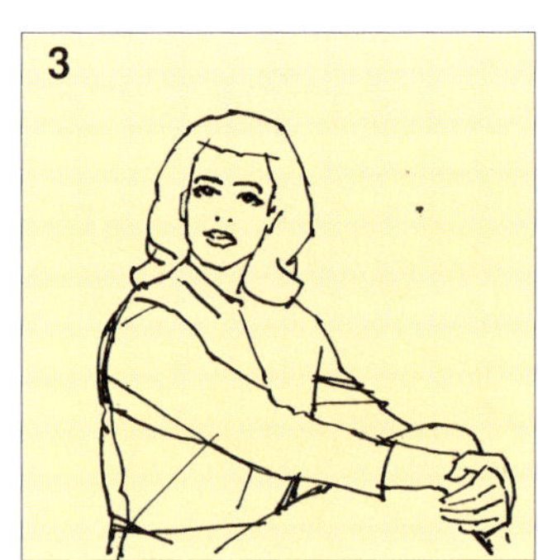

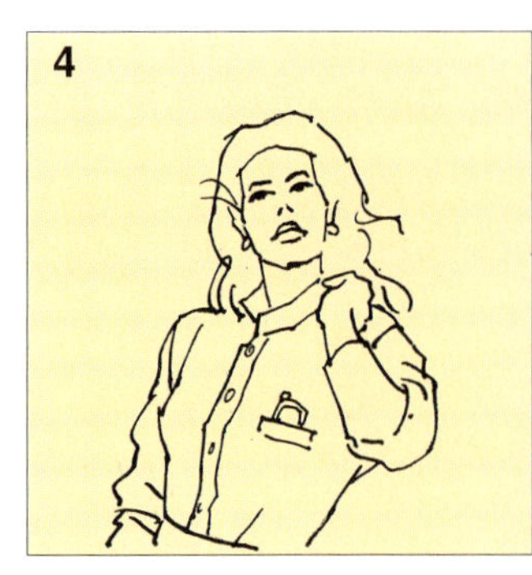

1. *This pose is excessively frontal and centered on the paper or frame. It is too rigid and lacks visual interest.*

2. *Here's a dynamic pose despite its stillness. It's enough for the head to move in a different direction from the body to generate interest.*

3. *This relaxed pose is also dynamic. The only problem with a pose like this is that the model will tire easily.*

4. *A pose such as this is, although dynamic, is difficult to resolve. It belongs more to the snapshot genre than to painting.*

The pose

We have mentioned the importance of trying different poses with the same model before beginning a portrait. In other words, adapt the pose to the respective model by keeping in mind the model's appearance, and peculiarities, among other things.

Now, let's focus on the aesthetic possibilities of the pose. We will begin to paint people in poses that are attractive and that facilitate interesting compositions. The famous painter Ingres gives us a clue on how to do this: "The body should not follow the movement of the head." His quote is exemplified by the drawings on this page.

As always in art, words of wisdom are advice rather than absolutes; there are no fixed rules in art. However, for now it might be easier for you to create a good portrait by trying out this experiment: Have the model turn his or her head one way and body the other. Notice how the pose becomes more attractive, less rigid or formal.

Using the model's hands

There are some people who know how to pose for a portrait. They ask no questions and need no explanations. They know how to place their hands with grace and style. On the other hand, there are those who are uncomfortable posing. You could chat with models to distract or relax them, thereby gaining their confidence. In difficult circumstances, you could give models a book or another object to occupy their hands. Remember, this should be done only as a last resort in difficult cases; it is not a generally applied rule. The more spontaneous the pose, the better.

Avoid foreshortening

With a model seated in the frontal position, you see the thighs foreshortened. With the model seated to one side with the chair half turned you see the back of the chair under the arm—the model possibly resting an arm on the chair back. Again there is foreshortening. Although this is not a rigid norm, try to avoid these and other types of foreshortening, as they are generally difficult to resolve and are not very appealing.

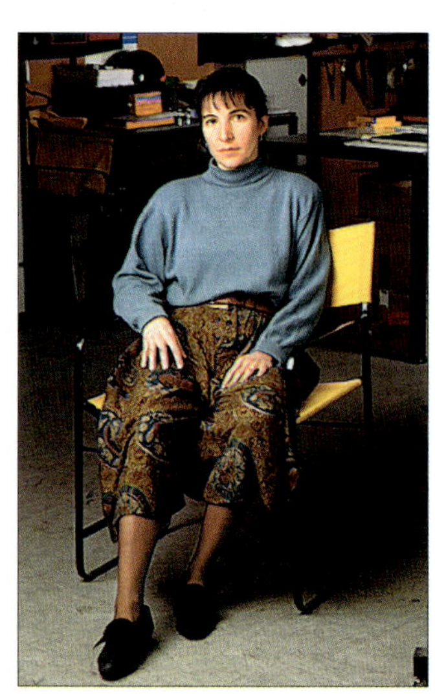

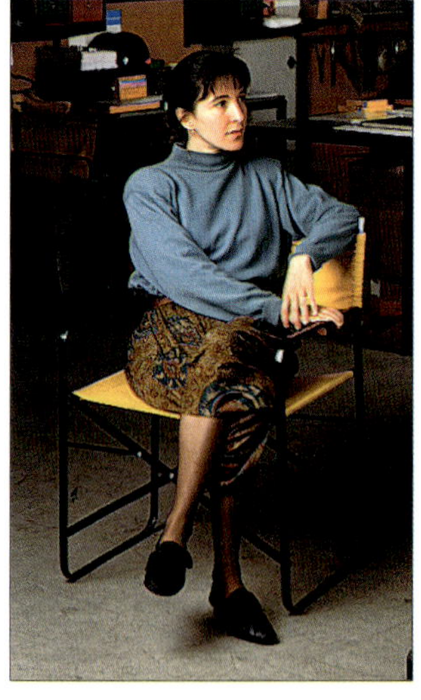

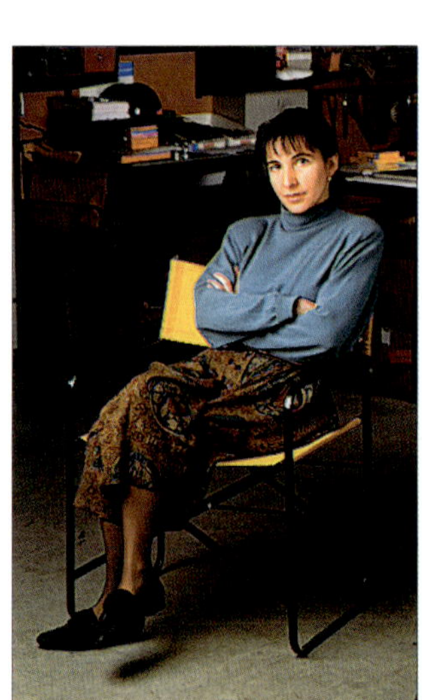

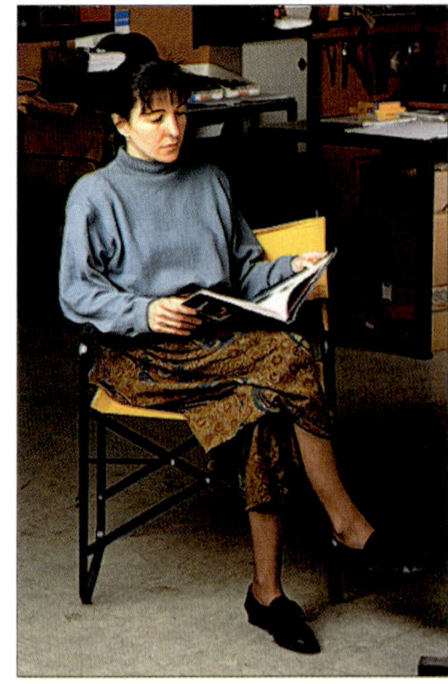

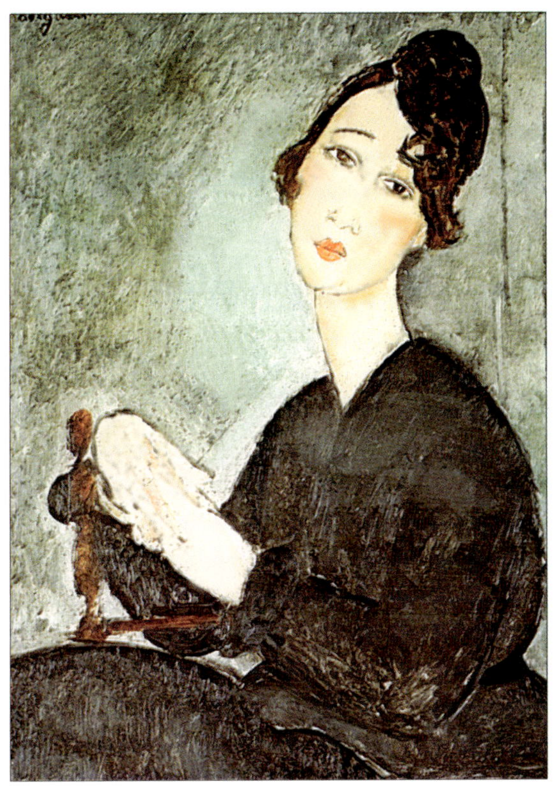

Amadeo Modigliani, Dedie Hayden. *This is a superb example of a pose in which vibrancy is perfectly balanced with tranquillity. The artist knew how to avoid foreshortening though surely it was present in the original pose.*

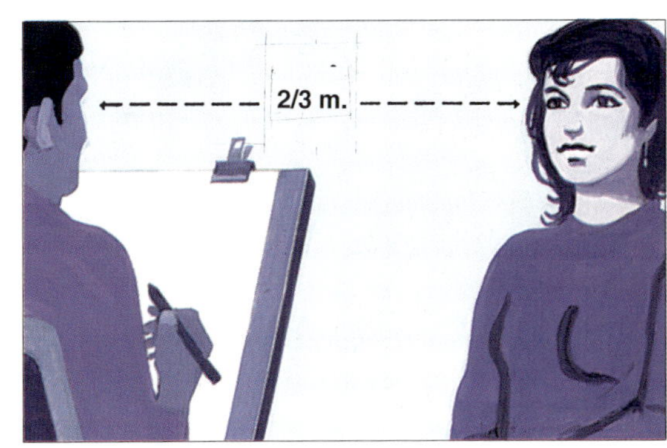

The distance between the painter and model should be between 7 and 10 feet (2 and 3 m) to obtain the best results when painting a half-body pose.

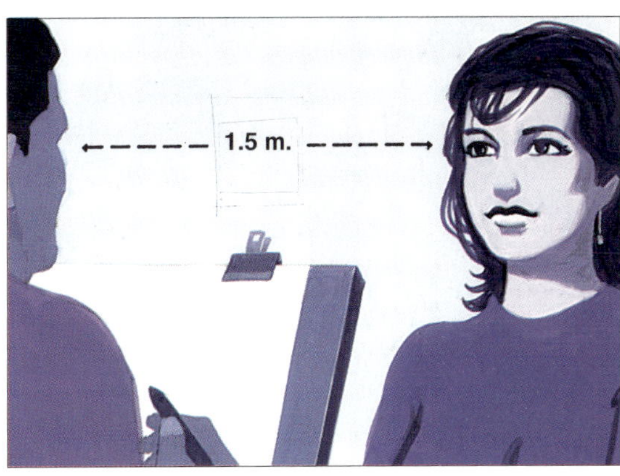

For head portraits your distance from the model should be less, approximately 5 feet (1½ m).

The best way to avoid this sort of problem is to try different poses. Ask the model to cross or uncross the legs, move the arms, cross them, rest one on something, turn the head one way or the other, etc.

Distance from the model

The distance between your chair and the model's should be 7 to 10 feet (2 to 3 m) when painting a half-length portrait. If the portrait is of the head only, the distance should be reduced to approximately 5 feet (1½ m).

When doing a full-length portrait, it's best to maintain a distance of about 10 to 15 feet (3 to 4 m).

A possible process for finding a pose is shown in the series of photographs below. You will have to ask the model to stand up, sit down, lean this way or that, pick up a book, turn her head, cross her arms, etc., until you find a suitable pose that fits her character.

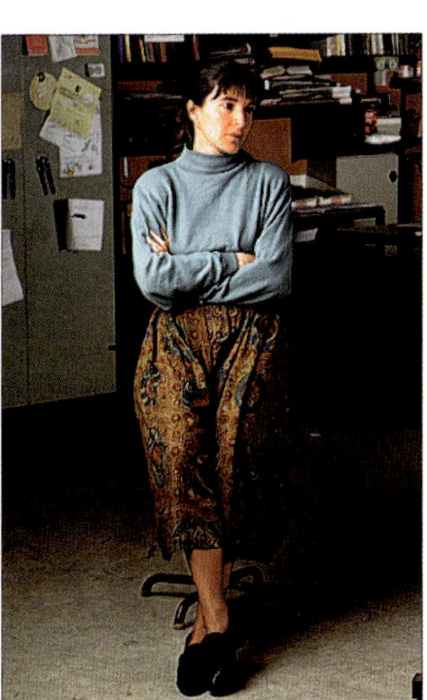

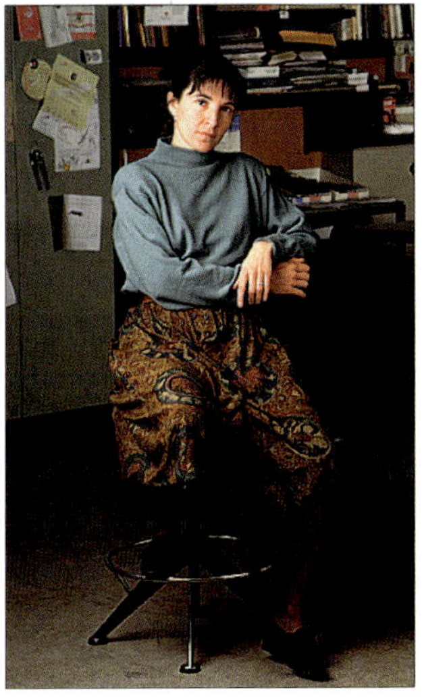

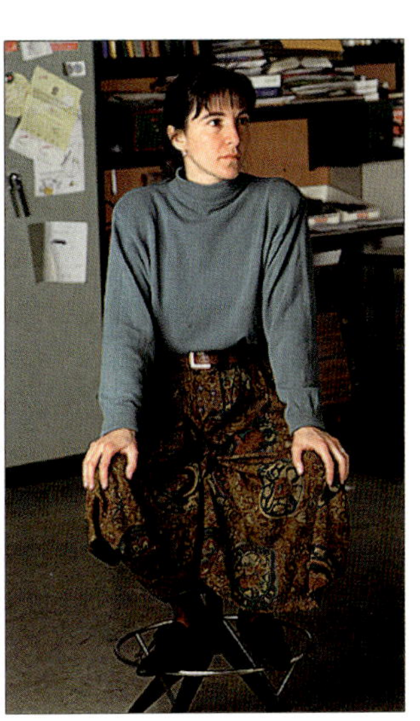

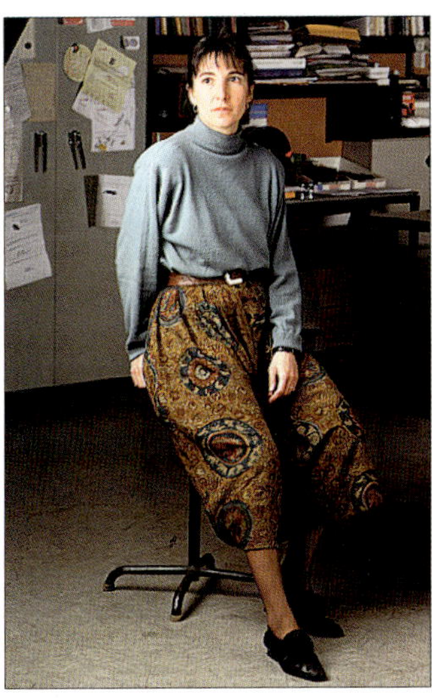

Lighting

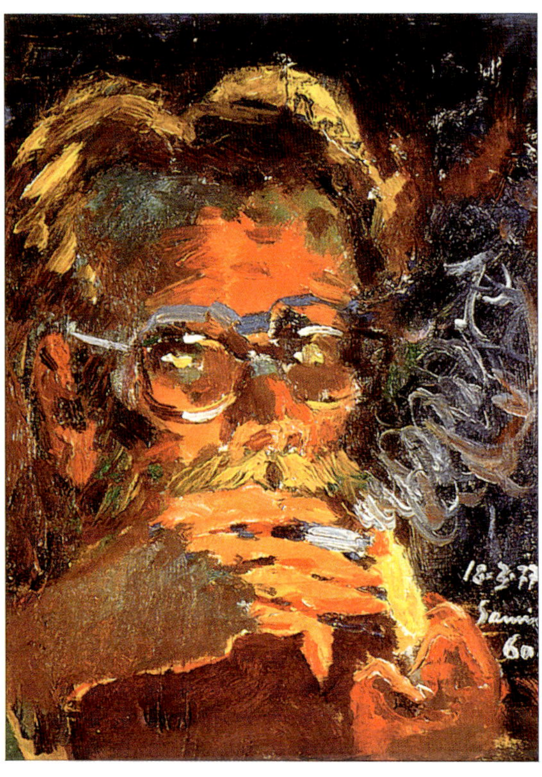

Ramon Sanvisens, Self-Portrait. *The lighting from below in this painting creates sharp contrast. This style is rather uncommon; however, the expressive and atmospheric effect justifies the experiment. In any case, it's not advisable for beginners to attempt this, at least not until they have a command of the technique.*

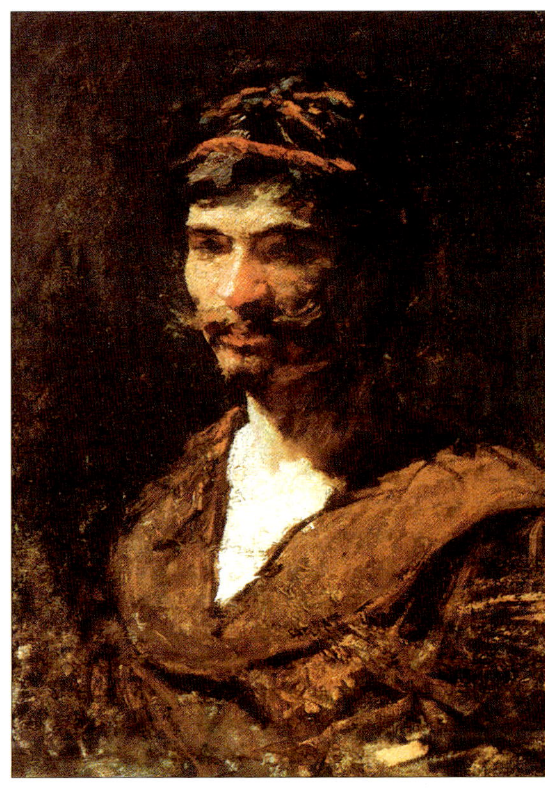

Mariano Fortuny, Bust of a Man. *The lighting in this portrait is typical (zenithal and lateral); yet it is very intense and contrasted with chiaroscuro, which creates a notable dramatic effect.*

Natural light or artificial light

As with all other elements that come together in a portrait, there are no absolute rules regarding what type of lighting is the most appropriate. As always, we have some suggestions, if only to get enough lighting possibilities in the studio, to allow you to begin sketching, then painting.

The essential difference between natural light and artificial light is that the former respects color. If it comes from a window, it's usually soft and balanced. On the other hand, artificial light is somewhat more defined and allows you to illuminate the model with the direction and intensity you wish. Artificial light is perfect for sketches and possibly for painting. However, if possible, you should experiment with natural light when painting. It's cooler than artificial light and it does not alter the colors.

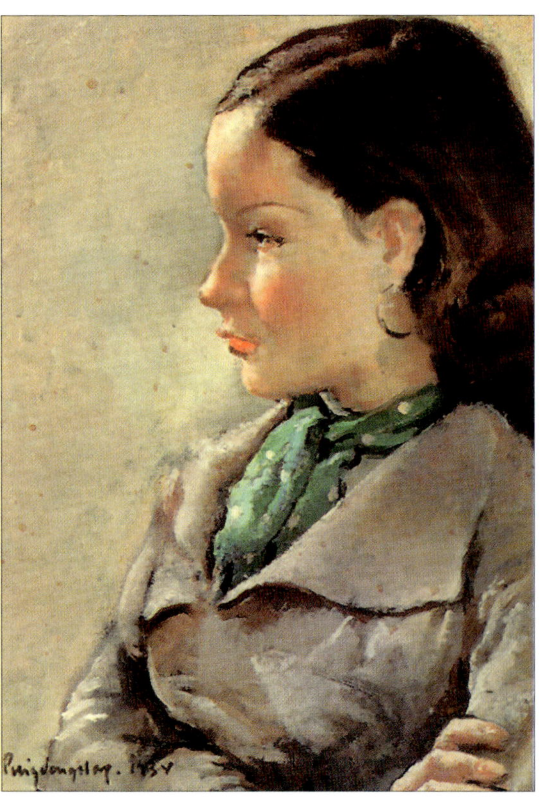

Josep Puigdengolas, Adela. *Lateral light used in a profile creates an original effect. In this case the light is diffused and the face's softness stands out. There is contrast, but it is subtle. The delicate and subtle facial features reinforce the image of tenderness and fragility the artist wants to express.*

The appropriate use of light

The face must be well lit. To do so, you should use frontal and lateral light. The light should not be fully frontal, as it diminishes the volume of the face. Neither should it be fully lateral because this creates hard shadows and very confusing areas. These options are best left for when you have a greater knowledge of portraiture. One last important point: The most illuminated part of the face is normally the side that is closest to the artist.

Now is an ideal time to pause before we plunge into the exercises contained in the rest of this chapter. Let's talk about self-portraits, which are, perhaps, painting "par excellence."

Throughout art history, artists have created a vast and enigmatic gallery of self-portraits.

In truth, the term "artist" is vast, and it becomes even more so when you understand that making art is an extension of life. The term "artist" need not be reserved for a few; creating art is what defines being human. We can go even further and say that understanding art is what makes us human. The typical aesthetic experience, the capacity to express emotions, belongs to everyone.

It happens whenever someone decides to express his or her emotions in one form or another, whether through the fine arts, literature, or the theater; it happens whenever someone becomes aware of the strength of universal communication through art. This force is nothing more than a representation of reality filtered through the creative spirit. If the message we send through our inner images can reflect reality onto a canvas, then it will become a powerful monologue, a truthful introspection of the self-portrait artist. With such knowledge, all creative barriers can be overcome. A self-portrait is a search for excellence within oneself; it mirrors the soul of the creator. You show yourself naked before yourself, and of course, before the spectator.

In a self-portrait, you don't try to translate the image in the mirror onto the canvas. The mirror need not be more than a guide for concentrating on your own gaze. In other words, when you do a self-portrait, you are virtually unleashing feelings deeply rooted inside yourself. These feelings could emerge in any other representation of yourself, but in a much more hidden and muted manner. It can be safely said that in a self-portrait we not only look for a way to represent ourselves on canvas, but we liberate the inner force that's reflected in all the work we do.

The necessity of self-portraiture exists in every artist. Sometimes, it's for pleasure; other times, it's more profound. The act of sitting in front of a mirror and constructing an image of oneself from one's reflection somehow shatters the normal boundaries of time. It is a deep and purely contemplative inner quest. Each time you do a self-portrait, you will be digging deeper and deeper into yourself.

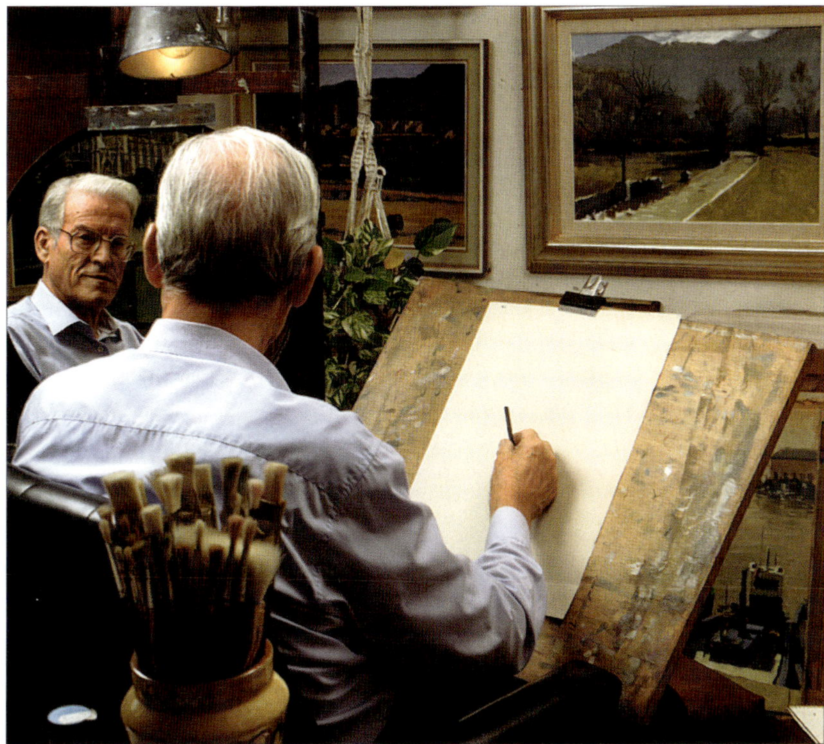

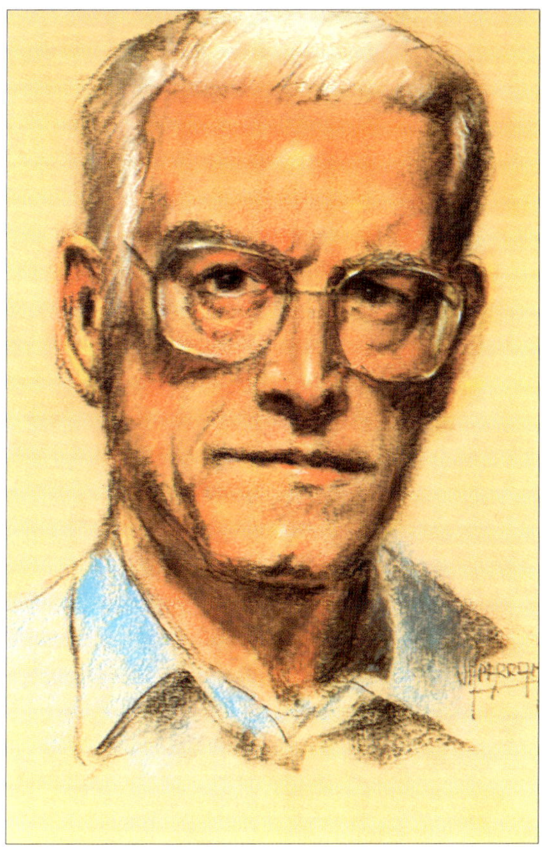

The mirror plays a fundamental role in self-portraiture. The distance between you and the mirror will determine in part the composition of your painting, as well as the plan you develop. Place yourself at a distance that allows you to capture all of the details; however, don't sit so close that you lose the sense of wholeness.

The importance of composition

Composition is essential for representing a human figure on canvas. At some point, you may have been moved by a painting that seemed simple. Apart from its pictorial quality, there was a secret hidden within it that made it unique. This secret can be unveiled by studying the lines of its composition.

In representing the human figure, once the pose has been analyzed and sketched, you must decide on its composition; that is to say the portion of the figure you wish to represent, as well as the space surrounding it. It's very important to represent the figure correctly, surrounding it, for instance, with an atmosphere that is harmonious with the space it occupies. The model's clothes will help you create this composition centered on a human figure. The human figure can be boiled down to a series of forms in the space. When further reduced, these forms can be seen as pure geometric forms.

The distance between you and the model does not change the composition, only its framing; that is, the part of the composition that you see. For example, a triangular composition of a human figure remains triangular even when seen up close—the compositional lines simply will have an imaginary prolongation outside the painting.

Compositional work should be done prior to, and maintained throughout, the pictorial development of your painting. Despite the changes that take place, the basic lines of the composition must not be lost. This way, you can be sure that the composition's balance will be maintained until the work is complete. As there is a wide variety of compositional models, you will find there is no exact formula for finding the perfect composition. Despite this, a formula has been sought throughout art history. As you know, the famous golden standard or canon of the Renaissance consisted of a series of relationships of measurements within the painting itself and was the embodiment of proportional rationality for each of the forms in it. Today such techniques are no longer used in painting; the trend is more toward a balance between forms and colors. Curiously, however, most of the masterpieces by classic, contemporary, or abstract artists conform to the golden standard. Perhaps we should return to the classic view.

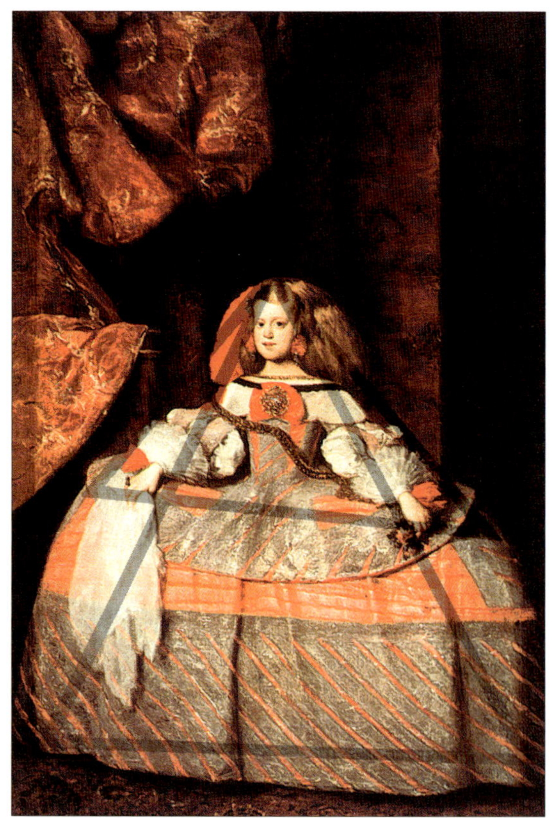

Velázquez, La Infanta Doña Margarita de Austria. *This is a clear example of symmetrical composition. This type of composition can be very risky given the repetition of forms. However, if you observe the compositional scheme, you will see that the triangles that form the figure are tilted at the base, subtly breaking the monotony.*

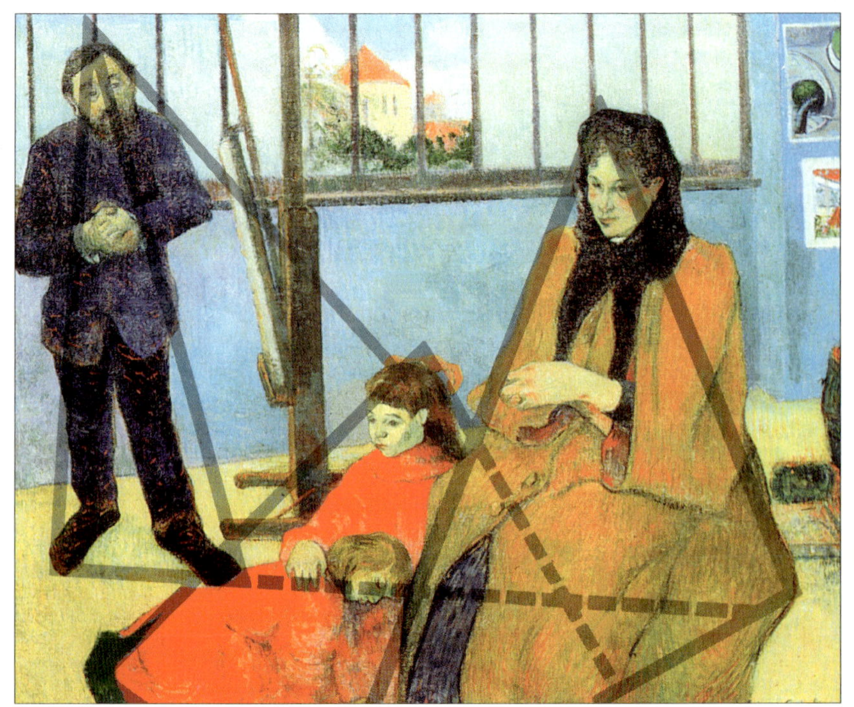

Paul Gauguin, The Schuffenecher Family. *In this type of composition, perspective among individual figures and the rhythm of forms keep the interest.*

Composition in landscapes

To compose is to arrange. Landscapes are made up of a multitude of elements such as fields and skies in a variety of colors, all with their own lights and shadows. The painter must know exactly how to distribute these elements in order to get a coherent arrangement.

Frequently, the very nature of the motif provides the painter with a composition. The artist must know how to exploit such occasions; however, if the artist relies too much on them, the theme will quickly become confusing without a preliminary sketch of the composition.

To a certain extent, the landscape's compositional scheme depends on the position of the horizon. A high horizon allows the painter to include a large stretch of terrain: forests, plains, valleys, etc. It also allows the artist to include effects of depth and distance. A low horizon, on the other hand, heightens the perspective and the contrasts in size of the landscape's different elements.

Artists have always arranged their landscape painting by basing them on simple, usually geometric forms such as diagonal lines that cross the surface of the canvas from corner to corner, curves, triangles, and L-, C-, and Z-shaped configurations, among others. Rubens, for instance, composed with a complex system of spirals, thus creating works of great dynamism. The English painter John Constable, like many Impressionists, used diagonally based compositions, but the Impressionist Paul Cézanne created many varied and original compositions—curves, rhombuses, and even circumferences are forms that frequently crop up in his paintings.

These forms should not be used arbitrarily. First, the painter must study the theme—the landscape—carefully and try to discover the composition. Sometimes, the composition becomes evident immediately, but this does not happen frequently. In most cases, you will have to distribute and compose by adding, increasing, or removing elements of the landscape until a coherent composition is found.

We have provided you with a series of examples that will help you to interpret the compositional outline that each painter has used in his work.

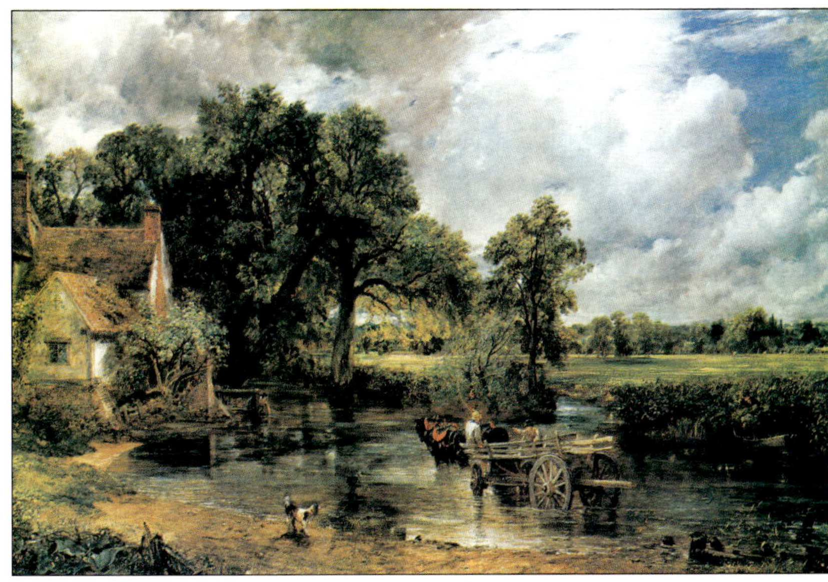

John Constable, Landscape at Noon. *This English landscape painter was a genuine precursor of the Impressionist movement. This is a classic composition of the genre; the canvas is divided into two halves by a diagonal line running from corner to corner.*

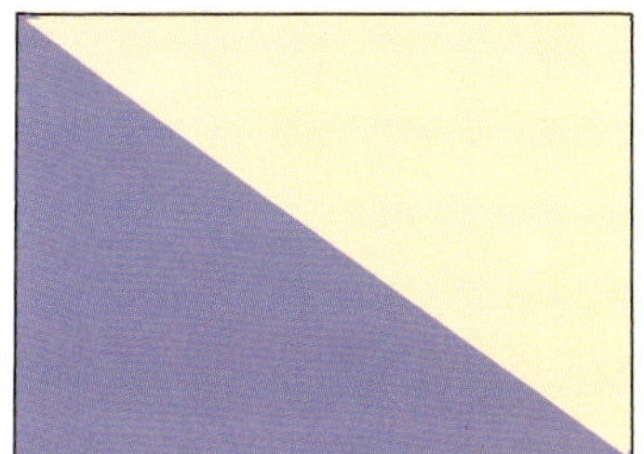

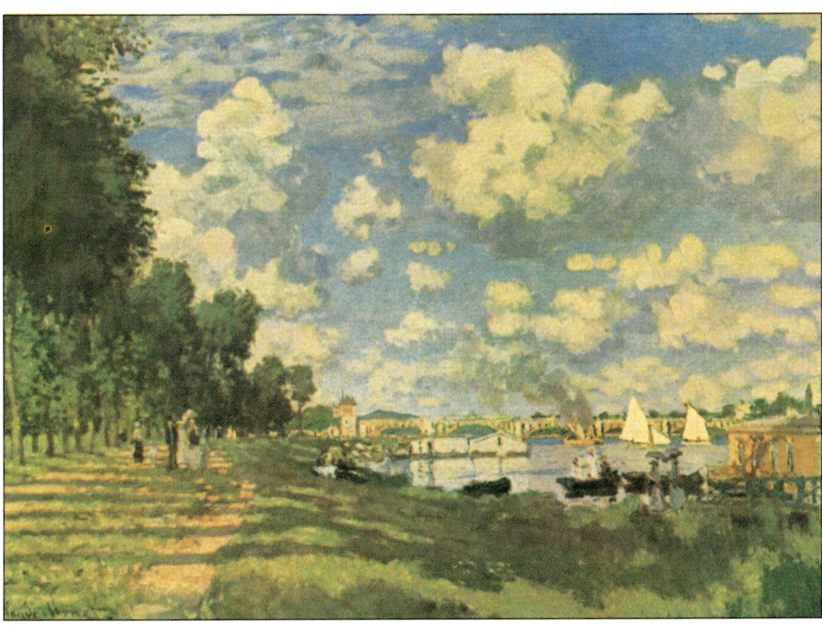

Claude Monet, The Lake at Argenteuil. *The composition is based on a parabola that helps create an effect of depth. This type of composition has been very popular among landscape artists since the Impressionists.*

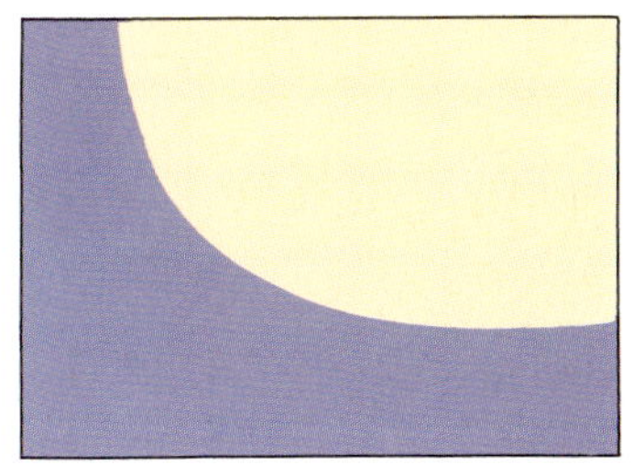

Composition in depth

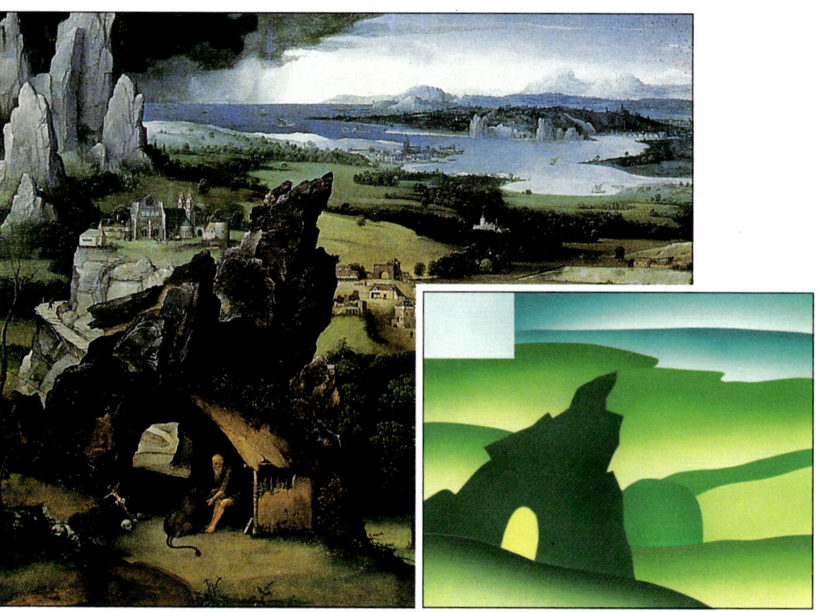

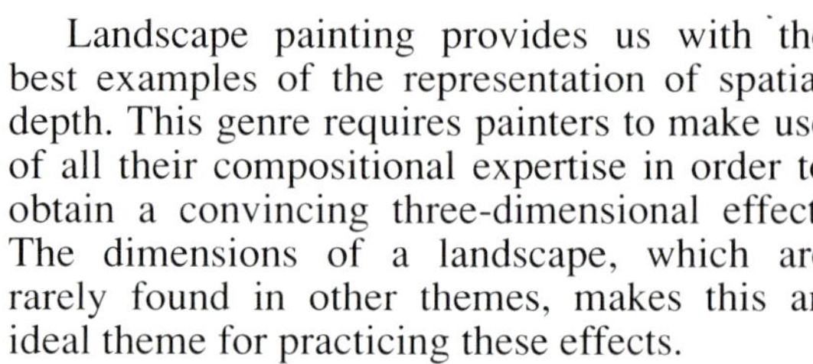

Landscape painting provides us with the best examples of the representation of spatial depth. This genre requires painters to make use of all their compositional expertise in order to obtain a convincing three-dimensional effect. The dimensions of a landscape, which are rarely found in other themes, makes this an ideal theme for practicing these effects.

There is also such a thing as the "flat" landscape, the characteristic two-dimensional backdrop of Gothic art—a type of landscape that is used to great effect by certain contemporary painters. Most artists, however, paint their landscapes in depth, following the rules laid down in the European tradition since the Renaissance.

Painters have achieved spatial depth through a variety of different compositional techniques. Although the use of perspective has always been recurrent among them, it is only one of several possibilities.

From the representation of a landscape by means of "screens," or superimposed planes, to spatial expression based on color contrasts distributed over the canvas, artists have experimented with a wide range of methods for creating depth on a two-dimensional surface. A study of the works reproduced on these pages will confirm this.

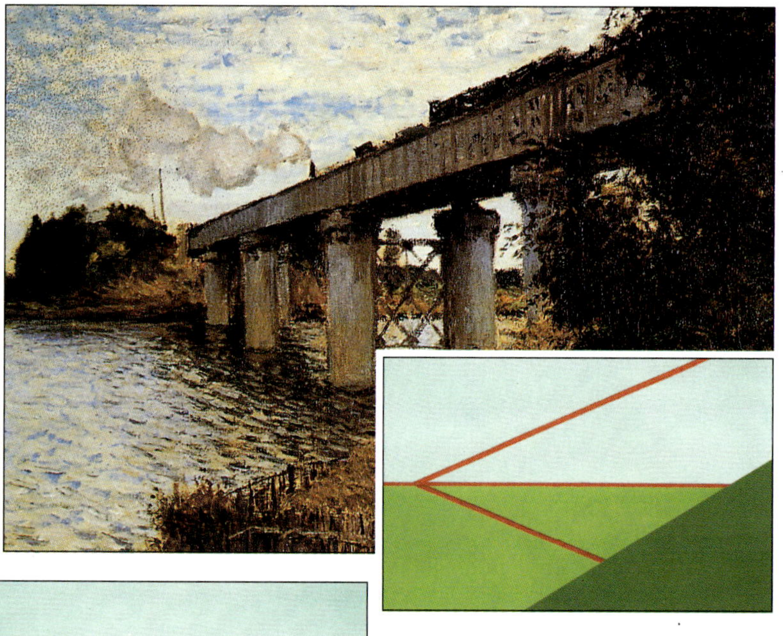

Joachim Patinir, Landscape with Saint Jerome. *This is a classic example of depth using planes or "screens," similar to the way wings are used in a theater. The contrasts of intensity or chiaroscuro between the different planes create the sensation of depth.*

Claude Monet, The Railroad Bridge. *Perspective in this painting is based on the vanishing lines of the bridge that create in the center of the canvas a sharp angle whose vertex coincides with the horizon.*

Edward Hopper, Sunset on the Roadside. *The artist's use of horizontal and parallel lines checks the effect of perspective, but the sensation of depth is convincing, due to the alternate planes of light and shadow.*

Vincent van Gogh. Haystacks in Provence. *The sensation of space in this picture is the result of the contrast between the highly saturated yellowish ocher tones and the light blue sky.*

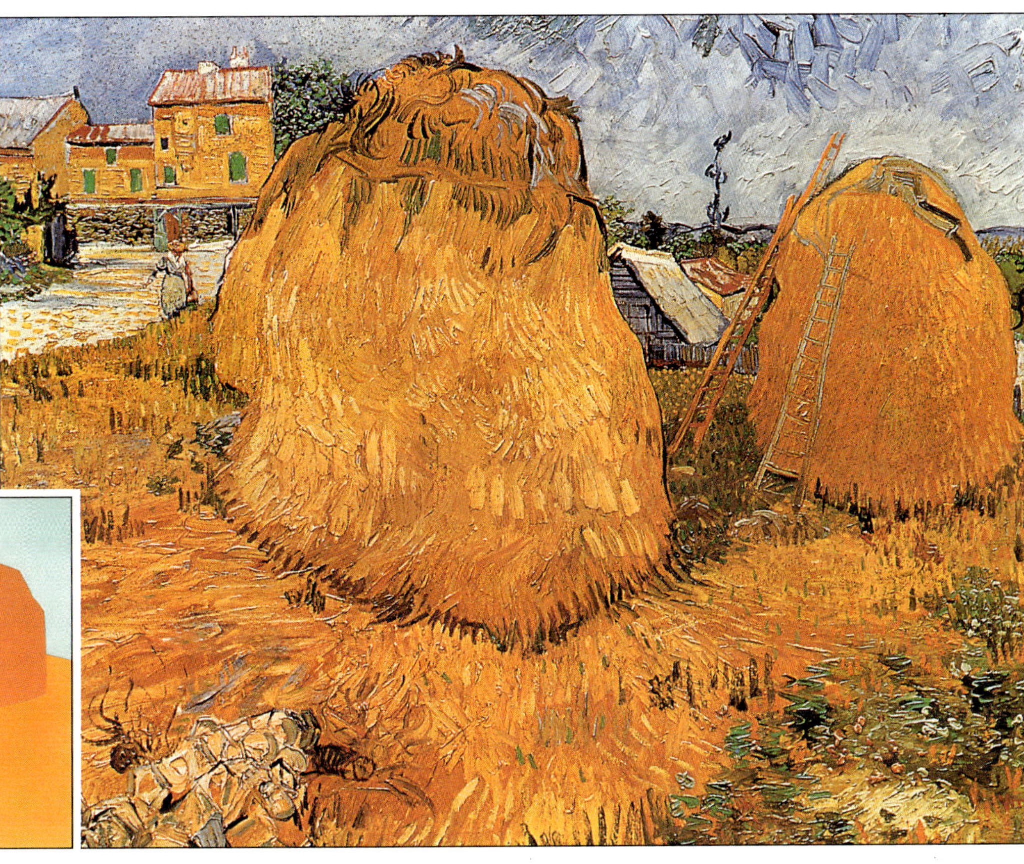

Jaume Mercadé, The Bastion. *The painter represents depth by painting his work as a geometric construction with superimposed planes.*

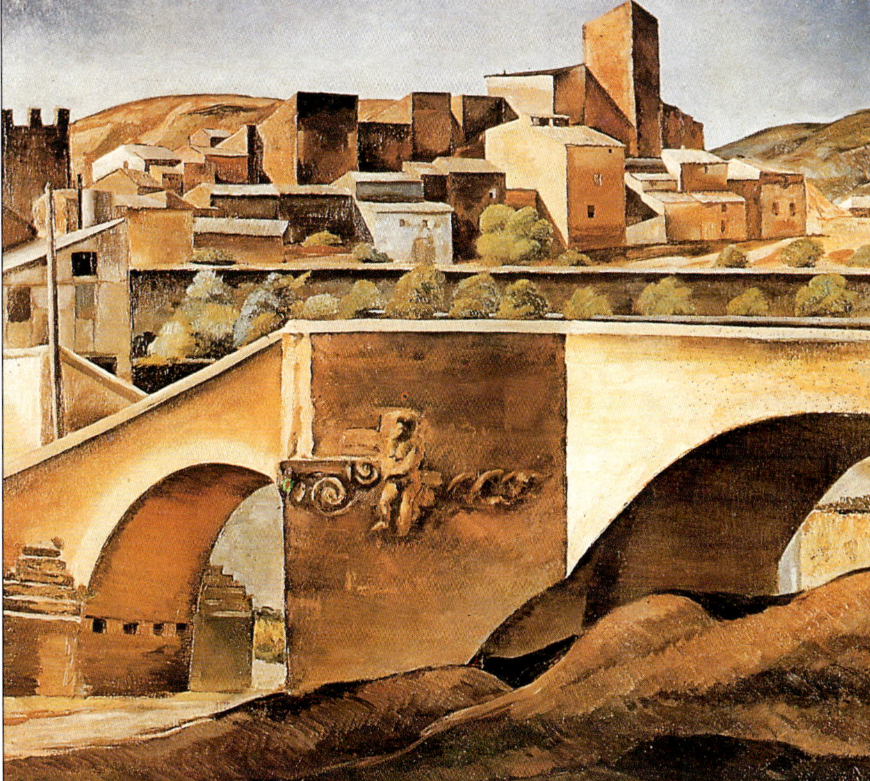

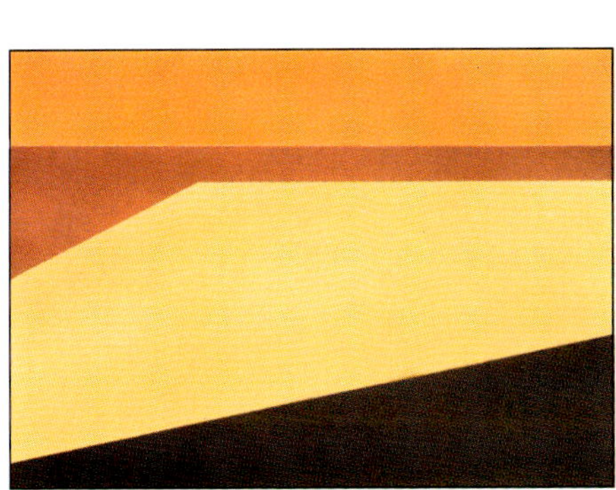

Composition in an urban landscape

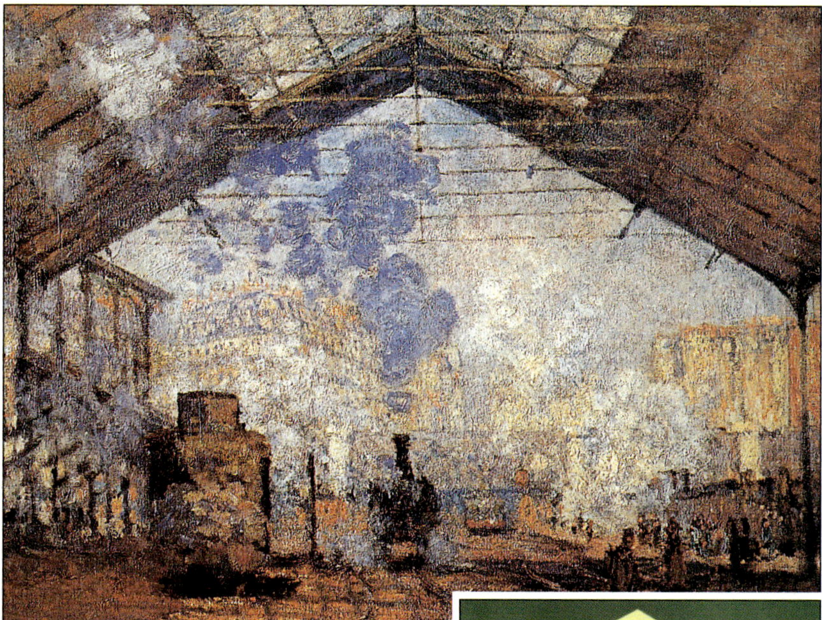

Claude Monet, Saint Lazare Station. *The vivaciousness and chromatacism of the scene are governed by the dominant compositional triangle formed by the station's roof.*

Albert Maquet, Rooftops of Paris. *The dominant geometric construction of this urban landscape is established by the triangle that divides the canvas in two and creates the foreground.*

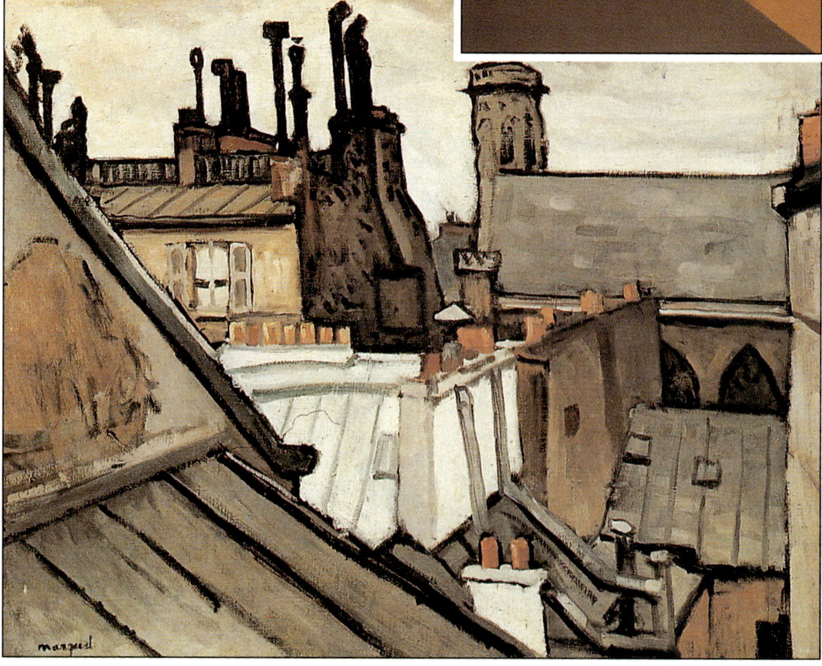

While the composition of a landscape is essentially organic, articulated from the irregularities of nature, the urban landscape is almost entirely geometric by definition.

What is an infinite diversity of shapes and sizes in the countryside, is precise definition in the city. This extremely important factor must be taken into account when composing an urban landscape.

Everything in the city appears to be already composed: the facades containing rows of windows and balconies, the sidewalks, the lines of the streets, the profile of the slated rooftops. We need not look far to find vertical, diagonal, and other lines. This is all very much to the painter's advantage, but it also entails certain risks.

In effect, geometric precision can create impeccable paintings, but rarely does it give way to works of art.

The temptation to design rather than paint an urban landscape is something that affects many painters. The results may be "perfect" but cold and dull.

What is the solution? As is often the case, the answer lies in the painter's own sensitivity and experience. Corot stated: "*Never lose the first impression.*" In other words, it is the painter's first aesthetic impression of the motif that counts, and any other considerations, such as exactitude, should be relegated to second place.

The abundance of motifs in the city makes it an ideal place for searching out your own personal aesthetics. Not only are there attractive avenues, streets, squares bathed in light, nighttime illumination, and endless perspectives, but the urban viewpoints from which to see them are also extremely varied—sidewalks, windows, balconies, etc. It all comes down to choosing your favorite place and interpreting it from an interesting viewpoint, using a clear and simple compositional scheme to achieve it.

A city scene can be composed from as many viewpoints as you want. It can be seen from a purely constructivist viewpoint, based on lines, searching out an abstraction of forms, or it can be interpreted organically, as if the city were a living being related to the forms surrounding it. If you study any urban landscape, the artist's compositional layout immediately becomes evident.

Camille Pisarro, The Bridge at Boïledieu. *This zigzag composition is recurrent in Impressionistic landscapes and, above all, in Pisarro's urban landscapes.*

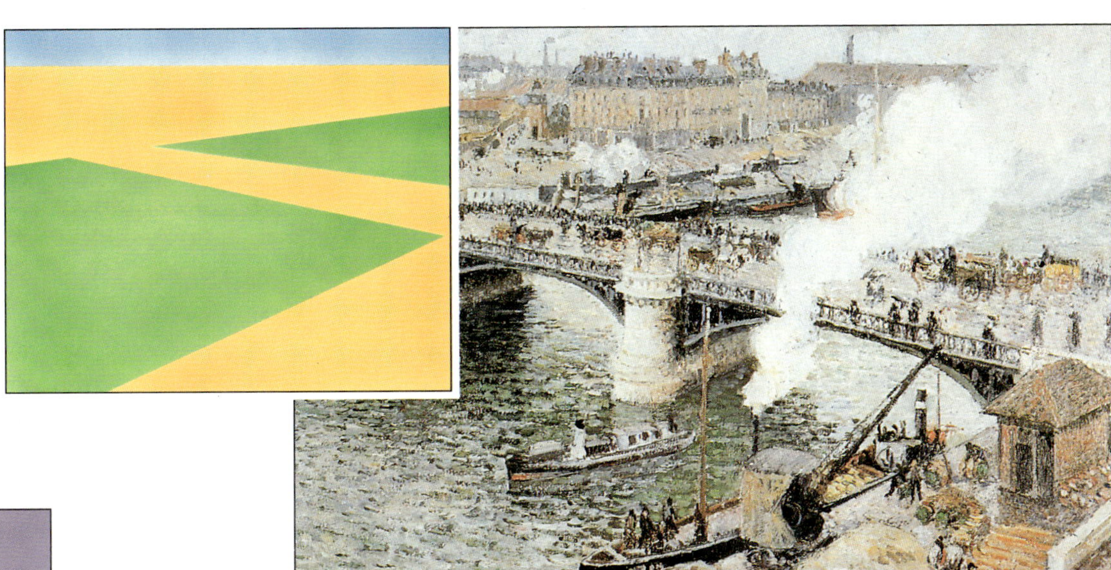

Ernst Ludwig Kirchner, The Red Tower at Halle. *In this composition, all the shapes form a series of rhombuses that reverse or distort the perspective, creating a sensation of vertigo.*

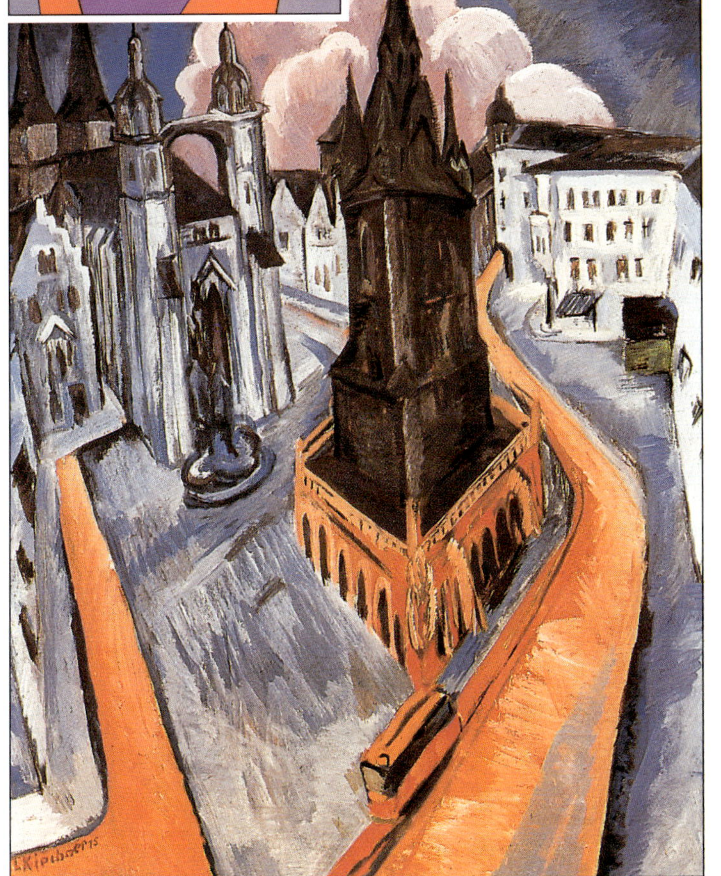

Johannes van Troostwij, The Raamportje, Amsterdam. *The serenity emanating from this work is the result of its predominant horizontal lines and the large "empty" spaces reserved for the sky.*

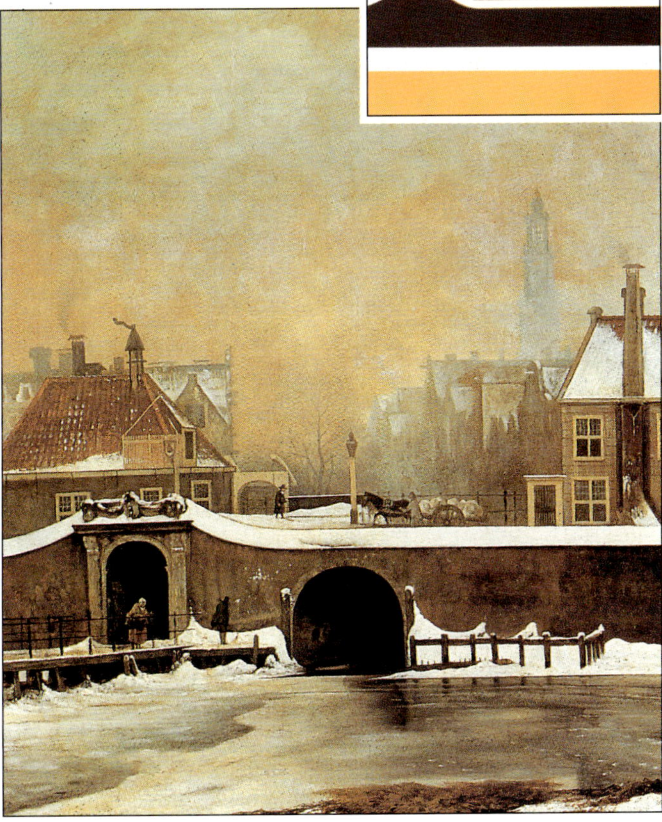

Drawing as a compositional study

Before you begin painting an urban landscape, it is essential to define its architecture. A drawing of the theme that accurately conveys the painter's aim is what lends each composition its unique character. We have already shown that no two compositions of the same theme are ever identical.

To paint an urban landscape it is essential to study drawing. You have to measure, size up, relate sizes and forms, and draw with a loose wrist.

Artists must practice their drawing skills constantly. They must exercise their powers of observation, as John Singer Sargent never stopped telling his students. One should never tire of making fast, improvised, spontaneous sketches. In other words, scribble to your heart's content; with practice you will gradually master the technique.

Drawing can be defined in a variety of ways and, logically, none of them is perfect. We could define the art of drawing as a means to establish and explain the landscape that we are trying to represent, as a way to express or arrange its composition.

To arrange in this context means to relate, compare, and classify the artist's sensations. There are many factors involved in achieving this arrangement, such as blocking in, proportions, evaluation, contrast, and perspective. Although all of these are useful for drawing, it is important to remember that each theme requires the artist to concentrate more on one or another of these aspects. Some motifs, for instance, stress perspective; others are better represented through contrast and evaluation, or by getting the correct dimensions and proportions in order to represent what is most characteristic.

It is important to bear in mind that, whether we are talking of blocking in, evaluation, or perspective, we must always compare the different parts of the model, its values of light and shadow, lines, and other elements.

Finally, it is up to you to choose your theme; every artist—every person, in fact—has his or her own particular thematic taste, a fact that must be respected.

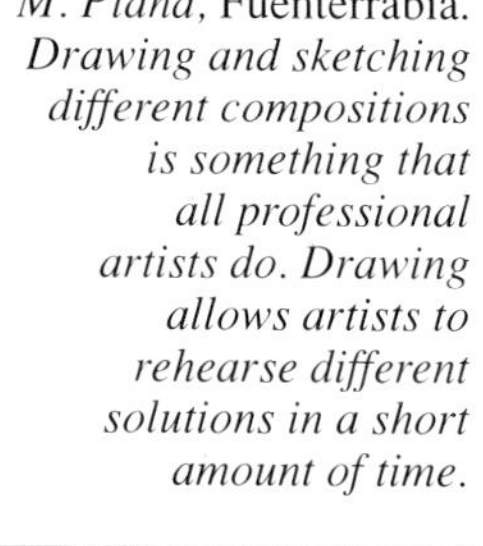

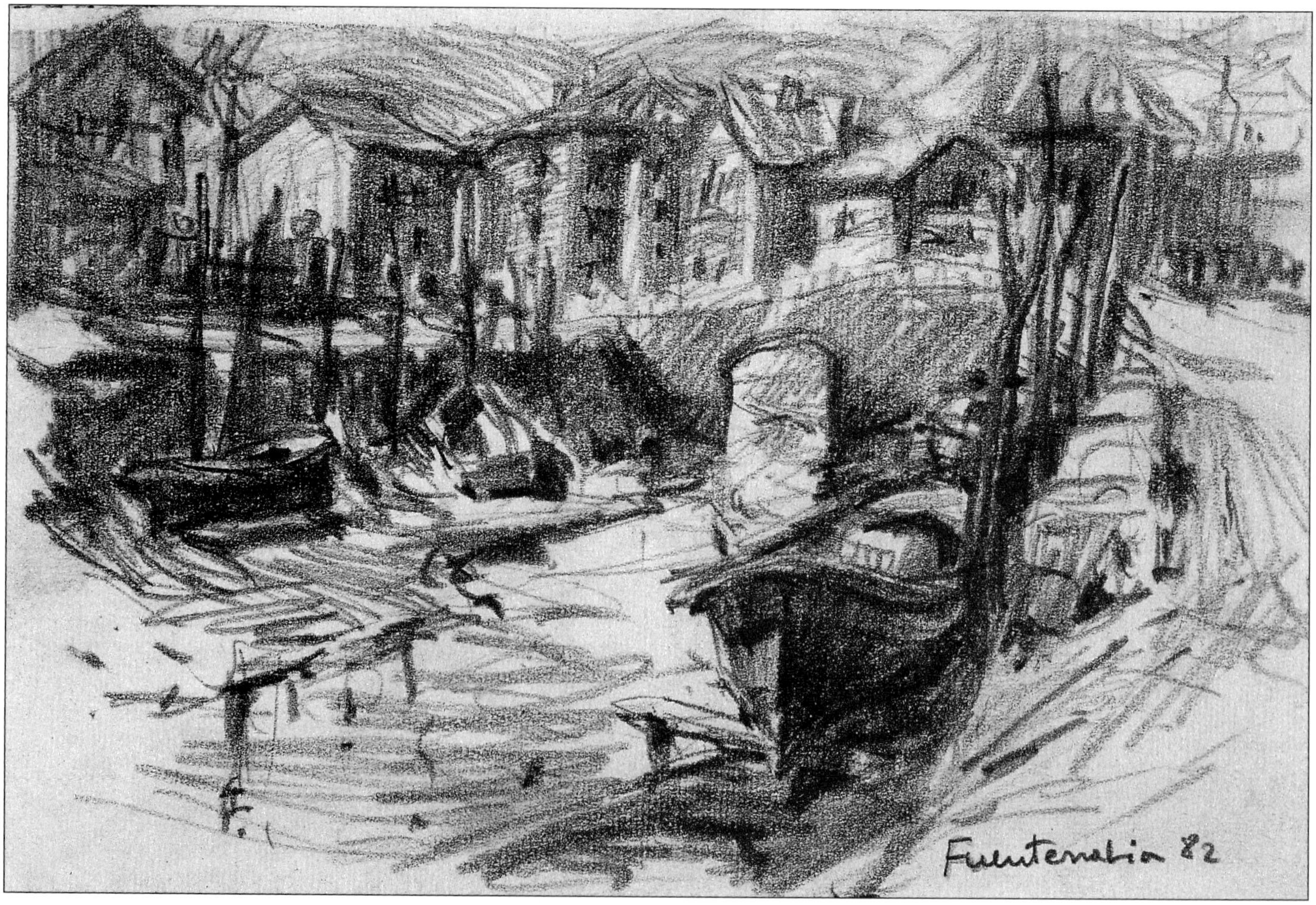

M. Plana, Fuenterrabía. *Drawing and sketching different compositions is something that all professional artists do. Drawing allows artists to rehearse different solutions in a short amount of time.*

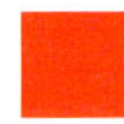

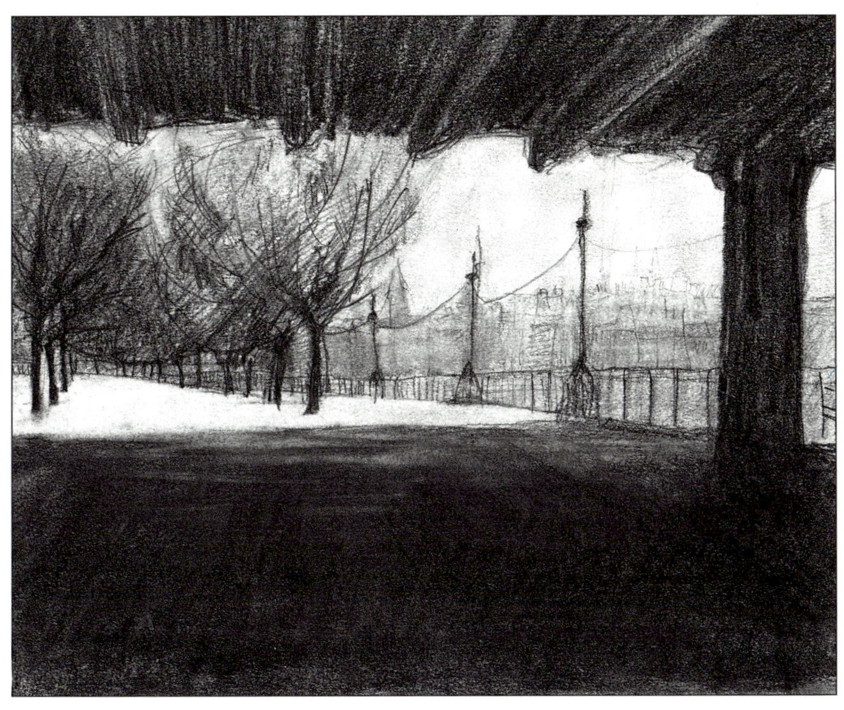

Muntsa Calbó, By the Thames. *The artist has perfectly defined the theme using three shades of gray and the white of the paper. The drawing has a parallel composition in the foreground, with a triangle-shaped vanishing point. The center of attention is situated on the horizon line.*

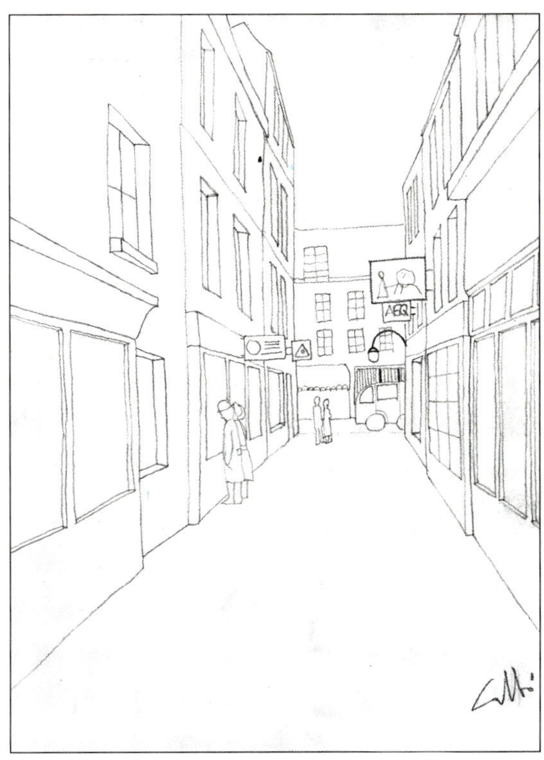

Muntsa Calbó, Street in Bath. *A purely linear drawing style is ideal for an urban landscape, since it allows artists to clearly establish the compositional aspects of the future work. Here we have an X-shaped composition in which the space is distributed proportionally in each one of the picture's sections.*

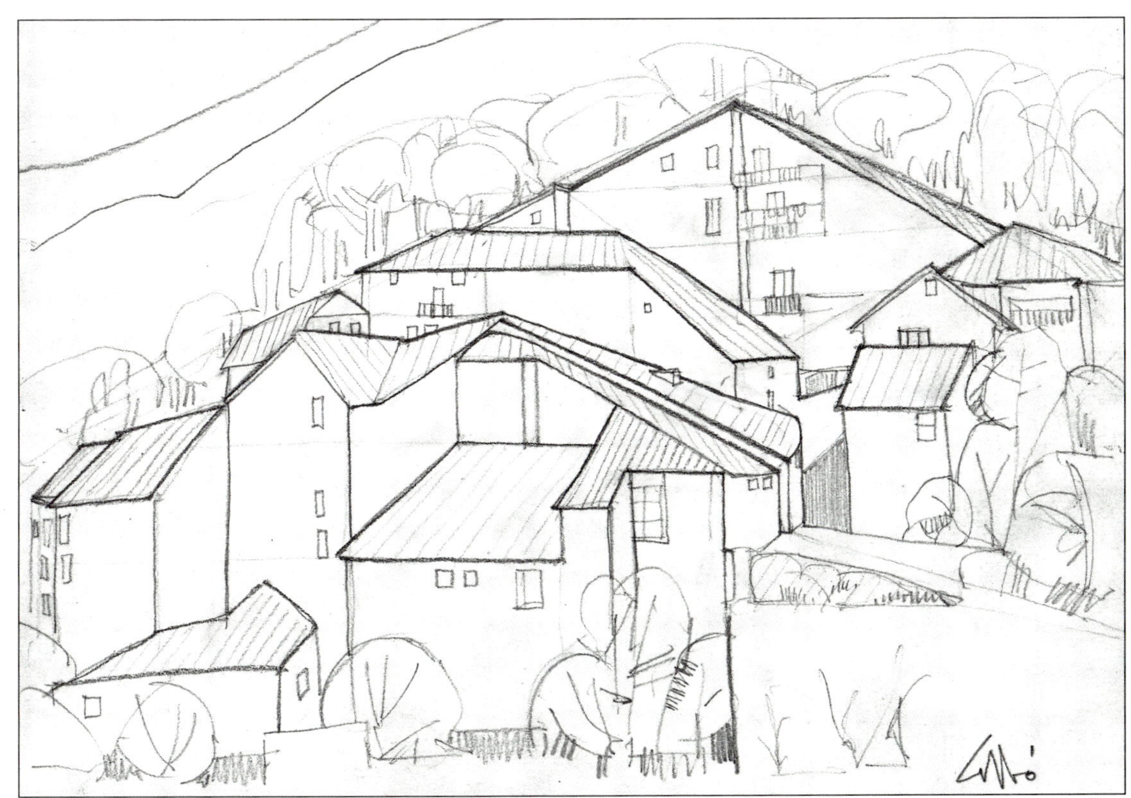

Muntsa Calbó, Durro. *In this case, the artist has based the drawing on the large triangular form created by the roof of the house farthest up the hill. This type of composition, which appears to be more complex that it really is, is in fact based on a diagonal line that defines the entire compositional space.*

Composition of an oil landscape

1 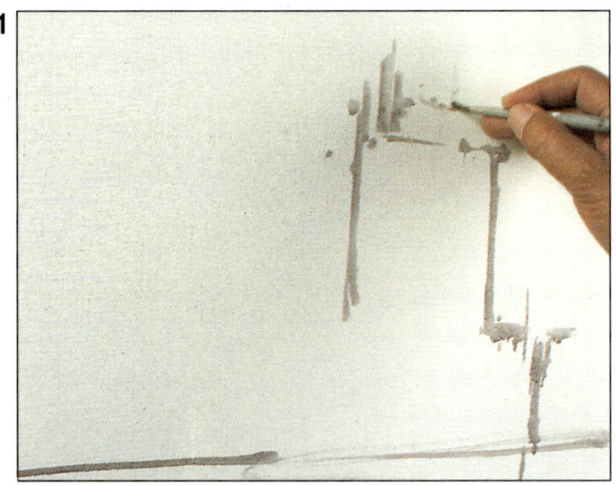

2 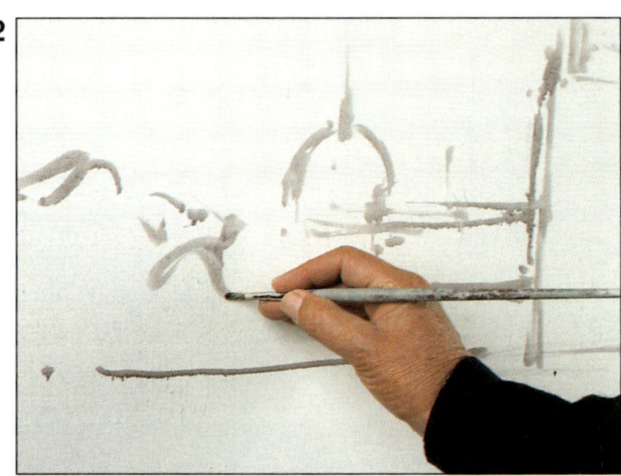

1 and 2. Casañé sketches with a fine brush. He uses a neutral bluish gray color diluted with plenty of turpentine, which lets him work freely, allowing the brush to glide over the canvas. It doesn't matter if the color drips, since this sketch is used only to work out the general structure of the composition, starting with the horizon at roughly the same height as the division of the golden section.

1. Preliminary drawing

Josep Luís Casañé is going to paint a landscape in his studio, using one of the many sketches he makes during his excursions into the country. He has chosen an essentially linear sketch that he will interpret from memory, using his extraordinary sense of color and bearing in mind the relative importance of the different masses, places, and details of the landscape.

The painter begins the preliminary drawing with a neutral bluish gray diluted with turpentine. This drawing, which sets out the painting's basic compositional characteristics, is a simplified version of the original sketch.

Casañé starts by dividing the canvas into two. The dividing line follows the rule of the golden section. This intuitive division, used by many painters to place the horizon in their landscapes, is one of the most time-honored methods of composing. Casañé places the buildings above this line and brings out the plane of the ground below it.

Even though the artist is painting a sketch, there is already ample definition at this stage.

Casañé holds the sketchbook in his left hand while he paints with the right. The artist explains that he always sketches from nature, either in pencil or watercolors. He also takes photographs of the theme. "Photographs," he tells us, "are useful for remembering certain details that can help to define parts of the painting, or to suggest a color or form."

3. *Here we can see how Casañé consults his sketchbook, which he holds in one hand, while he continues to draw with the other hand. The original sketch is specific enough to allow the artist to suppress certain details when the time comes to apply color.*

3 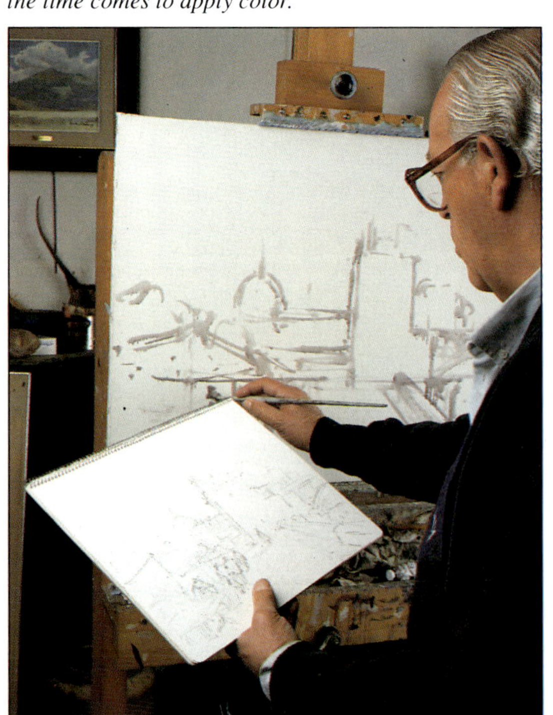

4. *Casañé finishes the sketch. Notice the abundant space left for the sky. The painter believes, as did the Impressionist Sisley, that much of a landscape should be reserved for the sky. A well-defined sky with the right color can bring out any landscape.*

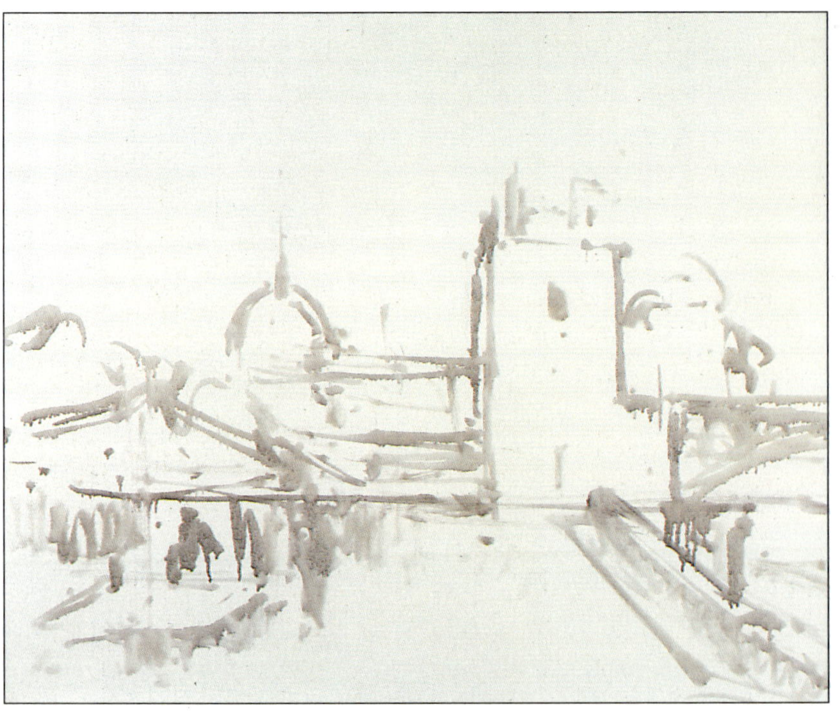

2. General staining

The artist begins by painting the sky with a flat, rather thick brush. He applies violet gray tones, obtained from a mix of ultramarine blue, carmine, a touch of ocher, and white. Each time Casañé loads the brush, he tones the color according to the area he is painting by adding blue, white, or ocher. With white paint the artist draws some of the shapes of the buildings while staining the area of the sky.

The first stains are general; they are applied to cover the canvas while allowing the original color to be seen through the paint. The barely diluted paint is thick, and is applied by vigorously scrubbing the canvas. This technique produces very discernible, directional strokes. The painter only applies flat color to the dome and the shadow cast by the side of the bridge.

Casañé works with neutral colors that he constantly mixes together. He creates blends of blue, carmine, ocher, and white; green, carmine, and white; and ocher, green, Prussian blue, and white. Mixed together, these colors produce neutral, cool colors.

The painter frequently changes brushes, especially when he changes color or requires a smaller brush for adding a detail. Up to this point, he has painted with four brushes, all flat, ranging from a number 8 to a number 12.

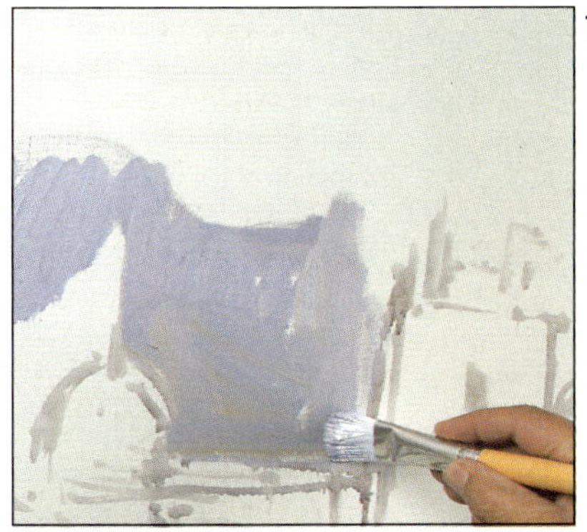
1

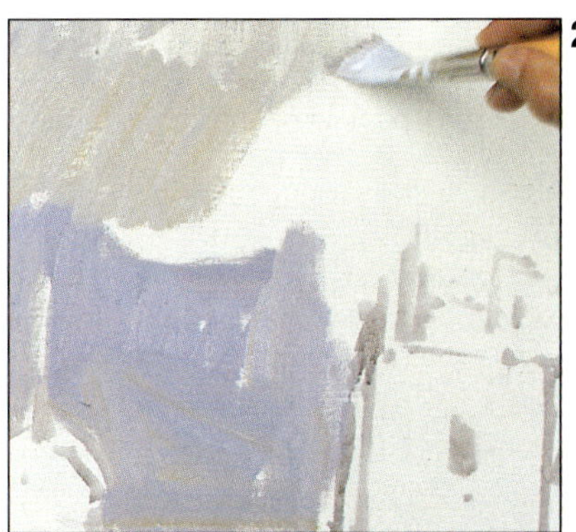
2

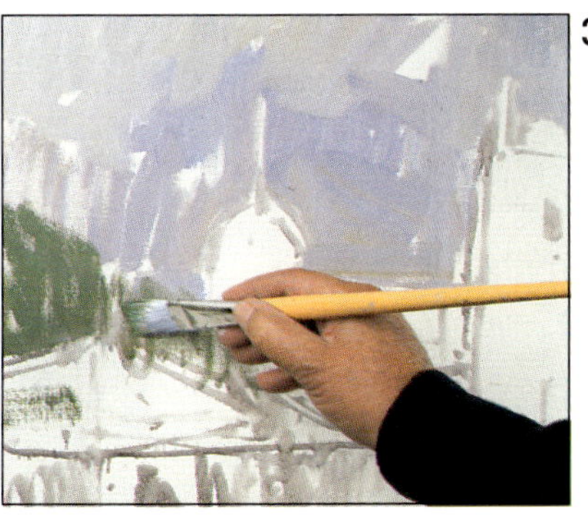
3

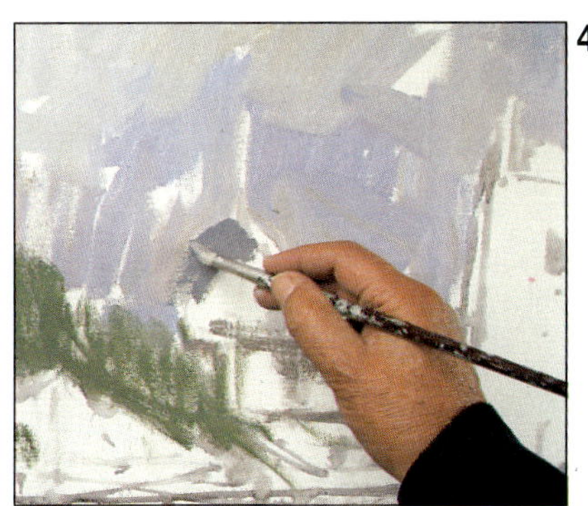
4

5

1 *and* **2.** *The artist begins by painting the sky with a host of blue tones: ultramarine blue with white, black, ocher, carmine, and grayish blue tones, all applied with the brush.*

3 *and* **4.** *The painter continues with the same brush, this time applying green for the trees and a very grayish dark blue for the dome. From the outset, Casañé harmonizes colors, staining with turpentine.*

5. *By the end of the second phase, Casañé has painted a large part of the canvas, working on everything at the same time. Evidence of this can be seen in the painting, which has now acquired a compositional balance and a synthesis of light and color.*

Composition of an oil landscape

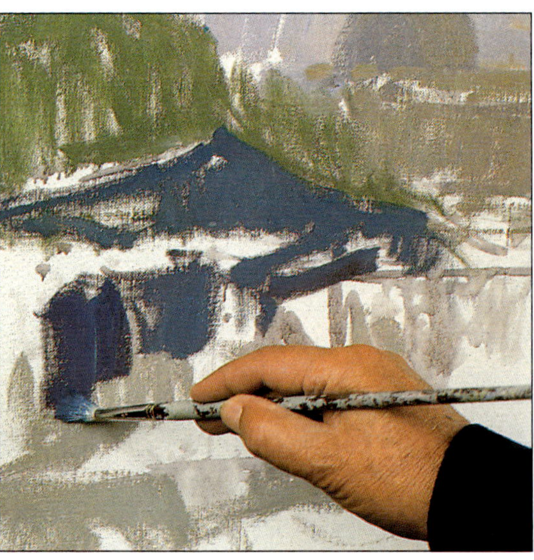

With various hues of dark blue, the artist stains the area of the stalls. This produces a stark contrast with the background that indicates the proximity and distance of the objects. This same color is applied in the background to define certain shadows.

3. Chromatic composition of the theme

Casañé continues staining the parts of the painting that are still unpainted. Using medium-sized brushes, he begins work on the stalls in the left corner of the foreground, which were barely defined in the preliminary sketch. The artist paints these stalls and their respective canvas roofs with dark, neutral colors so as to blend them in with the general harmony of colors. However, these colors are not as neutral as the gray tones applied to the sky and the buildings in the background. In other words, since he is painting the objects in the foreground, he uses purer, cleaner colors; colors that are not altered by the effect of distance.

Now the painter stains the tower bathed in sunlight with light colors—mixes of yellow and red with abundant white and a touch of ocher; that is, toned down colors again. The contrast with the sky is resounding and highly appropriate since, with the grayish blue background, the light colors of the tower appear lighter and more luminous. Each time Casañé loads some paint from the palette he mixes it, adding a touch of yellow, orange, or white. Toning it continuously, the artist applies it to the steps in the background and the ground in the foreground.

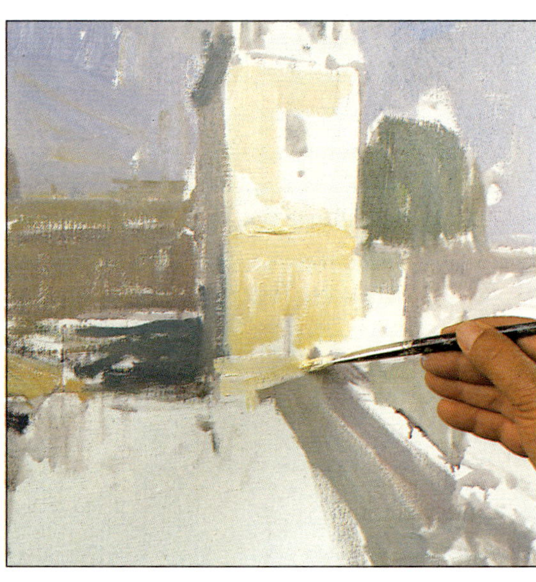

With white mixed with ocher and yellow, the artist obtains a pale, opaque color that he uses to paint the part of the tower in sunlight.

Quickly he paints the same color over the blue in the background, helping to suggest the steps with several narrow brushstrokes.

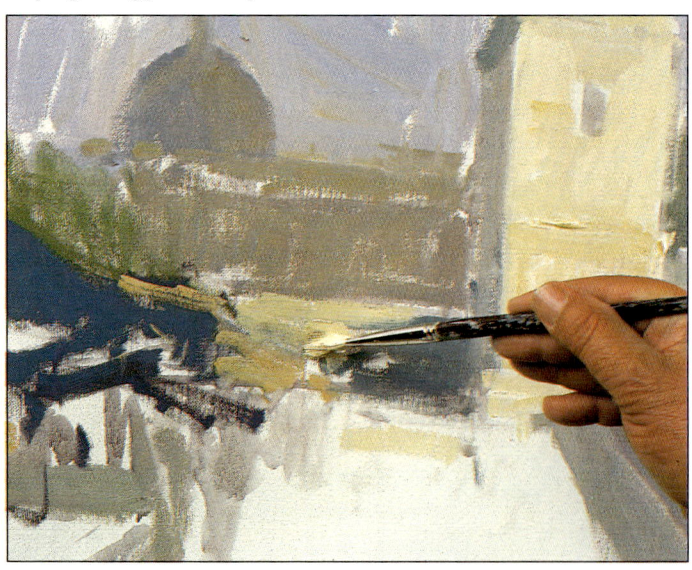

With short and vertical brushstrokes, the artist continues with the same color to paint the ground, leaving white spaces between them.

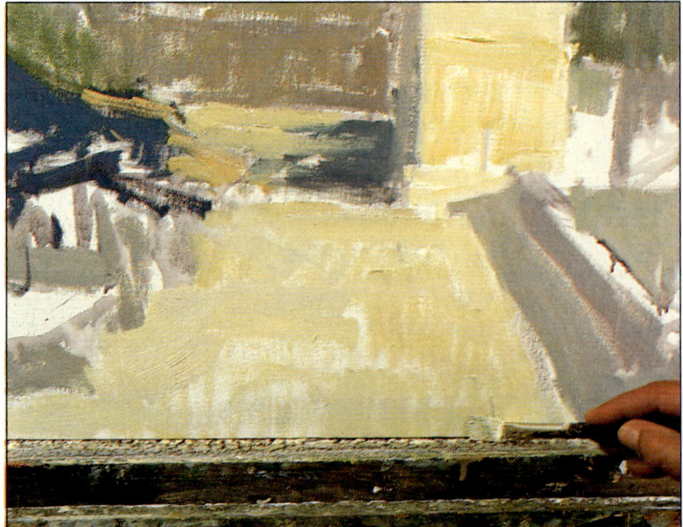

4. Evaluating the theme

The artist continues painting, this time on top of the still-wet paint, mixing the colors directly on the canvas. He starts to suggest volume by evaluating tones. For instance, in the mass of trees on the left, Casañé paints dark green over light green in order to represent volume and illumination, always in a schematic and synthetic form.

Casañé comments: "*I don't enjoy the preliminary staining of the canvas. What I mean is that I hate to start paintings. It would be great if I could buy them already primed, even if they were badly done.*" For those who are learning to paint, the preliminary staining session is often fun and satisfying, perhaps because they think this is the least important part of the work and find that the painting gradually loses its fresh appearance as more layers of paint are added. But the first few strokes play a vital role in the final result of the painting; they determine the composition. What Casañé likes most about painting is working on the difficult aspects; that is, modifying, toning, and finishing off the picture. The way in which the artist works on everything at the same time, instead of concentrating on individual aspects of the painting, is a clear demonstration of his experience.

It should be noted how Casañé has shown the illumination from the outset with direct and diluted stains, a method that Corot recommended to his students.

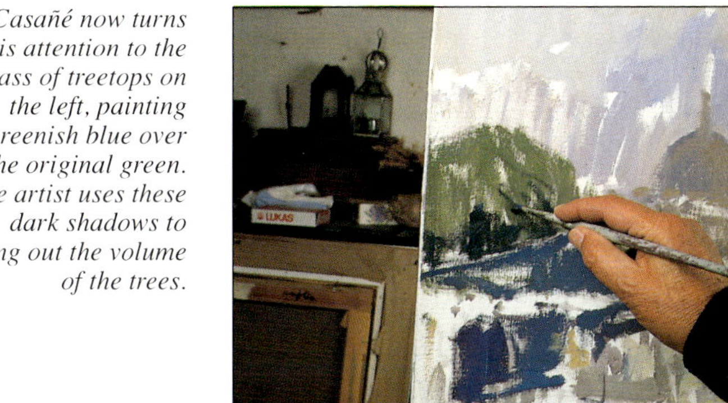

Casañé now turns his attention to the mass of treetops on the left, painting greenish blue over the original green. The artist uses these dark shadows to bring out the volume of the trees.

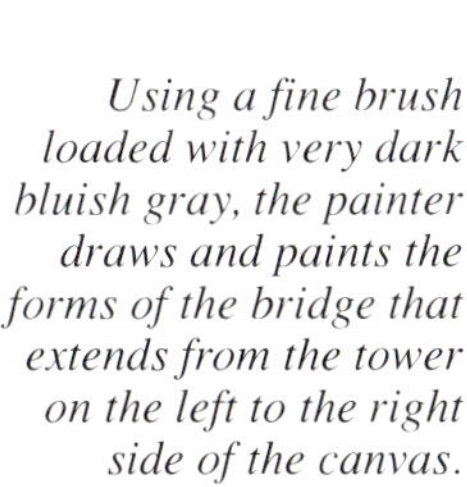

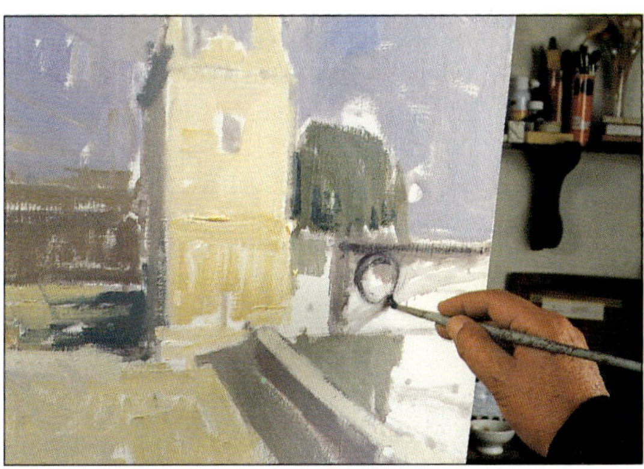

Using a fine brush loaded with very dark bluish gray, the painter draws and paints the forms of the bridge that extends from the tower on the left to the right side of the canvas.

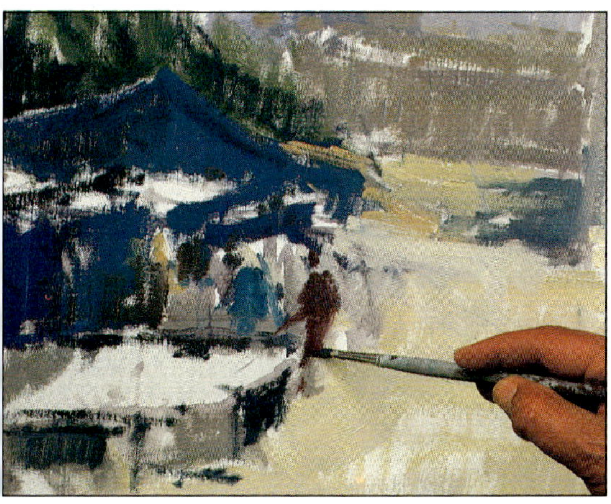

The painter begins to give greater definition to the color and forms of the flea market. The figures, tables, and covers begin to take shape from the apparently confusing mass of brushwork, a task that is effected with simplified and correctly calculated brushstrokes.

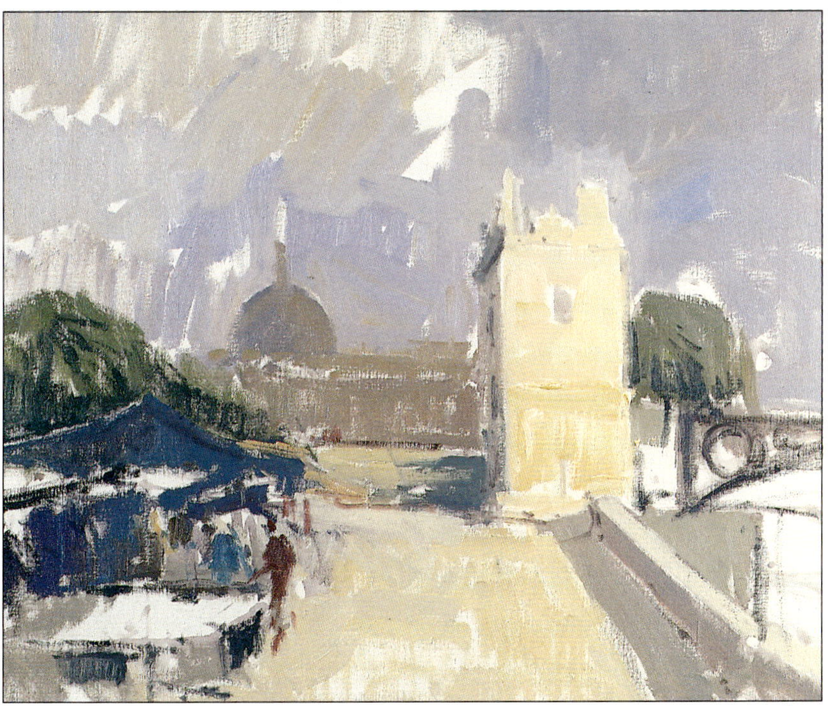

Doing what all painters do, Casañé stands back a few feet from the painting in order to study its current state. After a short silence, the artist says: "The fundamental part of the work, the overall color scheme, is complete."

5. Adding details

Casañé has stopped painting in order to study the theme for a few minutes. Then he starts rummaging for tubes of paint in his boxes, in leather pouches, and on top of shelves. Finding the ones he was looking for, he squirts generous amounts of paint onto his palette.

He is getting ready to paint over the initial layer of color. He will cover most of it, leaving only bits and pieces of it visible to create the desired effect. A reminder: In order to be sure that the paint dries properly on the surface and to prevent cracks from appearing later on, you should always begin by painting the first layers with plenty of turpentine, then proceeding with thick layers and impastos.

With several thick, almost white, zigzag brushstrokes, Casañé paints the ground in the foreground, which is now much brighter and more consistent. Using the same flat, wide brush, loaded with the same type of impasto, he paints the details on the steps and the building in the background, applying light over dark and then, dark over light. The resulting harmony remains within the neutral range of colors.

He begins to paint tiny figures around the market stalls, on the steps, and in other areas, with highly abstract blobs of pure color. The artist says that these tiny stains help to "create a sense of proportion," so that the sizes of the different elements of the painting are perceived coherently.

1 *and* **2.** *The painter applies a thick layer of pale paint above the building's dark carmine tones. Then he applies dark blue over the pale tones of the steps. This continuous overlaying process is used to lend greater definition to the forms.*

3 *and* **4.** *After countless neutral color mixes, Casañé begins painting with pure color. These tiny stains, representing the people in the street, allow him to create a sense of proportion in composition. While he's at it, he uses these same pure colors to finish a few details in the market stalls, painting over the previously painted layers.*

1

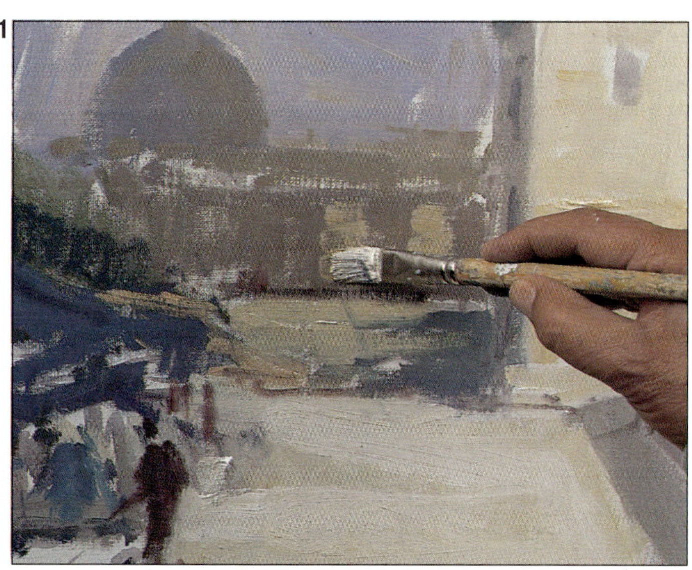

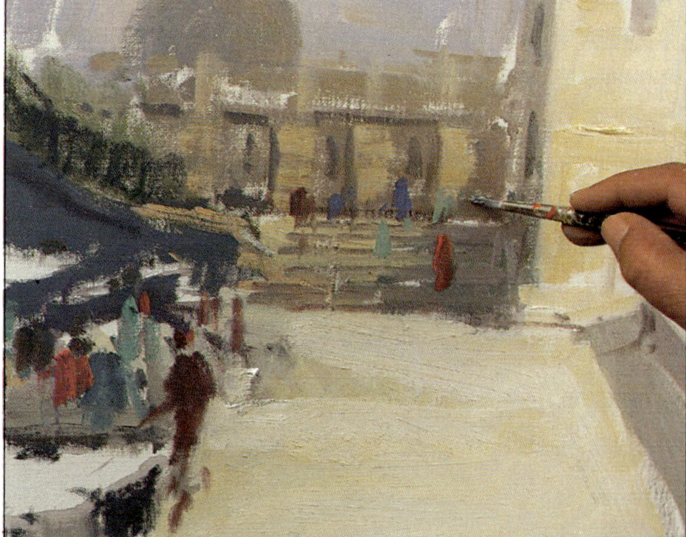

3

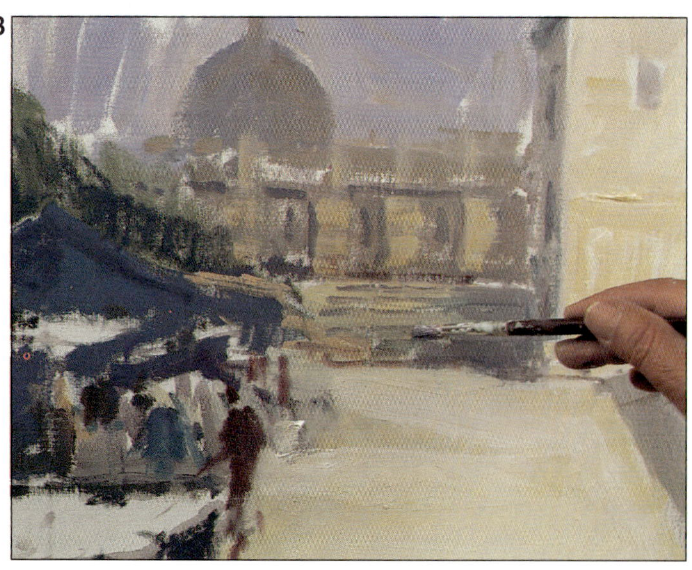

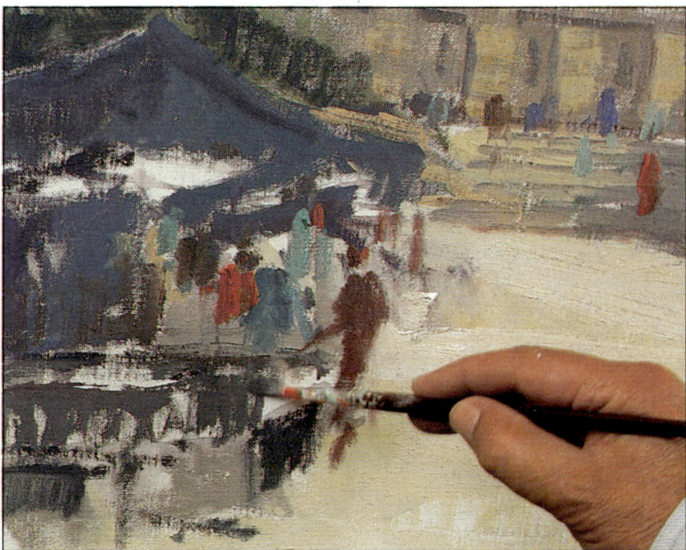

6. Finishing the work

Carried away by the joy of pure color, the artist applies thick impastos, but uses a fine brush to add details to the market stalls. The throng of objects, sellers, browsers, etc., are expressed with orangish tones, red, and celeste blue, all bright and defined.

Casañé works with narrow round brushes to paint the forms with short directional strokes, which construct the thickness of the trees and the walls. This brushwork is superimposed on the original color applications.

Then he switches brushes, choosing this time a thick flat one. Casañé prepares some dark gray on the palette, placing it on top of the remains of other colors that turn it into a opaque neutral gray, which he applies in the sky. He then adds some white and blue to it and continues adding patches of color all over the area of the sky.

The blue of the sky lightens the gray and turns it into a greenish tone. The result makes the sky appear darker above the horizon. Now we see how lighted parts of the trees and houses are almost as bright as the sky. This effect can often be observed when the sun directly illuminates forms.

The painter is now at an advanced stage, although some parts still require intensifying.

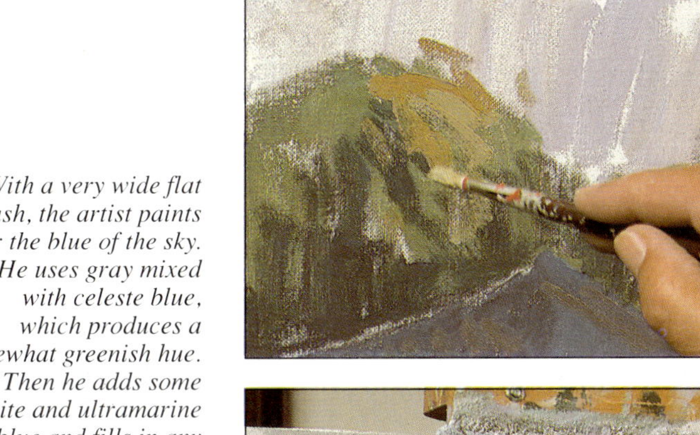

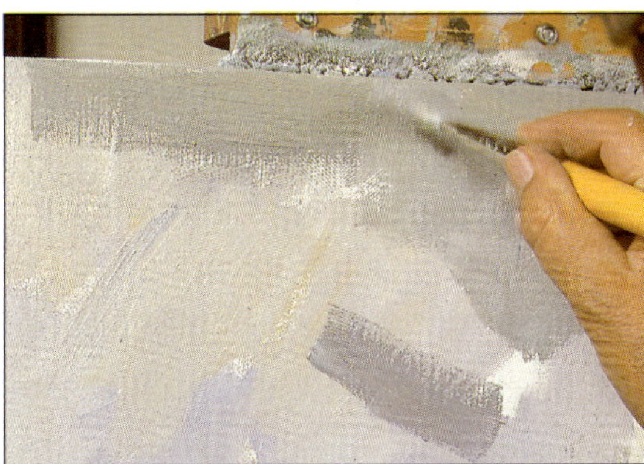

With a very wide flat brush, the artist paints over the blue of the sky. He uses gray mixed with celeste blue, which produces a somewhat greenish hue. Then he adds some white and ultramarine blue and fills in any gaps where the white of the canvas remains visible.

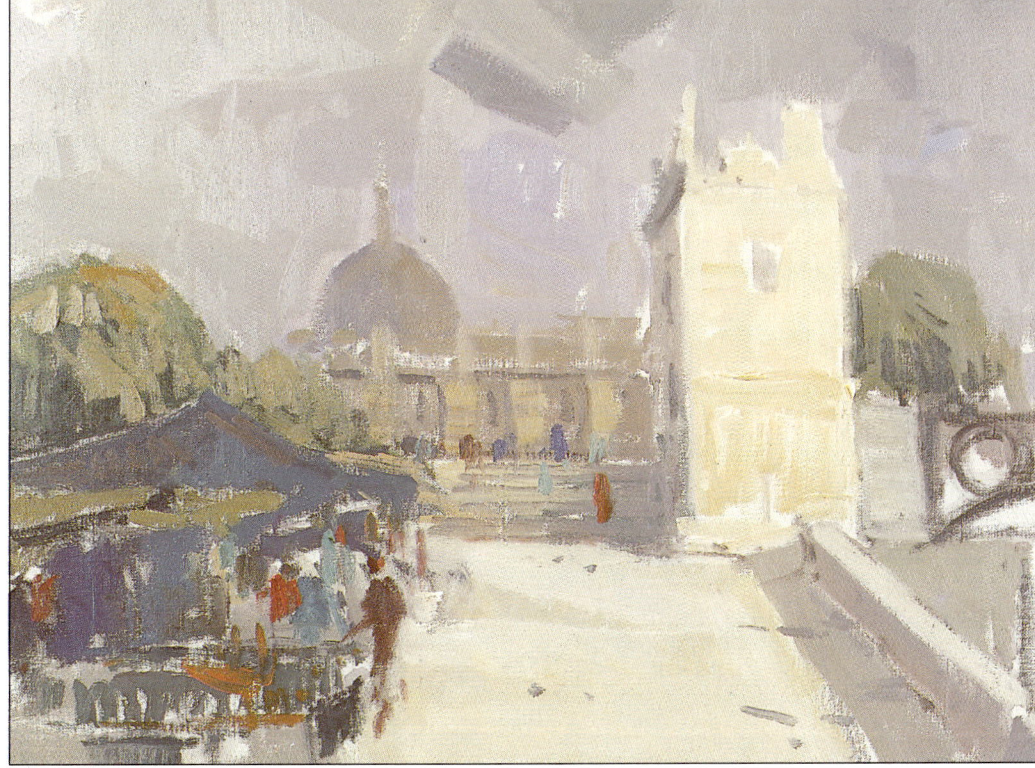

At this stage, the painting is almost complete. Notice how the most recent brushwork is superimposed over the original colors without mixing. Notice also the large zigzag strokes that cover the ground in the foreground, making it appear even more luminous and consistent and allowing it to blend in with the play of lights and shadows that predominate in the composition.

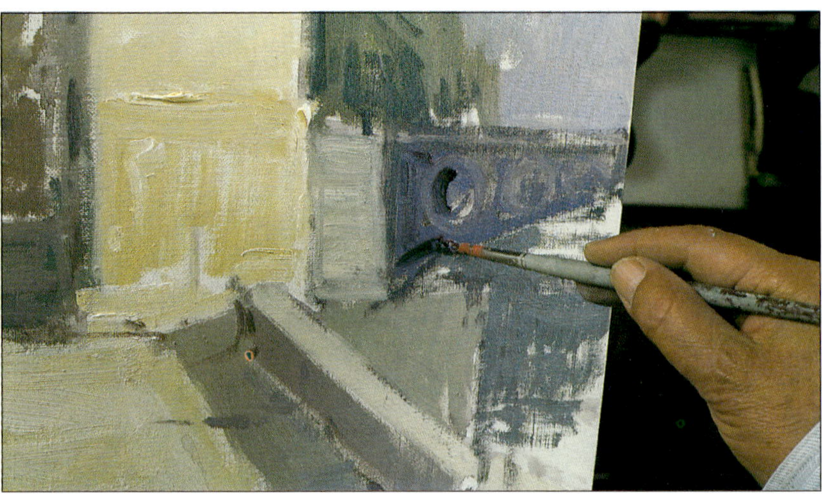

Casañé paints the bottom of the bridge. He paints the shadows of the iron structure with a cool grayish blue tone.

7. Details: Shines and reflections

Casañé runs his brush in a zigzag direction over the palette to load it with paint and mix colors. The forms that the brush draws on the surface look like knots, snakes, etc. He doesn't check to see what color he actually loads as his brush darts to and fro between the palette and the canvas. It does not matter, since these new and surprising colors make the grayish mix resound.

Then the artist paints the bridge, constructing the iron girders with light and dark violet tones. He returns to the stalls and adds some dark tones to lend them more definition.

The painter now constructs the trees with grayish green tones, adjusting them to the general color harmony of the canvas. Casañé paints at a more relaxed, although constant, pace. He paints standing up, often standing back from the canvas, more so now that he is in the final stage of the work. He switches brushes, depending on the detail he is working on. First, with a fine brush loaded with ocher he paints the arabesque at the top of the tower. Then he outlines the shadows cast by the bridge and touches up the shadows cast by the trees with a very dark gray. With an almost identical color he darkens the tower's windows.

He adds several touches of pure yellow in the area of the flea market, which he then mixes with the bluish tones that predominate in this area of the composition. The painter outlines the canvas covers of the stalls with white mixed with ocher to express the light that illuminates the canvas roofs, in contrast with the cool, dark atmosphere below. Casañé also works on the part of the river, below the bridge

More detail and an improvement in the construction. Casañé deals with these problems, while he continues the work at a more relaxed but constant pace.

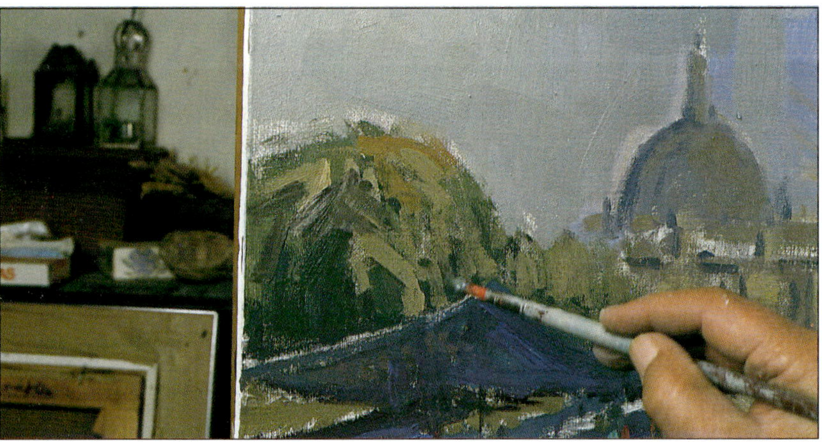

Here the artist goes over certain details, bringing out the light and dark areas of the composition.

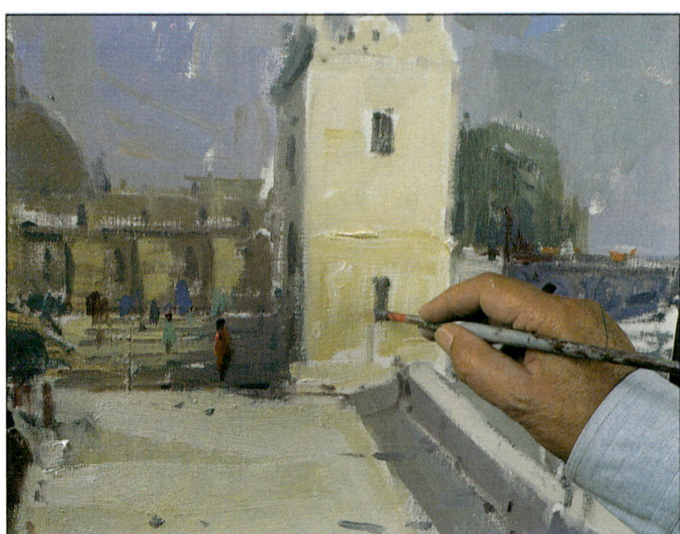

The greater the pure colors, the livelier the forms of the flea market look. The dozens of tiny brushstrokes give this area of the painting coherence and unity.

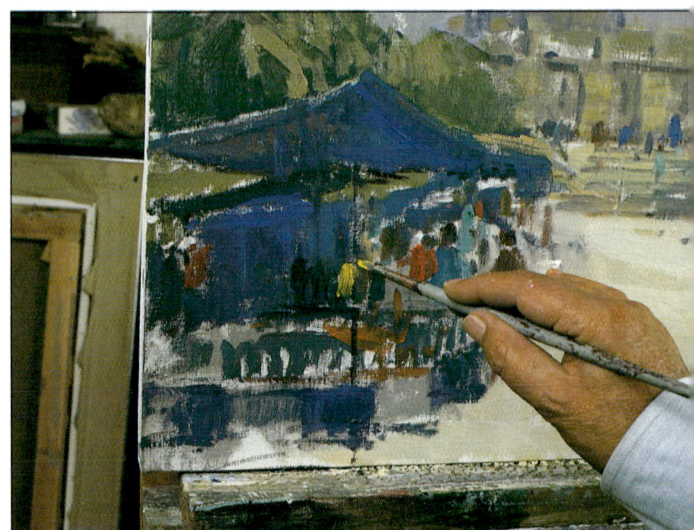

which until now has barely been touched. Patches of the white canvas have been left visible, but the artist covers them with tiny strokes, creating, at the same time, the reflections on the water. Next he adds several tiny brushstrokes over the entire surface of the painting, similar to notes of color that harmonize the colors of the composition.

Now it is time to add the odd detail, correct a color, etc. While Casañé studies the painting, he comments on the way an artist selects the theme: "*The theme is everywhere; the theme is nothing more than an excuse; it has to be imagined, interpreted; that is, you shouldn't wait to see it, but reflect, think, and search for the composition and the color harmony that will make it interesting. The theme, the real theme, is the painting, the painting itself, the pictorial resolution of something interesting.*"

And this is precisely what Casañé does now; he looks at the painting and checks specific features. At this point they are essential for obtaining a truly unified composition.

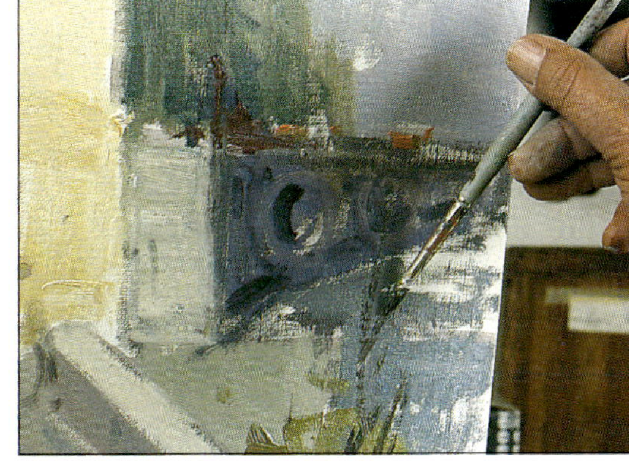

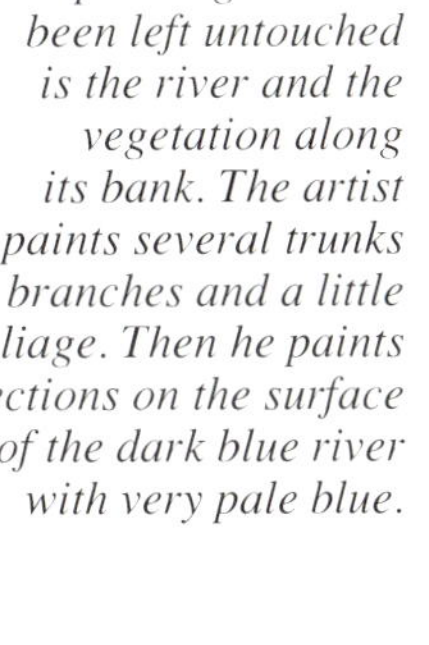

The only area of the painting that has been left untouched is the river and the vegetation along its bank. The artist paints several trunks and branches and a little foliage. Then he paints reflections on the surface of the dark blue river with very pale blue.

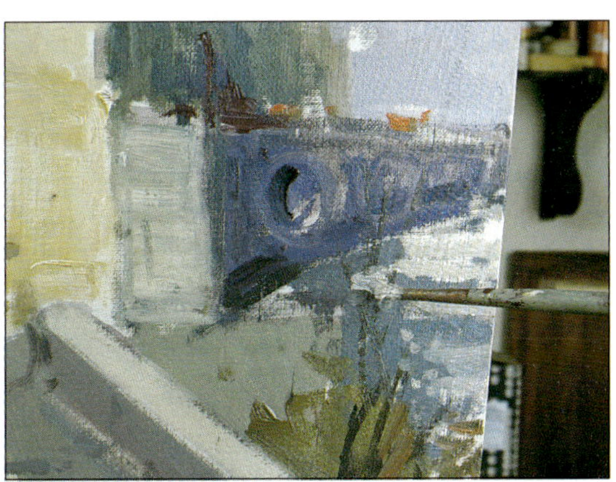

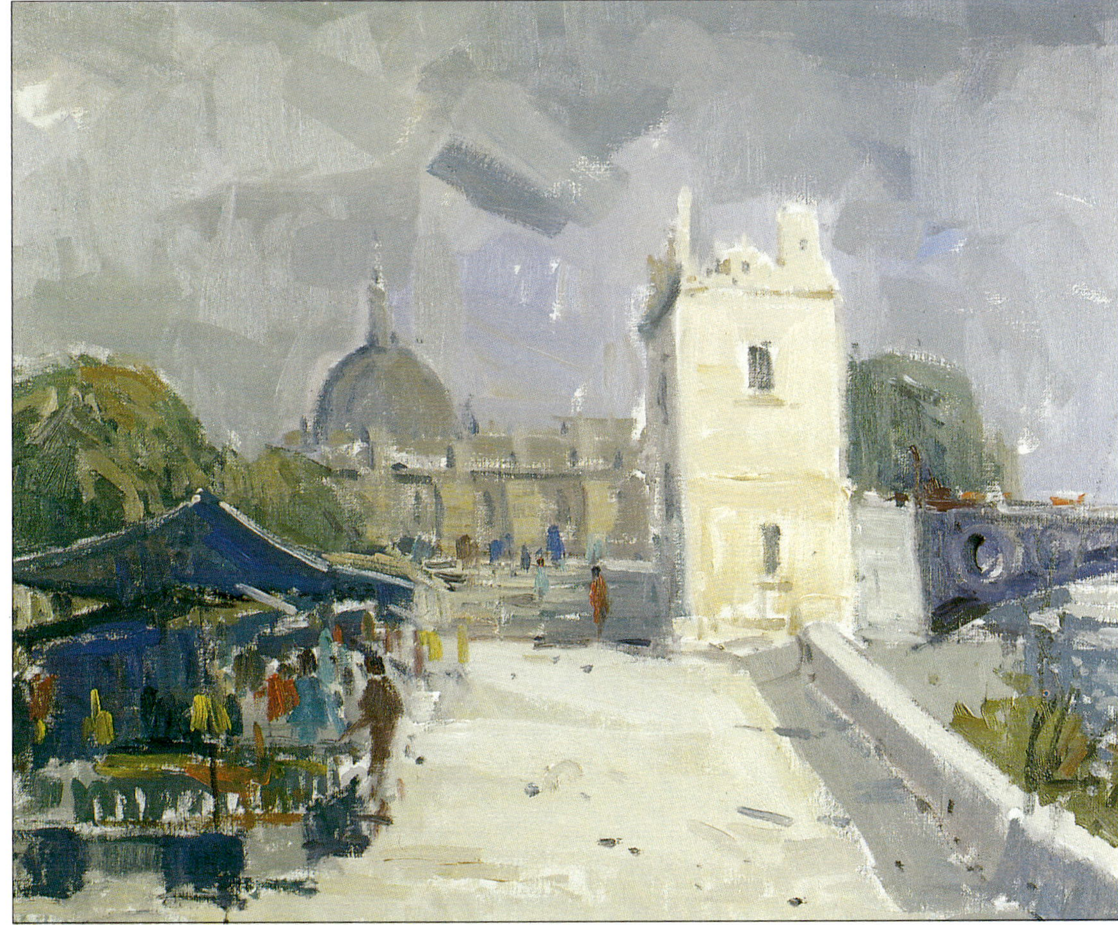

This is the state of the painting at this stage. Casañé is uncertain as to whether he should leave it as it is. It is almost complete; the white lines painted on the top of the canvas tents lend them their definitive shape. The tiny touches of light and shadow lend unity to the whole. Even the tiny specks on the sidewalk help to integrate the colors further still.

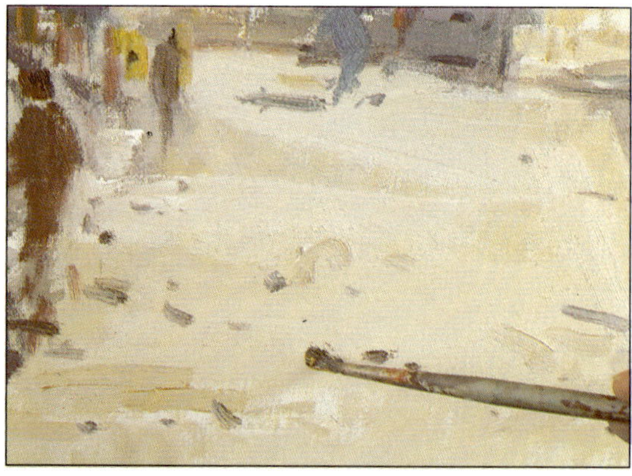

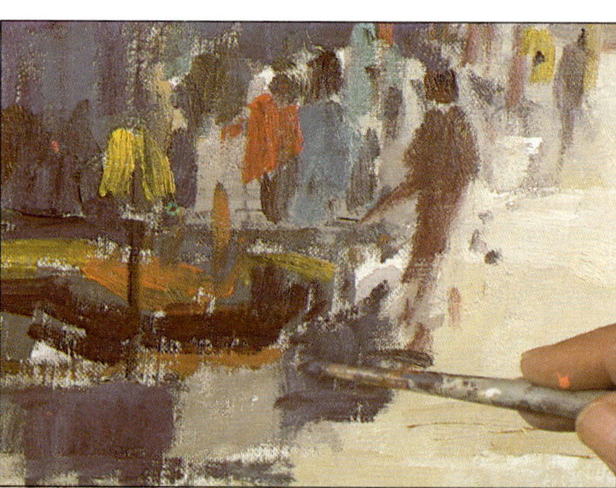

These two illustrations show the last brushstrokes that the artist applied to the canvas. Although the tiny brushstrokes may appear at first glance to be somewhat unimportant, these bold and vigorous impressionist strokes bring out the definitive form of the elements in the painting.

8. The finished painting

We can consider the painting finished. This is an important decision. A good painter must know when to finish a painting, since any unnecessary details can weigh it down excessively and give it an ugly appearance.

Since Casañé perfectly dominates the theme, he decides to continue a little more, elaborating certain elements further still. He adds more detail to the street market, lending it more consistency. He outlines the tower once again, adding several warm tones and some cool tones in the shadows with a color that makes the gray deeper, which defines a reflection. At this point he decides to conclude the work.

We believe that this demonstration has proved a valuable lesson in the evaluation and expression of light; the color range has been perfectly executed, without shrillness but with countless mixes and plenty of "palette work."

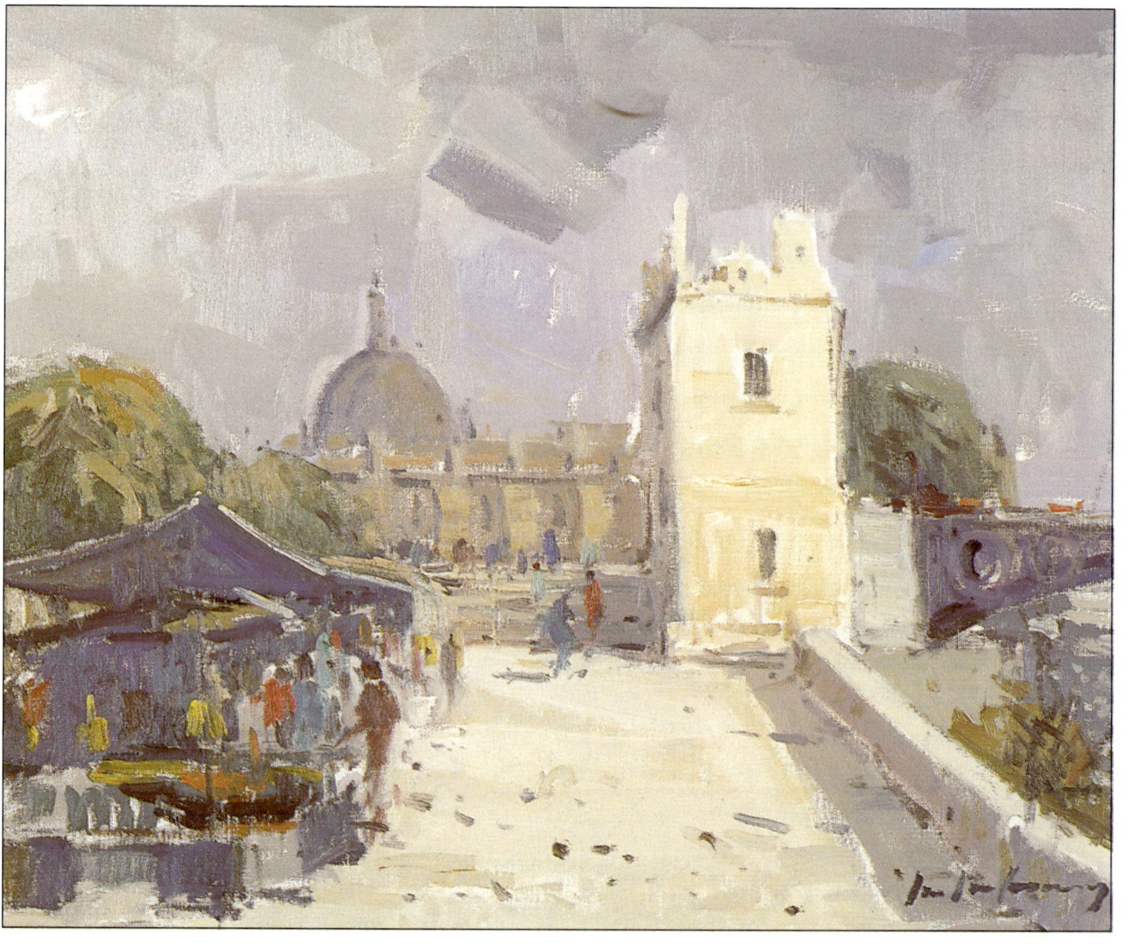

At this point—the definitive state of the painting—there is little left to add. Casañé has reoutlined certain elements, such as the towers and the dome, and has redefined anything that appeared to be flat or ambiguous. The artist has added warm tones over the cool tones of the shadows in order to create detail and create some contrast with the gray reflections, such as those at the side of the bridge. The variation of hues is subtle, often minimal. The whole, however, is more coherent and better balanced. A brilliantly resolved painting.

Abstract theme. Textured paint and collage

1. Introduction

The majority of great artists have made their mark, conceptually and stylistically, by using conventional techniques. Contemporary painting, however, breaks with these principles and reaches extraordinary heights by exploring new expressive forms and increasingly distancing itself from traditional artistic concepts. Having surpassed those limits, twentieth-century artists find their identity, half-way between the intimate and the relative, by exploring the expressive forms and formulas of what is known as "abstract art."

Saturo López, the renowned academic artist, whose work illustrates our pages, broke away from his conceptual background to discover that one of his main strengths was the fusion of figurative art with abstract art.

Our artist, an easygoing but private person, reveals a special talent for abstract painting in his wide-ranging work. His painting changes as rapidly as his mood—from soothing and relaxed to hard and aggressive. In his work, however, the aesthetic concept and the harmony of colors show a great respect for the more classical trends in his choice of materials and style. We hope that, by looking at his work and how he does it, you will learn how to express yourself, and conceptualize your own work, using the different techniques available.

In addition to abstract art, we'll also explore three-dimensional "matter" painting later in this chapter. In particular, we'll look at how textures are applied in two contrasting subjects, a bookcase and an urban landscape.

Two of the paintings that Saturo López paints for us in this section.

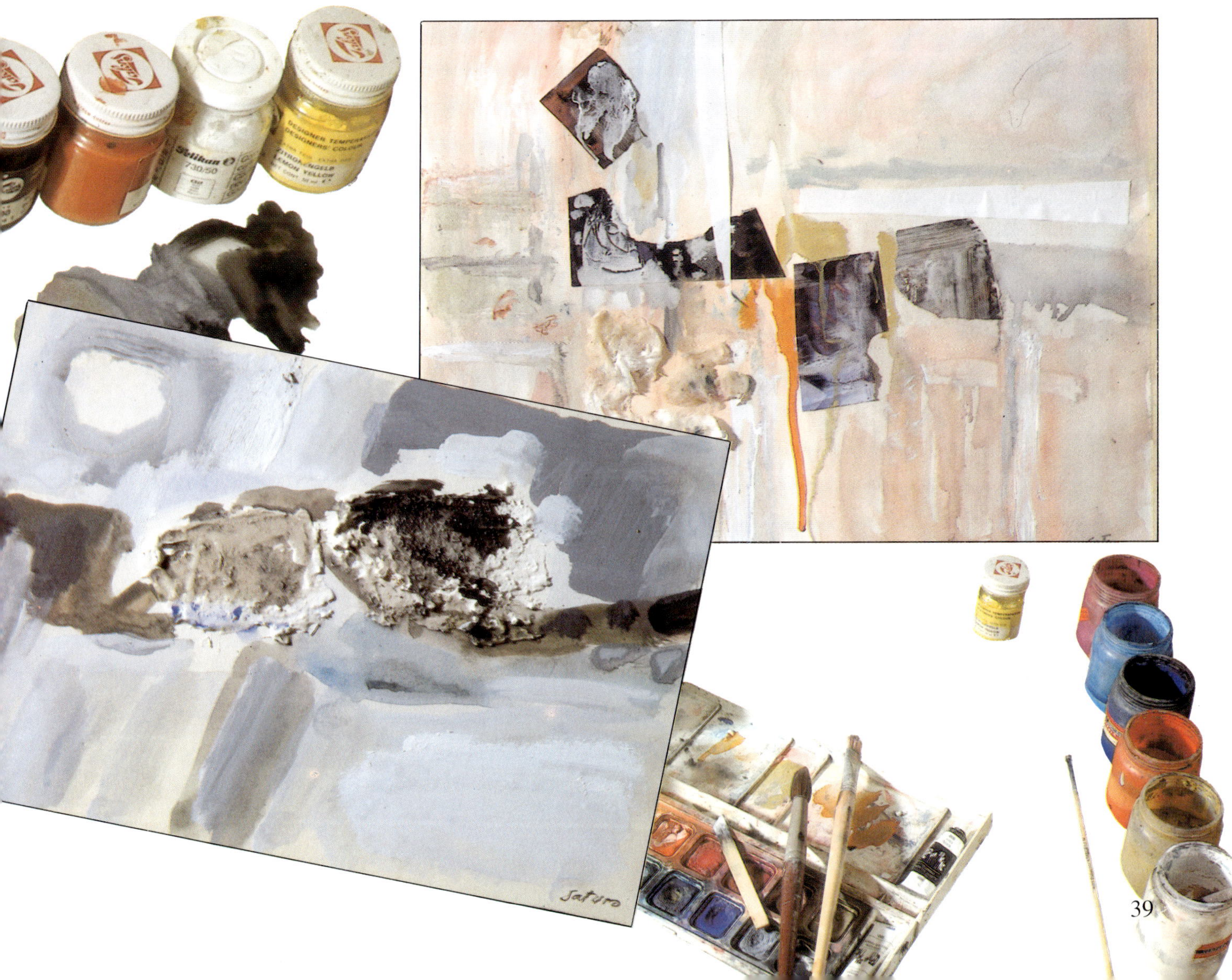

Abstract theme: Textured paint and collage

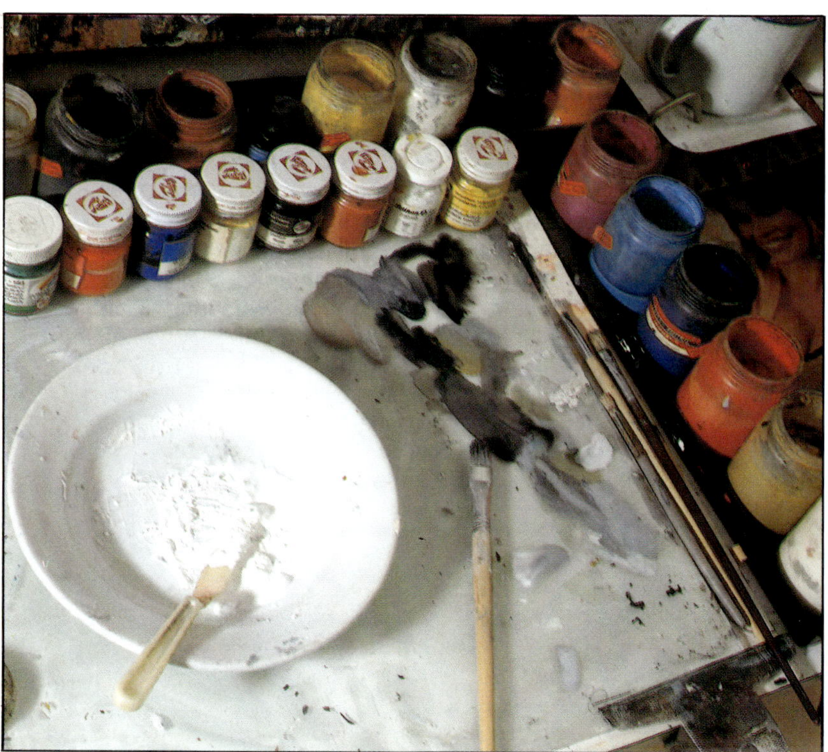

Still life showing the materials that Saturo López used for this work. Although you will see a wider range of colors than those mentioned here, the mixes on the palette were obtained from the colors we suggested.

The artist has applied a very subtle wash of ultramarine blue watercolor, leaving a space in the middle; he now spreads the relief paste with the palette knife.

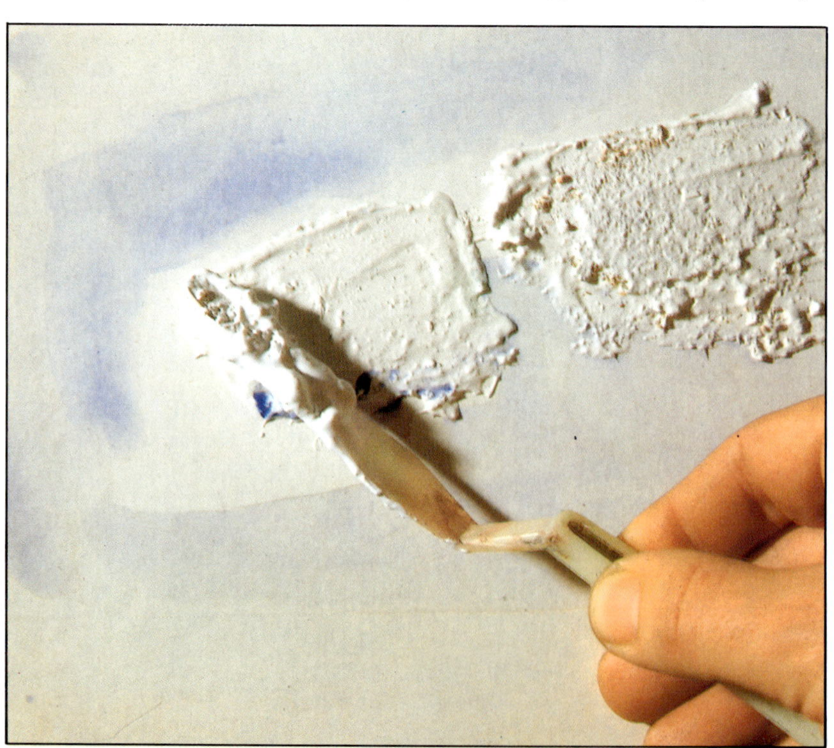

2. Materials and techniques

You might think that an abstract composition gives us the freedom to improvise everything. Many people equate abstract with chaotic when, in fact, just the opposite is true. For work to reach a high standard, all its various components should be well-thought-out: materials, techniques, composition. Technique is crucial in abstract art. While the level of expression in a painting is basically the result of the artist's conceptual capacity, that capacity greatly depends on the variety and richness of the technical means used. Thus, the artist's textural and compositional choices determine the degree of content and creativity.

In this first work, the painter deliberately takes advantage of the type of surface that can be achieved with tempera to turn the textural effect into the visual focus.

The following materials were used: a 11.8 × 7.8 inch (30 × 20 cm), white cardboard support, a round No. 12 hog hair brush, and white, dark blue, English red, black, and cadmium yellow tempera paints. (These colors are within the grayish, black-and-white tonal range of our work; you are free to use any other range.)

For the textural effect, a paste was made from acrylic modeling paste, latex, and gesso. A bowl or plate and a palette knife were used to get the right consistency for this textural paste, as well as a palette for mixing the colors. Given its relatively small format, you can do this type of work on a table, although we recommend that you get into the habit of using an easel.

You'll note that we have recommended mixing gesso for this relief paste due to its quick drying qualities, which allows us to carry on with our work after having applied the textural impastos.

3. The process

Deliberately using color mixes based on black-and-white tempera, Saturo López starts the process by reflecting on the intellectual compositional criteria. He applies a dark gray tone to the upper right side that surrounds part of one of the reliefs. He also creates a new pole of visual attraction by using different grayish shades, alternating with brushstrokes, to produce a spherical shape.

Given the complexity of this type of work, if you want to experiment, we recommend that you first do some preliminary sketches to avoid making fundamental mistakes in concept, compositional balance, and color.

Although we have already mentioned our artist's capacity for improvisation, we would suggest that you take your time and practice.

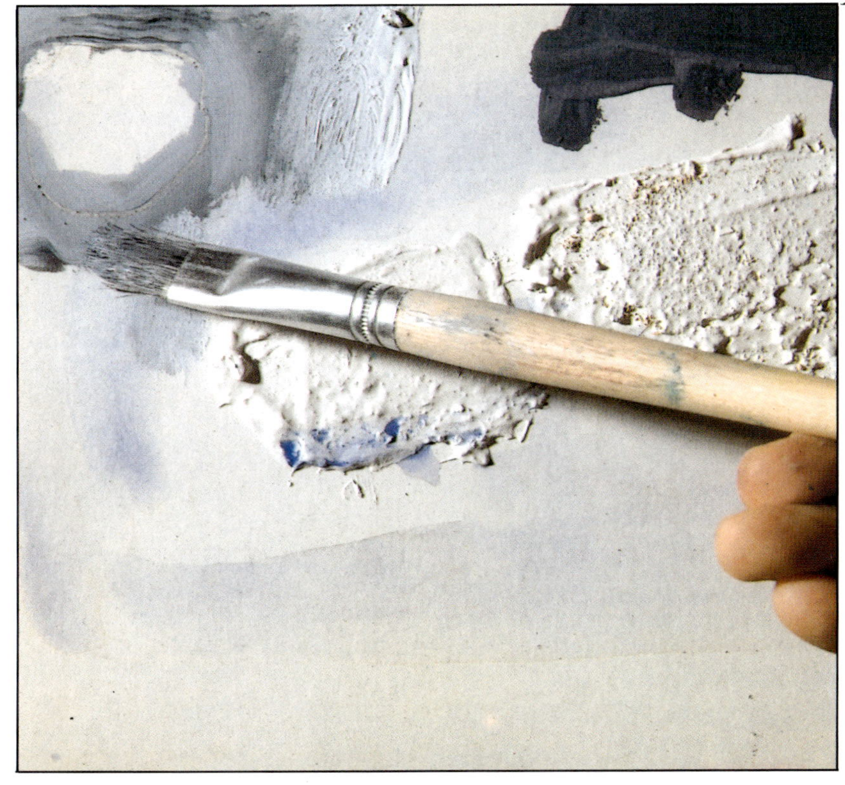

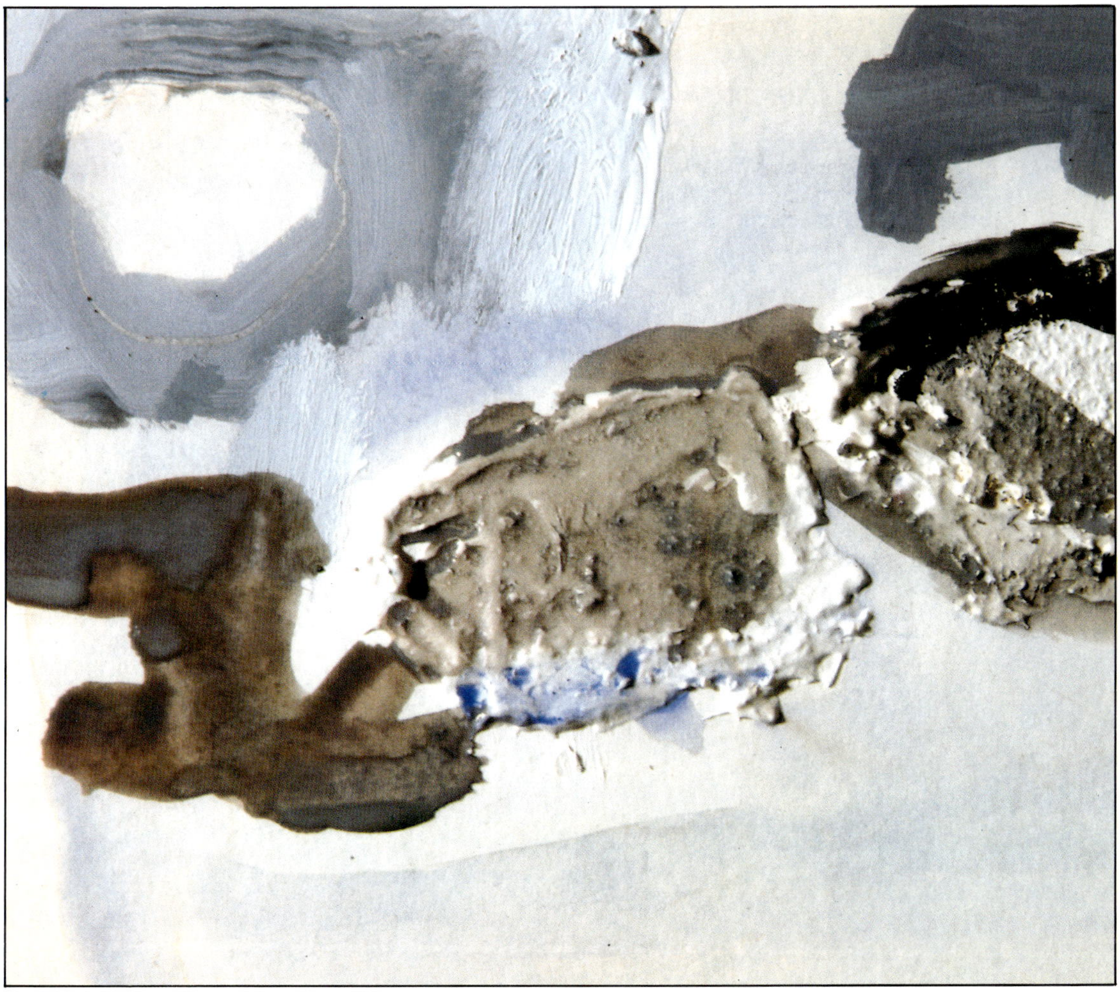

The artist adds a touch of English red to the grayish mix obtained on his palette, to warm the color tone. This produces a series of stains that are more watery than the previous ones, and that simultaneously intervene between the texture and background. The comparative warmth that can be seen in relation to the upper part, and the gestural movement that is imprinted on this sequence of stains, will establish a border difference in color that will mark the horizontal line of the composition.

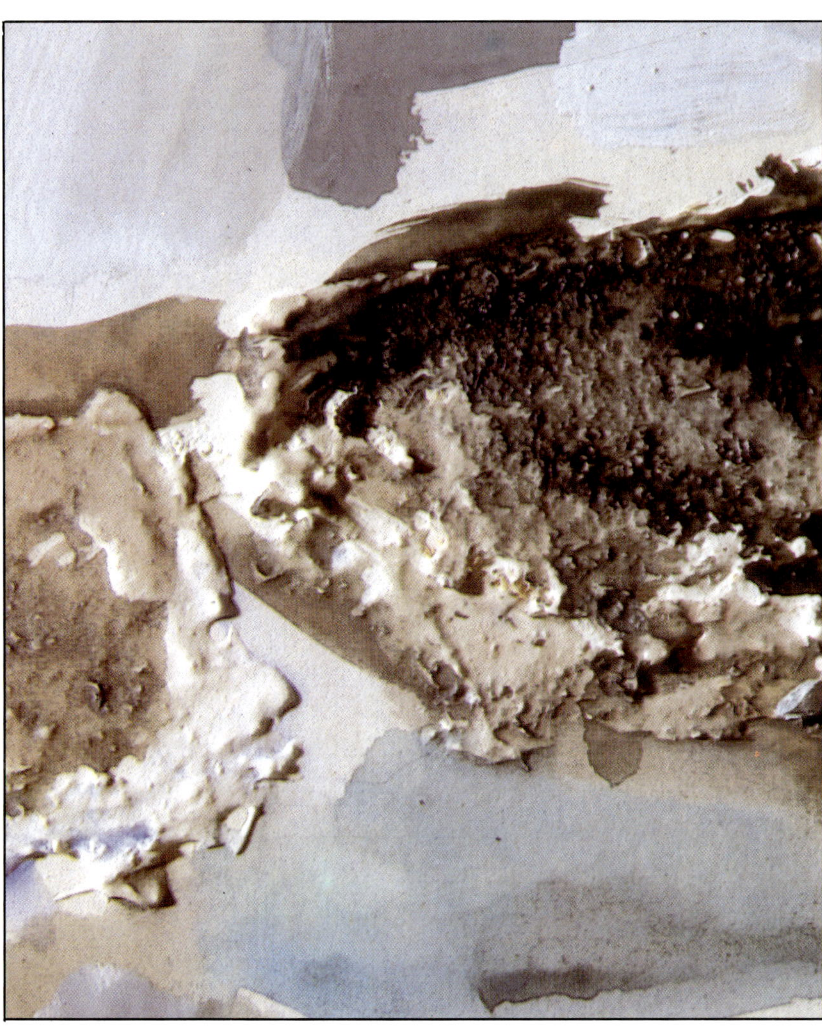

In this fragment, observe the richness of the colors produced by the variety of materials employed and the different moods established by the textural effects, as well as the way they now become an integral part of the composition through the stain.

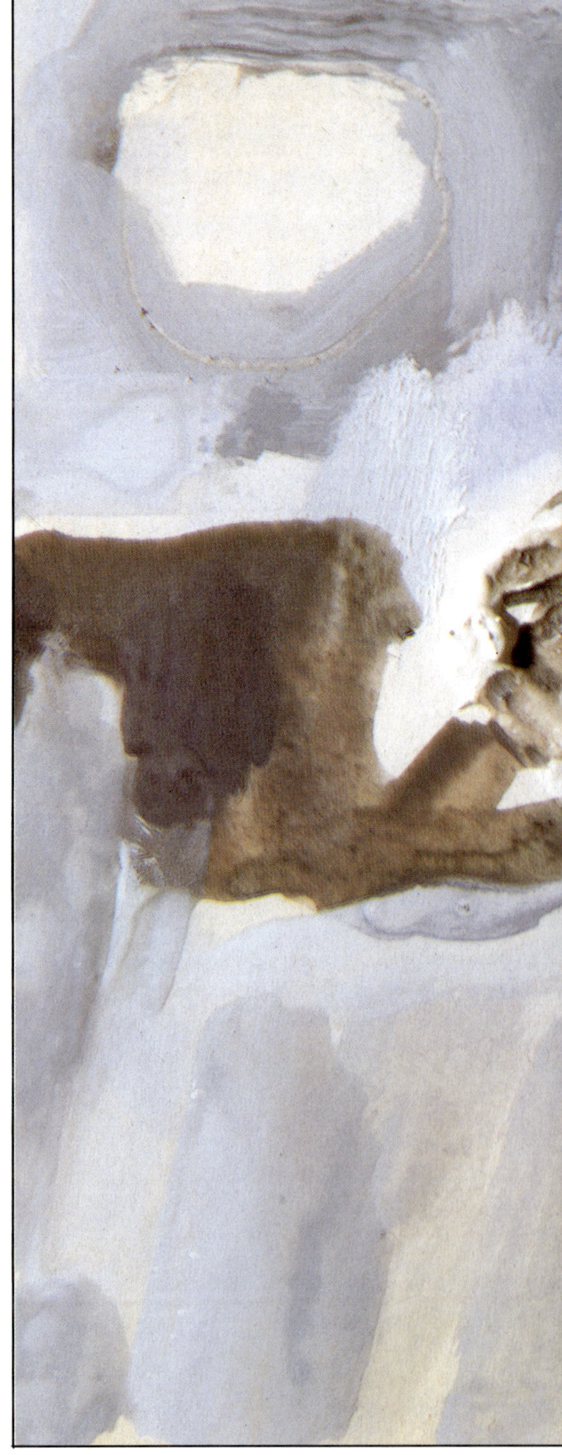

4. The completed work

To complete the work, the lower part has been rapidly resolved using the previous color base of dominant grays. Two fundamental features should be mentioned here: First, the vertical line that appears in the center of the base and that, connecting with the upper right stain, crosses and breaks the horizontal line, establishing the rhythm and compositional character that our artist desired; second a turquoise blue shade that defines the artist's central color variant.

The boundary of the composition has been defined in a logical manner, by filling the empty spaces and creating a tonal fusion that yields the definitive result seen here.

This is Saturo López's completed work, a good example of the technical and conceptual characteristics demanded by abstract art. Now that you have seen the completed work, go back and review all the stages of its creation so you can reach a better understanding of its composition and the way in which different elements are employed for special effects. This is something we suggest you do not only now, but also when you study other paintings.

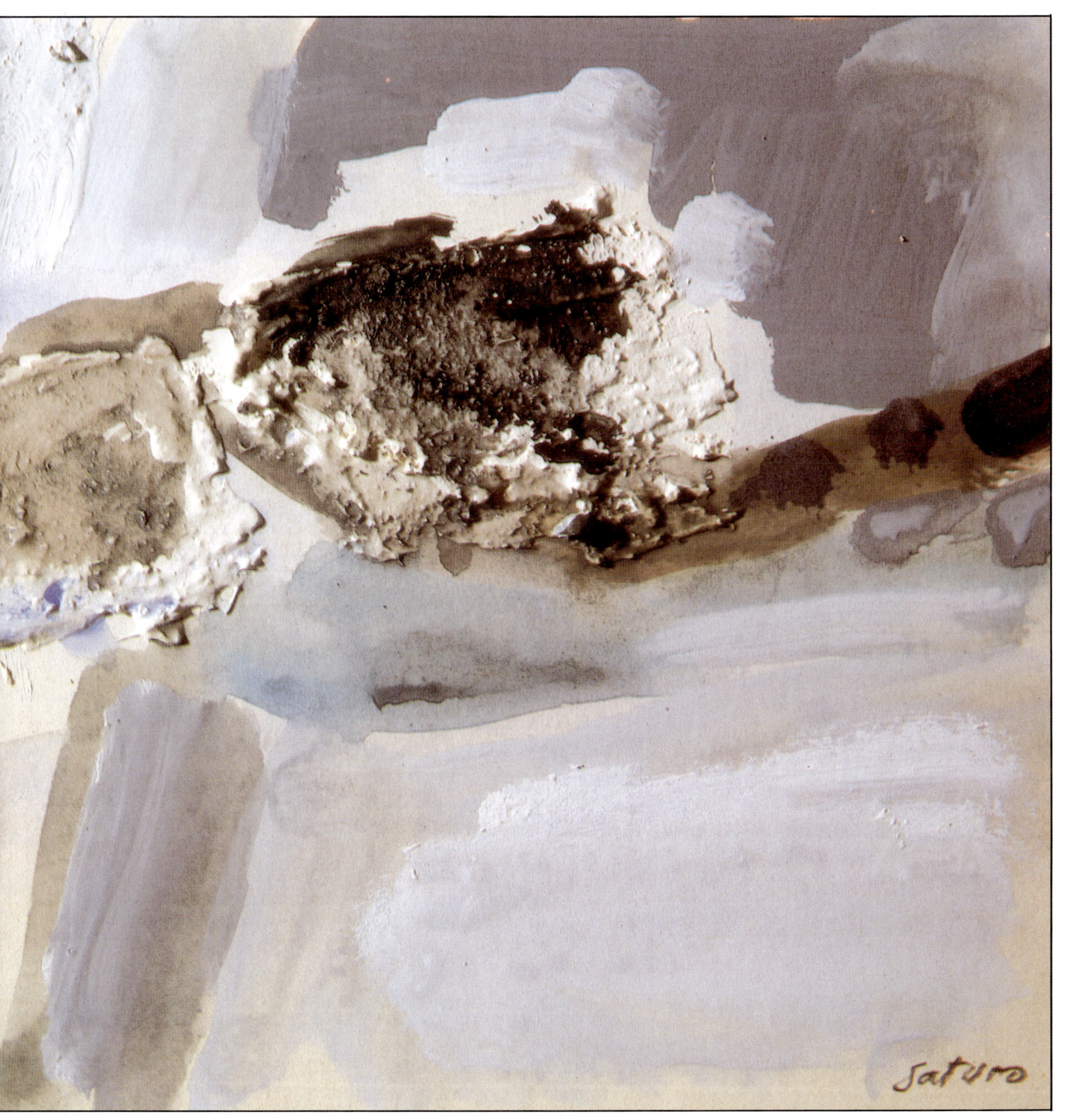

Abstract theme with mixed media: Gouache and collage

1. Introduction

The main characteristic of mixed media is the level of expression that can be achieved by using different materials. We have a great deal of scope here, bearing in mind that abstract art feeds on the visual attraction that the simultaneous alternation of different techniques creates for the viewer.

Nearly all abstract artists have resorted to collage in some way or another, as a means of expression. In this section, the possibility of alternating textural surfaces and the effects of combining collage with gouache will be the main objective of our analysis, along with the aesthetic and compositional concepts.

2. Materials

We have already pointed out that the tools and materials to be used in this type of exercise depend on their flexibility and how they interact. However, you must remember that improvisation requires careful thought. For the work presented on these pages, we used the following materials: as a support, a 14 × 18 inch (36 × 45 cm) sheet of 290 grm matte Geler paper, a wooden panel, and adhesive tape to attach the support to the panel.

A round No. 20 hog hair brush; a wide No. 15 brush; a round No. 20 watercolor brush; a reed stick; a box set of Karan d'Ache gouache with 14 colors in pans; and an incorporated palette were also used.

For the collage: newspaper cuttings treated with "Triqui" stain remover, toilet paper or similar paper, and a bowl of gum arabic.

Still life showing all the materials used to complete this work.

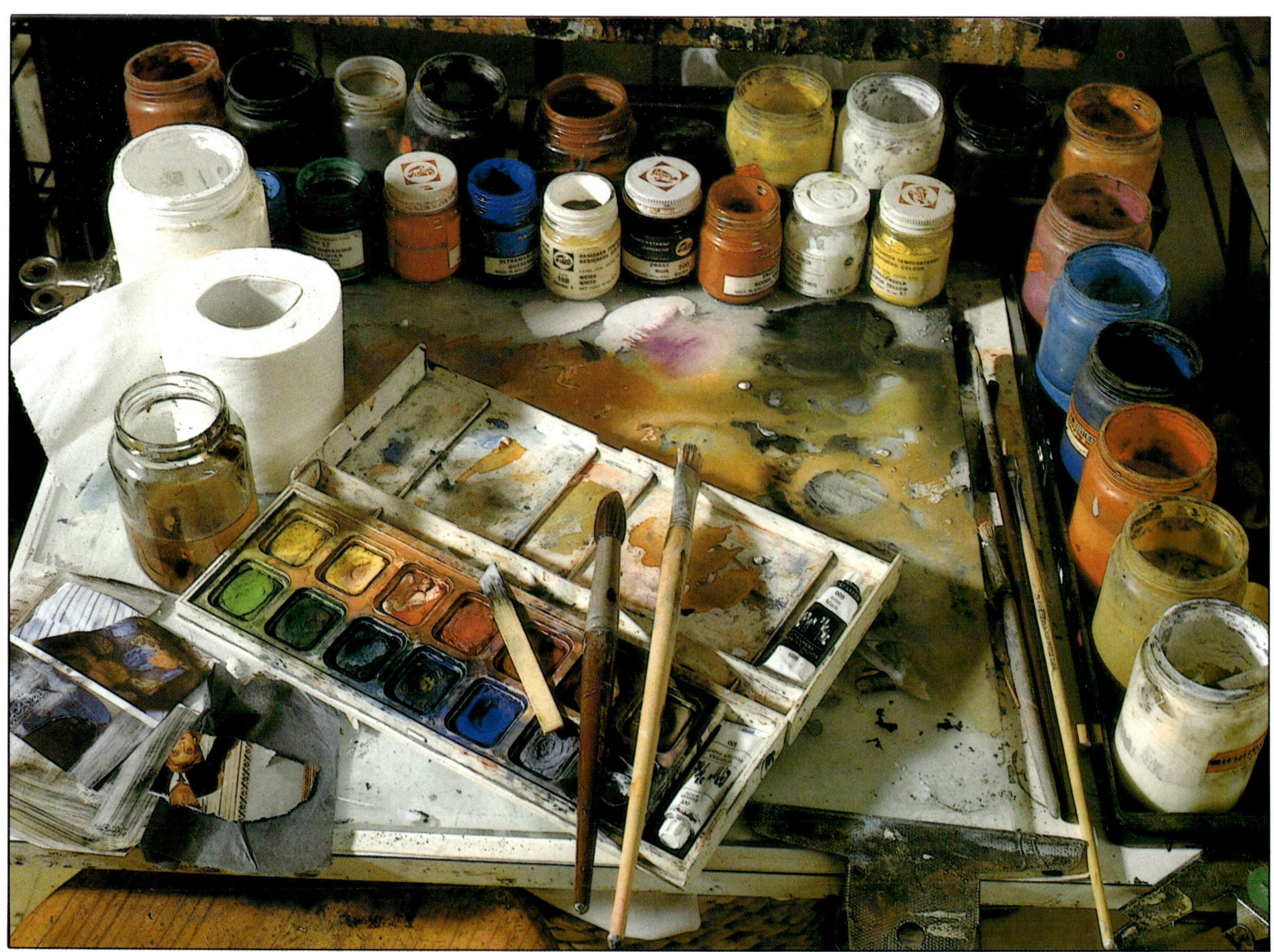

3. Subtle from the outset

"The type of composition and its essential characteristics are in the artist's mind," says Saturo López, "thereby making it very difficult to give a conceptual description, as there is always the risk of not being exact. My idea will be determined by the simultaneous alternation of special three-dimensional and linear rhythms, technically combined with very subtle transparencies and textural surfaces that give volume without creating excessive hardness."

Our artist first prepares a very smooth and watered-down background that will act as the color base on which the composition will be developed, using the gouache as a watercolor to create a mood of tones that contrasts with the cold and vigorous brushstrokes in the center.

The background is being prepared in a transparent and extremely watered-down grayish violet gouache, applied with a wide brush. Observe the vertical lines of the brushstroke.

The general outline of the background is characterized by its elegant tone and clean transparency. The emphasis on blue and cadmium yellow tones will constitute the composition's starting point.

Abstract theme with mixed media: Gouache and collage

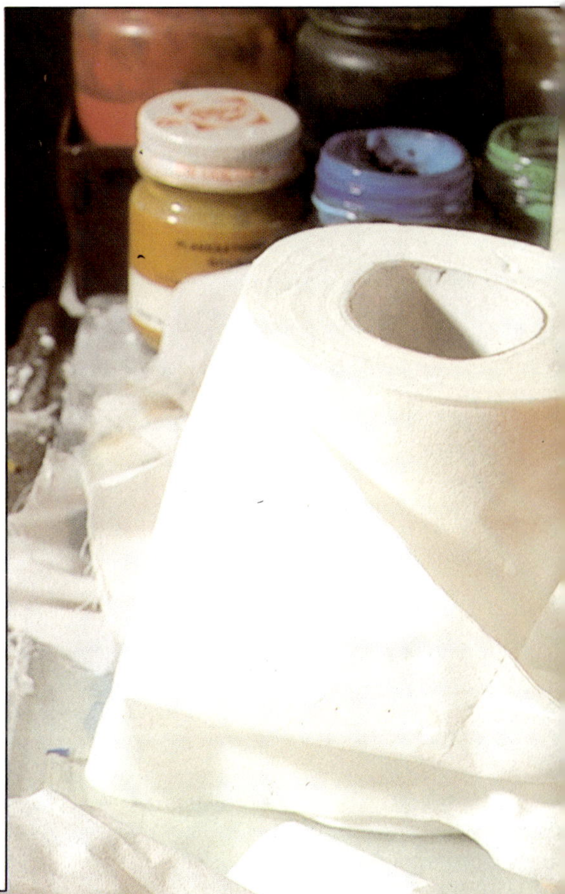

Make sure you thoroughly saturate any thin pieces of paper by immersing them in gum arabic.

4. Unusual reliefs

Our composition is progressing. The painter wants two aspects that he considers important in this work to be clearly differentiated: the compositional sketch and the technical and textural components of the collage itself. López will differentiate the compositional sketch through his use of technique and texture in collage. For this, he has used magazines and cut-out shapes in potent grayish shades that he has decolored using the solvent. Our artist contemplates the space and swaps and moves the shapes around until he finds their ideal position.

Only when he is sure that the shapes are suitably positioned does he attach them onto the support using gum arabic applied with a brush. López uses gum arabic to attach his collage because it is a natural product made from resins, and it does not damage or affect the materials he uses in his work.

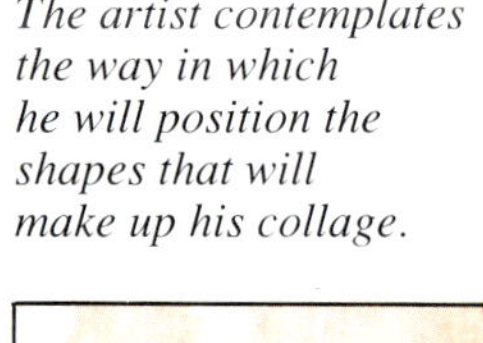

The artist contemplates the way in which he will position the shapes that will make up his collage.

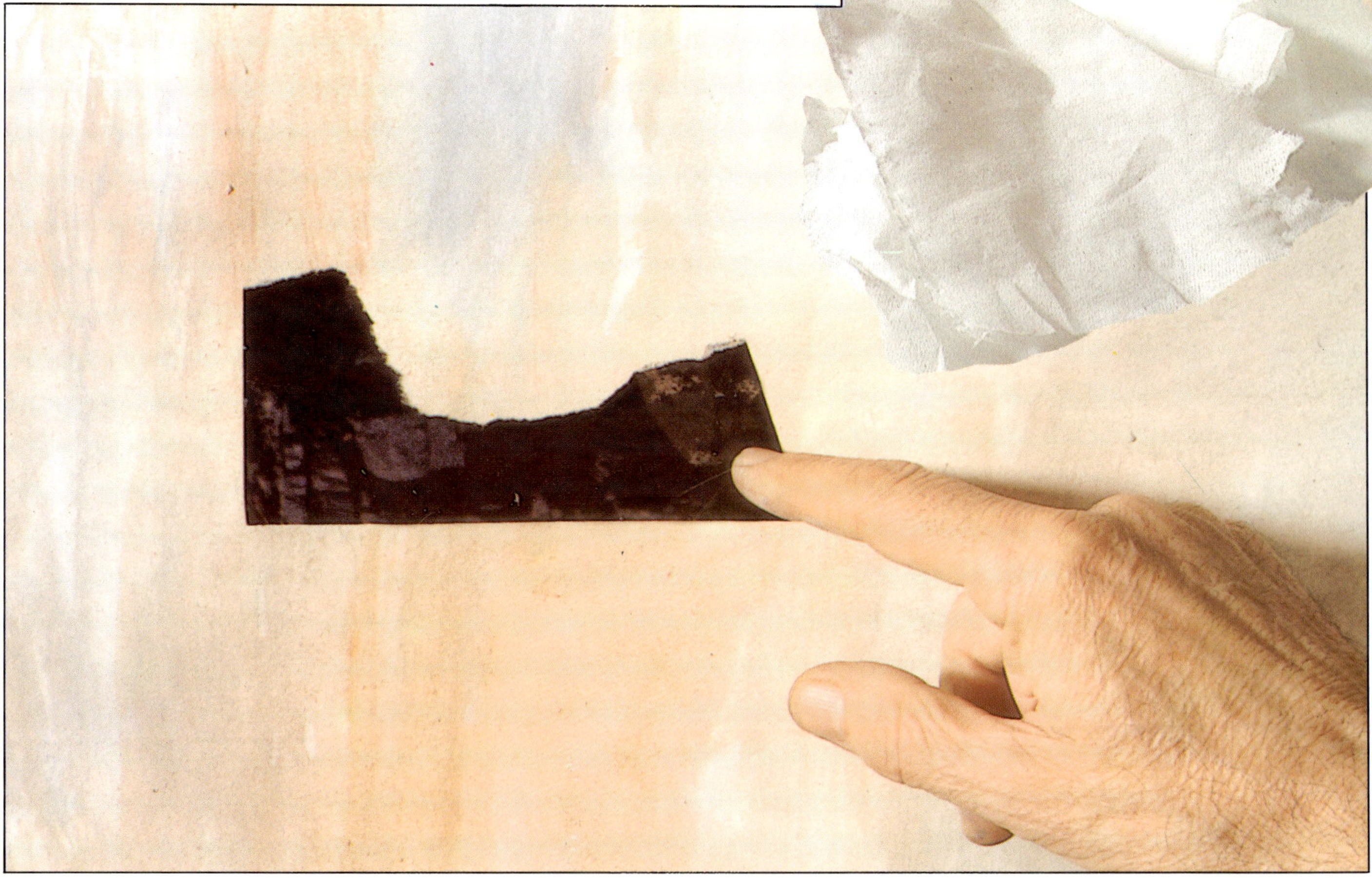

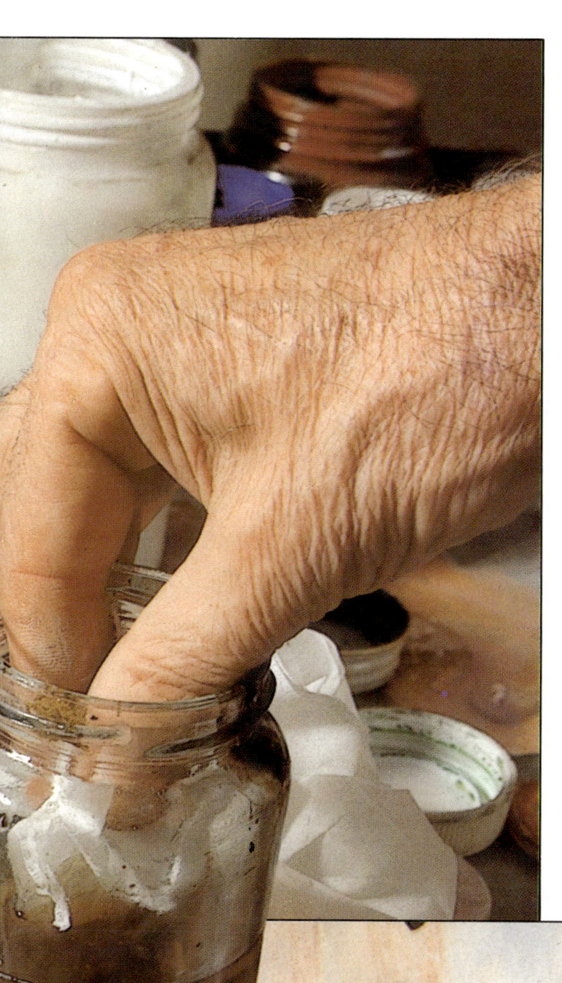

The time has come to establish a reference point to draw the viewer's attention; López uses toilet paper as a textural stain. As this type of paper is fragile, he first soaks it in gum arabic and then positions it in the place and shape he considers appropriate.

5. Gum arabic

Gum arabic is made from organic resins secreted by certain trees. When these resins are mixed with gum they are called gum resins.

Resins are traditionally used to prepare varnishes and lacquers because of their fixing qualities. This glutinous characteristic is the reason they are used for making water colors, temperas, etc., and why they are useful for our work.

Remember, when using thin paper as a textural surface, it should be completely soaked in gum arabic to be sure it will adhere correctly. It is also one of the best ways to prevent the work from deteriorating with time.

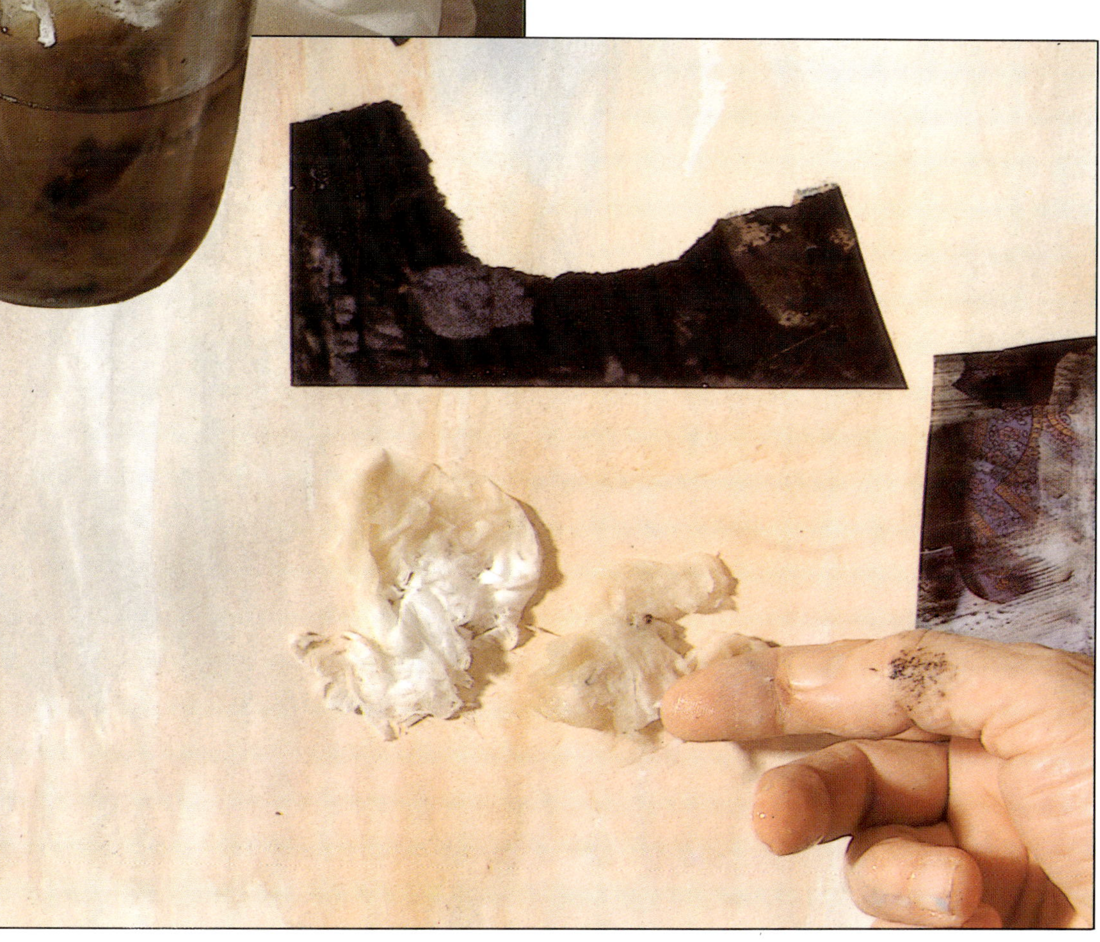

Here we can see how the textural forms of gum-soaked toilet paper are positioned. Because the paper is damp, it is easier to mold it into shapes.

Abstract theme with mixed media: Gouache and collage

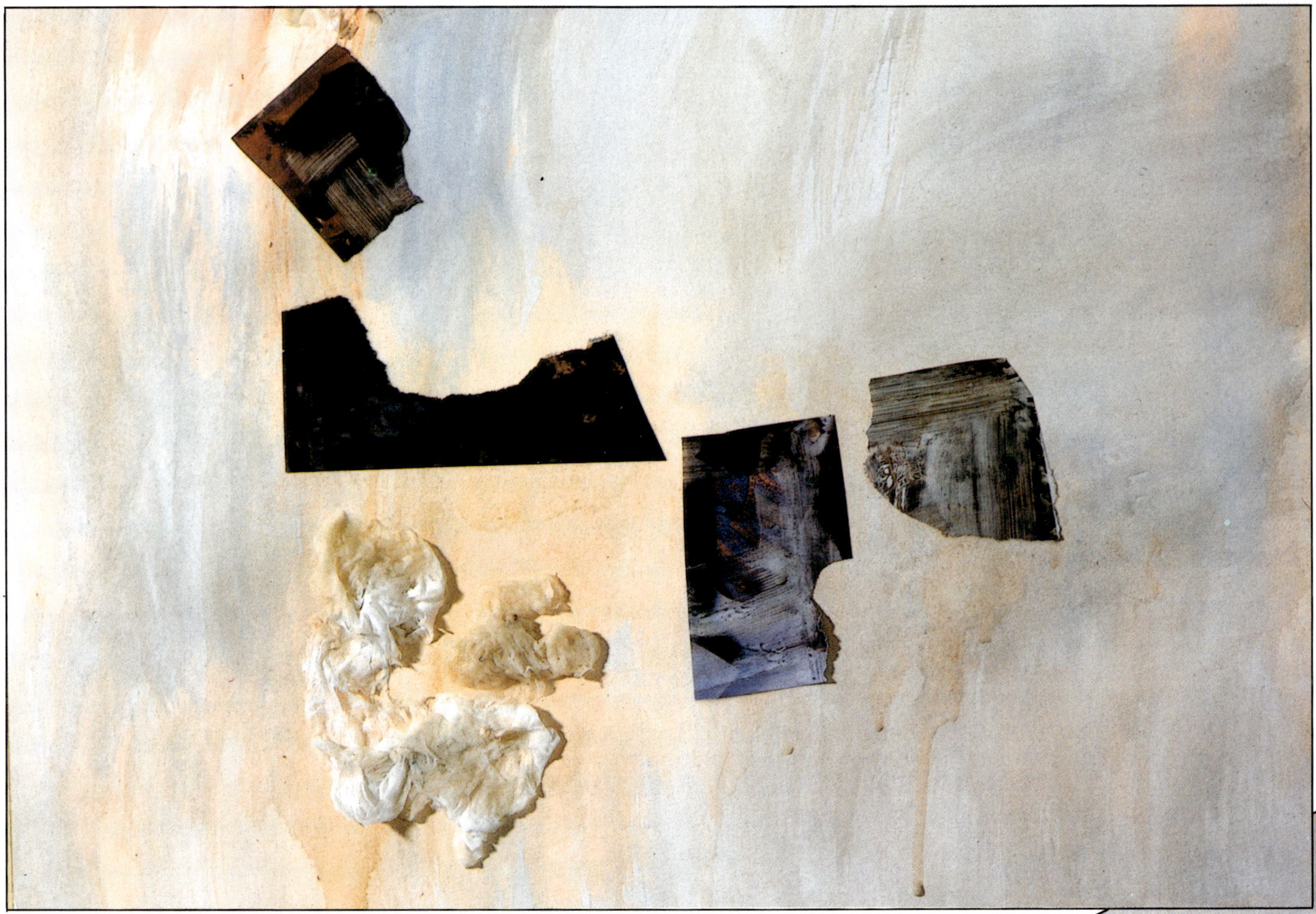

6. A first outline

The image above shows the first compositional outline of the subject now being clearly defined. The artist has already formed the collage by carefully selecting from the compositional sketch certain matter-texture forms and has intuitively considered how to establish the rhythmic and tonal fusion between the collage and the background. For this, our artist now intensifies the compositional rhythm through his choice of golden tones and brushstrokes, alternating opaque pictorial forms and subtle glazes to gradually define the dominant tone of the color criterion.

The way the shapes have been positioned constitutes the collage and firmly establishes the compositional character that will prevail throughout the entire work.

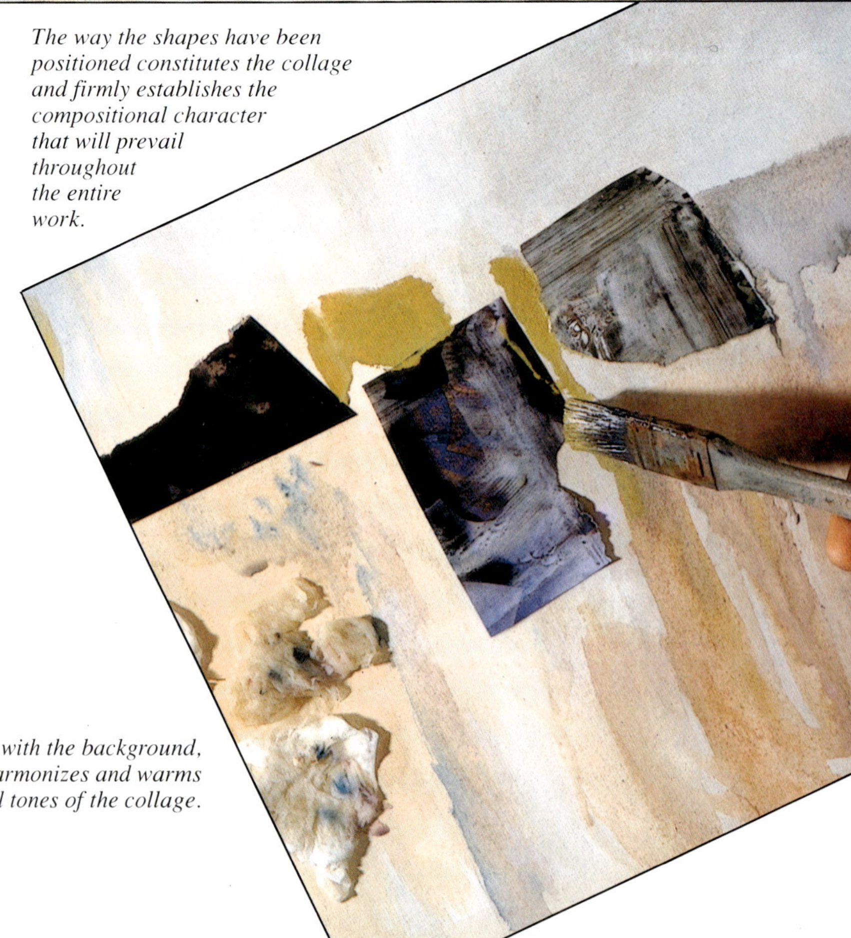

The painter blends the shapes in with the background, using an ocher color that harmonizes and warms the cool tones of the collage.

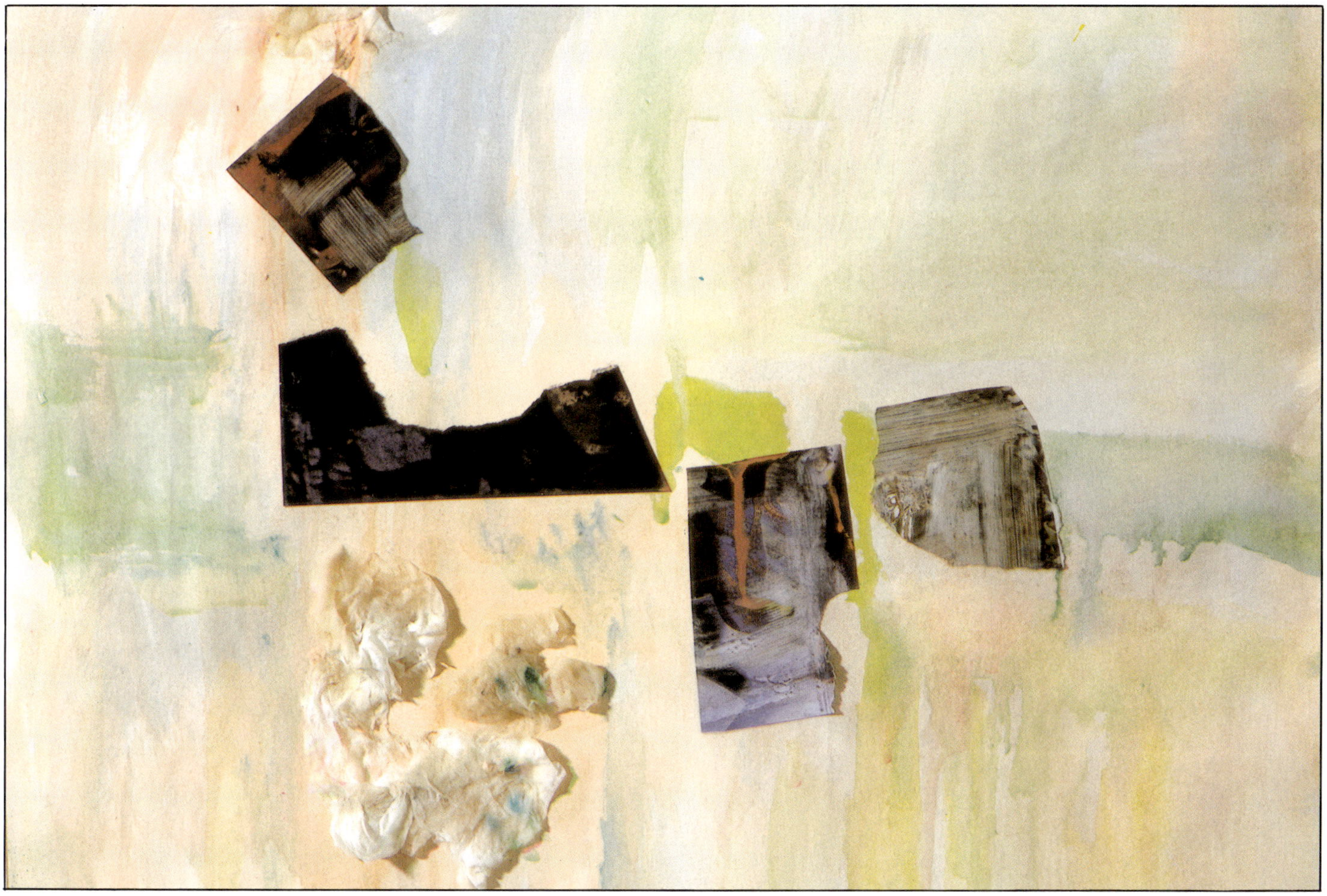

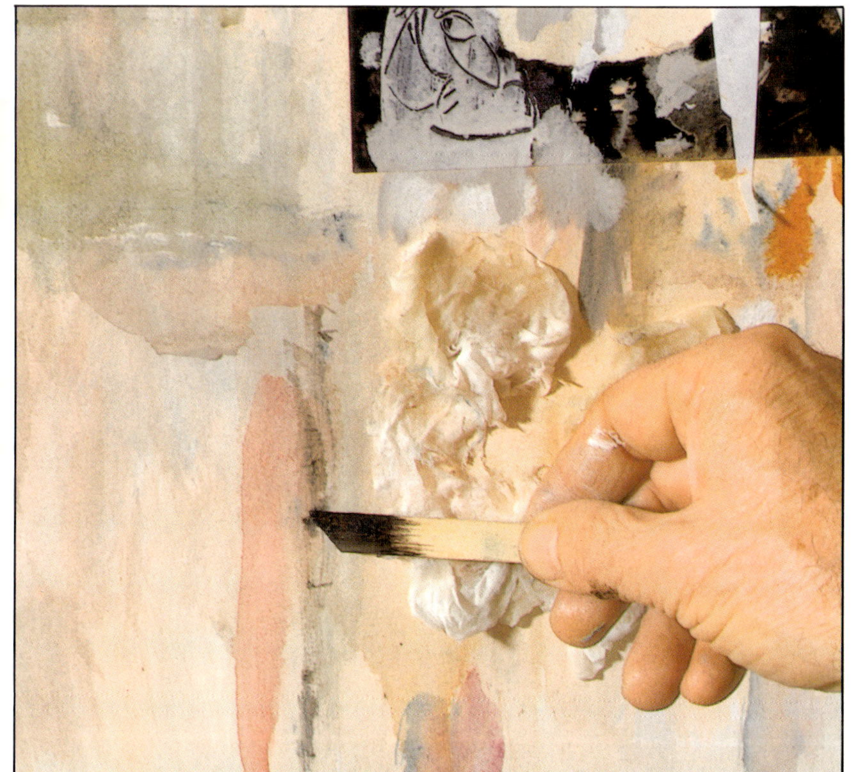

We can see how the simultaneous use of different techniques producing rich textural effects constitutes the main attraction of abstract painting.

7. The work is being defined

During the third stage the work has progressed in terms of color and composition, and the elegant and harmonious colors and the movement produced by the informal brushstrokes stand out.

The blendings and transparencies that can be observed in the work represent an interesting watery textural effect and denote López's intention to create four-sided boundary spaces in order to determine the compositional criteria of the work.

Notice how the work is completed using the stick to define spaces; the collage is also becoming an integral part of its surroundings through new color effects that simultaneously intervene between the textural surfaces and the background.

8. The final product

López has made final, overall adjustments in his work, completing the textural effects and the definition of his compositional spaces, and alternating a wide range of flat matter/texture.

The viewer's attention is grabbed by the work as a whole, the result of the textural effect achieved by the collage, which has been integrated into its surroundings with the degree of harmony and balance sought by our artist.

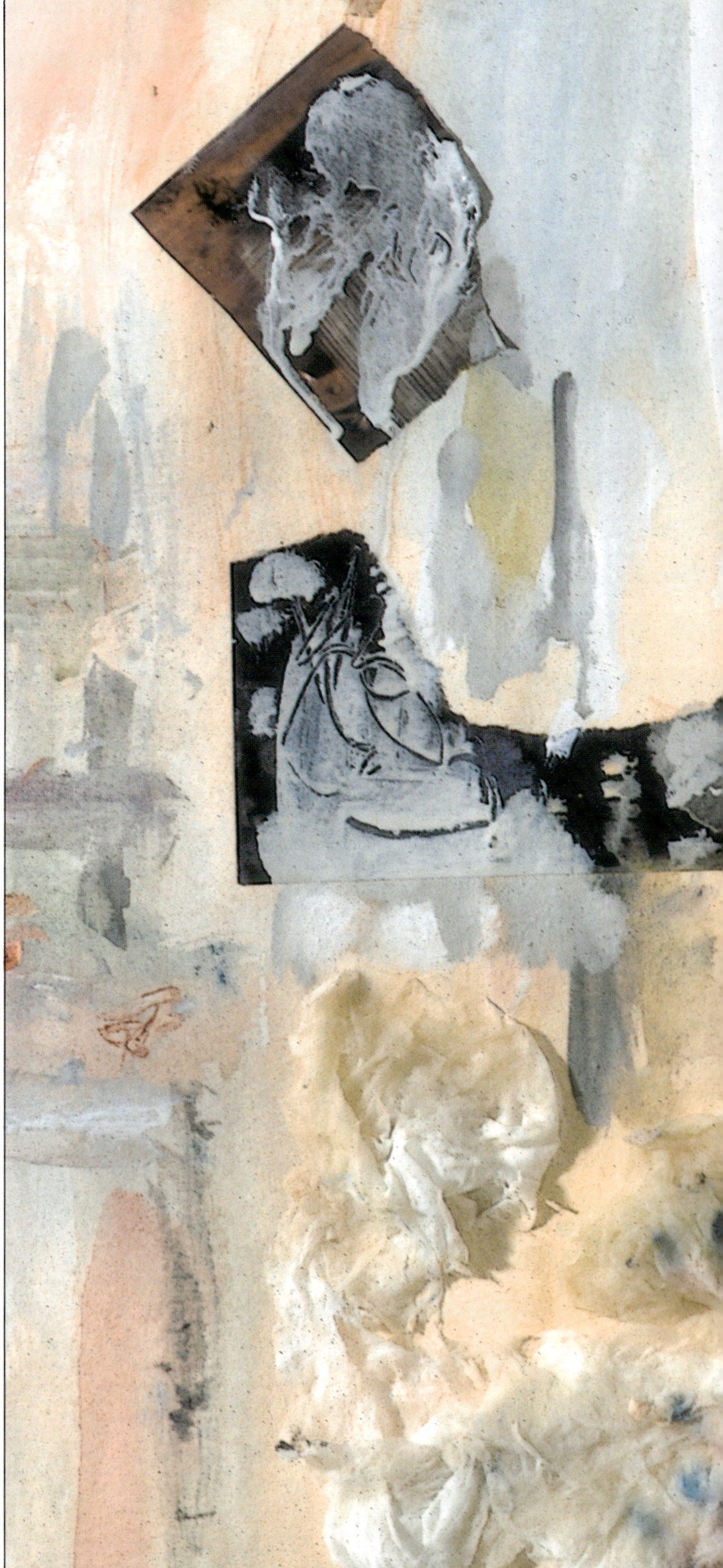

López's finished work. Notice the elegant rhythm of the composition, as well as the color alternation of the mixed media used. Now is the time, as you look at the finished work, to review the entire process and the materials used in order to see just how much you have learned. This is also an ideal time for you to think about what variations you could introduce and which materials you could change to achieve a different, yet equally high-quality result.

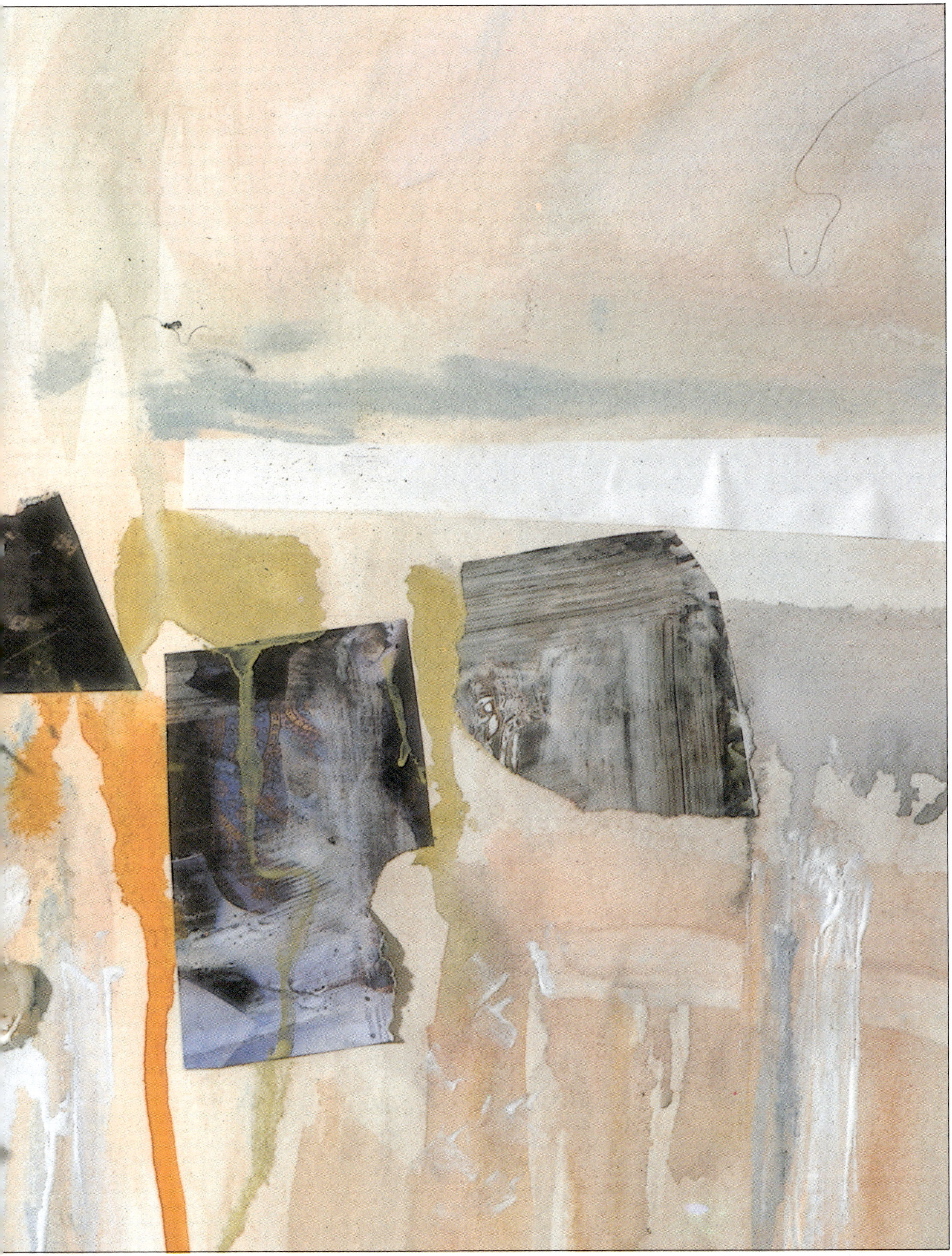

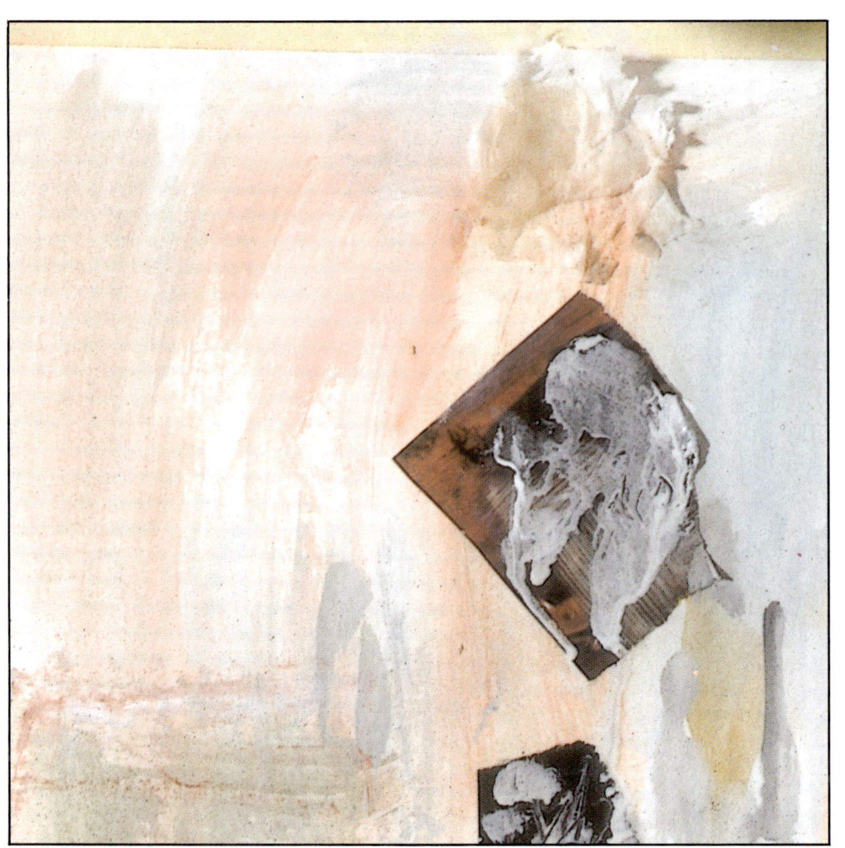

9. The hidden work

This is a good time to draw your attention to the principal characteristics of abstract art. Generally speaking, the color element of the textural effects is what attracts the viewer. The interest generated by them makes them the artist's main expressive and communicative target.

The artist's preoccupation with the aesthetic aspect of his or her work determines the personal level of commitment toward the viewer. Abstract art has the capacity to arouse sensibilities—this should be the artist's principal objective.

The importance of the materials used to create a collage becomes apparent in the compositional power that it exerts in the work as a whole. Therefore, if we consider the balance and color element resulting from the use of different materials to be the main objective of a work, we can find hidden levels of compositional interest in López's work.

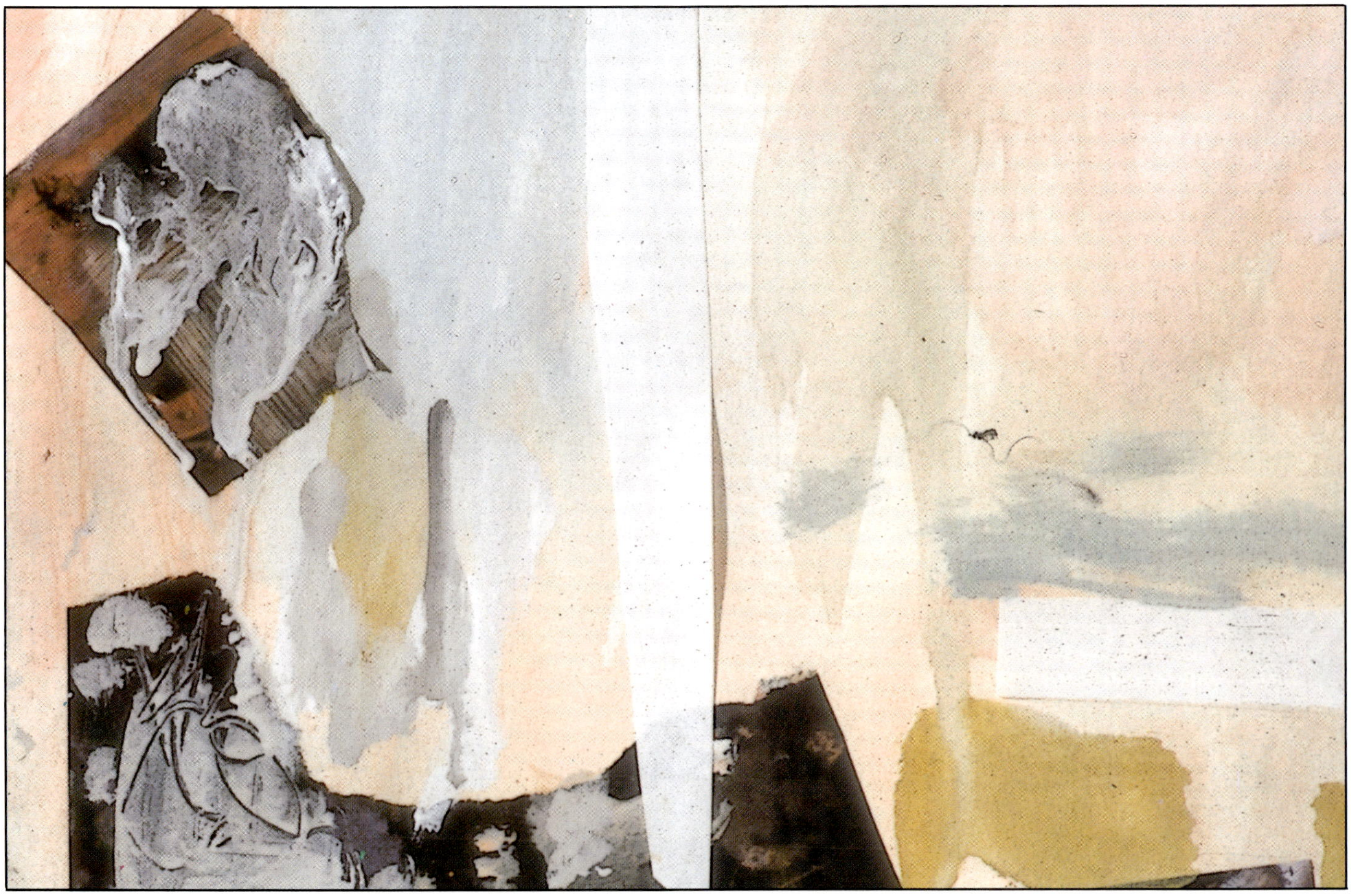

With these images, we will try to focus your attention on new pictorial ideas that are produced by the fragmentation of the work, and that can and should stimulate new compositional ideas. One aspect that you should always bear in mind is that the apparent ease with which any abstract work is produced is just that—apparent. When referring to good abstract art, we mean work that is valid when taken as a whole, but that is equally valid if, after being fragmented, each fragment manifests its own distinctive personality. If this is not so, you should question the apparent or supposed quality of this type of work. For you to apply this principle to the work that Saturo López has just completed for us, here are several fragments with which to check the truth of our statement.

In addition to the high content of rhythms and effects within this work, you will be able to observe how each of its fragments makes us feel the need to engage in a partial and detailed analysis. Some fragments open up a wide range of new compositional possibilities, starting with their global compositional structure.

The simultaneous alternation produced by the use of comparatively heterogeneous mixed media, as well as the process and criteria followed, also contribute to the great pictorial interest of the work.

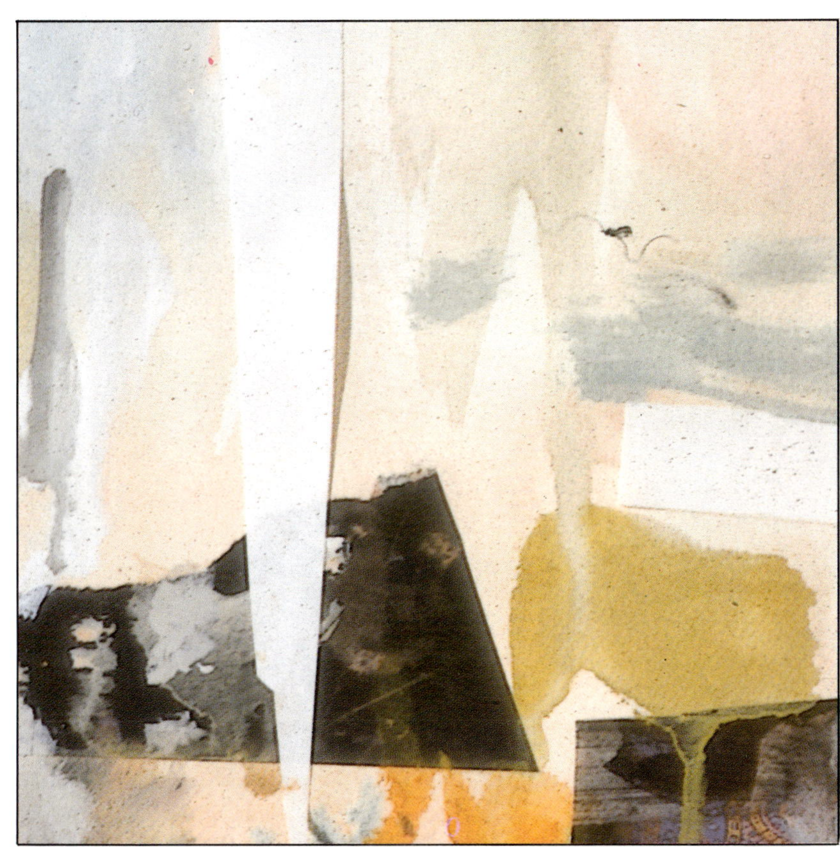

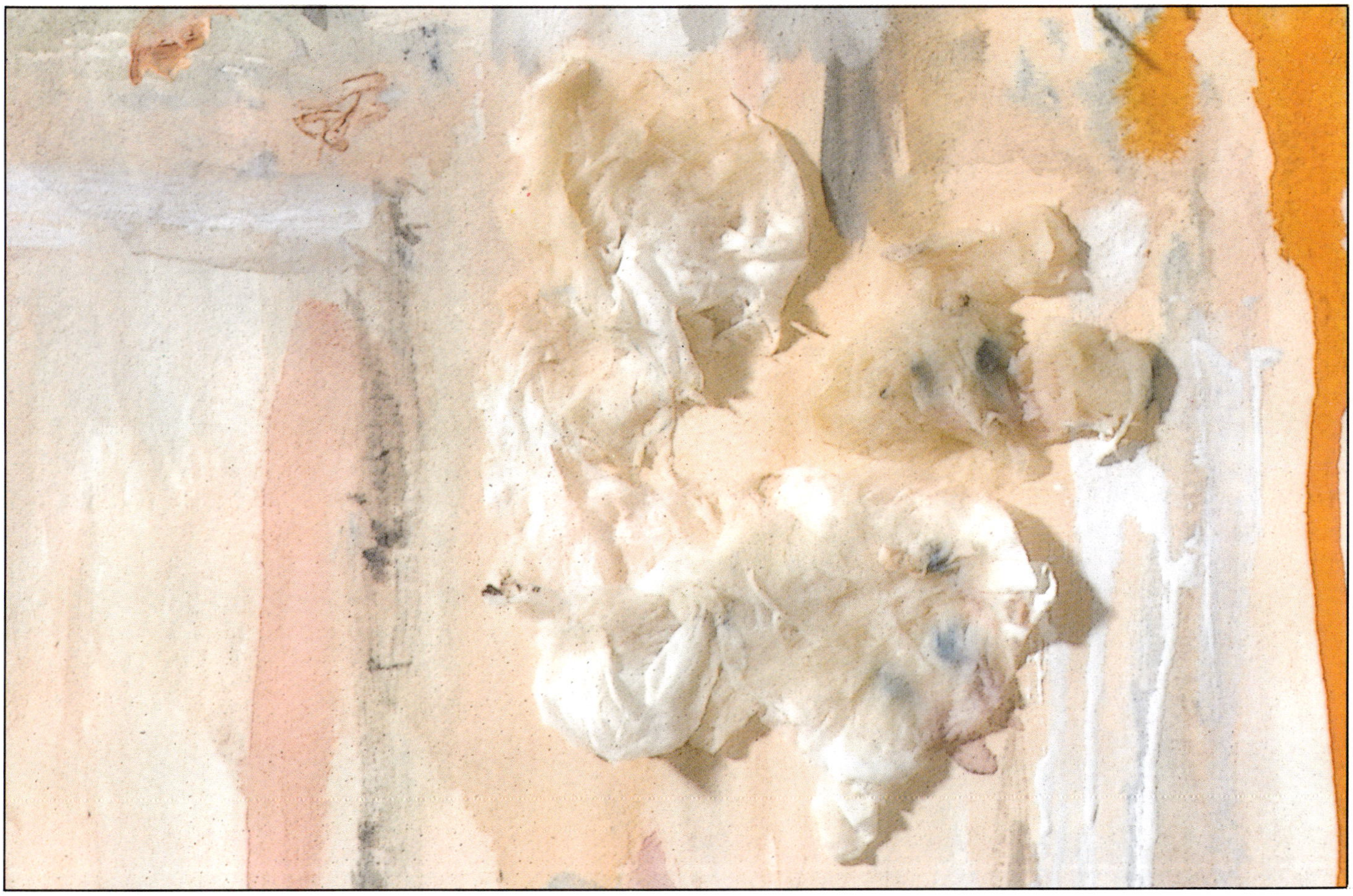

An old bookcase

1. Ground dust, ground marble, and sand

Today, there is a large variety of materials available for creating textures. One of the most traditional types is ground alabaster. Another common material is ground marble, available in different degrees of thickness, each of which produces a different texture. Not only ground alabaster and marble produce texture; oil and acrylic also can be used to create considerable volume and relief. Although many types of material can be used to thicken oil and other mediums, we will concern ourselves here with those previously mentioned.

By the time you have finished these exercises, we hope you will have learned enough to be able to attempt your own creations.

What will the choice of ground alabaster, marble, or sand depend on? Nothing less than our own desire to communicate. You must try not to become a slave of the medium chosen. Media and techniques are to be used by you—always make sure that they are not using you. If we decide to use a material to obtain texture in a painting, there should be a good reason for doing so; the artist must never use it for the sake of it. It would not be appropriate, for instance, to use a palette knife in order to achieve a hyper-realistic portrait.

The artist should learn different techniques and apply each only in the right context. In the next exercise we will use ground alabaster to thicken the oil paint, since we will need a rather viscous medium. Given the size of the work we are going to paint, we cannot use thick-grain ground marble because it would produce a rather coarse texture. Had we been interested in creating relief in a larger painting, we would have then chosen a mineral that creates a more abrupt surface, such as ground marble or washed beach sand.

2. The theme, a preliminary drawing

We are going to paint a robust theme, in which the incorporated "matter" will feature prominently. The subject of our work is a drawing of an old bookcase, which looks promisingly attractive as a motif. As you can see, it is not a difficult motif; quite the opposite—it is a simple drawing executed with india ink on old paper. The theme suggesting dust, heavy books, and the passage of time is particularly attractive and suitable for the use of materials that evoke these same qualities.

The drawing was executed from nature with a round brush and india ink from a bar. The highlights were added with white pastel. Instead of striving for originality with this subject, we prefer to concentrate on practicing the use of materials.

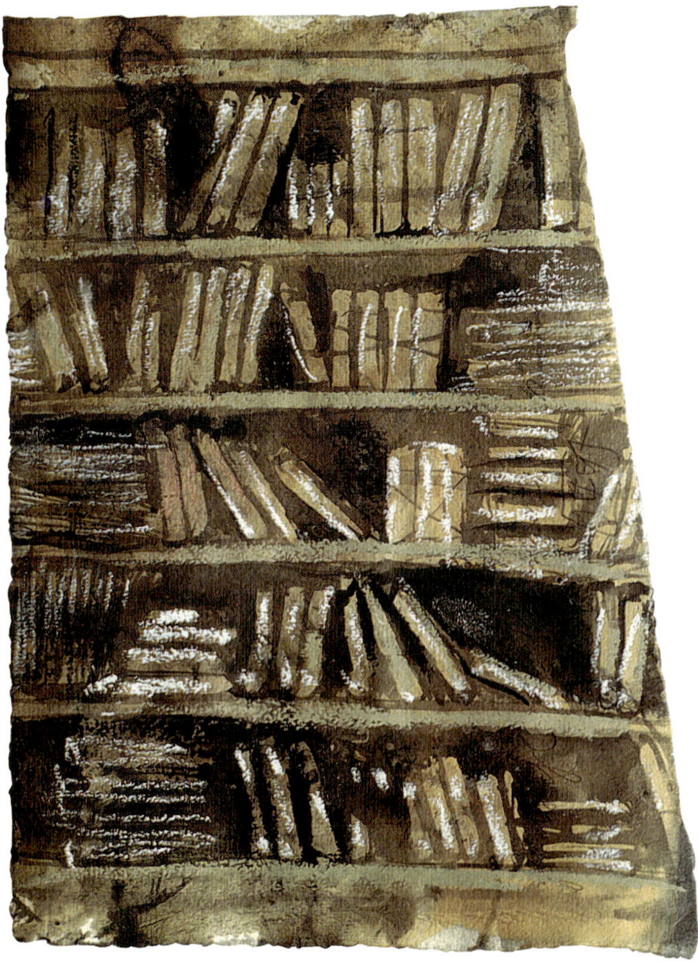

An old drawing gives us an enticing subject for our next painting. The drawing was executed with india ink with white pastel highlights. This is the original that we are going to use for our exercise.

3. Drawing on canvas

The first stage consists of copying the drawing onto the canvas. It is not necessary to get an exact copy since, in most cases, sketches and preliminary drawings are used only as outlines for developing ideas. First we mix a touch of dark oil paint with a little turpentine; the liquid will become blackish brown. The edges of the shelves are drawn by sticking a strip of adhesive tape to the canvas; this is not essential, but it helps us to divide up the spaces. Then we dip the brush into the dirty turpentine, paint the guidelines, and immediately remove the tape without taking too much care. There is no need to be concerned if the paint runs; the main lines of the painting are sufficiently clear that this should not be a problem. We now draw the shelves, leaving the same amount of space between each one. The lines of the drawing will be the main guide for our painting; we should not worry about covering them, since they will always emerge in the painting. Indeed, the success of the painting rests solely on the preliminary drawing. Once all the contours of the shelves have been drawn, we will quickly sketch the entire bookcase. It is important to keep in mind that what we are dealing with here is a collection of light and dark masses; the light masses will balance the dark ones. First we draw the whites and distribute the spaces destined for the heavy books. In the painting we are going to create, expressionism and a certain amount of gestural drama will play an important role.

Note how clear the shape of the painting already looks at this stage.

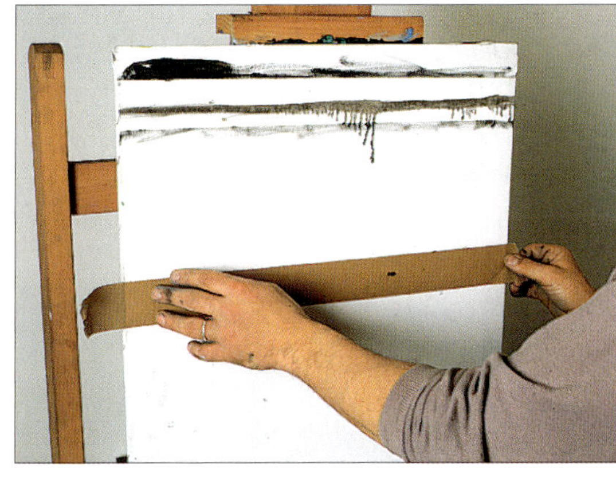

The drawing is our guide. We simply want to create a linear framework on which the paint will rest.

Now we will begin to distribute the spaces, as if we were building a real bookcase. The drawing is completed in one move, rectifying directly on the canvas before the painting begins.

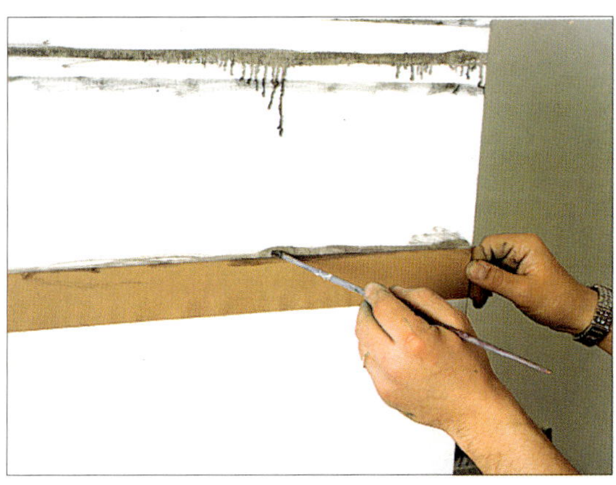

We use a strip of adhesive tape to draw the shelves. There is no need to press down too hard.

We run the brush along the edge of the tape to obtain the line of the shelf's edge.

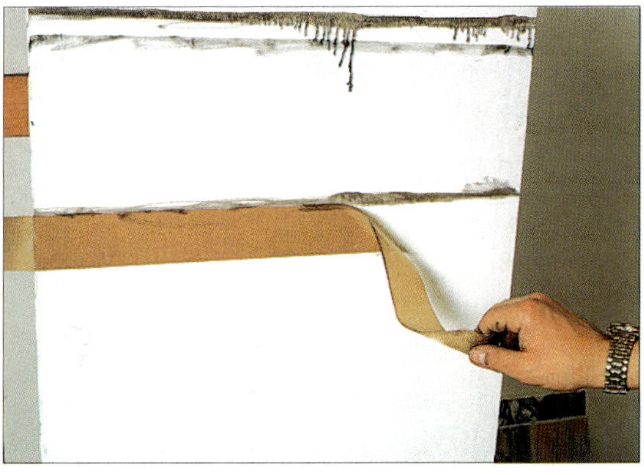

Removing the tape, we can see the line that we will use as a guide for the development of our painting.

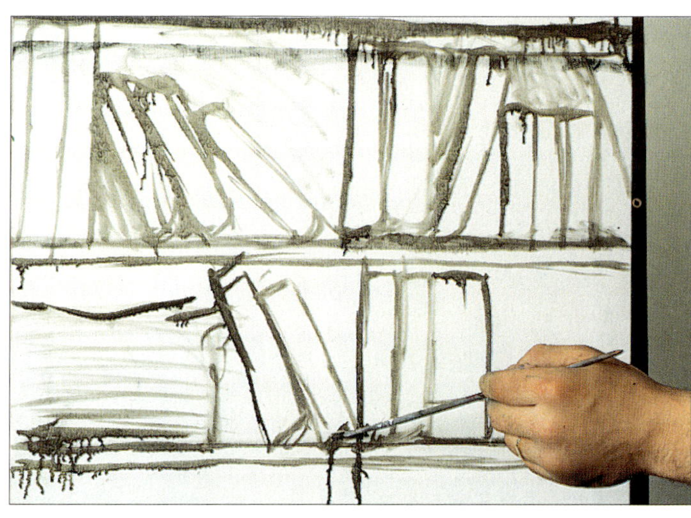

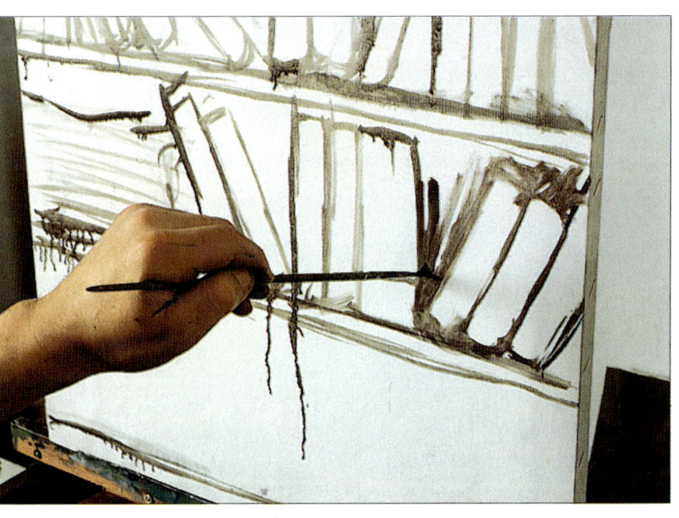

4. Do you want to make your own oil colors?

The drawing made with oil and turpentine will soon be dry. While we wait, we can prepare our palette. This time we will not use an ordinary palette because we will be working with large amounts of oil paint. It is more practical to work on a larger surface. We have chosen a white formica board of 19.7 × 19.7 inches (50 × 50 cm) with strips of wood attached to the edges to keep the ground alabaster in.

One important point to bear in mind: This type of work requires abundant paint; the usual oil paint tubes will not suffice. You will need 1.1 pound (½ kg) containers. For many people, especially amateurs, the cost may be prohibitive, but there is a cheaper and more satisfying alternative. Why not make your own paint? It's not difficult. All you need is some spare time and the following materials: pigments (sold in fine art stores) turpentine, linseed oil without cobalt siccative, a little beeswax, and damar varnish. They are all easy to obtain and inexpensive.

Let us now follow the correct procedure for making good-quality oil paint. It is possible to make oil paint simply by mixing the pigment with oil until it forms a paste. Indeed, I have often done this myself. However, to get truly amazing results, you should follow these instructions carefully: Tip about a fistful of powdered pigment onto a slab of glass or marble. If the powder is not fine enough, grind it down with a pestle. Using a flexible palette knife, such as the type used to fill in cracks in walls, mass the pigment into a pile and pour a small amount of linseed oil around the bottom. Then tip a small amount of pigment over the oil with a palette knife. Still working with the palette knife, move the pigment and oil to one side where you can grind the mix; it doesn't take long for the pigment to absorb the oil. Continue grinding the pigment with an up and down movement until the pigment and oil have been completely mixed together. Depending on how fluid you want the paint to be, add more pigment or oil until you obtain a consistent mass; then continue adding more oil and pigment to get the desired quantity. With the aid of a palette knife, grind the pigment for 10 or 15 minutes; leave it to stand for a while, then repeat the procedure again. It is essential to carry out several grinding sessions because the pigment envelops the oil but doesn't actually absorb it, so the artist must continue mixing and grinding to break down the pigment particles and bind it to the oil. Then put the oil in a pot along with a quarter of its total volume of wax, the same amount of varnish, and a little turpentine. Heat the pot in a double-boiler until the ingredients have melted, all the time stirring it in order to maintain a homogeneous substance. Taking care not to get burned, pour the liquid over the oil and continue mixing and grinding until it is ready.

You will have noticed by now that the color is much darker than the pigment was at the beginning. This can be avoided by adding Spanish white. Don't use white since it makes the color take on a paler tone. The oil paint is now ready. We can keep it in glass or plastic pots. All we need to do now is place some paint on the palette with a palette knife and use it.

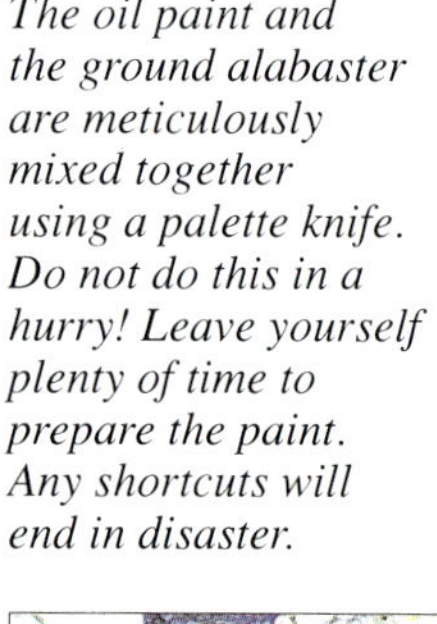

The oil paint and the ground alabaster are meticulously mixed together using a palette knife. Do not do this in a hurry! Leave yourself plenty of time to prepare the paint. Any shortcuts will end in disaster.

With the palette knife, we model the "matter"; the texture must never be left to chance.

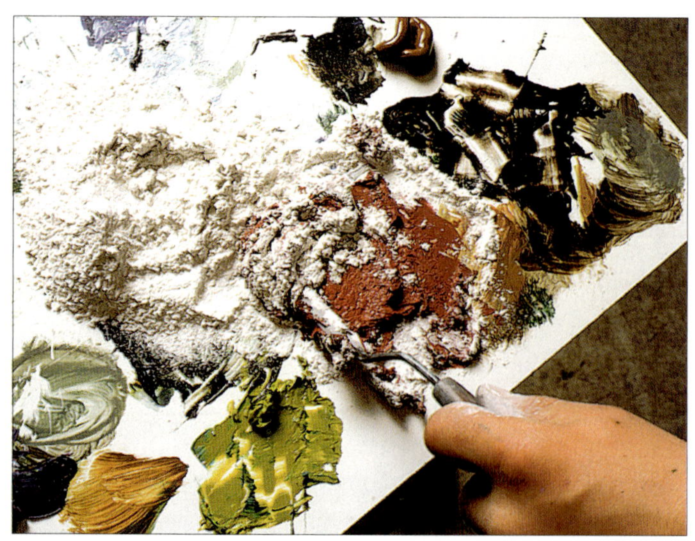

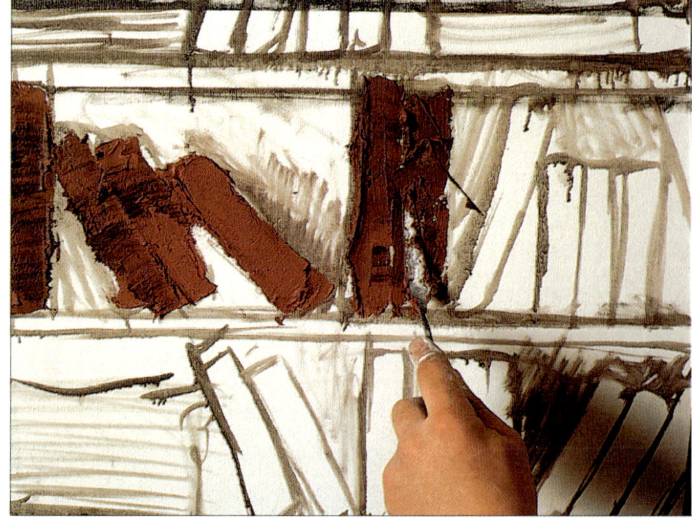

5. Before painting

We now have the following colors on our palette, from right to left: ivory black, cobalt blue, Prussian blue, brown, burnt umber, raw umber, English red (lots of it, since it is the predominant color), yellow ocher, dark ocher, and white. At the center of our palette, we have placed about a glassful of ground alabaster. The sequential placement of colors on the palette is a question of method; you may change the order if you want.

Now we begin to thicken the paint with ground alabaster. Following the same procedure used for making our oil paints, we begin to add the alabaster powder to the paint. You will see how, at first, alabaster "floats" on top of the paint; it may even form lumps, but don't worry, the oil paint has not been ruined. We must persist until the oil has "devoured" the powder, and has acquired a more pasty consistency. Once the quantity has been kneaded, make sure that it contains enough powder; we can always make a less dense mass simply by adding a little of the initial paste to a new amount of oil, thus obtaining paint with less mix.

6. The first stains

Now that we have mixed the alabaster with the paint, it is time to apply the first colors. For this purpose we have carefully prepared some English red mixed in with a small quantity of sienna. Using a long palette knife, we begin to apply it carefully over the areas occupied by books, as shown in the photo below (left). The paint has to be constantly kneaded, adding oil or powder depending on how much weight and texture we want. It is important to keep in mind that if we apply a heavy impasto over a layer of paint containing too much oil, the former will slide. This is an effect that we can play with on occasion; however, it is not advisable to "abuse" it—these effects should be used only when really necessary. Notice how, as we gradually build up the color, the textured paint overlaps the boundaries of the preliminary drawing. It is necessary, therefore, to constantly redefine those boundaries by using the tip of the palette knife, although not too carefully, since the patches of color already define the volumes on their own.

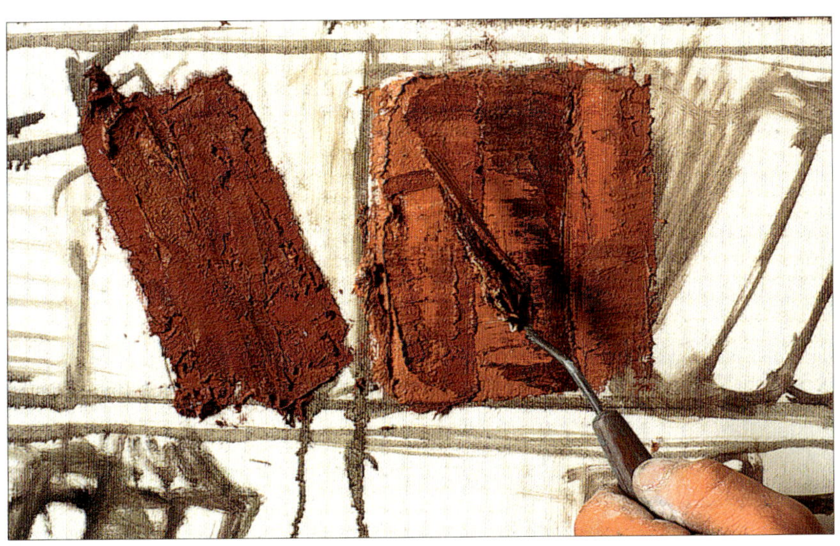

Notice how we scrape matter paint over an underlying layer, allowing the texture and color of the original layer to remain visible.

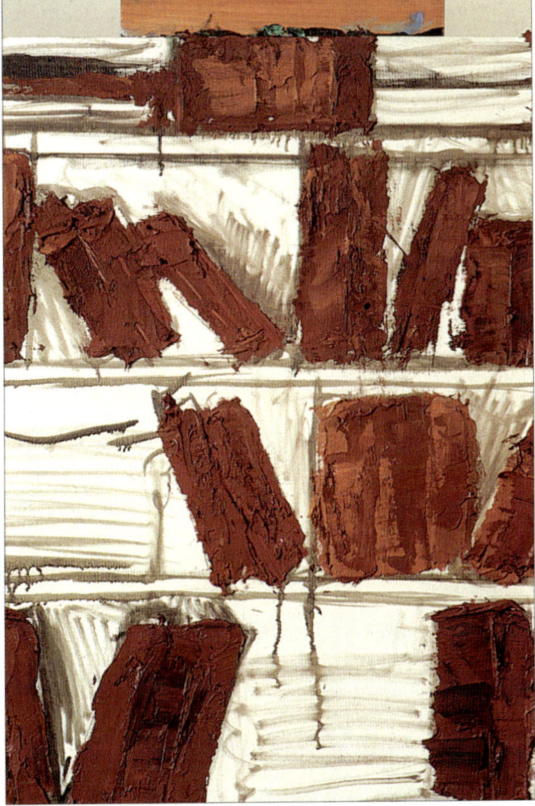

At this stage of the painting, we can picture the separations among the main books.

7. The palette knife as main tool for this painting

At this stage of the work, it would be handy to give a little advice on how to use a palette knife to paint.

By now, we hope that you have gotten the feel of your palette knife; if you already know how to use a brush properly, then it will be easy to get a grasp of this new tool. At the beginning of this project, you probably felt tentative when using the palette knife. By now, you will have learned to mash colors on the palette, mix them with ground alabaster, and spread them over the canvas.

By running the point of the palette knife across an area of paint you can create effects to resolve problems in empty spaces. For instance, if we paint red over a dry area of green, we can then scrape away parts of the red to reveal the underlying color and create vibrant contrast. We can use the same technique to obtain lines, blobs, splashes, etc.

The palette knife can also be used for blending. This is done by using the flat part with the corner, just as you can see in the photograph. Returning to our painting, we once again prepare some paint, this time with less ground alabaster and darkened slightly with Prussian blue. We apply it in different areas of the picture, "placing" it on the canvas.

When we are working with a lot of paint, together with matter, we can overlay different types of materials. We can use this technique to create different textures in the painting, substituting traditional varnishes with eroded surfaces, which reveal the "archeological remains" of the first layers.

One of the most common uses of the palette knife is to form impastos and create textures. This exercise provides an excellent demonstration of this. The palette knife is easily cleaned with some old newspaper. We should apply each color without worrying about it getting mixed with adjacent colors; eventually, the drawing will be seen in the painting itself.

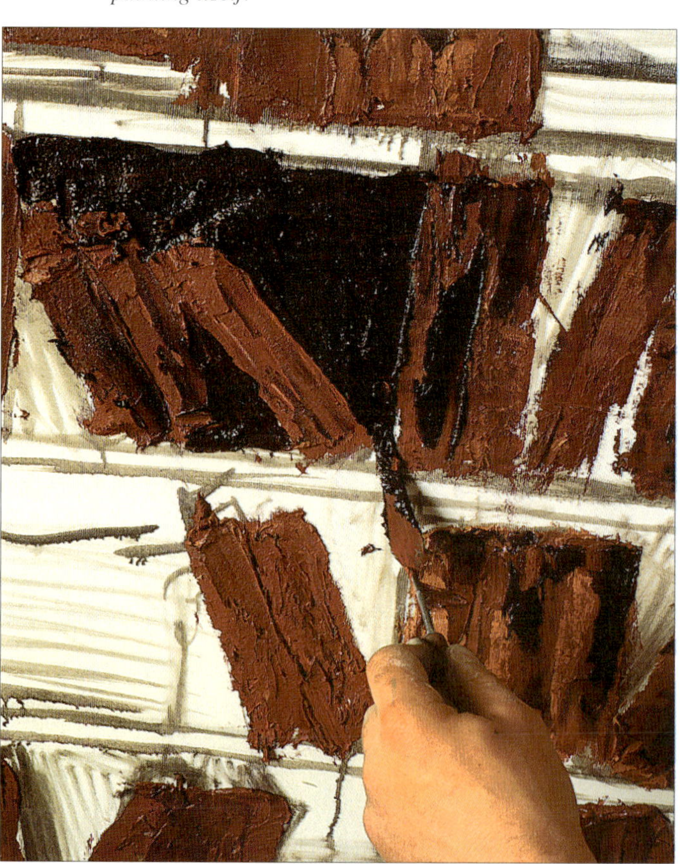

This is what the painting looks like after the largest dark masses have been added.

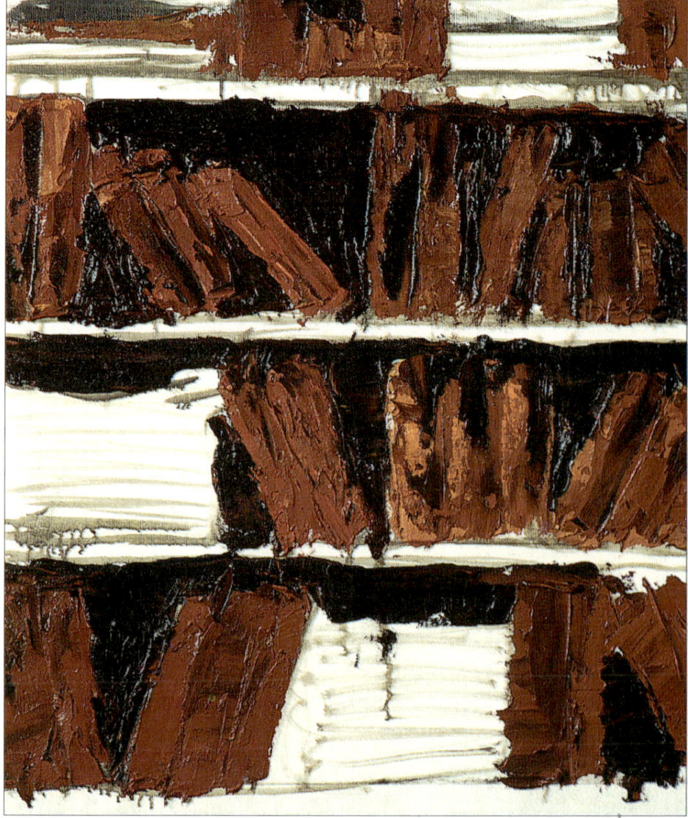

8. Applying dark impastos and highlighting

It is now time to begin making the painting darker. The reason for this is that when black oil dries below another color, it tends to "open up," producing cracks. Therefore, given the amount of paint we have used, we should define the main mass of the painting before using black.

Some painters never use black in their paintings, but black is a color like any other. Opposition to black began over a hundred years ago, at the time of impressionism, one of the most splendid periods in the history of painting.

We mix black with turquoise and several drops of wax heated in a double-boiler inside a pot containing turpentine.

Turpentine will lend the mix a velvety touch, making it stand out from the rest of the colors.

Having added the appropriate amount of ground alabaster following the procedure already described, we knead the result using a palette knife and begin to paint.

When you do this type of work, never think that you are filling in an empty space; you are painting the space. This change in concept will dramatically improve the result of your work with the palette knife. You must play with the color you are painting with, without caring about retaining the original shape of each book; it does not matter even if they seem disfigured.

We use the same technique to outline several books in shadow; in certain cases, a mere stroke of color will suggest the shadow. It is important to note how the amount of pressure applied produces different effects. Light scrapes are good for mixing color; more pressure applied on the palette knife allows the artist to sculpt the different planes between the books. Do not neglect the dark areas, since they are as essential as the light ones.

We can also juxtapose colors to obtain the desired effect; this will work provided the effect is not gratuitous. (A technique used in a gratuitous way is only effective when gratuitousness itself is a conscious aesthetic choice.)

Having prepared the white oil, we clean the center of the palette with a long palette knife and some newspaper, something that is easily done. If necessary you should also wipe it with a cloth dampened in turpentine. The reason for so much cleanliness lies in the fact that white is an especially delicate color. It should not be altered unless we want it to be. It is essential to avoid accidents that can alter our perception of the painting.

We place the white color in the center of the palette, tip a large amount of ground alabaster next to it, and start mixing again until a uniform paste is obtained. The oil must be mixed until it has acquired enough consistency to be able to transfer large amounts with the palette knife to the canvas. Before doing this, we first touch some earth colors on the palette—not red, however, because it turns pink when mixed with white. Then we spread the color in a horizontal direction in uniform applications. The color variation produces a streaky effect. Once the white parts have been painted, we create horizontal lines by scratching with the edge of the palette knife the areas of the painting that represent stacks of paper. Then part of these lines are covered, using the flat side of the palette knife, and new textures are created, producing earthy tones in the light part of the painting.

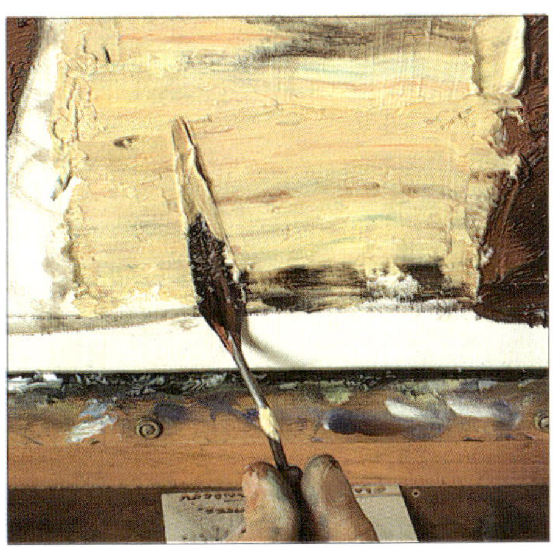

The light stains are applied in the form of large impastos that will later be modeled with the aid of the corner of the palette knife.

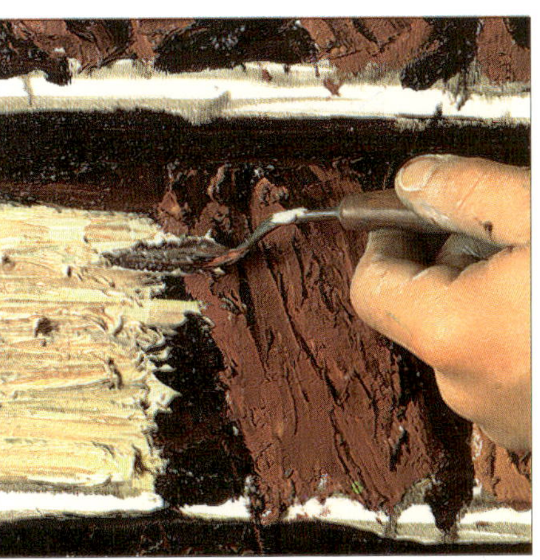

With the sharp side of the palette knife we create a horizontal array of lines that will provide the painting with both relief and color.

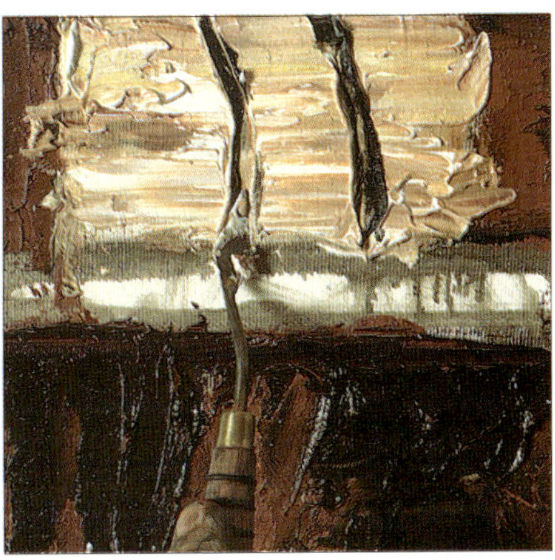

The edge of the palette knife is used to define the volume of the papers on the shelves. The palette knife is then used to shape—even sculpt—the masses of paint.

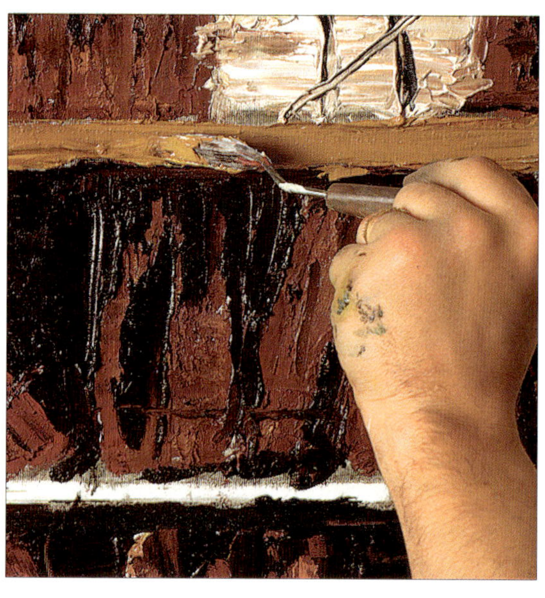

With the flat side of the palette knife we draw the supports of the shelf. Here we have barely used any matter with the paint, since the focus should be on the books.

A detail of the final touches. Basically, we go over one or two lines, and touch up a white area that appears too shiny, in order to create the right contrast.

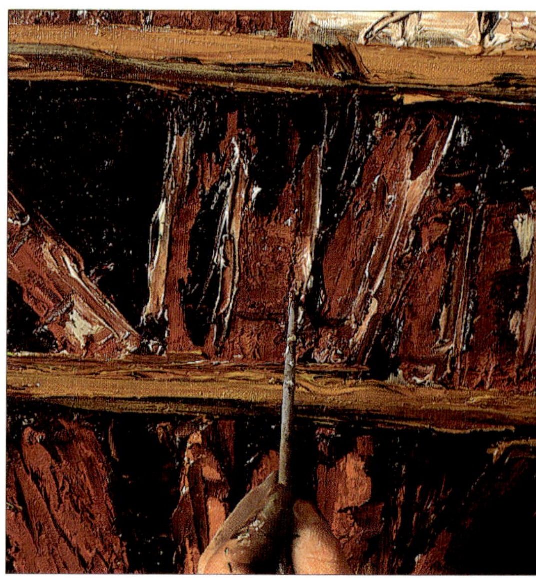

The painting is finished. It will take a long time to dry. Don't apply varnish until it has been left to dry for several months.

9. The final touches

Having used white to create several new compositional masses, the painting is considered complete; however, the whole still lacks life. It still requires certain touches to lend it vibrancy.

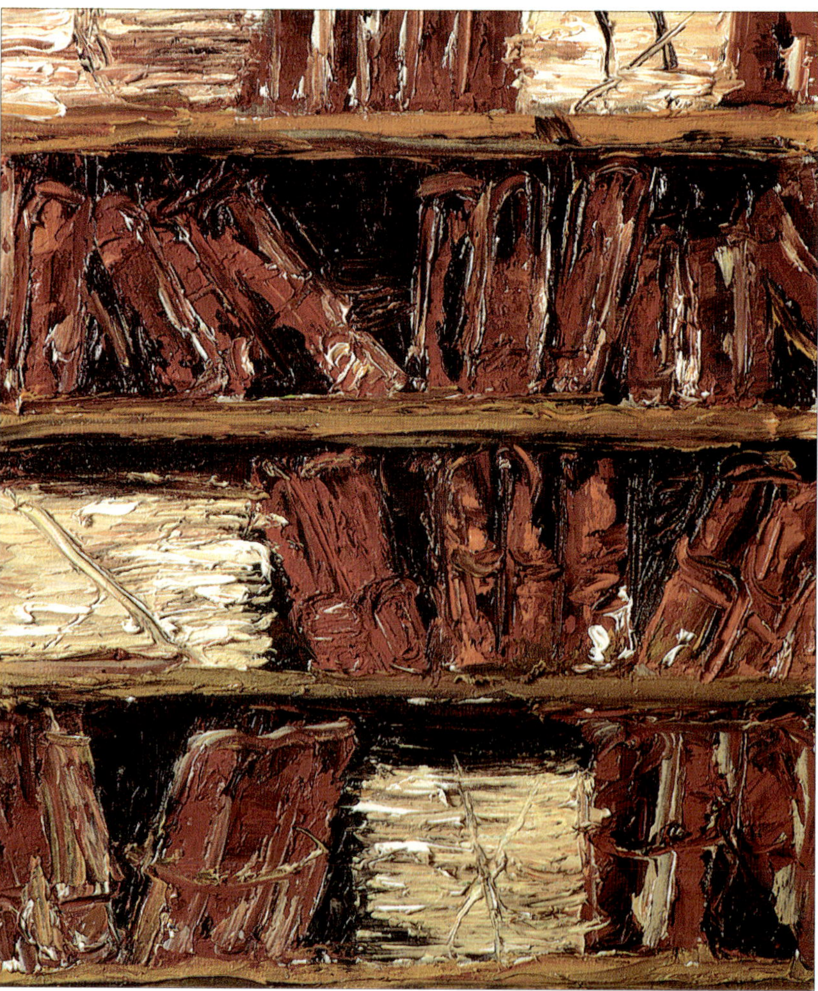

If we look back a few pages and examine the original drawing this painting was based on, we will see that, although monochromatic, the drawing does possess a life of its own, thanks to the white pastel highlighting.

It is curious that, while we did not copy the original idea onto the canvas, we do end up treating light as in the original. This time we will not use white from the palette. Although it may appear rather unorthodox, we will use paint direct from the tube; in fact, we will paint with the tube itself, leaving as much oil paint in the areas of light as is necessary. These white highlights give the painting a greater plasticity. We continue with the palette knife, applying touches of white wherever necessary, again mixing certain colors. We do not do this everywhere, only in the areas that are excessively opaque. We leave the shelves until last. They are easiest to resolve: a little ocher, to which we add a touch of sienna, simply to modify the tone. Here we barely add any material to the paint. Homogeneous applications of color are then painted with the long palette knife.

The painting is finished, although to speak of finishing a painting is a delicate matter. There are one or two things that could be improved, but, as previously mentioned, it is important to know when to stop and save your yearning to paint for another work.

We hope that this demonstration will motivate you to experiment along the same lines with your own creations.

An Amsterdam canal

1. Introduction

The painting we are about to follow is an excellent example of matter painting using ground alabaster. The model we are going to paint is an urban landscape. We will put into practice everything we have learned about matter painting to execute the scene in this photograph, but our aim is to transcend any simple representation of reality.

We will apply the material onto a previously prepared canvas.

Matter painting, as you will have discovered by now, can be used in the representation of any theme. On the other hand, with matter painting the purely pictorial is taken to a new dimension, creating relief in a traditionally two-dimensional art form.

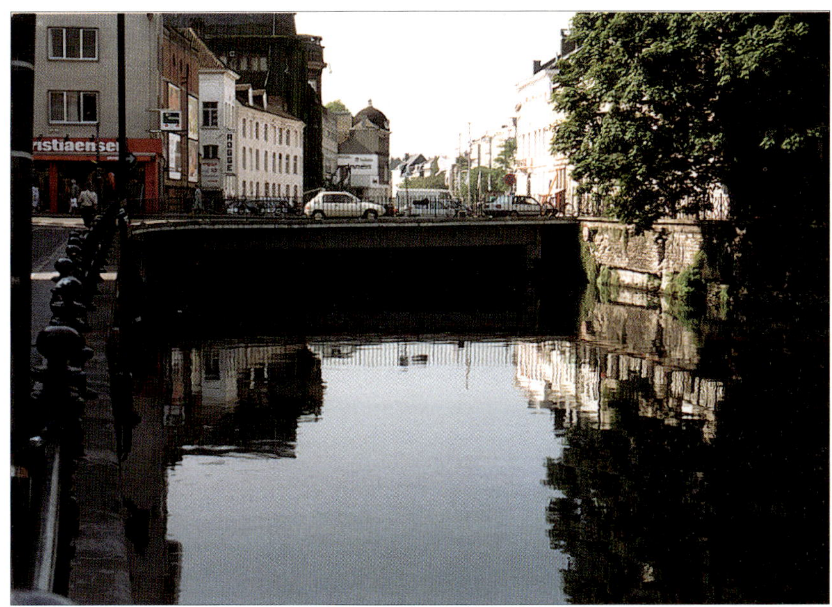

This photograph of a canal in Amsterdam will be the subject for the painting we are about to follow. Note the vanishing lines and reduction of definition in the farthest planes.

Following a common practice that we highly recommend, we begin our work by painting a study of the theme in watercolor. This will help us to establish different aspects of the composition and the color range.

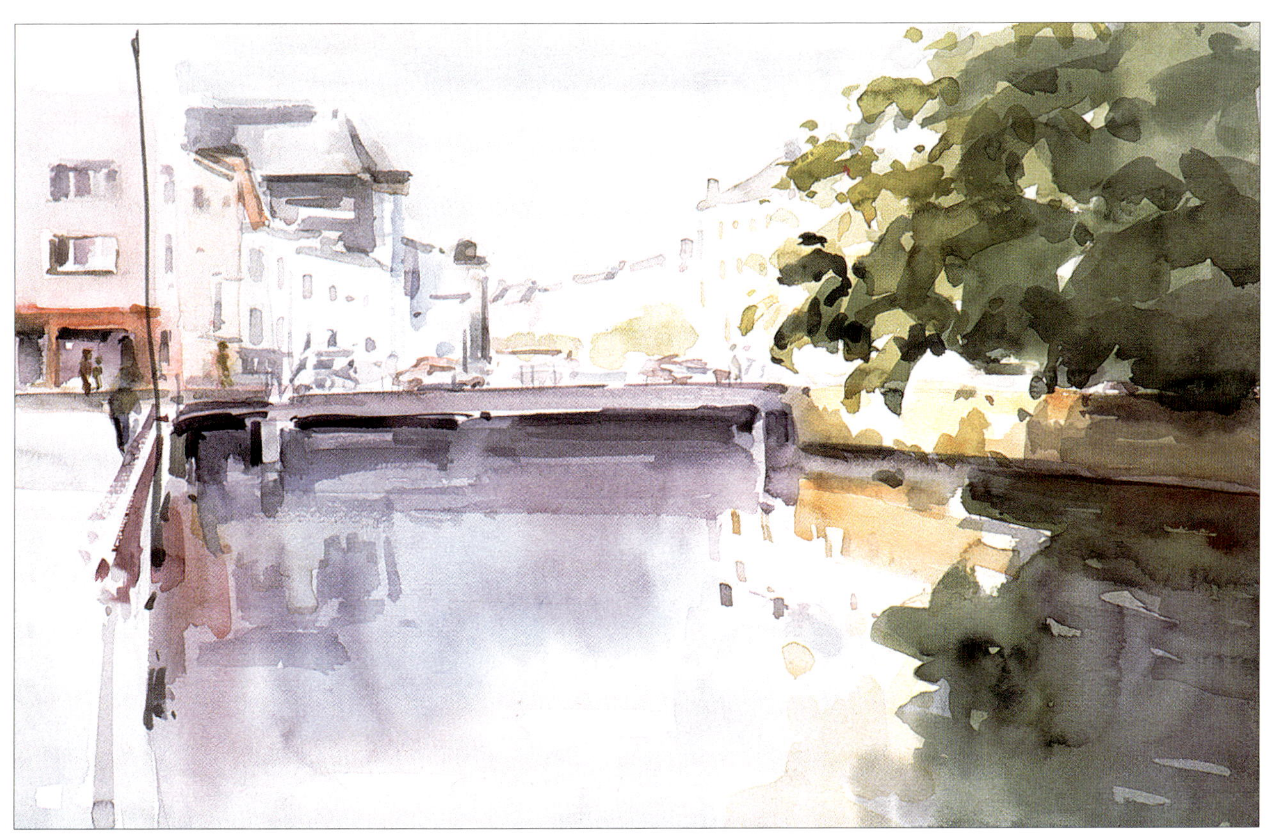

An Amsterdam canal

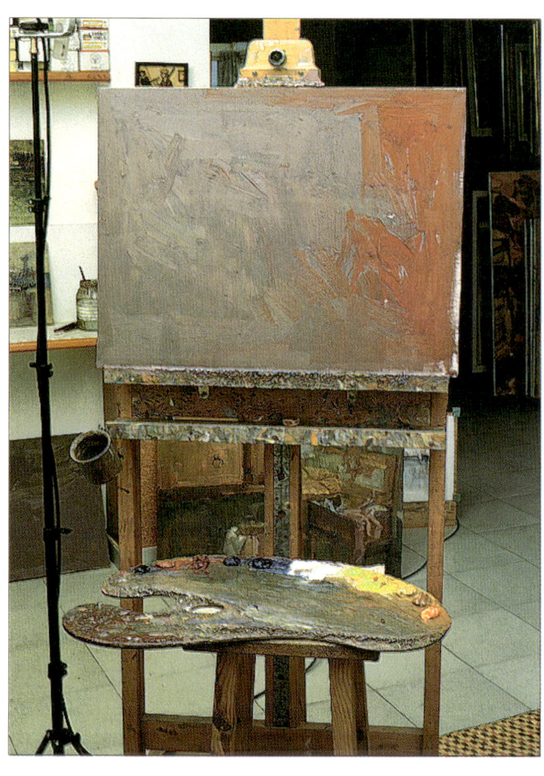

Notice how the painter holds the brush, both for painting and for loading paint from the palette.

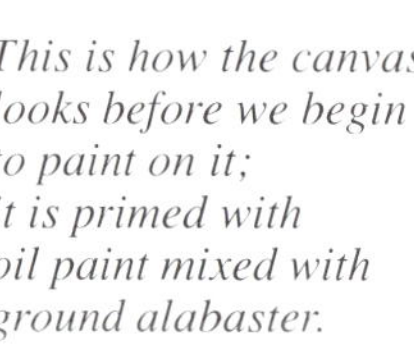

This is how the canvas looks before we begin to paint on it; it is primed with oil paint mixed with ground alabaster.

2. Painting on a prepared canvas

You can see in the photograph the prepared canvas, primed with a dark grayish oil color, to which some English red has been added on the left. As you can see, the canvas already has a rough texture, which we will use in our painting. The canvas must be primed several days in advance because oil takes time to dry, as we have mentioned in earlier chapters.

It is handy to have more than one canvas ready, with different color backgrounds, cool and warm, so we can match them with the theme we choose.

We begin by painting and drawing at the same time, applying a dark gray patch mixed with ultramarine blue. Before using the palette knife, we have to establish the general outline of the theme using various paintbrushes. Our brushstrokes are hard. From the very outset our aim is to give priority to texture.

Once a few of the structural lines have been drawn, we paint directly with neutral colors, always with thick hog hair brushes. Using the brush as if it were a palette knife, we apply thick and flat brushstrokes, all the time working with large quantities of paint.

Once the first color stains are in place, we must be more decisive with color. We apply a thick yellow impasto containing a small amount of ground alabaster. This technique of applying large impastos allows us to paint large masses or remove areas without hardly dirtying the color. This allows us more freedom and spontaneity in our work.

Besides, since we are painting with a great deal of paint and a thick brush, the color does not mix with the underlying layer of paint. The painting is now outlined.

Colors are always mixed on the palette, not on the canvas. This way we can keep them pure.

Notice in this photograph where we begin to paint: at the center of the canvas, indicating clearly the painting's most important compositional line, which divides the theme horizontally.

With the flat part of the brush we trace the space and masses that define the main elements of the painting.

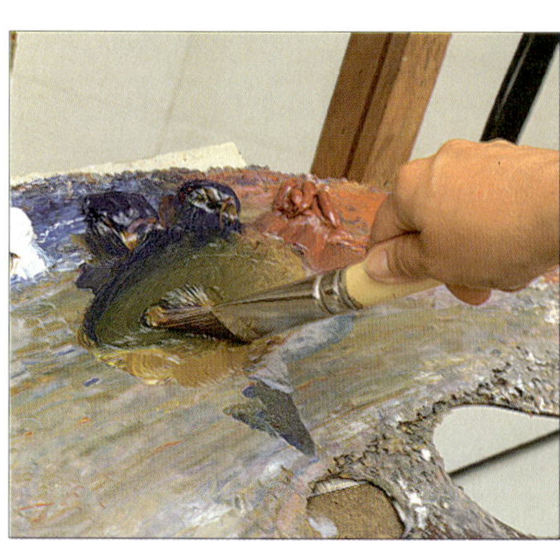

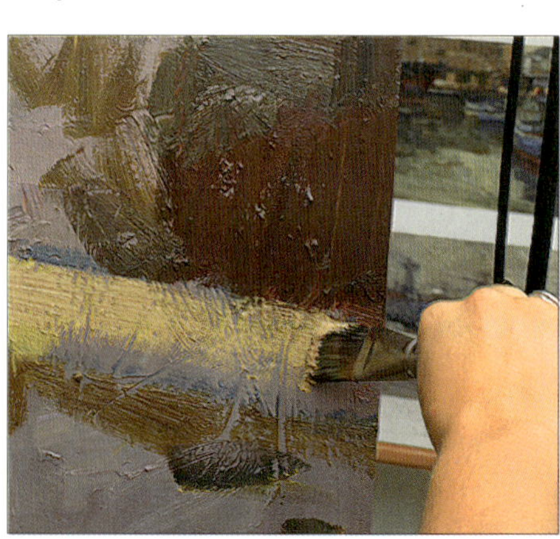

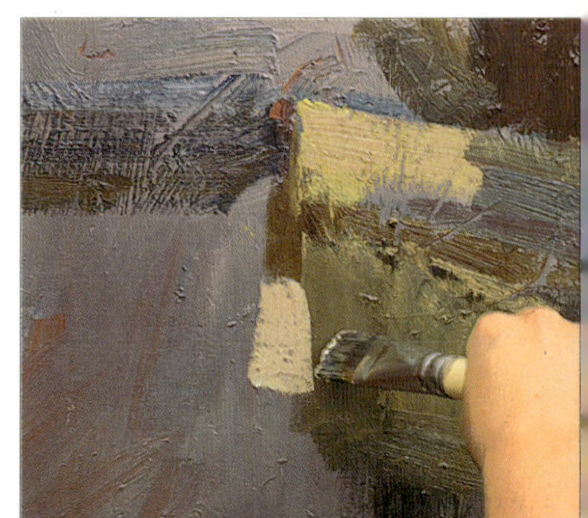

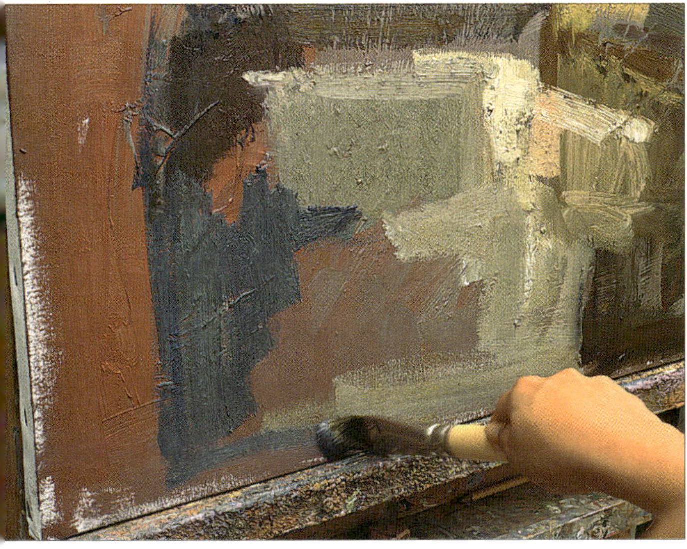

We start to cover the canal with Prussian blue and white, painting over, where necessary, the red patch in the background, but without covering it entirely.

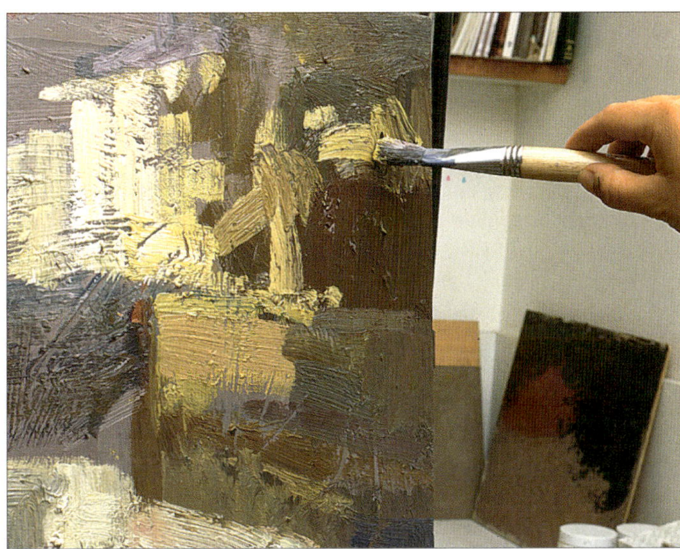

With several very small brushstrokes of yellowish ocher, we stain the treetop area.

3. Establishing the contrasts

Quickly, and with a loose wrist, we start painting a series of large, well-defined flat masses, corresponding to the buildings, trees, and other elements that comprise the main structure of the painting. We are now working at full speed, continuously scraping, mixing, and massing paint.

With a mix of Prussian blue and white, we stain the large area that was primed with red, while allowing some of it to remain visible in order to create a contrast with the other colors that will make up the reflections on the water.

We continue painting with light colors. The walls of the buildings are defined with cadmium yellow and lemon, both of which are saturated with white. These luminous stains stand out on the still unpainted background.

Now, with the side of the brush, we paint white to suggest the bridge that divides the composition in half.

We have also painted, with small disorderly patches, an area of trees, using yellow and greenish ocher tones. Next, we apply green to help suggest an area of water, indicating, while we are at it, a reflection or two.

We now turn our attention to painting light gray tones in the sky and adding some broken violet tones to a good part of the building.

With pure white we drag the edge of the brush over the canvas to define the bridge.

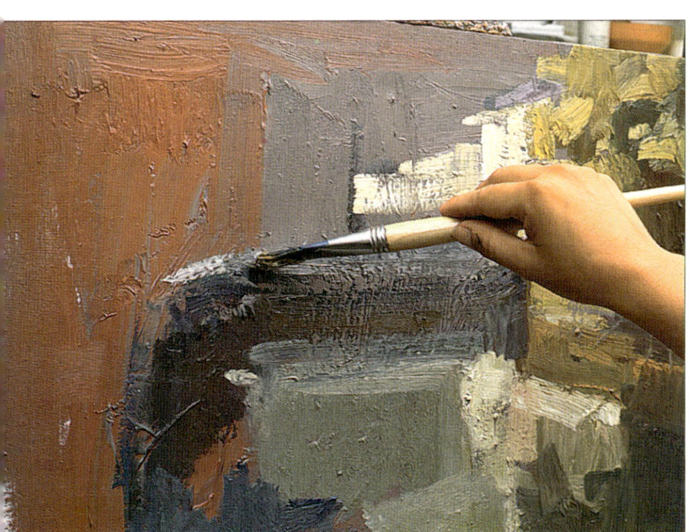

We continue working on the houses; some are illuminated with very pale yellowish colors; others, in the shadow, will take violet gray tones.

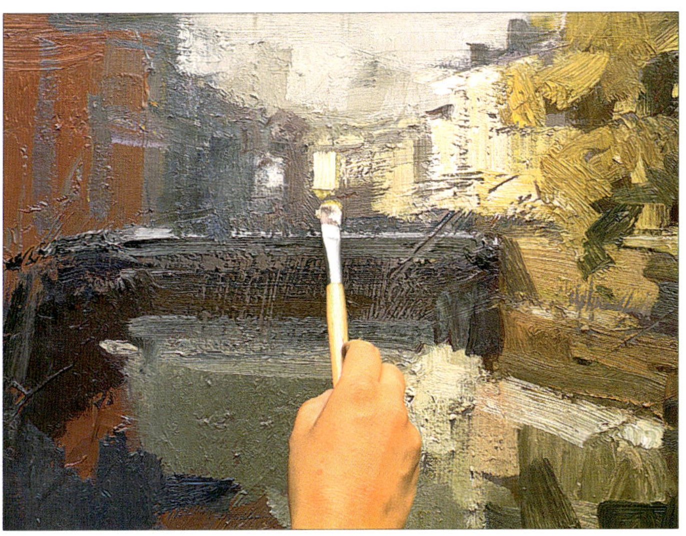

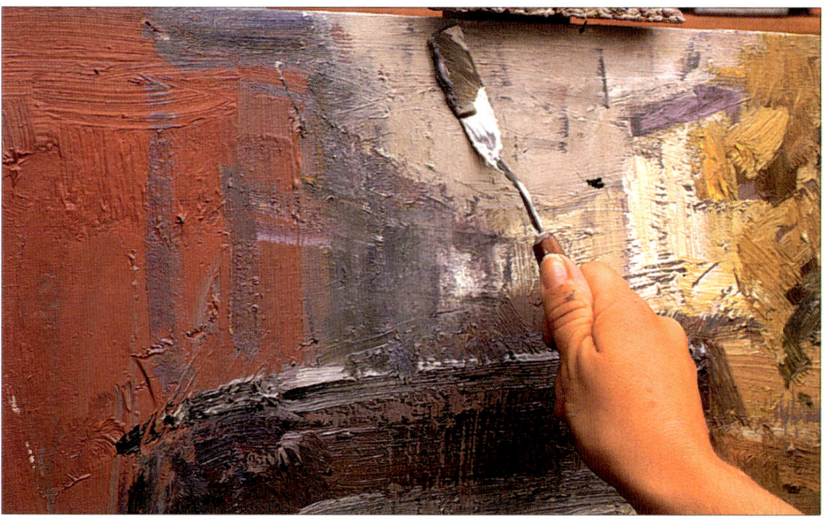

Applying the palette knife on its flat side we define the sky with a gray-violet color, bearing in mind the predominantly horizontal flow of the painting.

4. Working with the palette knife

We now begin to work with the palette knife especially in the area of the sky. We can see how the palette knife is used to create different textures that complement one another. By applying the palette knife in uniform parallel strokes over the surface, we can obtain a smooth texture; we can also use it as we see fit to create planes of impastos. Now that the general outline of the painting has been established, the palette knife will play a decisive role in bringing the whole together. We paint by mixing colors directly on the canvas, while at the same time scraping and thus obtaining a neutral color range, the result of the colors previously used.

As mentioned in earlier chapters, the palette can be cleaned with newspaper. For this type of work requiring a great deal of paint, we use paint pots, since tubes are used up too quickly.

We are achieving a series of really interesting textures. The thick impastos are alternated with flat applications of paint mixed with ground alabaster.

The palette knife allows us to work freely and spontaneously. As the painting takes shape we notice how easy it becomes to work on it. The painting itself seems to compel us to go faster, and the layers of color overlap each other naturally. Quickly, we clean the large palette knife with a piece of newspaper and, with a mix of ivory black and cobalt blue, separate some of the lines within the painted surface. With the side of the palette knife we draw some almost invisible lines and then scrape paint over them. Although there is still work to do on the dark areas, and contrast with highlights and whites, we can already begin to make out the fundamental parts of the painting.

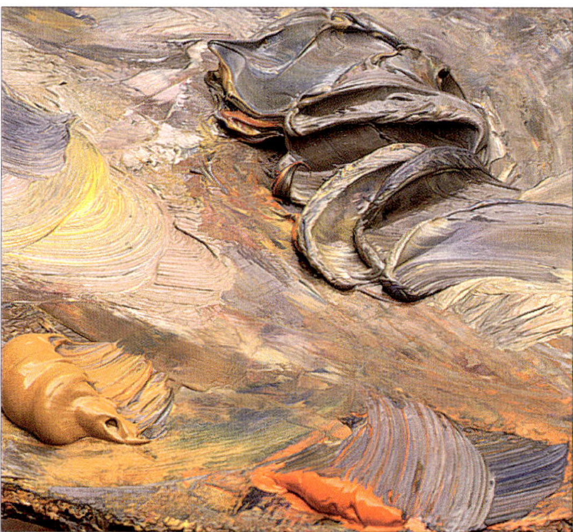

A close view of our palette. We have created good-sized color mixes, kneading the oil paint thoroughly.

We create masses by means of color planes, but we do it in a most concise form, only suggesting shadows, lights, and volume. The texture of the canvas, and of the paint itself, play an essential role.

This photograph shows how the artist mixes paint on his palette. Note the grayish tone obtained from the rest of the colors.

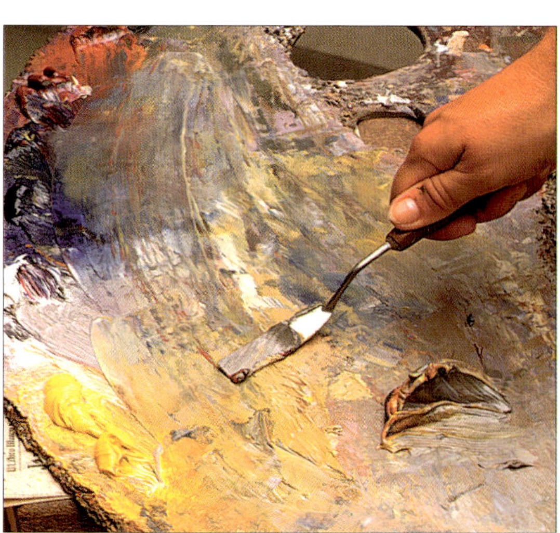

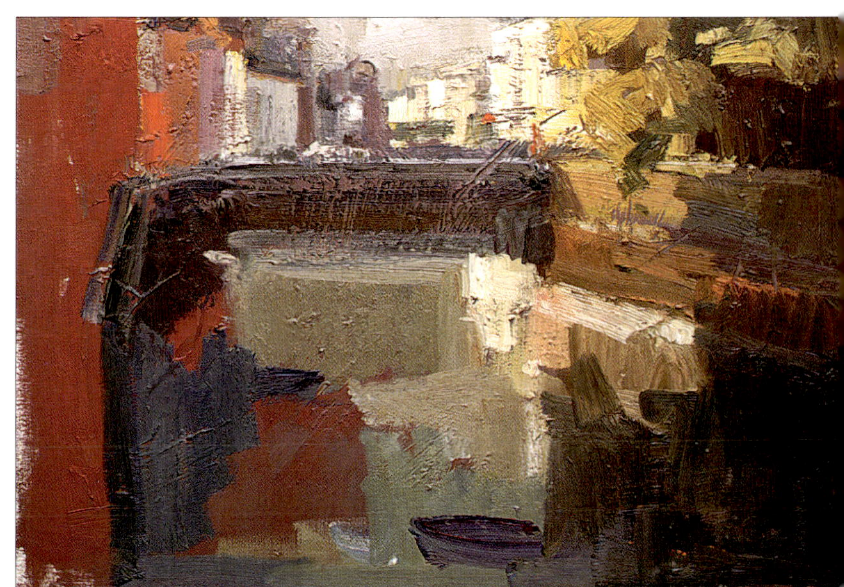

5. Creating planes with color

The best way to understand the theme as a whole is to stand back and look at it through squinted eyes. This allows us to make a better overall assessment of the piece. Our technique of alternating between hog hair brushes and palette knives is increasingly making a mark on the development of the painting.

It is essential to always see the theme as one. We begin work on the left side of the painting, barely altering the large red mass. We paint with neutral colors from a warm range, including ocher, cadmium orange, carmine, etc. Several sweeping brushstrokes of pinkish violet are used to finish the house on the left side of the canvas. In contrast, the areas of the street and the edge of the canal are painted with a cooler violet.

We constantly return to the background to add various dark-hued planes, so that we can later add colors or impastos that outline the forms, thus attempting to create the appropriate contrast and color vibration. The reflections of the building are treated in the same way—superimposing orange and carmine tones on top of darker tones.

We are painting while standing up, with the palette placed on top of a stool in front of us. The colors we are using for this painting are: orange, cadmium orange, ocher, gold ocher, yellow ocher medium, lemon yellow, titanium white, ultramarine blue deep, Prussian blue, madder, English red, and ivory black.

This selection of colors allows us to build up the atmosphere in our painting. Note the effect of dragging a brush loaded with paint over previously applied layers. We should not be concerned when doing this about the resulting mix. The increase in tones and hues will contribute greatly to the overall look of the work.

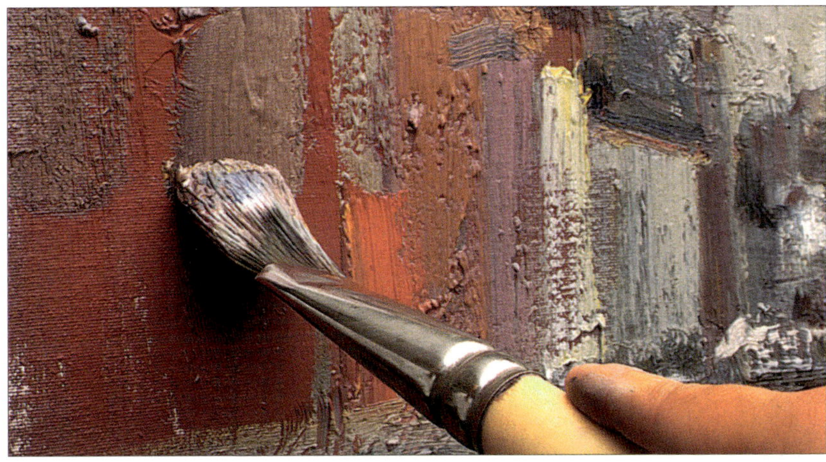

We paint with sweeping brushstrokes, applying light colors over dark ones, searching for contrast. Notice how the brush is held as if it were a palette knife. We have worked on the left side of the canvas, partially covering the English red background and defining the house with several loose strokes.

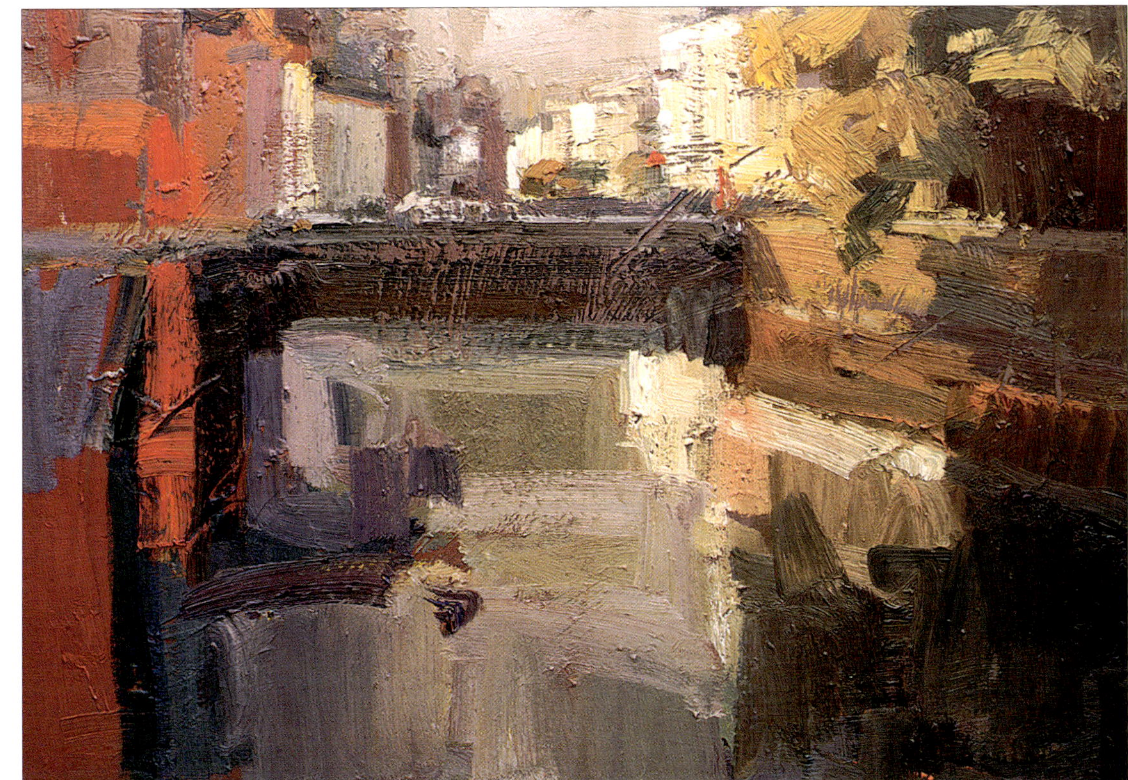

The painting is at an advanced stage, with main masses and the general structure completely defined. Working with the palette knife has left some underlying layers visible.

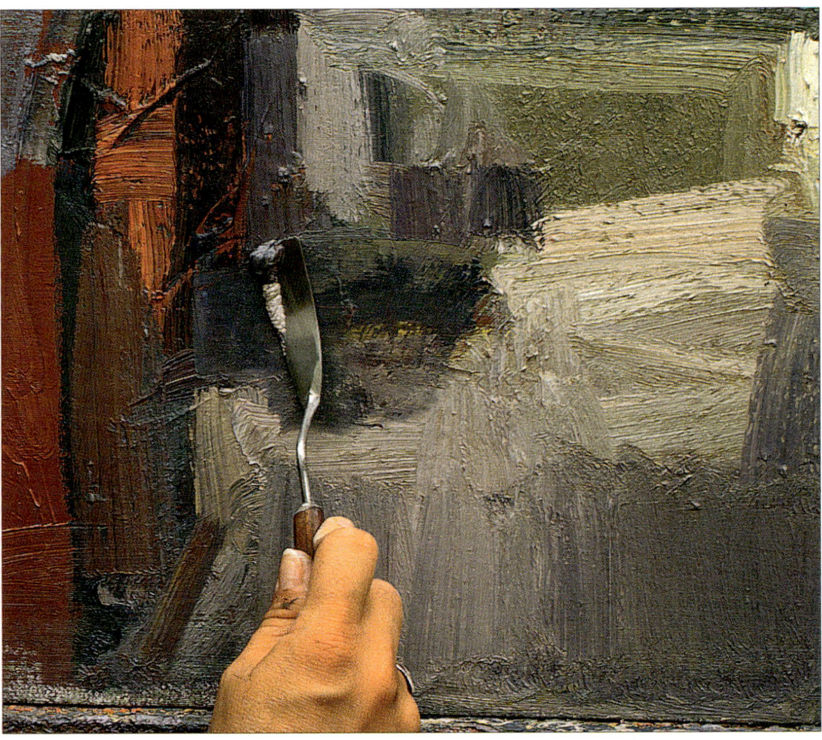

The palette knife is extremely useful both for removing paint and for achieving gradations among the reflections.

6. Interpreting forms

Until now we have used thick brushes and palette knives to avoid details, drawing, painting, and overlaying paint without any apparent concern, although taking the utmost care to arrange these elements so that they do not define the theme too clearly. Every time we painted a curve or a contour too accurately, we instantly "broke" it. The reason for working this way is to make sure that we continue to see the painting as a whole.

Alternating brushes with palette knives, we continue painting the left side, which is the warmer, more shadowy area. Then we return to the opposite side, indicating forms, tones, and values on this much lighter side.

The painting gradually begins to acquire unity and coherence with the buildings in the distance taking on a more definitive shape.

We are painting everywhere now, careful not to get stuck in any particular area of the painting. A sharp shadow will be indicated with a small, brisk brushstroke of a very dark color. Later we will work on the more precise shapes of the buildings on the left, using small patches of paint to represent windows and other projecting parts.

Now we move on to defining the reflections on the water; we build and rebuild, add and suppress, constantly turning the painting around. Occasionally, we leave the part of the picture we are working on and concentrate on another area, thus allowing us to see clearly anything that may cause problems. We return to the theme of the model, which does not have to be interpreted as it is seen in reality. It is up to us to interpret it according to our own criteria. This is especially true of the way we paint the reflections on the water. We must develop our personal view of reality.

Brushwork and palette knife continuously alternate to transform the image of reality into painting. By adding different amounts of ground alabaster to the paint we are using, we gradually turn our picture into a personal vehicle of artistic expression. It is essential to give your painting a personal touch. Each artist leaves his or her own mark—the thing that makes a painting an extension of the artist's personality. In this case, we are attempting a visceral expressionistic view of reality.

This photograph depicts that time when we return once more to stain on top of highlights, insinuating a shadow that outlines the wall of the canal. This is done with a rounded, very dark brushstroke.

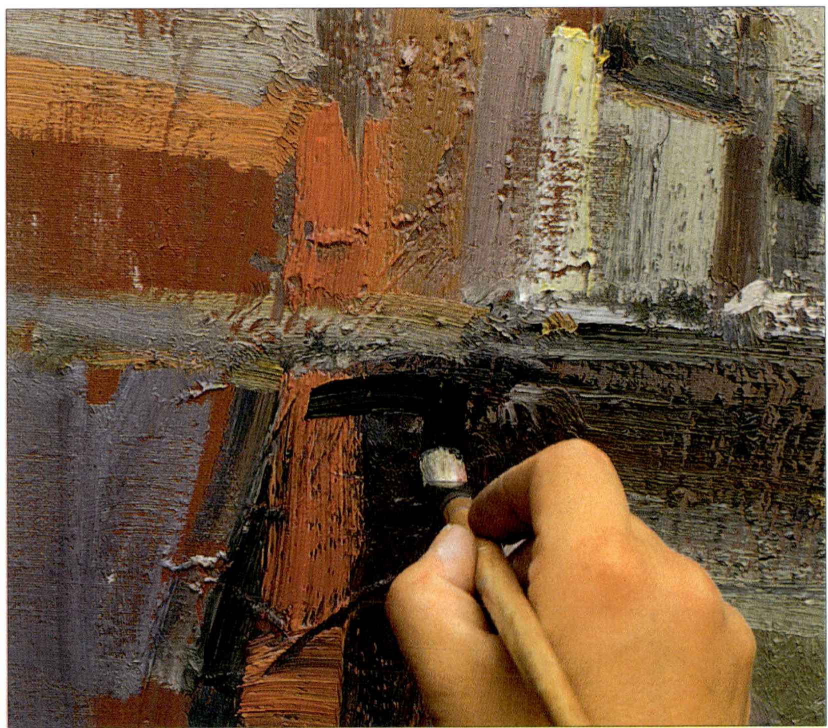

7. Several details

The arduous work of painting with brushes and palette knives continues. The technique used for building up the work is almost architectonic, painting the planes of the buildings alongside the organic lines of the green zones, as well as the treatment of the sky.

The reflections on the water have been resolved with several touches without attempting anything too intricate. Many outstanding paintings are especially so because of their simplicity. Our objective here is expression and sensibility.

We begin to paint in a more decisive manner over the reflections that we have just worked on. We paint a wavy shadow that brings out the wall of the canal. The style of the work requires that we make it darker, with a sharper and more angled stroke.

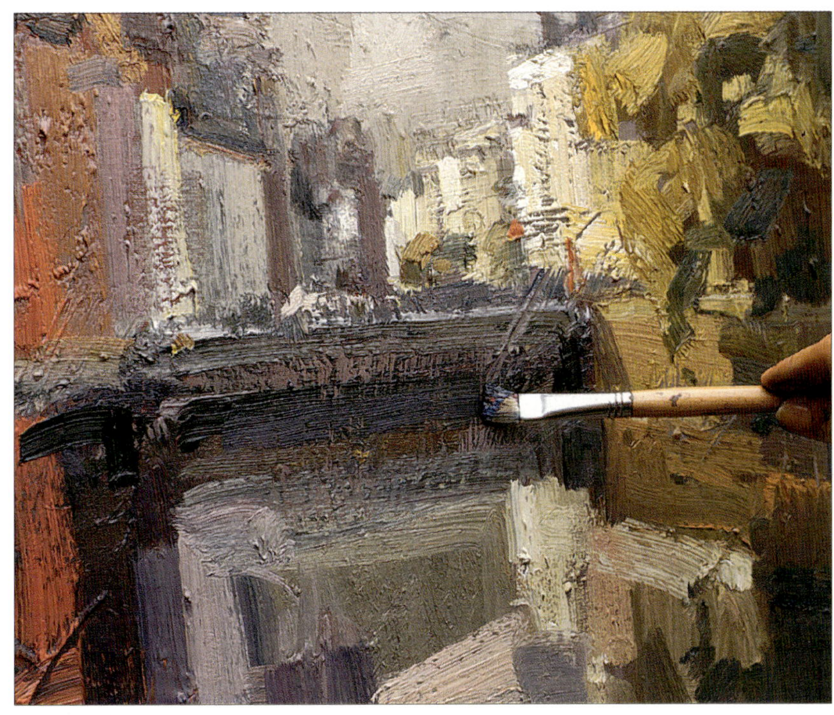

We continue working on details, making the reflections on the water cleaner. We do this by using a slightly lighter tone, lightly graying a blue with delicate, horizontally applied brushstrokes.

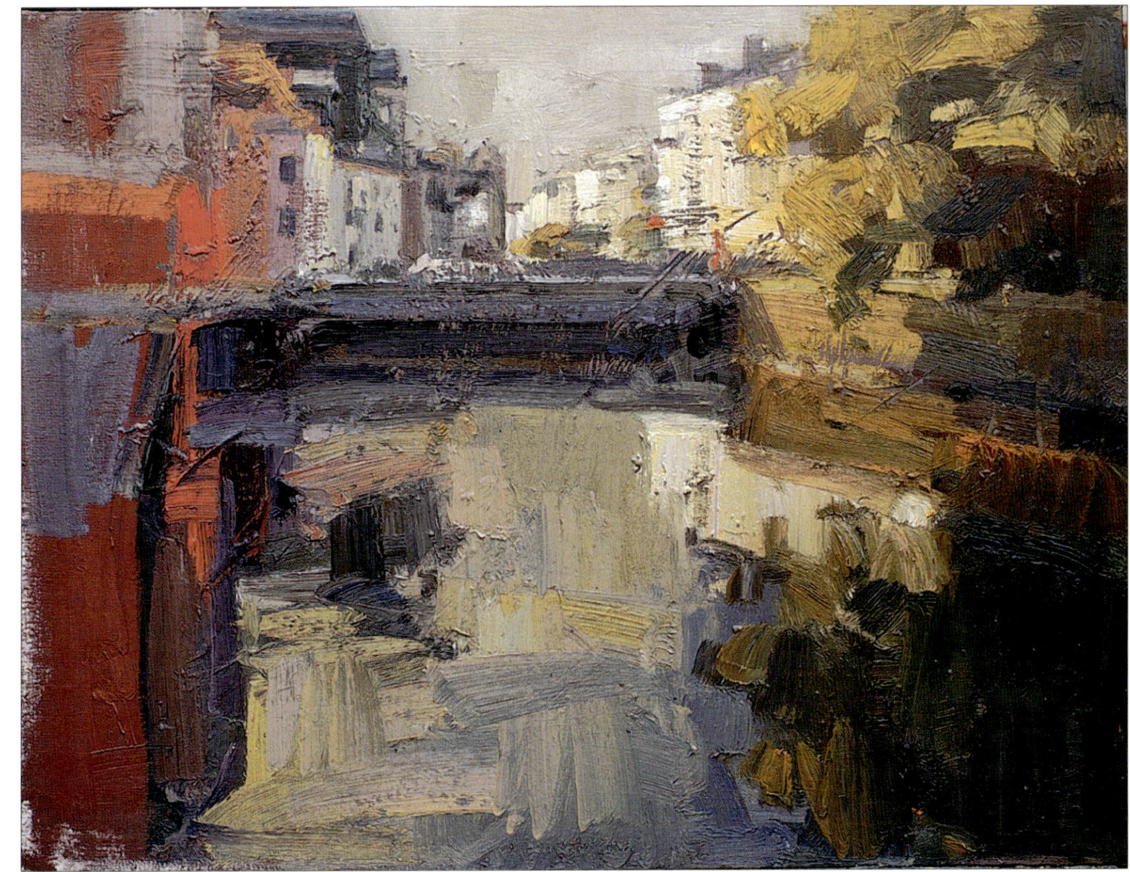

The painting appears almost complete. Note the continual work of the brush and palette knife to execute this composition; compare the current state of the picture with earlier stages; and analyze carefully the profound changes it has undergone. At this point, the work has depth and atmosphere.

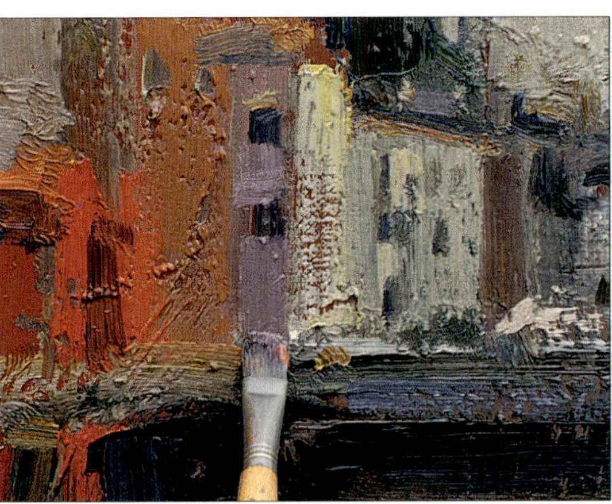

Notice in this photograph how the artist automatically transfers color from the building to the water.

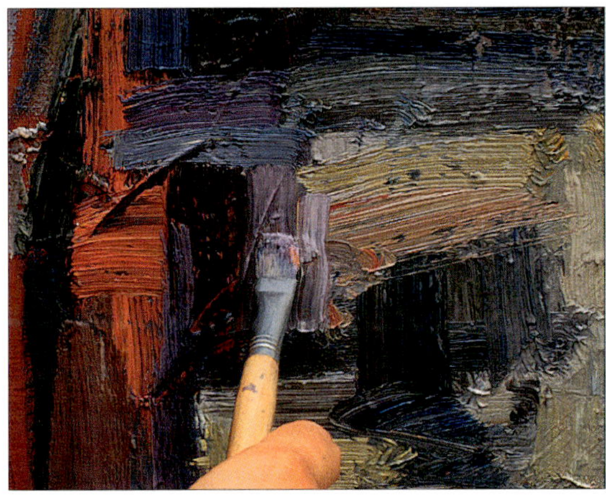

A final detail is applied directly over several underlying layers.

8. Finishing the painting

We turn our attention to the left side of the canvas, establishing the forms of the buildings without going into too much detail. Using the same method, we transfer the colors of the houses to the surface of the water but without emphasizing any particular detail. It all comes down to achieving a color parallel between the lower half of the reflections and the houses. We restrict the color harmony to the warm range.

With the small palette knife, we build the house on the left. The walls of its ground-floor shop are red.

As you can see, the last touches involve painting rather undefined, almost abstract masses.

Our brushstrokes continue to be wide and flat. Their sole purpose is to bring out the horizontal feel of the work.

Finally, we paint several windows on the previously painted background, with one or two irregular strokes.

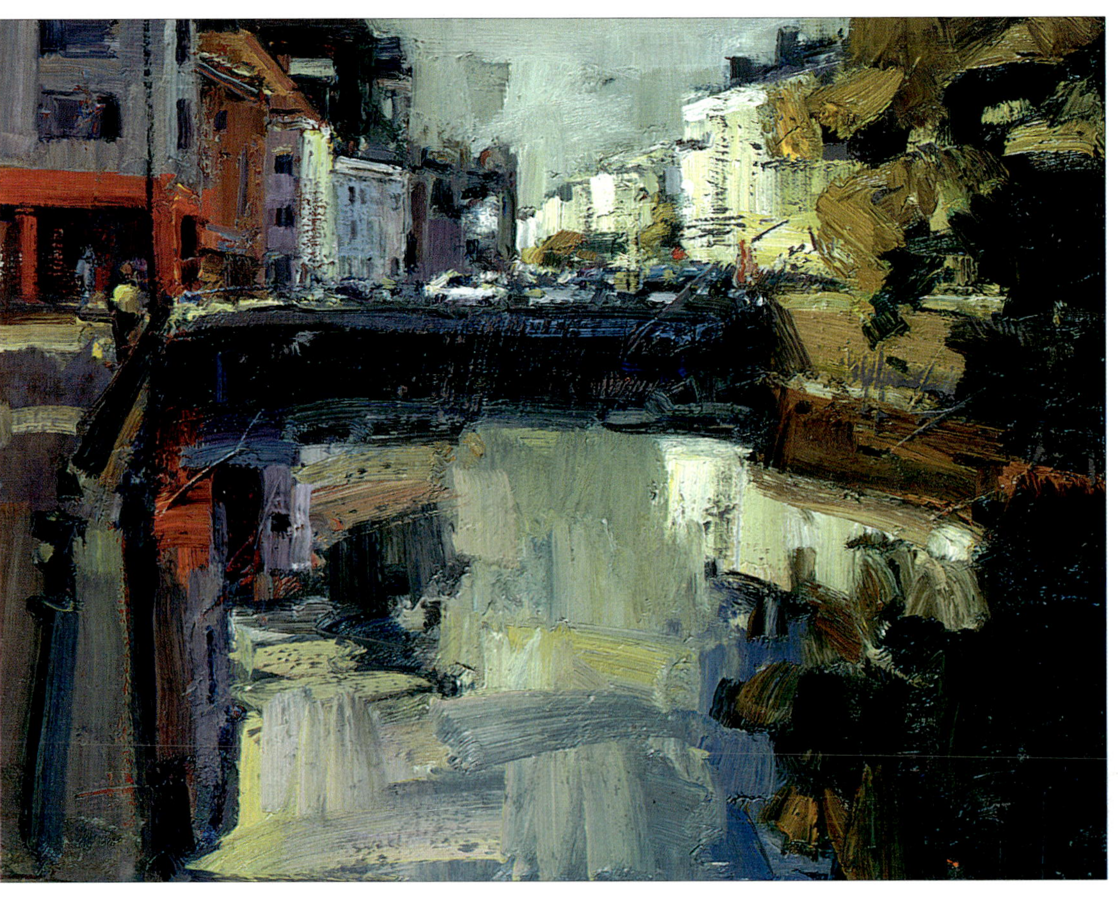

This is what the painting looks like once our laborious procedure has been brought to an end. See how light, contrast, and color have been handled. Check how colors blend and alter in the water. You can also appreciate the texture of color masses, a characteristic feature of matter painting.

Lesser-known techniques

Long before oil made its first appearance around the year 1410 in Bruges, in the hands of van Eyck, who discovered a method for allowing oil colors to dry easily, there were few painting media to choose from. Although widespread in their day, the pictorial techniques of tempera and fresco are largely forgotten today. Both methods were employed by Cimabue and Giotto to execute their works. Largely due to this fact, both are generally considered the founders of modern painting. Until Giotto painted the first realistic picture, painting lacked anything akin to naturalism. Giotto not only achieved this in his work but also made use of elements that are still relevant today, such as the expressiveness of the subject's face and body. His work bridges the gap between medieval art, in which he himself was completely immersed, and the future world of the Renaissance.

The media we will discuss in this chapter were extremely popular in their day. Today they have been relegated to art history texts, but this does not mean that they do not deserve an in-depth examination. Creativity knows no boundaries and it is important to know the origins of current materials and media. Of course, tempera paint and gouache are rather limited when compared with the chromatic qualities and plastic possibilities of today's media, but comparisons are beside the point. As you will shortly find out, it is possible to create modern paintings using these time-honored media; it is up to us to overcome any limitations. We must be prepared to forego the comfort of prefabricated and packaged paints and challenge the passing of time in order to discover the pleasure of painting with techniques used by masters such as Leonardo and Michelangelo. We will discuss fresco painting, if briefly, not only to complete our overview of all pictorial mediums, but to remind ourselves that it was the technique used to create magnificent scenes that have survived for centuries, works of art that can still be admired in convents, churches, and great cathedrals.

Giotto, Saint Steven, *Horne Museum, Florence. A fine example of a painting executed in tempera. Notice the artist's pure, faultless technique. The tonal variation is truly admirable.*

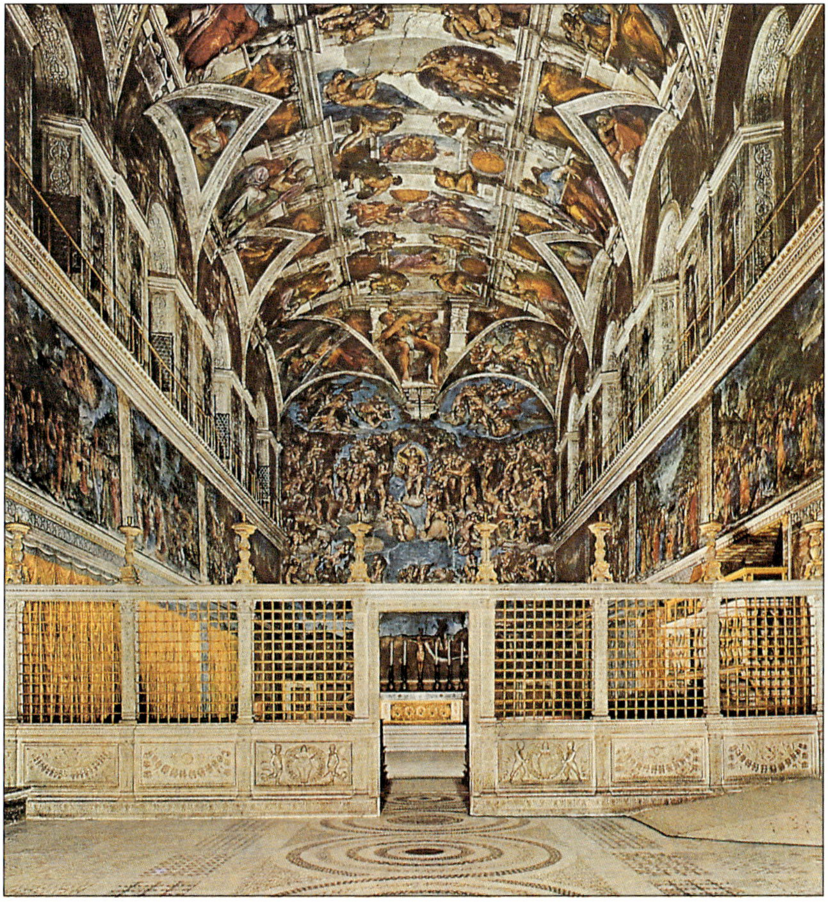

Michelangelo, one of the most universal painters in art history, used fresco in the most sublime form. One need only look at his most important work, The Sistine Chapel.

A still life in tempera paint with egg yolk

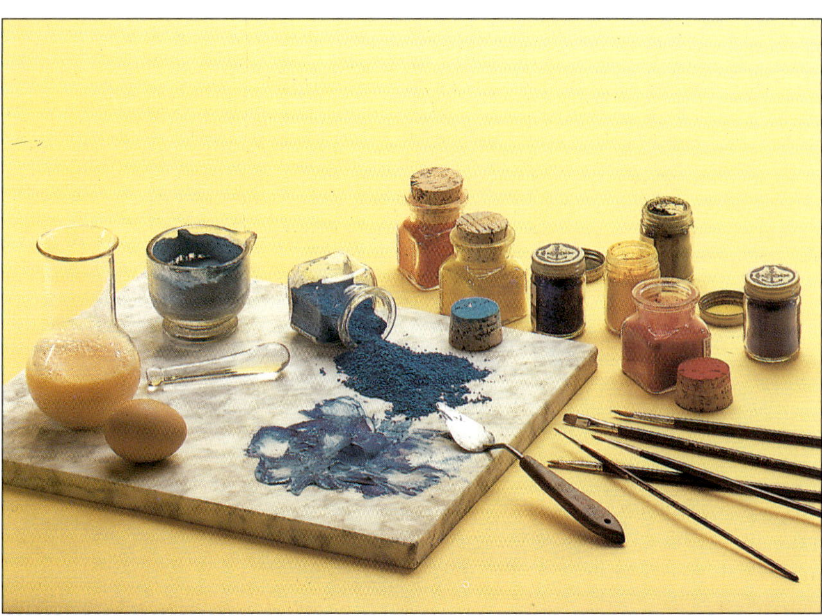

Although these are the basic materials for making tempera paint with rabbitskin glue, we are going to add some varnish to it.

1. Introduction

According to the *Dictionary of Art and Artists*, by Peter and Linda Murray, tempera is *"the pictorial medium that uses a binder to distemper the pigment color in order to paint with it."* Egg yolk was the most common binder in tempera until the end of the fifteenth century. We are going to paint in tempera with egg yolk, just as the anonymous artists of the Middle Ages did. We will paint our picture on a piece of plywood board, primed with Spanish white and rabbitskin glue, applied in various superimposed layers that are then sanded down to obtain a smooth finish.

2. Preparing the material

First let's make a list of the materials we are going to use: a piece of plywood board, rabbitskin glue, Spanish white, and fine-grain sandpaper.

To make the egg tempera we will need several additional items. Usually it would be enough to mix the pigment in water and then dip the brush in the egg yolk; however, we are going to attempt something slightly more sophisticated: egg yolk, varnish, pigments, and water.

The plywood board should be about 3/8 of an inch (1 cm) thick so that it does not warp when it becomes damp. First, sand the board down. Then, begin to prepare the rabbitskin glue. Take about a glassful of rabbitskin glue and leave it to soak in water for about eight hours. When the glue comes into contact with the water it will expand and become a dense, lumpy mass. The result obtained is placed in a container with three parts of water for each part of glue, which will be heated in a double-boiler until it is completely runny. Allow it to cool and then add enough Spanish white so that the glue turns white without becoming too dense. Now we can apply the glue to the board using a soft, wide brush. The first layers are applied with vertical strokes. Once they have dried, the glue is applied with horizontal strokes. It is important to apply several layers in order to be sure that the wood's veins and pores are completely filled in. Softly sand down the final layer, using circular movements.

3. Preparing the tempera

As we mentioned earlier, before oil paints were first used in the fifteenth century, the traditional technique of tempera paint required the artist to dip a brush in egg yolk before applying the paste (the pigment mixed with water). We are going to use a slightly different method, mixing the egg, varnish, and water. Once the paste has acquired a homogenous consistency, we add the pigment, thus obtaining a concentrated mass. We will do this for each of the colors we are going to use, keeping each one in a separate container.

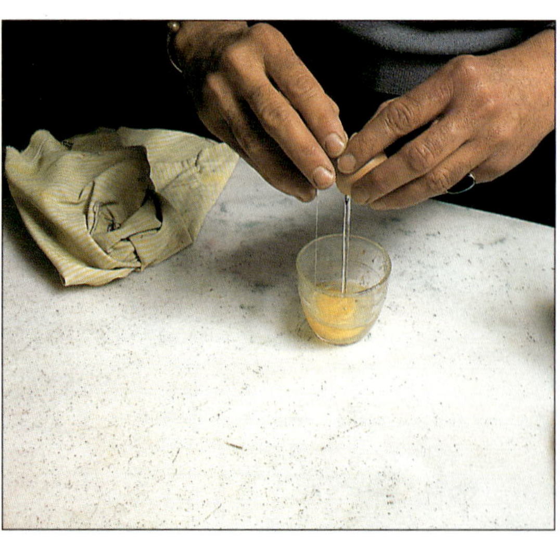

We place the egg in a glass and beat it well.

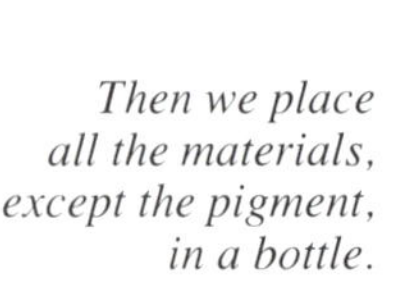

Then we place all the materials, except the pigment, in a bottle.

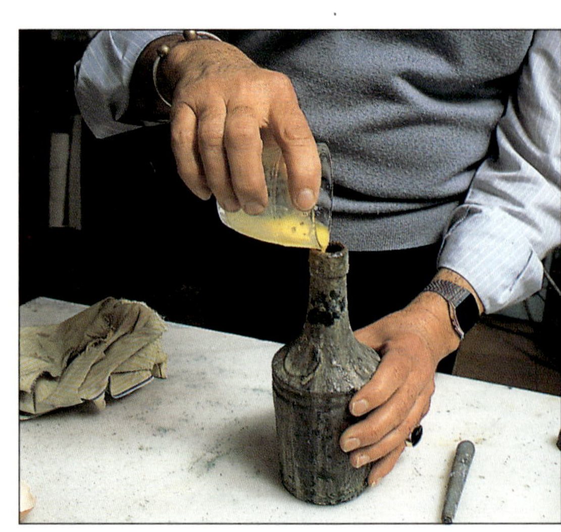

We place the egg yolk in a glass and thoroughly beat it with a brush. Once it is ready, we pour it into a bottle that we have prepared for this purpose. We add a similar amount of water and, last of all, varnish. Then we shake the bottle as if we were making a cocktail. The result is the medium, which we carefully pour over a small amount of pigment. We mix the two together using a palette knife. It is important to be sure that this is done properly and that no lumps of pigment are left.

In this chapter we are going to show you how to paint with two types of tempera paints. The first, tempera with egg yolk, is believed to be the oldest painting medium. Egg tempera allows greater transparency and produces a particularly fresh result in which the underlying layers can be seen through the uppermost ones. The second type of tempera paint we will work with is also known as gouache. It is prepared with gum and produces a far more opaque result.

4. Drawing on paper

We are going to draw a theme from our imagination. Imagining something is both an intellectual representation of reality and an abstraction of one's memories. Representation using one's imagination is, on occasion, a healthy escape that allows us to unleash our deepest feelings. We are merely resorting to the mechanism that children follow in their own drawings: all we want is to communicate an abstract image we have in our heads. During the time when tempera paint was in use, the artists, simple folk for the most part, did not concern themselves with realistic matters. They had other aims, such as communicating with the imagination, making the spectator see a different but parallel world to our own in which all manner of beings existed. To understand this, one need only look at the Gothic miniatures or any of the Romanic paintings that adorn monasteries.

So, we will use our imagination to paint a fictitious still life, a nonexistent reality. We begin by blocking up the larger masses with concise lines. It is essential to make sure that the construction of the drawing is correct, since we will apply the paint directly on top. We block up the forms and volumes, following the design we have in our head. We could have improvised, but it is better not to do so here because we are learning new techniques. We first draw several simple circles for the flowers using a lightly sharpened pencil. Then we draw the vase in which the flowers stand, the empty one next to it, and a series of circles to represent the apples. Once the general drawing is finished, we shade those areas that are in shadow. Now it is time to transfer it onto the piece of wood we prepared earlier. To do this we take a sheet of wrapping paper and cover the side that will be placed over the wood with blue pigment. Then the paper on which the preliminary drawing was made is placed over the wrapping paper. Finally, by going over the main lines of our drawing, we can transfer it to the wooden board via the pigment.

Now that we have obtained a perfect outline of the drawing on the board, using the same ultramarine blue pigment, only this time diluted in water, we again go over the drawing on the board.

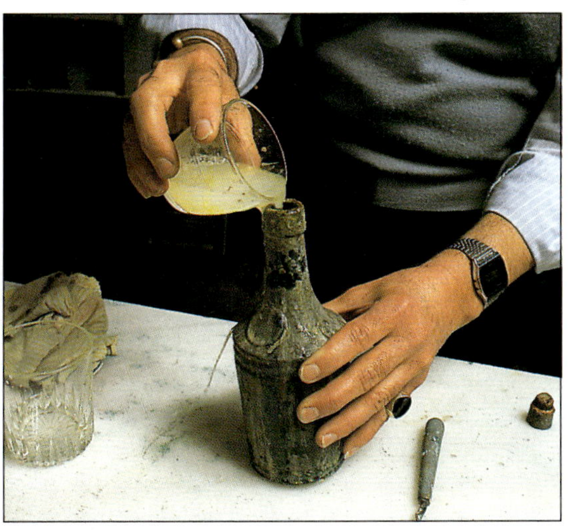

The varnish is included as an additive element to the traditional egg tempera.

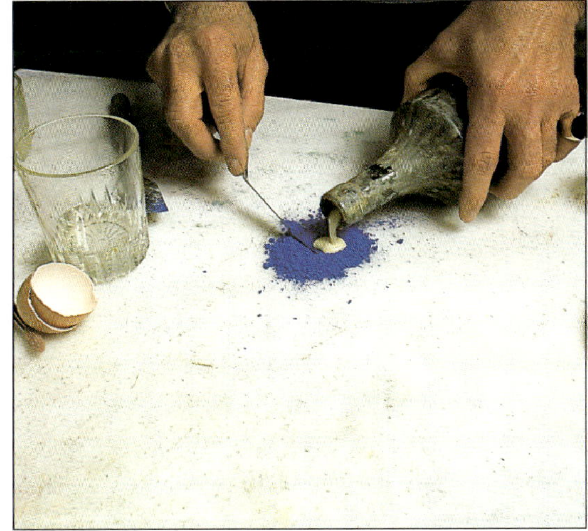

The paint must be prepared little by little in order to obtain a homogenous mass.

A still life in tempera paint with egg yolk

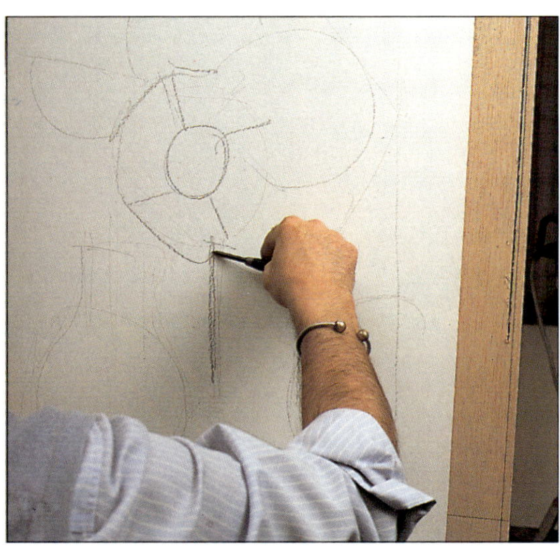

We draw the first circles, which will represent the flowers. It is important to be sure that the lines are clear, without going into any details.

This drawing will play a fundamental role in the development of the painting. Bear in mind that this is the framework of the painting; therefore it must be clear and concise.

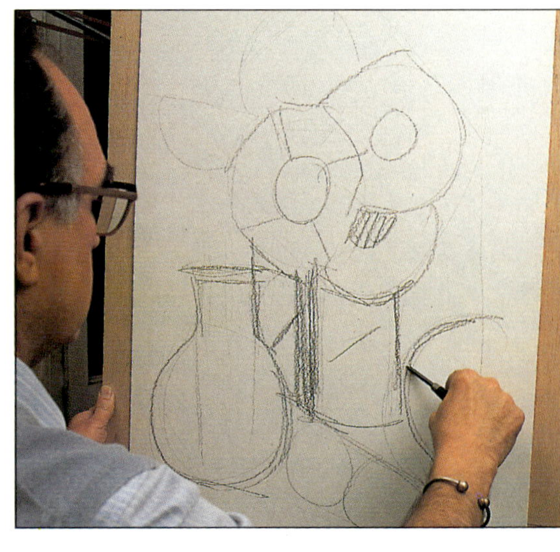

Still working with the same blue, we begin to indicate some masses and one or two shadows. We will start on the background and leave the main elements of the painting for last. Despite the fact that tempera is a quick-drying medium, we work slowly and deliberately.

5. The colors

Given the transparency of this medium, it is best to use a palette that allows the color to be seen clearly. The palette can be made of marble, glass, or transparent plastic. For this painting, we are going to use ultramarine blue, violet, vermillion, sienna, lemon yellow, cadmium yellow, white, emerald green, turquoise blue, and ocher.

We take a little water with the palette knife and lightly dampen the colors, since they dry remarkably fast. We prepare several pieces of sponge and a small washbasin filled with water, as well as a jar containing brushes.

6. Drawing in blue and painting the background

Having built up the forms with blue, we now begin to paint the board with other colors, absorbing any surplus color with a piece of sponge. We will make constant use of the sponge throughout our work, since tempera colors have a tendency to quickly saturate the surfaces on which they're applied. First we tackle the blue and lilac areas on either side of the flower vase.

Now we add shadows to certain parts of the painting. You may add both highlights and shadows as your personal style dictates, since this is not meant to represent reality.

Having saturated the wrapping paper with the blue pigment, we place the paper on the board previously prepared for transferring the drawing.

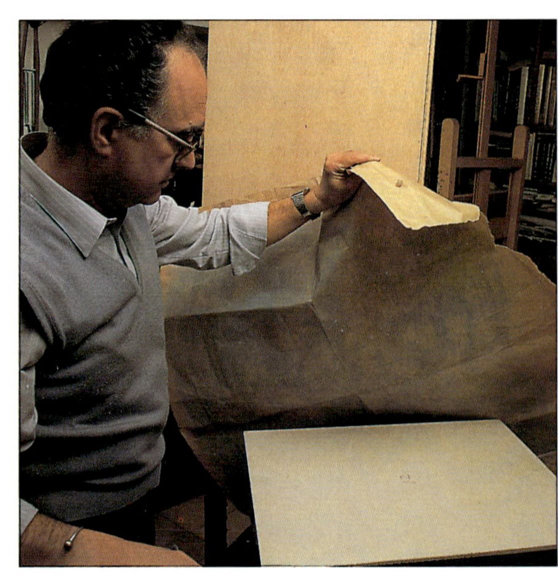

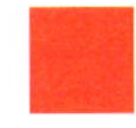

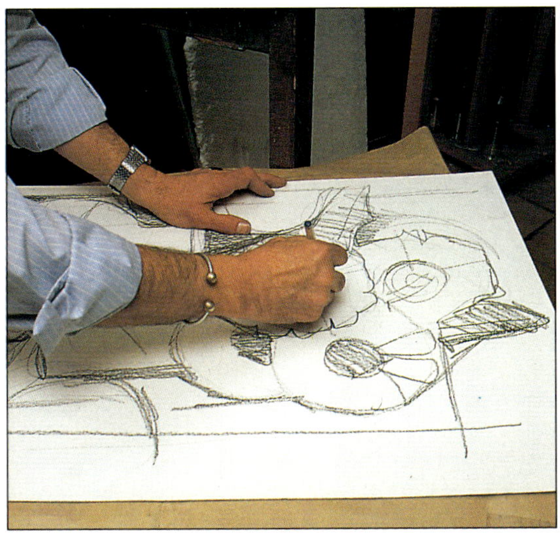

We meticulously go over the lines of the original model in order to transfer them onto the board. It is essential to be sure that the paper is not moved during this procedure.

Once we have finished tracing the drawing, we go over the lines transferred to the board using blue pigment mixed with water.

Notice the faded blue strip on the right side of the picture. We have done this by pressing down the sponge over this area. We now paint the areas surrounding the sunflowers, first with orangish ocher on the left, then with a yellowish ocher on the top part. In this painting, we begin work on the background, leaving the objects in the foreground white.

We start painting the sunflowers yellow. The general color range of the painting has been established, now that we have set the tones for the largest areas. This way, we avoid the risks inherent in painting the main elements of the still life before the background. Since a color is lighter or darker according to the color that surrounds it, if we paint an isolated object on a white surface, the color of the object may have to be altered once the background has been painted.

We are painting a picture that lacks shadow and relief. These questions will be dealt with as our painting develops. For now, we have only insinuated the color of the cylindrical vase; there is still no color for the element situated in the foreground, on the left side of the painting.

Now we are going to paint the background with oil paint brushes, leaving the most important spaces for last.

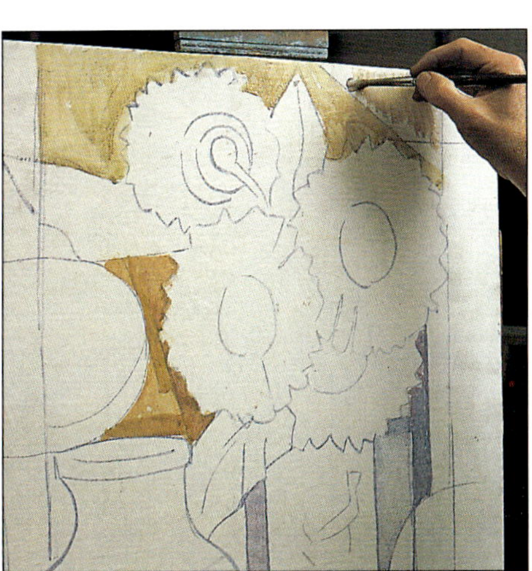

The sponge is essential for absorbing the saturated colors and for dampening the large spaces.

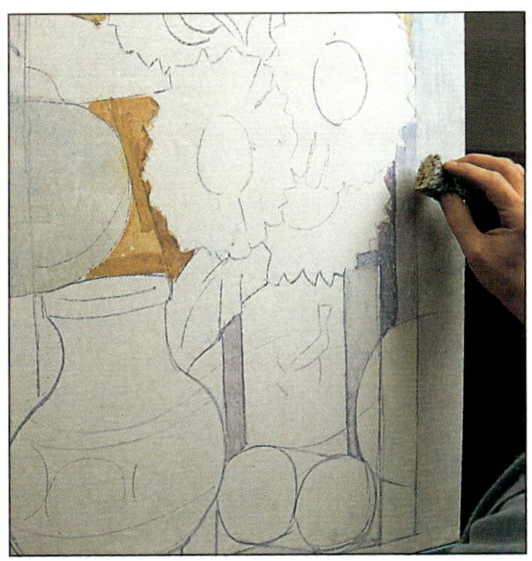

We start painting the sunflowers without relief or contrast.

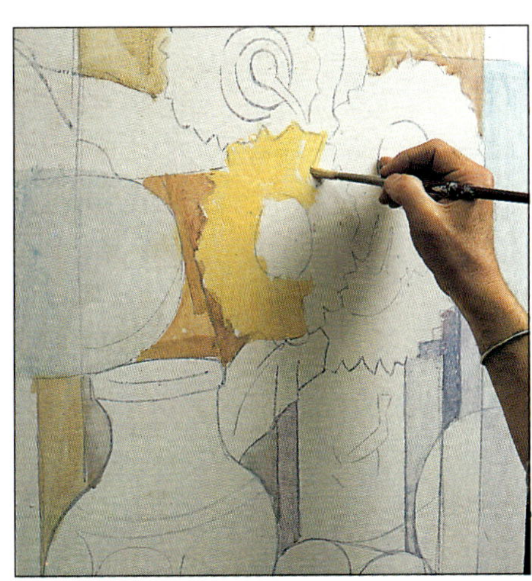

A still life in tempera paint with egg yolk

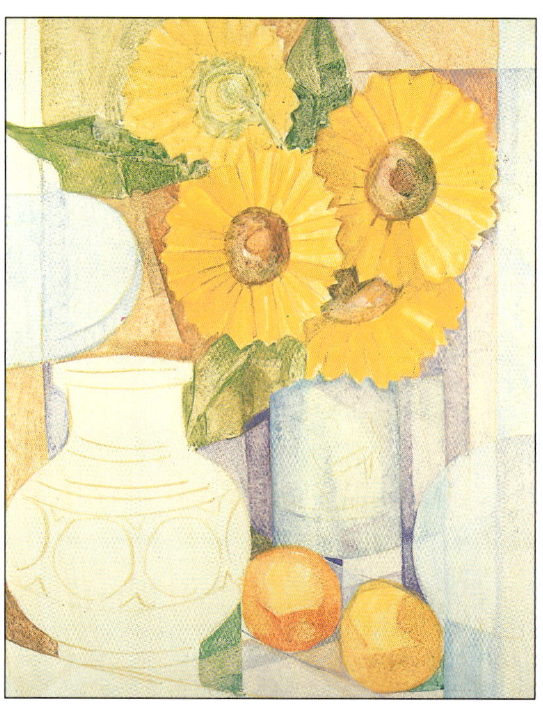

The background is ready. If we had started out by painting the main motifs first, we would have faced many more problems in bringing the painting to a successful conclusion. The green leaves and lighter hues in the yellow sunflowers have been executed, and some volume has been lent to the fruit in the foreground.

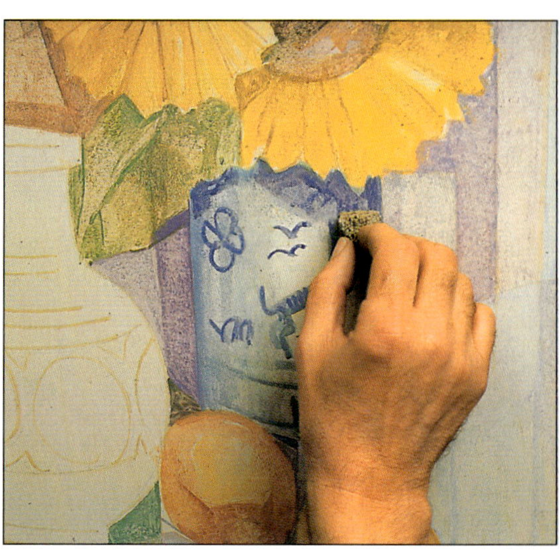

Using a fine brush we decorate the ceramic vases. The excess color is removed with a sponge.

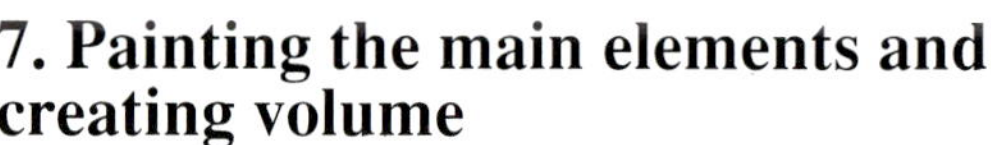

7. Painting the main elements and creating volume

We paint the vase with two different brown colors. Not only are they tonally different, but we have added ocher to one and a touch of carmine to the other. From the combination of these two values we obtain a balance in the foreground. Our work consists of alternating the brush with the sponge, on the one hand, adding color, and on the other, removing it until the entire painting acquires the same tonal level. In this type of work the sponge is used as simply another pictorial tool. Since we are not interested in creating very evident brushwork, the sponge helps us to create a homogenous surface. We create the volume of the vase with both the curvature of the drawing and the color that indicates the darker zones, since they help us to understand the volume of the object. Note, in addition, how we have obtained the color harmony, using two types of watered-down brown in order to bring out the volume of the inside of the vase's neck.

We are painting on an upright size 12 support. The format of the canvas always conditions the theme's composition, so it must be suitable. Format should serve composition.

We work as ceramists now, decorating our ware with a very fine brush; however, we still have to resolve the cylindrical volume of the vase in the center.

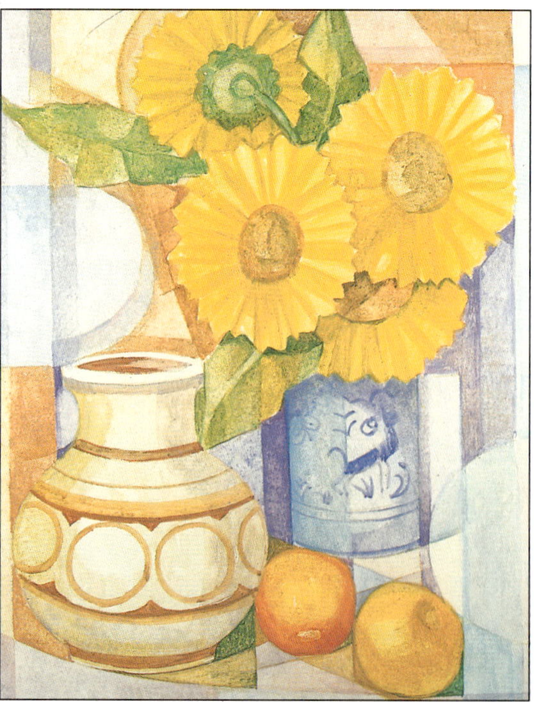

The foreground is finished. The ceramic vase on the left has been painted with two different tones of brown.

Now we paint the decoration on the vase on the left, exploiting its spherical perspective. We also incorporate shadows and light, concentrating on the aesthetics rather than attempting to imitate reality.

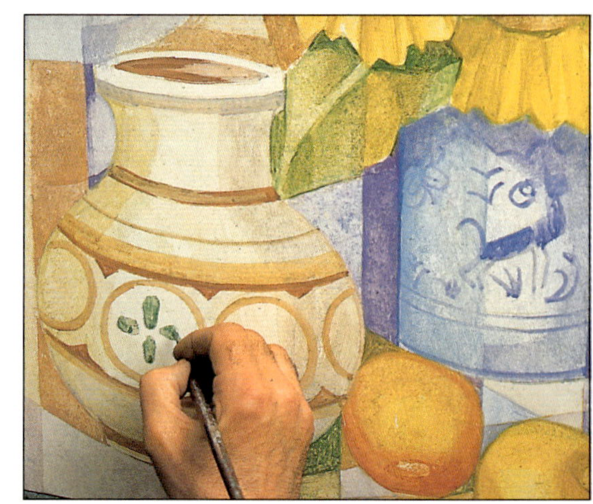

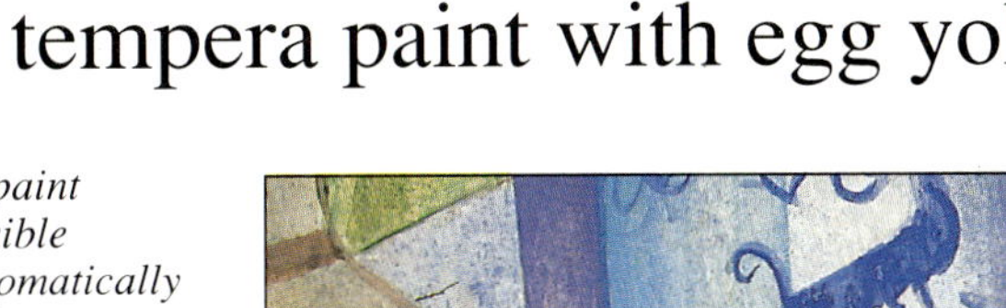

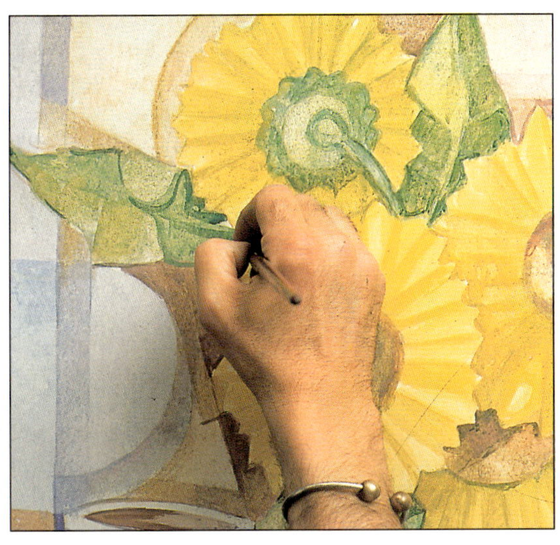

Gradually, we paint some barely visible details that chromatically enrich the work as a whole. A good example of this is the way highlighted green tones produce a slight effect of depth in the other planes.

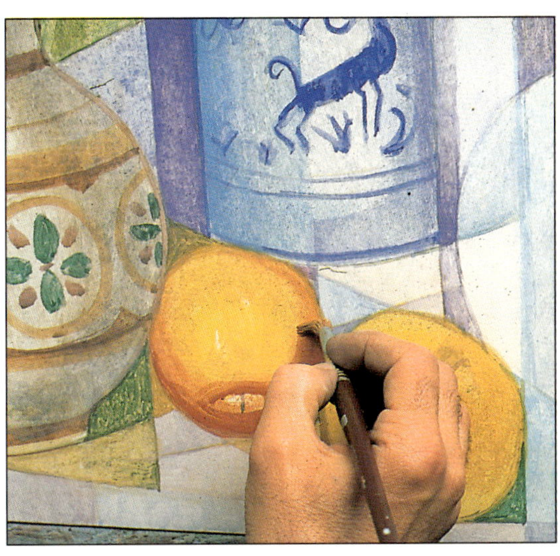

We increase the range of colors, searching out relief through the superimposition of planes.

8. Working on the details

With a fine brush and a sponge, we begin adding details all over the surface of the painting. We should not hurry during this phase, because, although it is true that tempera dries fast, if we attempt to paint over the surface of a still-wet layer, we will remove the underlying layer, damaging the painting beyond repair. Time is an important consideration in artistic creation. Our sense of time must fit the type of work we are doing. It would be absurd to try to create a Gothic-style painting, with the haste of late twentieth-century culture. The antidote of rashness is meticulousness.

In addition to painting the elements of the foreground carefully, we constantly revise the whole, slightly altering warm tones, bringing out the volume in the spherical forms, adding tiny brushstrokes that help to increase the volume in a painting that until now lacked all relief, and refining hues in areas that are perhaps only visible to our eyes.

We bring this meticulous work to a conclusion. As you have seen, this medium has allowed us to develop pictorial ideas that go far beyond mere realism. Now you can find new themes to paint using the techniques described here. Our aim is to provide you with the practical knowledge to be able to do this.

With patience, we have concluded this painting, which has a slight cubist air about it. We hope this will motivate you to paint your own themes in tempera paint with egg.

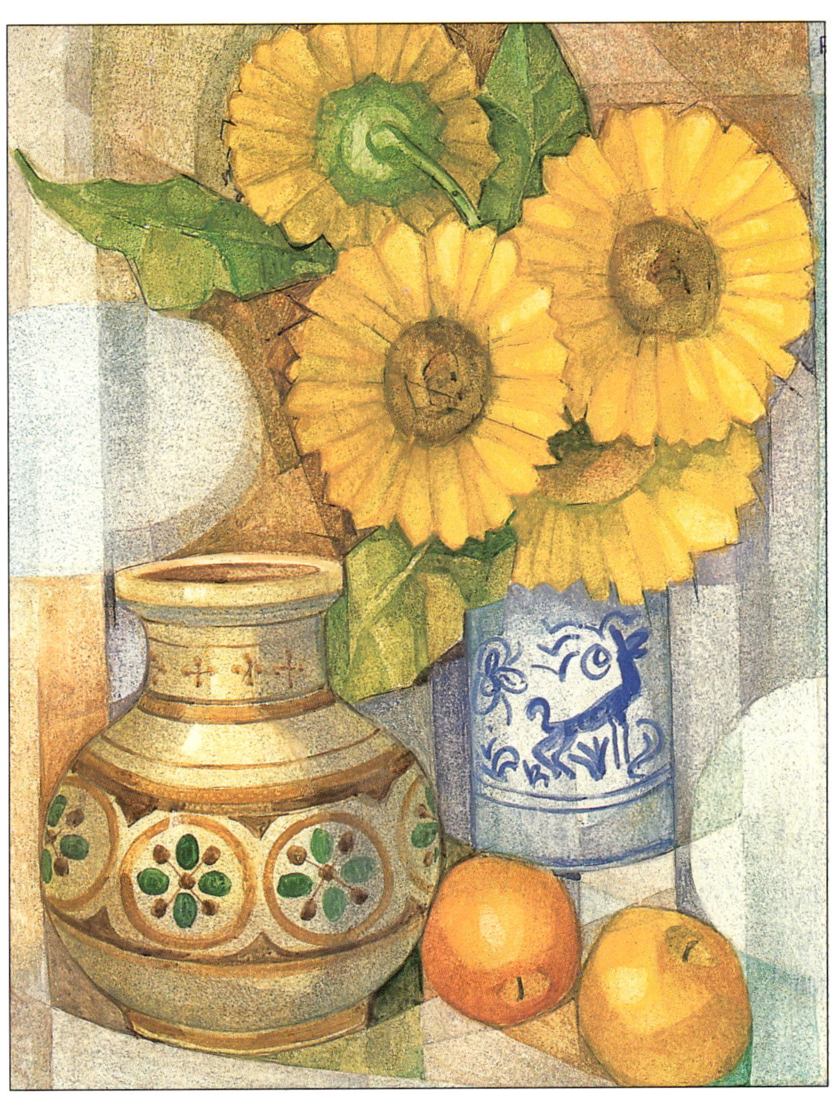

A still life in gouache

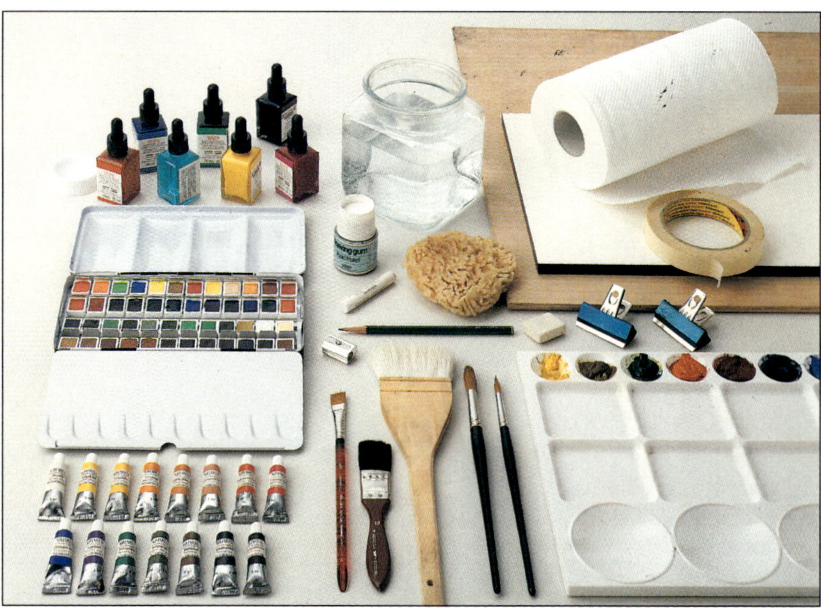

Gouache paints are packaged and sold in a variety of jars and containers. Like watercolors, gouache is made with gum. It can be bought in liquid form, or in hard or soft pans. In addition, there are various accessories available to make goache easier to use, including special boxes and water containers.

1. The material

Today, tempera with gum is commercially manufactured and sold in art stores as gouache. Of course, gouache is tempera with gum, as opposed to tempera with egg yolk.

Even though this type of paint is manufactured and packaged by all the major paint companies, we believe it is interesting and useful to know how to make it yourself. It is easy to make and does not involve getting dirty. You will need the following items to make gouache: color pigments (mineral, organic, or synthetic), distilled water, gum arabic (also known as senegal), a little glycerine, a touch of ox gall, phenol, and some sealable containers.

First we leave the pigment to soak overnight in distilled water. The amount of pigment should be greater than the quantity of water in order to obtain a viscous paste. There is no need to make a large quantity: three or four spoonfuls of dampened pigment will shrink considerably when dampened.

The dampened pigment is placed in containers that can be sealed with a lid to prevent it from drying. We now place a generous quantity of gum arabic in a jam jar and add a part of distilled water. We place this jar in a double-boiler and stir it with a stick or a brush handle until the ingredients are thoroughly mixed. As soon as the solution has cooled, add a teaspoonful of glycerine, together with a few drops of phenol and half a drop of ox gall. Stir the mix until it acquires a homogenous consistency.

Each one of the components we have used has a specific purpose. Gum arabic is used as a binder, making the pigment adhere to paper. Glycerine extends the drying time; thus, whenever you are working with a water-based medium, a few drops of this substance may come in handy for this purpose. The ox gall helps the color to spread evenly, without running. Finally, phenol conserves the medium when it has dried.

Once we have the two preparations ready, we can use them in two different ways: either by dipping the brush in the gum arabic solution and then loading a little damp pigment, or by pouring some solution into each of the jars filled with damp pigment and mixing pigment and solution well until they acquire the desired consistency.

2. Preparing the paper

Once the paints have been made, we begin to prepare the paper we are going to paint on.

You will need the following materials: a sheet of 18 × 24 inch (46 × 62 cm) Fabriano paper, a work space where you can wet the paper, and special tape that sticks to wet surfaces and wood.

When we paint with aqueous mediums, their dampness tends to make the paper crease, which renders it almost useless. So it is necessary to stretch the paper before painting on it.

Take a sheet of paper and immerse it in water for two or three minutes until it is completely soaked. Remove it from the water and attach it immediately to the surface of the wood with a strip of gummed paper. The paper will remain completely flat on the surface. Then fasten down the opposite side with another strip of gummed paper, and finally, the two remaining sides. Once the paper has dried, after a few hours, it will try to revert to its original position, but since it is fastened down on the four corners, it will acquire a degree of tension that will not alter when we wet the paper again, this time with paint.

We will paint with ordinary watercolor brushes. The best and most common types are those made of sable hair and ox hair. See the selection of basic materials on the opposite page: numbers 8, 12 and 14 sable hair brushes and a number 24 ox hair brush.

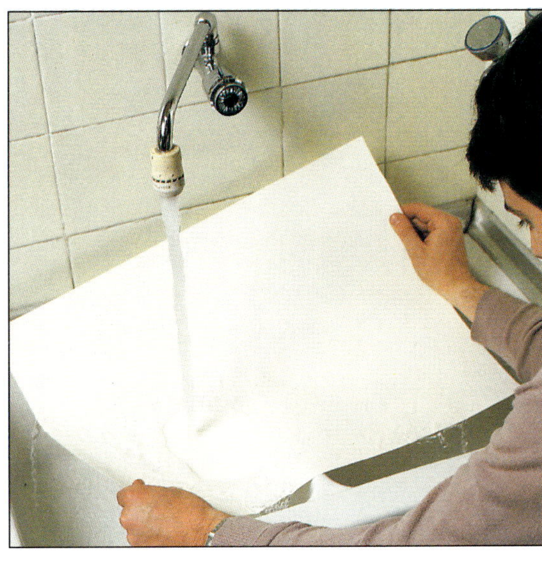

To prevent the paper from warping when damp, we have attached it firmly to a support. First we immerse the paper in water to help it dilate.

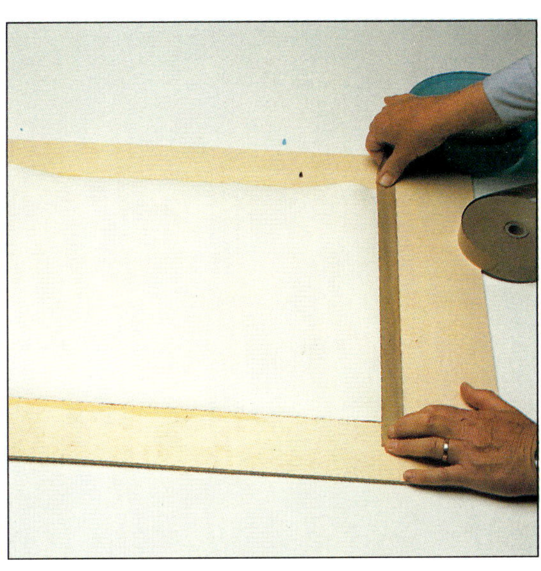

We place the paper flat on a board. With special adhesive tape, we attach each corner to the board. When the paper has dried, it will be taut and smooth.

In addition to the items shown here, other highly useful complementary items are a flat Japanese deer hair paintbrush, a roller-shaped sponge, and a small natural sponge. These additional items come in very handy, since they can be used to work on backgrounds, carry out gradations, and absorb water. Just one observation regarding the brushes: Sable hair brushes tend to be outrageously expensive and wear away easily. Windsor & Newton manufacture a brush made from a mix of synthetic and squirrel's hair. Unlike completely synthetic hairbrushes, this brush can absorb a large quantity of water. Furthermore, this mixed hairbrush lasts longer and is much cheaper that sable hair brushes. The last items you need are a number of glass jars and containers with a maximum capacity of half a liter.

3. Drawing our model

The simple elements of our composition will allow us to experiment with forms within a given space, as well as with the most important points of light. We have decided to arrange the fruit and ceramics of our still life on a white cloth. This way, although we start with an apparently simple model, we will have a wide array of textures before our eyes.

Of course, before we begin painting, we should wait for the base color to dry thoroughly. This paint was applied using a thick, wide brush; the color blotches were painted with round brushes alternated with flat ones.

It is important to make sure that our position in front of the model does not block light or create undesired shadows. The table on which we are working is slightly below our elbows and is set at an angle so that we can see our work from a perpendicular viewpoint.

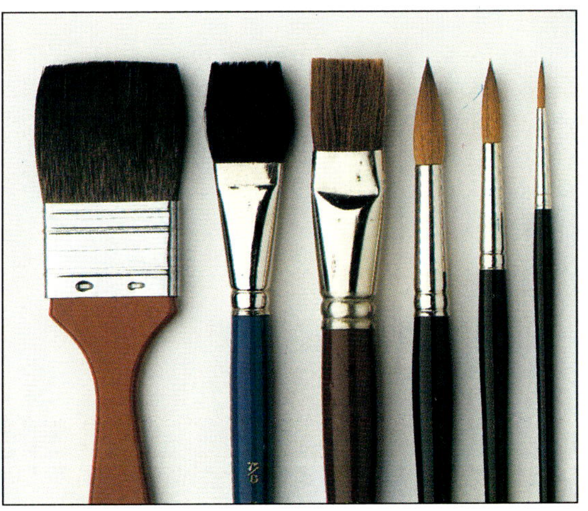

These are the most common brushes that we will use.

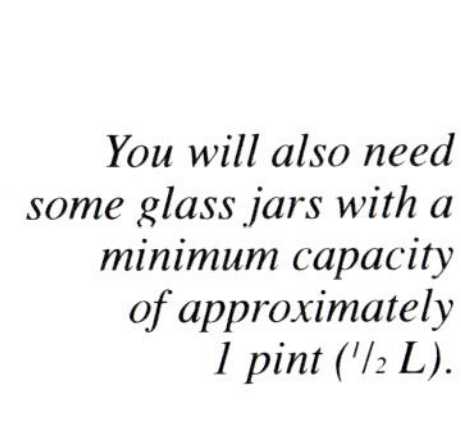

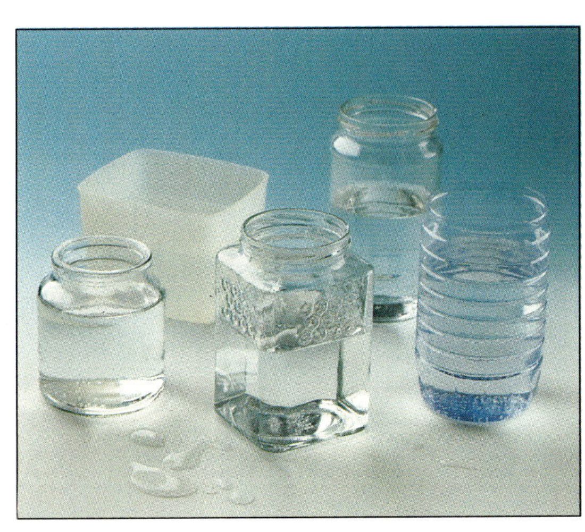

You will also need some glass jars with a minimum capacity of approximately 1 pint (1/2 L).

A still life in gouache

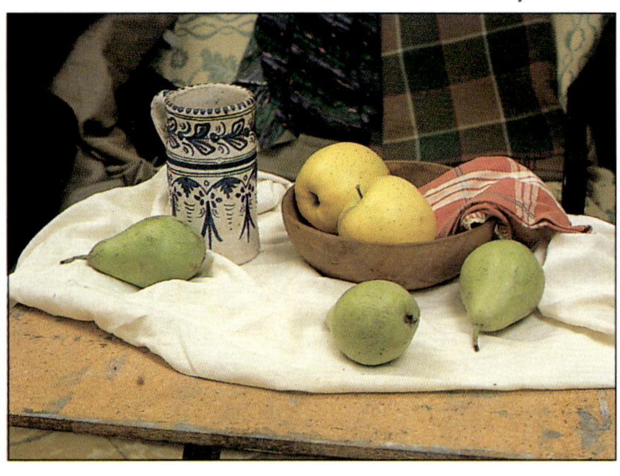

We will paint our model from nature, having made a careful study of the composition and illumination before embarking on the work.

The paper has been prepared with a base layer of paint in which gray, blue, and certain earth tones predominate. It is easy to obtain this kind of color base; we need only allow transparent layers of different colors to intermix, while making sure that the color distribution is more or less even.

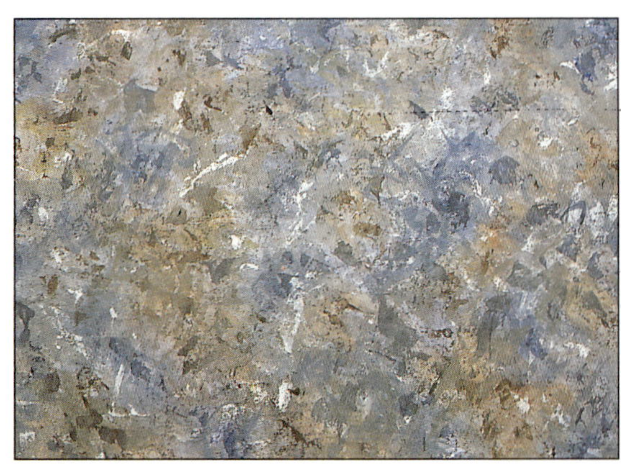

The tempera we are going to paint with has been placed in a special palette box. This, of course, is optional, since almost any nonporous surface can be used for mixing colors. We have decided not to use a simple plastic palette because the watery medium we're dealing with here could spill over the palette's edges.

The title of this section is more pertinent here than anywhere else because drawing truly is a crucial and vital part of the exercise explained here. We usually execute the preliminary drawing with an HB lead pencil, but this time we are going to be brave and take a few risks. In other words, instead of using a pencil, we are going to draw the basic outline of the theme, in a clean and concise manner, using a toothpick dipped in india ink.

We begin by directly attacking the textured spaces of the paper, aiming for a definitive drawing on the first attempt, since there is no possibility of correcting anything drawn in india ink once it has dried.

We will use our tempera with gum as if it were any other watery paint; that is, we will employ an almost identical technique as that used with commercial gouache.

4. The basic colors

Using a very transparent (watered-down) yellow gouache, we begin painting the apples with a rounded brush. When filling out the shapes, we do not necessarily have to respect the boundaries of the drawing. The transparent background will chromatically unify the whole. We are, in fact, painting and drawing at the same time, something essential in order to achieve a successful piece. Our theme should emerge as if we were developing a photograph—slowly, purposely. We should never lose sight of our theme. Drawing will be the fundamental structure of the painting, on which all end results will depend. Without it, the painting would lack a "skeleton," and would lose its internal structure.

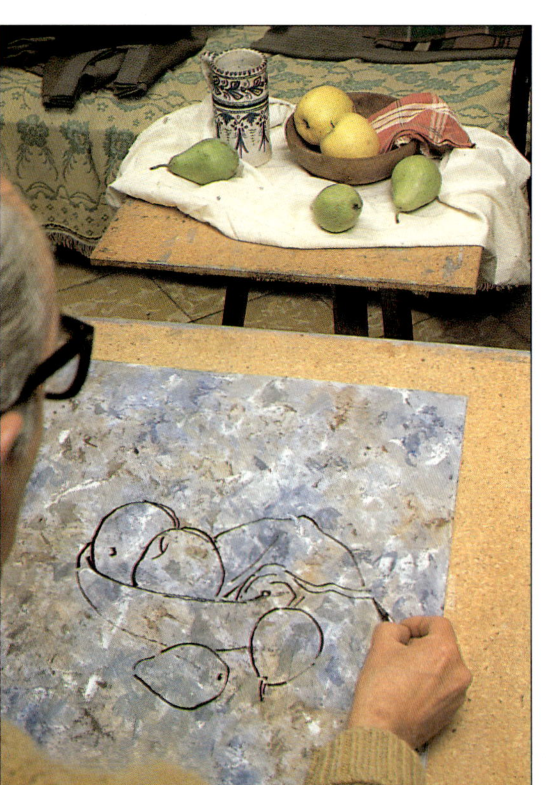

Now that it is completely dry, we can draw lines without the ink bleeding. There are two reasons for drawing in ink: Lead pencil would most likely dirty the color of the paint, and the line it produces would remain too visible through the transparent layers of paint.

This is how the piece looks once we have finished drawing the main motif. Notice how clean and sharp the lines are. This drawing is decisive for the final outcome of the picture. India ink produces an intense and permanent black line that cannot be achieved with any other water-based medium.

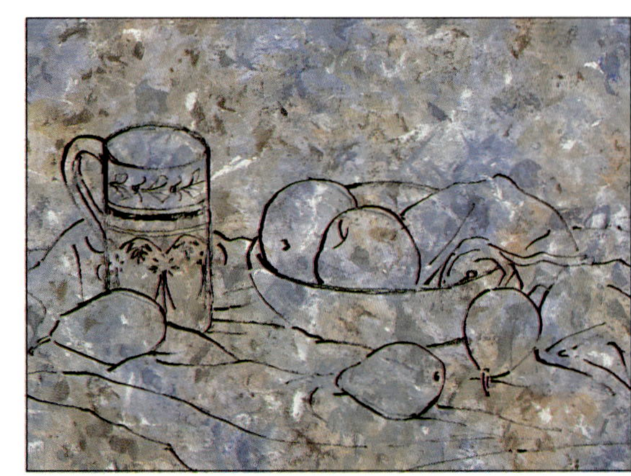

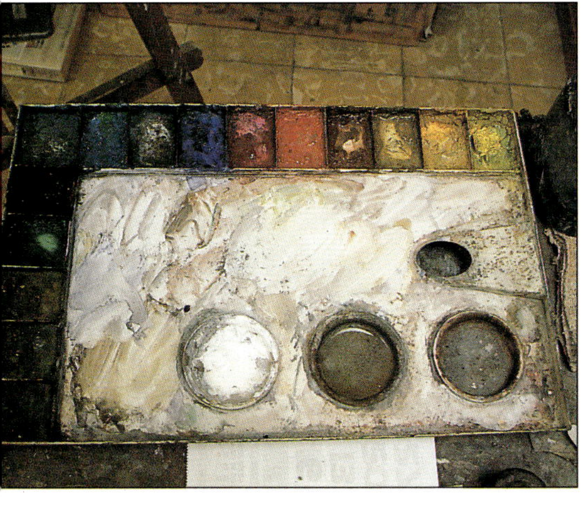

We are going to use all color ranges. We can buy a special palette box in art stores that makes it easier to work with gouache and allows us to safely mix colors in the wells of each box.

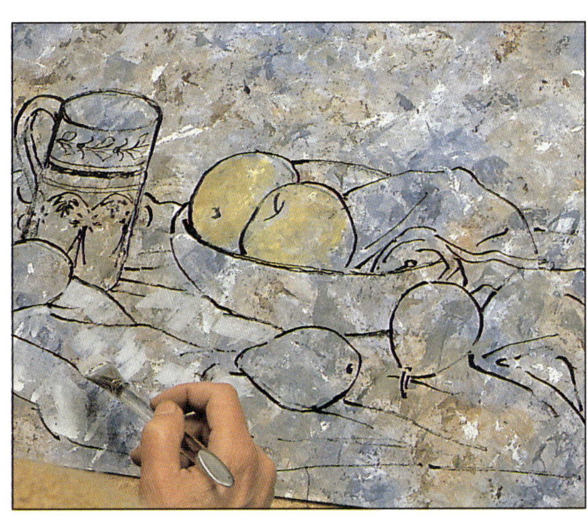

We begin by painting with watered-down gouache, creating a transparent effect and allowing some of the original color of the background to remain visible.

Now that we have finished the apples, we begin painting the white cloth supporting the still life. Although gouache is an opaque medium, it can also be used to obtain transparent effects similar to watercolor. In fact, tempera with gum and watercolors are made of the same ingredients, only in different proportions. To obtain an almost translucent effect, we have diluted some white tempera with water.

When we paint with impure colors, it is important to always carry out a few tests on a piece of paper to see what they will look like on your picture. We paint the basket with a light earth color, using a very watered-down gouache. In this first phase, color should be almost transparent. In watercolor painting, light is created through transparencies; in gouache painting, it can be obtained only through color.

It becomes increasingly evident that drawing here is the framework of painting. Taking the utmost care, we use our fingers to remove any paint that may have covered the lines of the drawing. We modify the blue background, although in no way do we attempt realism. With these alterations, we begin to unify the background and the other elements. By leaving some white specks—the original color of the paper—both in the objects and in the background, we help to suggest the texture of the background within the objects and the color of the objects in the background.

We must be careful when working around the original lines of the drawing; their purpose is to "enclose" the color. Note how the background helps unify the overall color scheme.

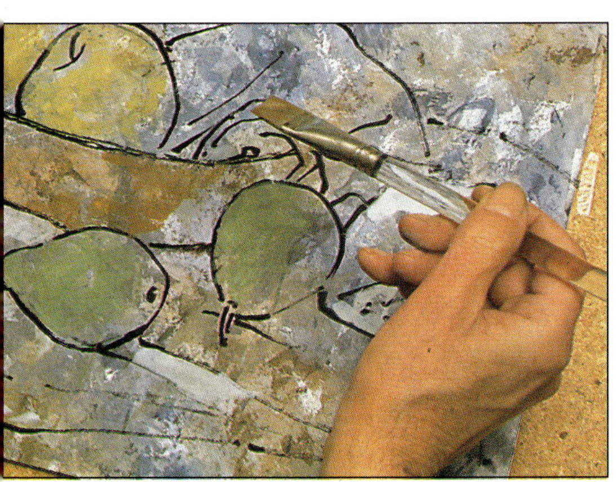

This is the current state of the painting: We have taken care of most of the problems of light within the figures by painting the lighter areas; the unpainted areas are the shadows.

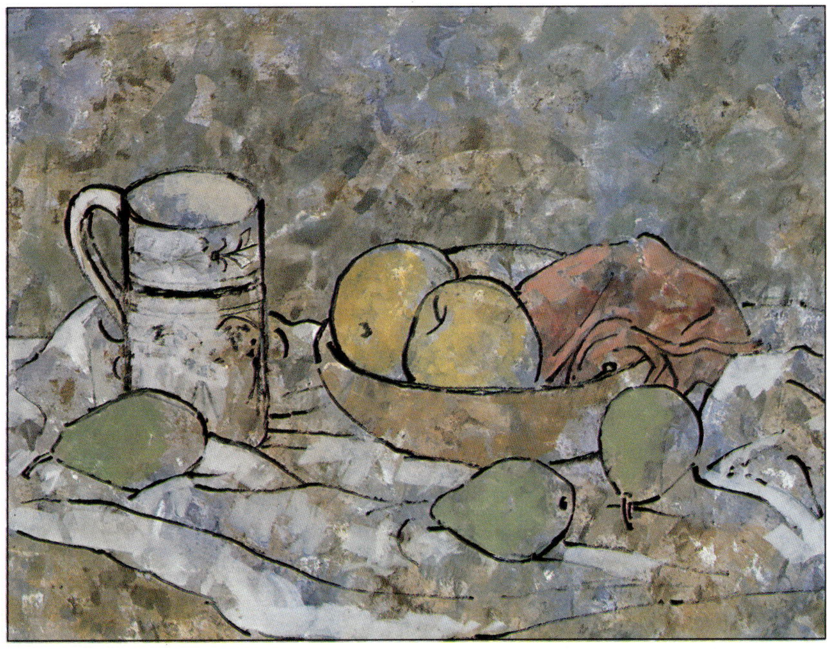

A still life in gouache

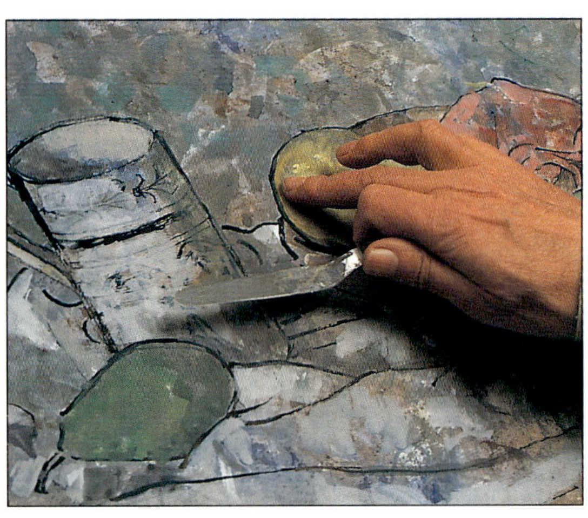

Before the paint dries, we use our fingers to blend the most recent areas with the ones previously applied.

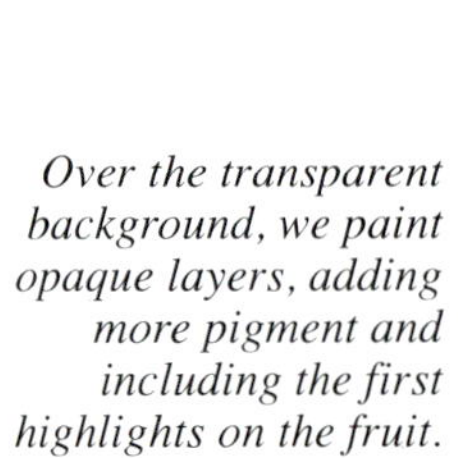

Over the transparent background, we paint opaque layers, adding more pigment and including the first highlights on the fruit.

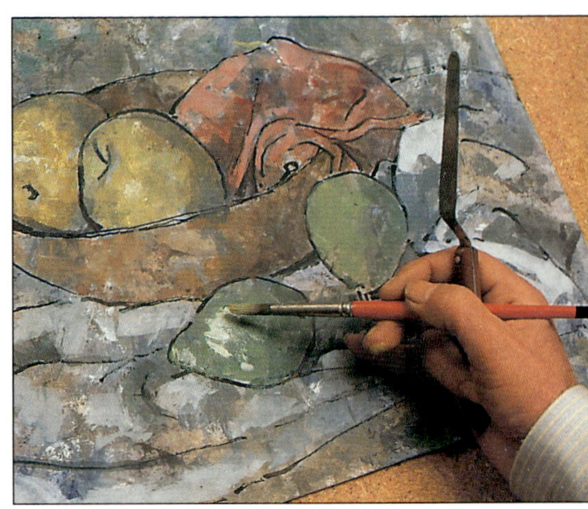

5. Defining forms

We are going to work with the palette knife on the lightest areas, smoothing down the paint we have applied with the brush. Now we apply opaque paint to cover the areas in the shadow.

Using palette knife, brush, and fingers, we begin to lend volume to the elements of the still life. It is important to remember that although tempera is a stable medium, it is soluble in water; therefore, we can alter or soften any aspect of the painting simply by dipping a clean brush in water. We continue painting with the deliberate brushwork appropriate for water-based painting media. Since we always work on a dry base layer, our painting will not bleed or mix.

The areas in the shadow also have their bright parts. We achieve this by removing paint with our fingers and adding yellow to the existing green, to obtain a notably lighter color.

In order to unify the color we are working with, we make continuous use of the palette knife to spread and blend it, making sure that the paint on the right side of the piece acquires a certain amount of texture and relief. By this stage, it is possible to see what the definitive painting will look like. The light and dark areas have been perfectly defined and the main points of light have been worked on.

The areas that until now had been left untouched are filled in by mixing paint with the base color. We are now applying the definitive colors. The overall color scheme of the painting has been established. We can add on top of it glazes and stains that will define and consolidate it. We keep certain light areas that will be later glazed over to create distant planes.

At this stage of the painting, many of the questions of color have been settled. Notice how we have dealt with highlights and the decoration on the vase.

We alternate the use of the brush, our fingers, and the palette knife, blending colors due to the fact that tempera paint can be softened with water.

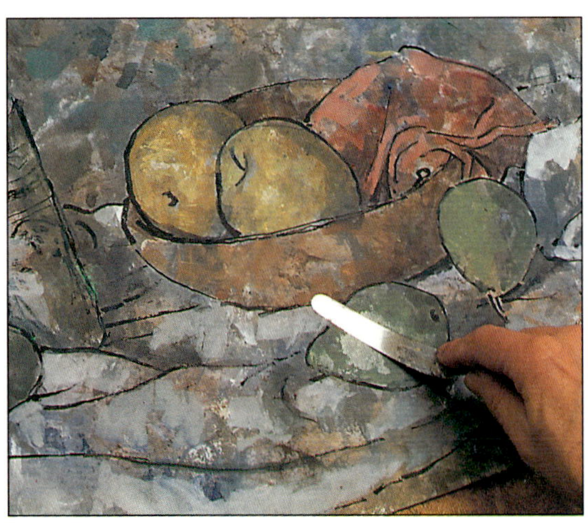

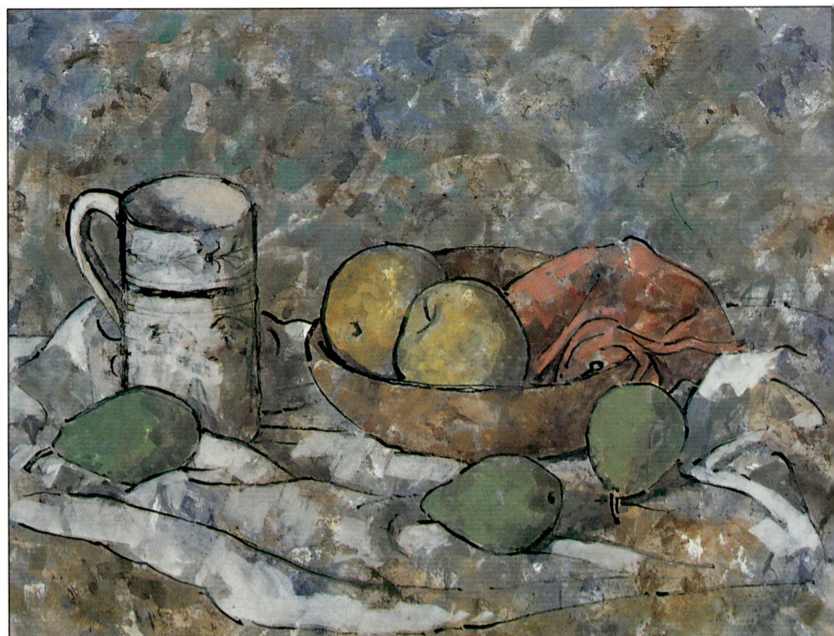

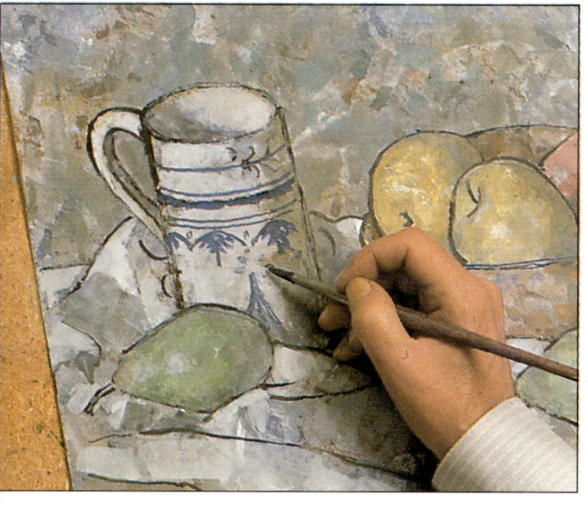

Notice how the predominant color hues are entirely dependent on the color background, providing unity to the whole. Likewise, each one of the painting's elements are chromatically heightened by the colors that surround them. We are not painting with flat colors here; volume is obtained through the creation of chiaroscuros.

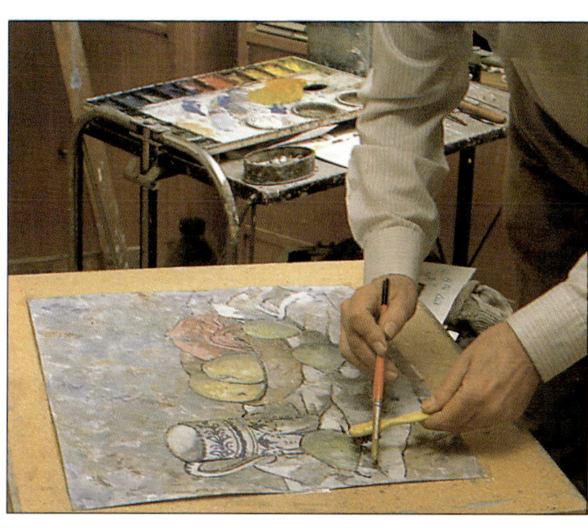

With the toothbrush, we softly flick small, uneven amounts of paint over certain areas of the painting.

6. Finishing the painting

With a wet brush we go over the arabesque decoration of the ceramic jug to emphasize its volume and make it look realistic. A loose type of brushstroke is required to execute the calligraphic lines of the pattern. It is worth noting that the more decorative aspects of your painting should not be attempted before the background color has thoroughly dried because the underlying layer will merge with the new paint and create unwanted effects. We spread small amounts of color, lightly altering the tone of the background to adapt it to the overall colors of the main motifs. Along with our fingers, the palette knife is the most useful tool for spreading or removing paint. By applying the palette knife softly, we can obtain broad opaque surfaces. If, however, we roughly scrape the surface of the paper with the edge of the palette knife, it is possible to create transparent tones.

We add some tones of pure white to the jug handle. The red cloth has been painted with carmine hues for the brightest areas, while the darker colors of the shadow areas have been deepened.

We wet our index finger and lightly dab the tip on those areas of the pear reflecting direct light. Then we add a touch of yellow to bring out the shine (when we mix yellow with green we create a paler tone).

We again wet the toothbrush in burnt sienna and English red and flick it over the surface of the picture. This final technique neatly rounds off the unity of the painting; the droplets form a filter, lending the theme a certain informal air, even though its basis is fundamentally classical. You will also notice how we chose to ignore certain features of the model, such as the pattern on the red napkin. We have used both a plastic and compositional analysis in this painting.

The picture is finished, but there is a little retouching left to do, both in the highlights and in the masses of the components of this still life.

The painting is finished. We have used two time-honored tempera techniques—tempera with egg yolk and tempera with gum, also known as gouache. Although the latter is often used in contemporary painting, it is rarely made in the artist's studio nowadays, since it is readily available in art stores.

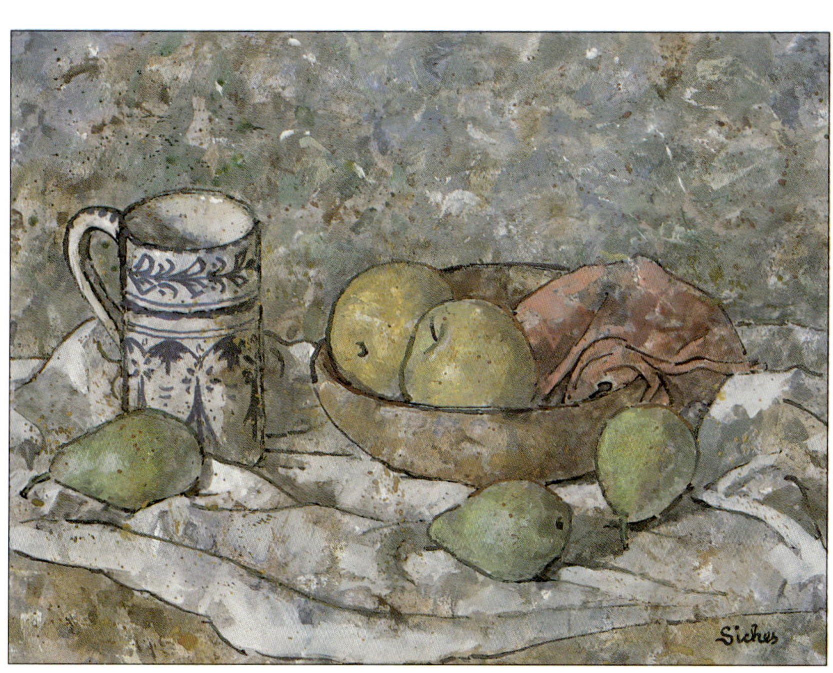

Fresco painting

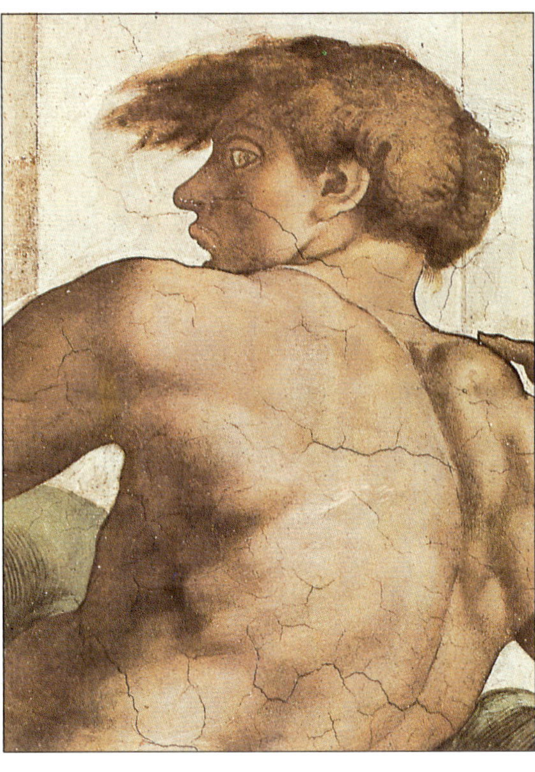

Michelangelo (1475–1564). Decorative figure from the Sistine Chapel. The fresco technique was perfected by the master Renaissance painter. Due to technical problems, the artist almost became blind when painting the fresco in the Sistine Chapel.

A legacy of antiquity

The first thing that probably comes to mind when you hear the term fresco painting is Michelangelo's colossal work in the Sistine Chapel, but there is more to fresco painting than that. When the great artist painted his monumental work, he was merely inheriting a tradition that goes back over a thousand years. In fact, the fresco is probably the oldest pictorial technique of all, since it can be traced as far back as the ancient Greeks.

From time immemorial the fresco has been the most common way of painting a wall. This technique has been somewhat forgotten in our modern times. We are not talking about the artistic legacy of Cimabue, Michelangelo, or Giotto, which is alive, but to the technique they used, which has been replaced by others, much easier to use. The fact is that it is difficult to equal with any other medium the luminosity of a well-executed fresco.

Due to the technical difficulties involved in fresco painting, many variants have been tried and tested throughout the history of painting, but none has been able to resist the passing of time like fresco. Even the great masters have failed. We need only look at the result of a different type of mural painting in *The Holy Supper* (Convent of Saint Mary of the Graces, Milan), in order to see how an erroneous technique can ruin even the most perfect work. In this piece, Leonardo tried to avoid the costliness of a fresco painting, using instead another technique that he himself had invented. A few years before his death, the painting had already deteriorated.

The development of modern painting begins with the technical advances triggered by fresco painting. This is a difficult medium; therefore, it is essential to understand its basic principles in order to understand its development. In this book we are only going to cover the fundamental aspects.

In this detail of The Holy Supper *by Leonardo da Vinci, we can see the result of his ill-fated attempt at substituting the fresco technique with an unsatisfactory mural style painting.*

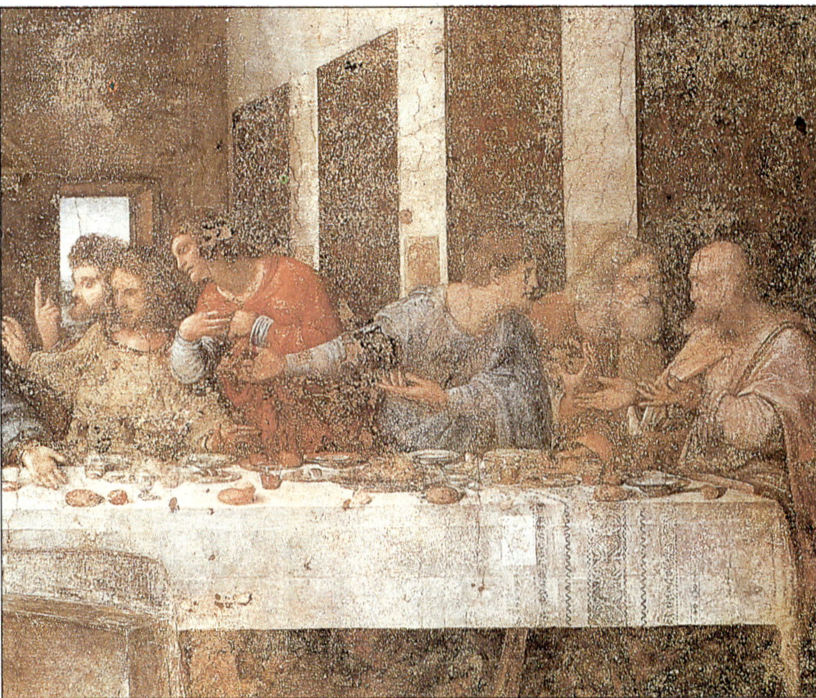

The basic technique

Il buon fresco, as the Italians call it, essentially consists of painting on a wall of damp plaster, prepared by the artist, in such way that the colors employed dry along with the wall, causing a chemical reaction that hardens and dries the paint. This is the secret of a fresco's longevity; it is not a painting on a support, but rather the opposite—the support is the painting itself.

The materials and tools required for painting a fresco are fine sand, plaster, a level board, a trowel, some wool, a ruler, a spirit level, rags, color pigments, a brush, paintbrushes, water containers, shredded paper, and a click wheel.

From the outset we must have a clear idea of what we want to achieve, so the first thing to do is to get it all down on paper.

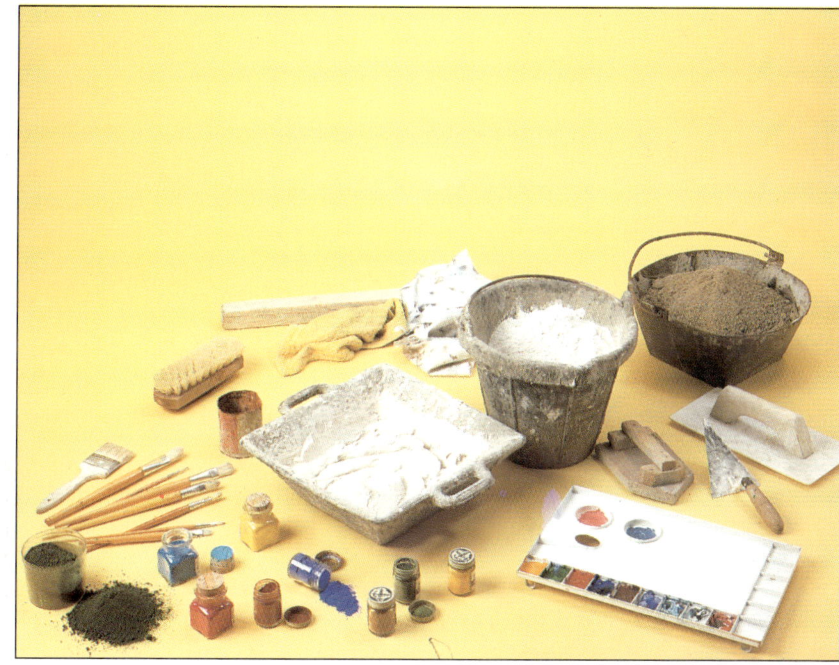

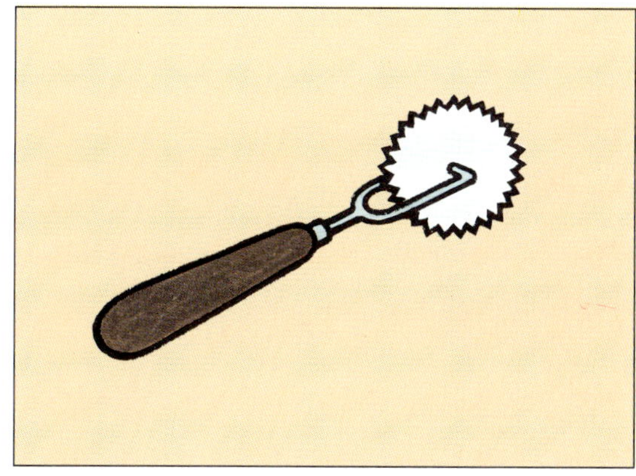

The click wheel is used to transfer the outlines to the wall on which you are going to paint.

The tools and materials required for fresco painting are much the same as those used by a bricklayer. The technique demands neatness and meticulousness, since we have to match the speed of the setting time with our pictorial capacity.

We will need only a small drawing, since it can later be enlarged using the grid technique. Once the drawing is completed, we go over the main lines with the click wheel in order to perforate the lines so that it can be transferred onto the wall. Care should be taken when doing this to be sure of having a satisfactory result.

Now it is time to prepare the wall. We have chosen uncovered brickwork that we have dampened after first removing dust and any other particles that might prevent the work from adhering properly. Fill a bucket a quarter way up with water and add plaster and fine sand until it has acquired a creamy consistency. Leave it to stand for a while until it begins to set. Then apply it with a level board at great speed, leaving the wall totally smooth. Later, apply a second coat.

When we have finished plastering, we smooth down the wall with a bricklayer's ruler. This procedure must be done very quickly, since the plaster on the wall sets almost immediately.

Having made the mix, we plaster the wall using a trowel; we must work fast because if the mix dries too quickly it will not stick to the wall.

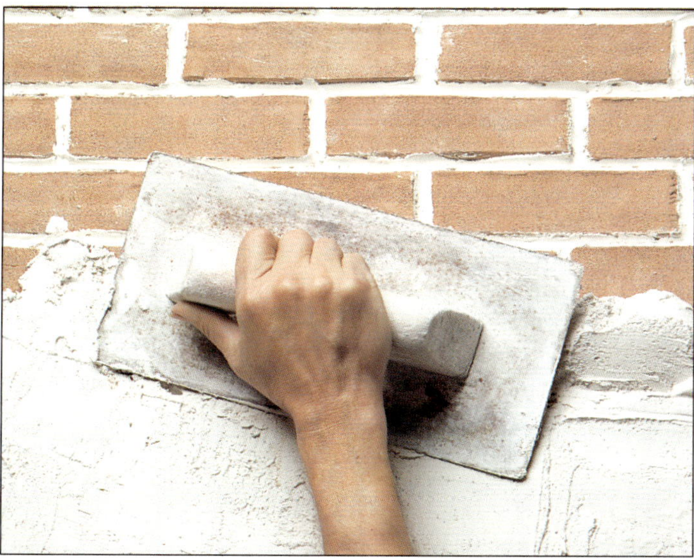

We apply a second layer, making sure that the surface remains even. This second application does not have to be as thick as the first.

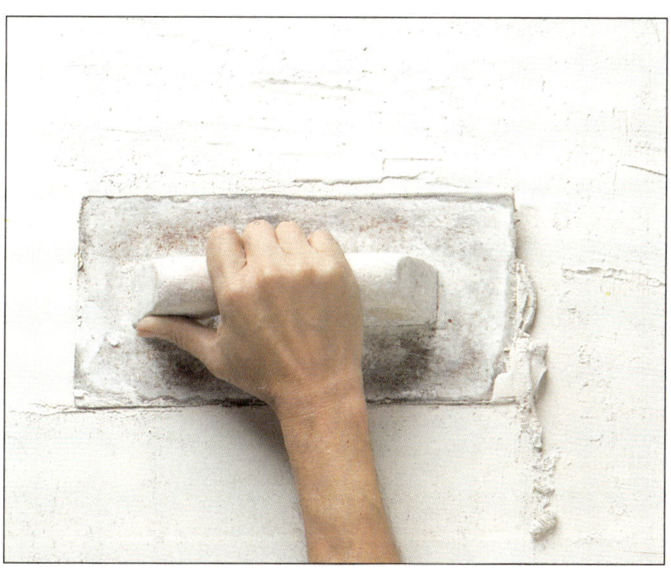

Fresco painting

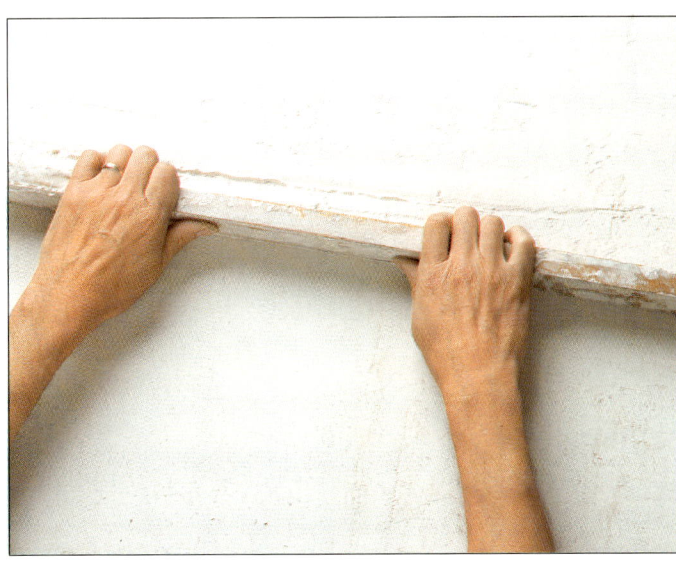

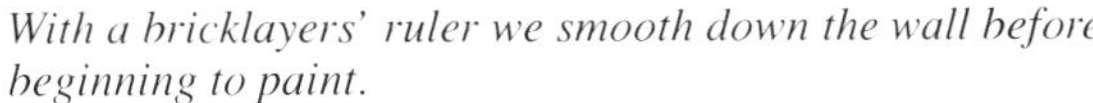

With a bricklayers' ruler we smooth down the wall before beginning to paint.

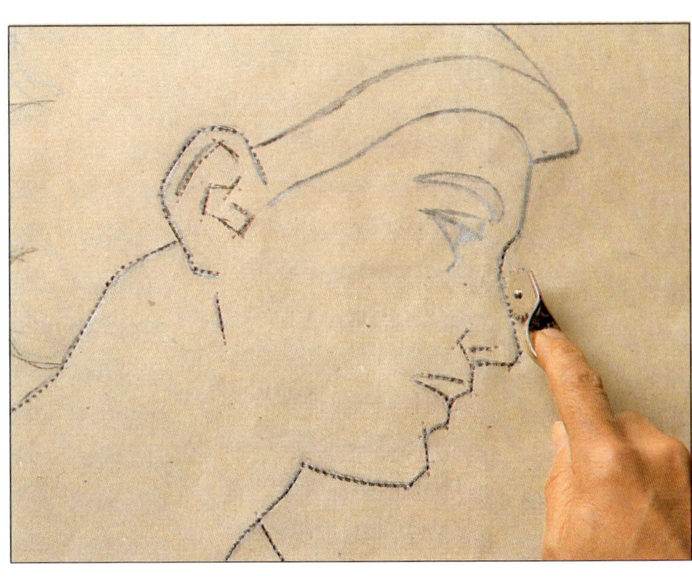

If you don't have a click wheel, you can perforate the contours of the drawing with any sharp object.

We take up the perforated drawing and use it as a mask. This process must be carried out using a fine fabric impregnated with black pigment. The pigment that filters through the pores of the fabric will transfer the image onto the wall.

The only thing left to do is to paint it. This we do directly with damp pigments, wetting the brush and applying the paint on the wall while it is still setting. The color penetrates the wall, becoming one with the plaster. A dry wall prevents the pigment from being absorbed, so, in order to continue painting, you may have to add some more plaster to those areas that have already dried.

Using a piece of fabric saturated with black pigment, we begin to transfer the drawing to the wall. The pigment goes through the perforations on the drawing.

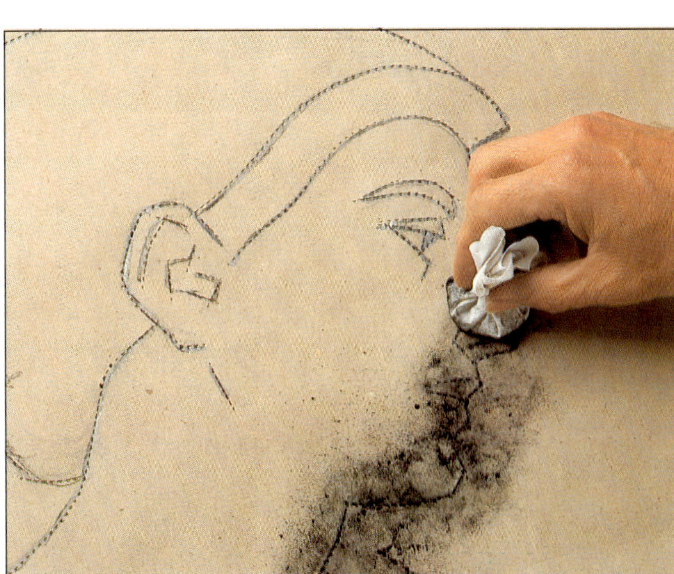

As you can see, we paint directly on the wall with pigment dampened with water and ordinary brushes. Color must be applied as quickly as possible, since it is absorbed by the wall as the plaster sets.

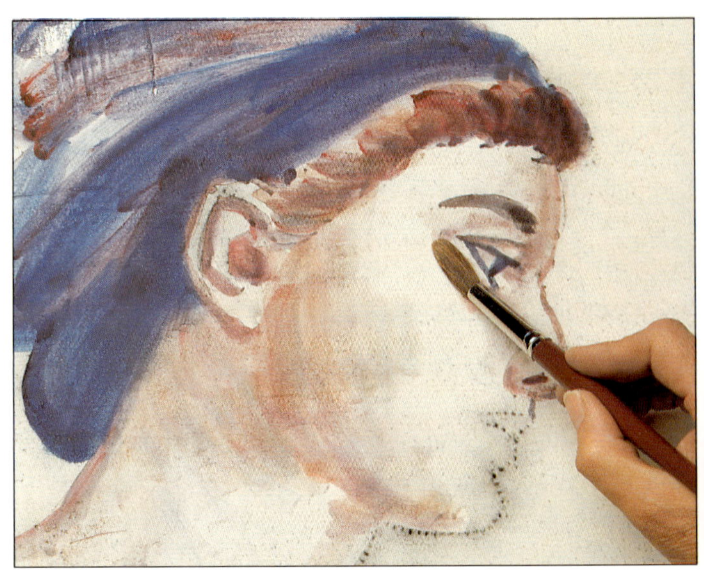

The art of engraving

Engraving was born the moment humans first used their hands covered in colored earth to leave their imprint on the walls of their cave dwellings. In its many facets, engraving has been present throughout art history. As early as the fifth century, blocks of wood were used in the Orient for stamping cloth. The possibility of making repeated reproductions of images has always been particularly attractive to artists. It is a way of reaching the largest number of people. It is also less costly than an original work, although some equipment is required that not everyone can afford.

In the fifteenth century, with the increased use of paper and printing, there was also an increase in the number of books published; many were illustrated with crude drawings made on blocks of wood. This process replaced the laborious work of the medieval illuminators. All that remained to be done was to color the illustrations by hand. In the Netherlands, where the paper industry flourished, woodcuts developed to a level of astonishing virtuosity. One of the most important exponents of this art was the German Albrecht Dürer (1471–1528).

Gradually, the woodcut was overshadowed by the development of other methods of reproduction, such as engraving on metal. It was not until the nineteenth and early twentieth centuries that the woodcut came into its own again, revitalized by the early avant-garde artists. They not only engraved the blocks but also took over the entire printing process, thus controlling the production from start to finish. Movements such as fauvism, with Paul Gauguin (1848–1903) at its head, and expressionism, with Edvard Munch (1862–1944), did much to revive the ancient techniques of engraving.

Linoleum appeared as a substitute for wood at the beginning of this century. Linocuts were produced by Pablo Picasso and most of the avant-garde artists of that time. They are perhaps the easiest of the various engraving techniques, because they are produced on relatively soft material. Etching, on the other hand, introduced most likely by William Blake (1737–1827), has a much shorter history than the woodcut. It consists basically of a metal, copper, or zinc being "bitten" by acid, leaving the image in relief. The areas protected from the acid are not eaten away and therefore remain in relief and will be printed; the parts bitten out will not be printed. This system of engraving is used more for defining areas than for drawing lines and requires no special instruments for engraving the metal since the acid does the work.

Drypoint engraving requires nothing more than a copper plate and a punch or steel needle with which to scratch the surface: all marks made on the plate will be printed on the paper. Drypoint engravings have a very fresh appearance, similar to pencil drawings. We will now demonstrate the various techniques used for producing the different types of prints.

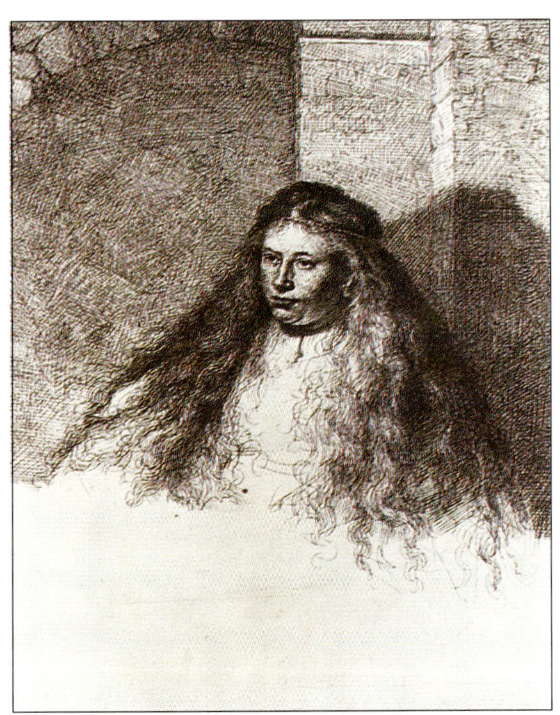

Rembrandt (1606–1669) was not only a great draftsman but also a skilled engraver. He was one of the masters of this technique, demonstrating such virtuosity of line that very few people to date have been able to equal his legacy.

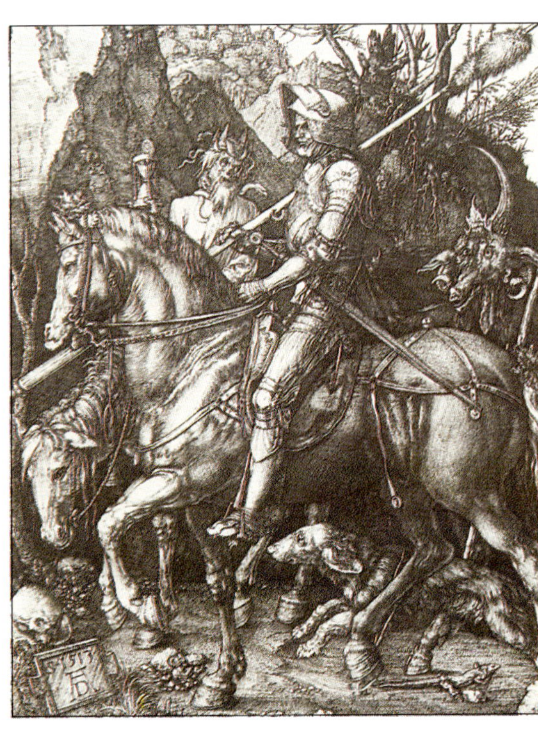

Albrecht Dürer (1471–1528), Knight, Death and the Devil. *In this engraving, done with a burin on a copper plate, the great engraver produced a masterful example of drypoint.*

Linocuts

1. An old technique

The linocut is an old engraving technique derived from the woodcut. It is one of the simplest methods and practically the only one that can be used at home without too many complications. Linoleum was used at one time as roofing insulation against damp, cold, and rain, until the invention of asphalt sheeting. Today, although it is still marketed for household purposes, its main function is as an engraving plate. Its great advantage lies in its ductility, for it is a very dense material with a smooth surface. It does not absorb ink but holds it well. Linoleum is made from cork dust, glued and pressed onto a sackcloth backing. As a cork by-product, it is very easy to cut and carve, and comes in different colors, depending on the tinting used during manufacture.

For a long time, linoleum was used for printing posters, since it is easily worked—no special etching press is required, and prints can be made with a small bookbinding press or even by rubbing with a simple wooden spoon.

We have all seen the great linocuts by Picasso, Toulouse-Lautrec, and the leading avant-garde artists of the turn of the century. Linocuts and woodcuts enjoyed considerable popularity in the Expressionist movement; Edvard Munch was one of their principal exponents and made good use of both techniques. Linocuts are usually monochrome, although several blocks can be used to make a polychrome print.

2. The material

As with any artistic technique, the materials used for making a linocut must be of high quality. Etching tools must be sharp. We will need at least a V-shaped one for making fine lines, as well as a U-shaped one and a straight cutter. We will also find the various cutters to be valuable allies.

For the following exercises we will use a Swedish paper called Invercote; it is not, strictly speaking, a printing paper, but it accepts the ink very well. One side has a very satin finish, whereas the other does not. We will use this other side.

One final item we will need for producing this print is alcohol, which we will use to clean both the plates and the roller.

Felt sheets are required if we are using a press, since they help distribute the pressure uniformly over the plate. They can be found in stores that sell household furnishings, since they are often used for covering walls. We will use a fairly dense, even type.

3. How to proceed

First of all, we need to start off with a specific idea. We know that for any pictorial subject there is one basic requirement: drawing, not only as construction but also as meaning. Linocuts have been produced on all kinds of subjects; what we are going to do here belongs to the field of illustration or posters.

The avant-garde artists at the beginning of the century took to woodcuts with enthusiasm. As a substitute for wood they used linoleum, which acquired considerable importance with the Expressionist movement, of which Edvard Munch (1862–1944) was one of the principal forerunners.

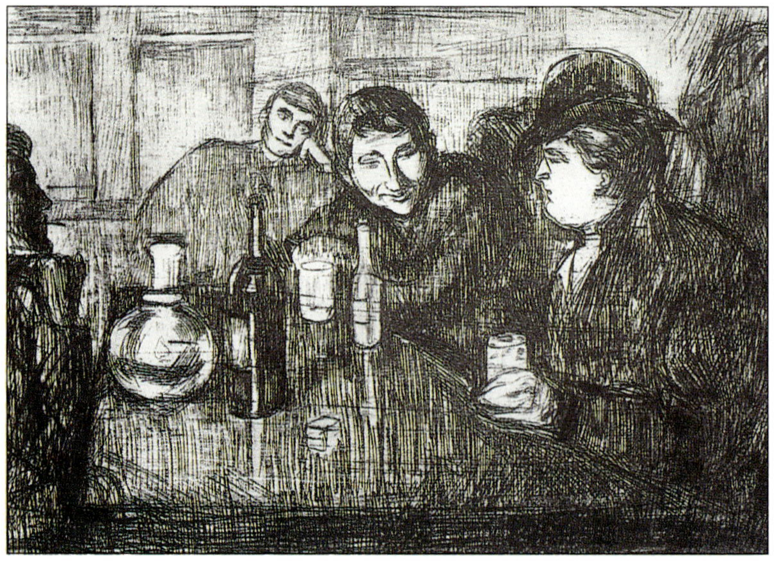

Cristiania-Bohemia I, *a drypoint engraving and etching by Munch that is a brilliant combination of both techniques.*

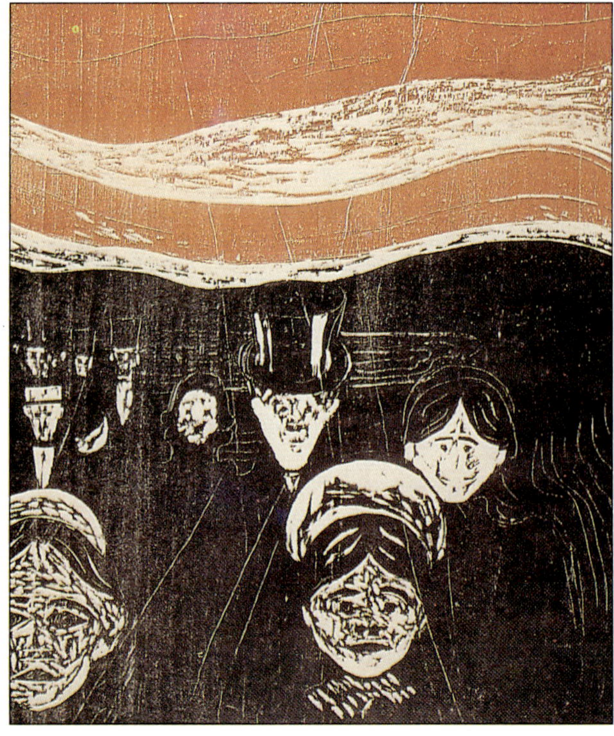

Giants are beloved by storytellers and their illustrators, so we are going to start with a drawing of a giant. This giant has been created entirely from imagination, with no natural points of reference. To produce this creature, we have started by making a sketch of the figure from a very low viewpoint, giving greater importance to the lower part of the body, which takes up two-thirds of the entire drawing. We have imagined it as if it were a large building, supported by two enormous columns. In order to increase the sensation of size, we have produced a triangular composition that takes up practically the entire picture. We will start by making a sketch in broad outline, concentrating on the general form of the figure and not paying too much attention to detail. We then work on this structure from within, adding lines that denote a body. Obviously, giants are notorious for their grotesque features, so we are not trying to make a lifelike drawing but an interesting, baroque caricature.

4. Preliminary work

The initial drawing has been produced without bothering with dark or white areas; it is nothing more than a general outline. The next step, using a light-table, is to trace the outline of the drawing with a thick felt-tipped pen in order to indicate some of the dark lines and the large shaded areas, which will be worked on at a later stage. In the next tracing, we can delete some of the many lines we consider superfluous in order to reduce our field of work to a more specific, graphic drawing. It is important that the final picture is not too complicated; otherwise, because of the limited precision of the method employed, the details could be blurred.

We will then finalize the design of the plate by defining all the dark areas and all the uninked areas, although this, of course, is not a definitive solution, since when we begin to work on the linocut, other interesting questions will arise. We have now produced the final drawing and marked the darker areas. We next have to transfer the design to the plate.

5. Transferring the design to the plate

If we want the image to be exactly the same as the one we have just drawn on paper, then once we start printing with the linoleum plate, we must work not only in negative but also back to front, as if we were looking at the drawing through a mirror. In order to do this, we must transfer the image the opposite way around. After cleaning the surface of the linoleum with alcohol, trace the image on tracing paper, but with the drawing placed face downward.

These are the materials we will use to produce a linocut, one of the most suitable engraving techniques for amateurs because of the simplicity of the process and the results obtained: lino plate, set of etching tools and cutters for working the lino, 1B pencil, sheets of paper for sketches, printing paper, printing ink, inking roller, thick felt sheets, and a glass sheet for the ink.

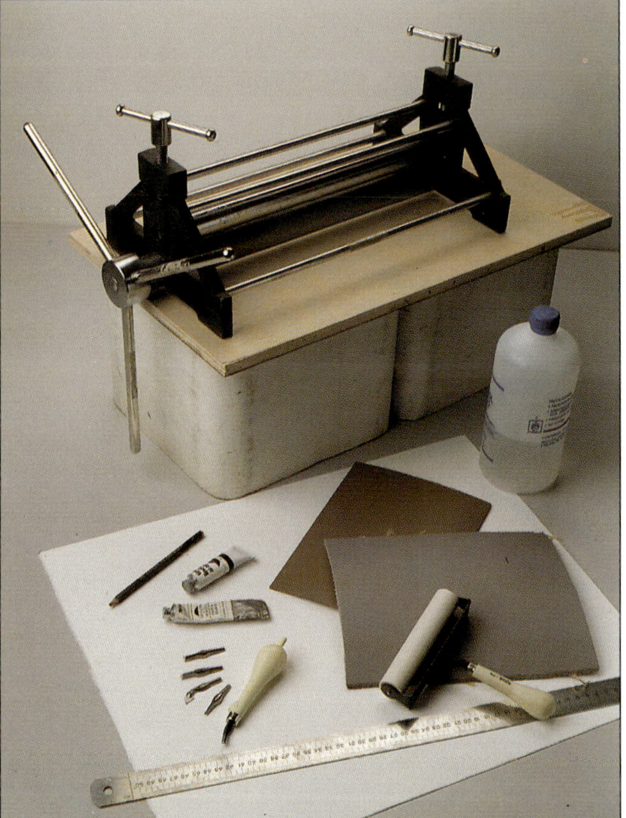

In order to produce the design on the plate, we first make a quick sketch that will serve as a template for tracing the final drawing, filling in the darker shaded areas.

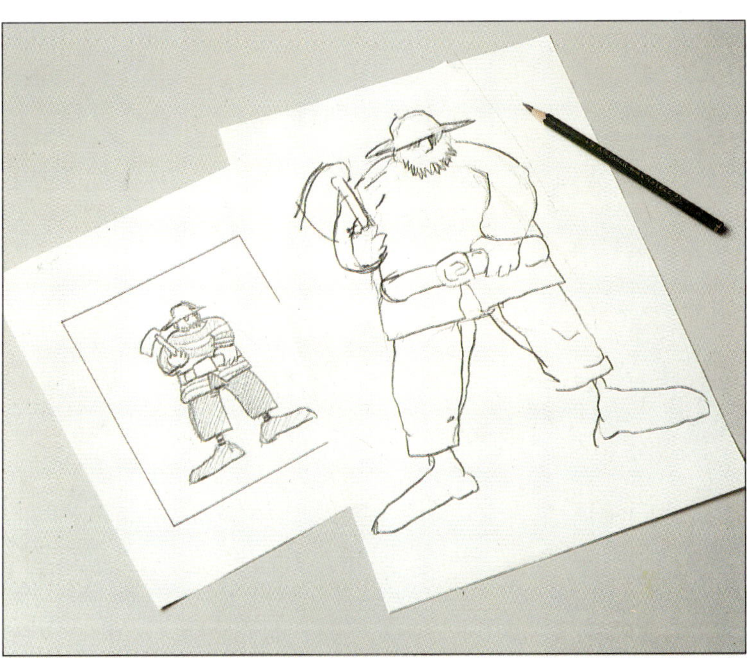

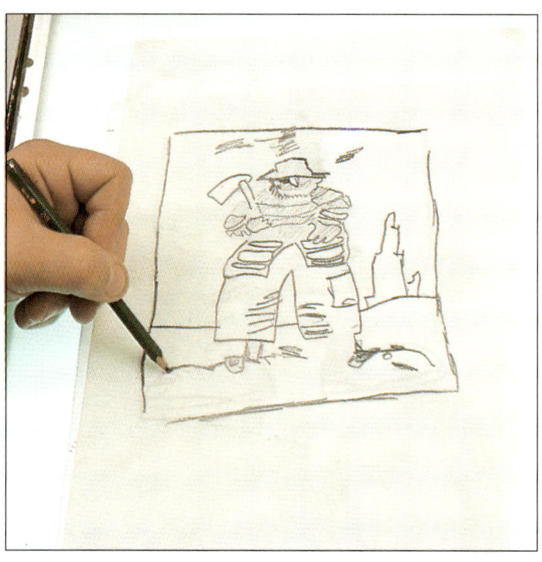

Place the final sketch on a light-table or a window in order to trace the dark areas that will later be traced onto the sheet of linoleum.

Thoroughly clean the plate with alcohol in order to remove any grease.

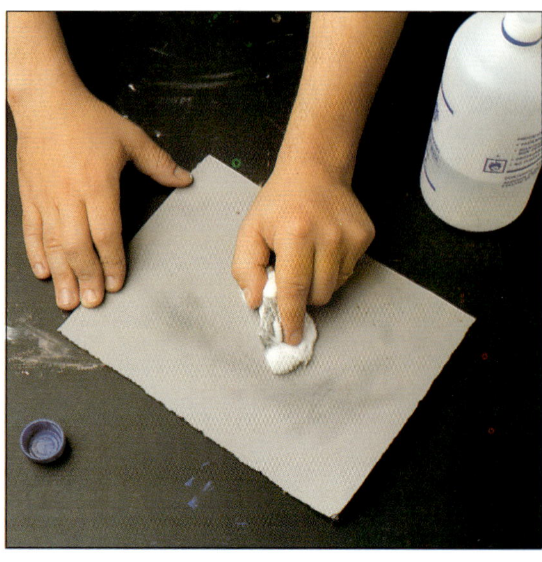

We can paint the linoleum with white gouache before transferring the drawing, in order to see the lines more clearly, though this is not altogether necessary. Using a sharp pencil, we trace the drawing onto the linoleum plate. We then ink the drawing on the plate with india ink and let it dry completely before starting to etch the unprinted areas.

6. Etching

Etching tools are delicate and dangerous instruments. We should never put a hand in front of the tool in the direction in which we are working as, if we are not careful, it could skid on the surface and cut us. These tools must be kept well-sharpened at all times. We will begin by etching away the upper part. First of all, we will cut along the edges of all the drawn lines with the aid of a cutter, so as to define the lines cleanly and sharply; if we later want to work on these relief areas, there is always time to do so.

Once we have "drawn" the outlines with the cutter—taking care not to cut through the plate—we can begin to scrape. The small areas and details, like the face of the figure, will be worked with a fine cutter. We must try not to etch too deeply, because of the softness of the linoleum, fine lines in relief tend to split. On the other hand, very fine lines are easier to achieve when the relief is not so high. There is no need to cut too far into the linoleum anyway, since the part that will be printed is the upper surface.

We can paint the sheet of linoleum with white gouache so that the lines of the drawing will show up more clearly.

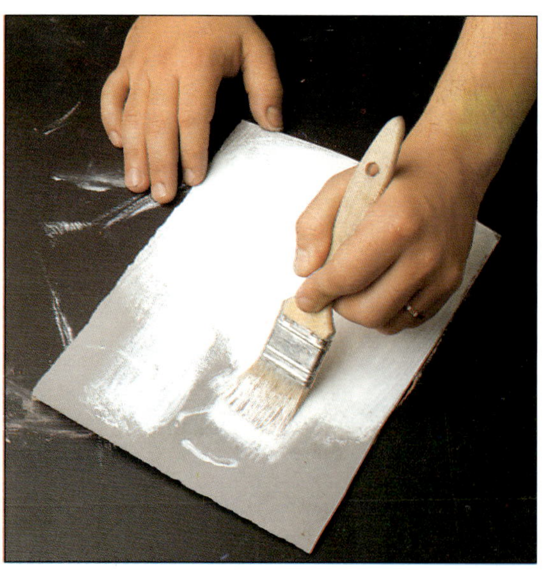

Place a sheet of tracing paper on the linoleum, and place the drawing face down on top of it. Keep in mind that the final result on the linoleum will be the negative of the drawing. Afterwards, we will ink the drawing with india ink.

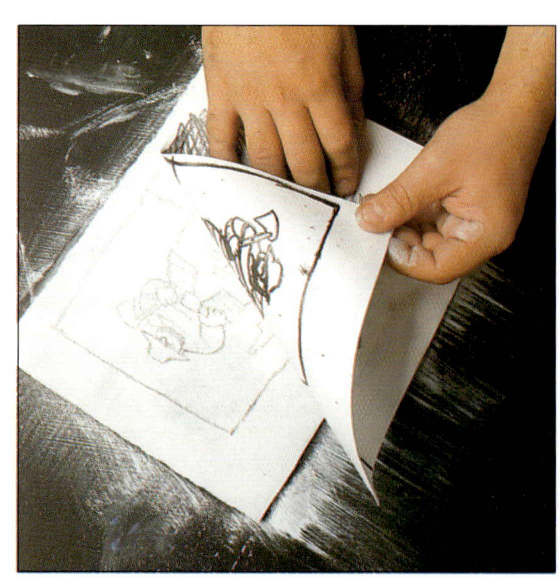

Once the area around the face has been scraped out, we continue down the body, working on the striped part of the giant's garments. Throughout all this section, we must be careful not to invade the area to be left in relief, since any mark would later show on the print. So, very patiently—for patience is what is required in this work—we continue scraping with the finest cutter until we reach the part with the large white areas. We now take a wider etcher and cut away in parallel lines, each line overlapping the next, taking great care when we reach the edges of the area that is not to be cut away.

Note that the areas to be left in white, around the legs, seem to extend beyond the picture. We must continue to respect the limits of the drawing and not scrape away too far beyond the figure because, once we have completed this task, we will etch a border to form the background of the illustration. Since we have previously outlined the entire figure with the cutter, we will have no problem following the lines as the cut-away areas will be clearly marked with a clean edge. Obviously we will make a few incisions to add freshness to the image we are producing, but we want to preserve the sharply defined form produced by the cutter. Remember that linocuts have a number of limitations that we must accept; it is therefore better to go for simpler forms rather than complicate matters by making thicker lines that will only blur them. This, however, is merely a word of advice; if you prefer more highly worked forms, just follow your own inclinations.

We continue scraping away until the entire image is represented on the linoleum sheet. We now have the basic black lines that will be the printing surface of the plate, but we still have some areas that are not distinguished from the background. It is time to make a border to establish the distinction between figure and background. To do this, we use the finest cutter and draw a series of lines parallel to the base of the plate. We need to achieve a fairly solid line, but we will not use the cutter because this would produce an excessively clean line that would detract from the lines of the principal figure.

When we have completed this work, we can still make a few alterations to the plate with a fine cutter.

After adding these changes, we clean the plate thoroughly and remove any shavings, using a clothesbrush and, for the finer lines, an old toothbrush or nailbrush.

7. Printing

An engraving is not completely finished until it has been printed. The plate itself is not the engraving. To say that it is would be like saying that a painting is the preliminary photograph or even the model. Of course, if we want to, we can produce the plate and leave it at that; but then it would not be an engraving, but something quite different. The very concept of an engraving includes its reproduction.

The type of paper we will use can vary. It is advisable to carry out tests on different papers, from very basic types such as newspaper or wrapping paper to high-quality handmade papers. These, however, are obviously much more expensive and delicate.

The bottom left photograph shows different types of etching tools, although the most common tools are the V-shaped etcher, the U-shaped etcher, and the cutter.

The first step is to cut around the entire outline of the drawing with the cutter, then scrape out those areas to be left white in the print, taking care not to cut through the plate and not to go beyond the edges of the picture.

After defining the cut edges of the figure, we use the V-shaped etcher to make the lines around it. See the bottom right illustration.

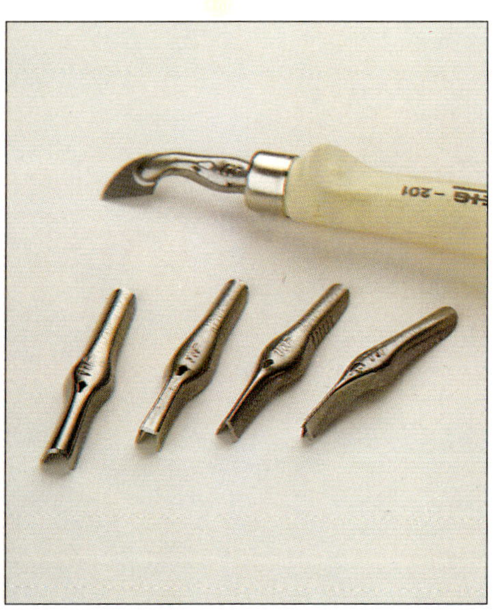

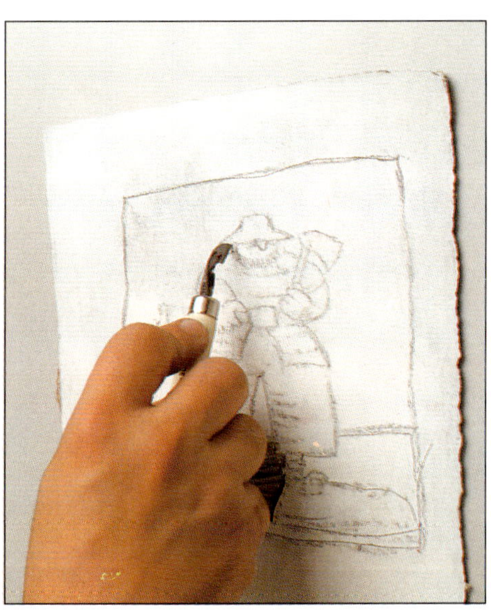

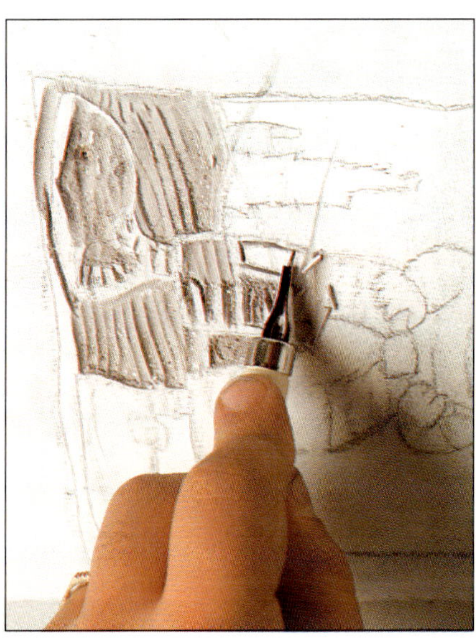

Linocuts

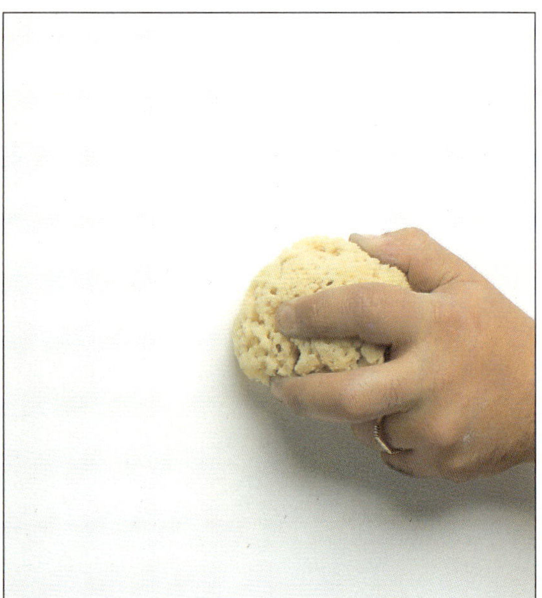

Before printing, we should dampen the paper to open its pores and facilitate contact with the ink.

After dampening the paper, we ink the roller and run it evenly over the plate.

Next, we lay a white backing sheet on the felt, and on top of this the printing paper.

Ink responds in very different ways on different papers, depending on the degree of glue they contain, their density, and even their weight. For the print we are making, we will use a thick paper that has a satin finish on one side and is slightly porous on the other side. If you want to use another, less stiff type of rag paper, we would advise you to dampen it first with water and dry it lightly between two sheets of paper.

For printing from this plate, we will use a simple bookbinding press on which we have placed a couple of pieces of thick felt so as to distribute the pressure uniformly and also prevent the plate from being spoiled. Using a spatula, we place some ink on the sheet of glass and spread it evenly over the surface, then run the cork roller lengthwise and crosswise over the glass until it is thoroughly impregnated with ink, but not saturated. If the roller has too much ink on it, we continue rolling it over another part of the glass until it contains the right amount—too much ink can even cause the lines to split under the pressure of the press. We run the inked roller twice over the plate, once crosswise and once lengthwise, making sure that the whole surface is inked. Next we place a sheet of white paper in the press, on top of the felt sheets, to serve as a backing. On top of this we place the sheet of paper that is to be printed, and on top of this the inked plate, with the inked side toward the paper. Then we exert pressure gradually, and hold it for a few seconds. Afterwards, we unscrew the press and with the utmost care lift the plate away; the paper will very probably stick to it. We peel it away carefully and check that the proof is to our liking. If it is not, we can touch up the plate, but if we clean it with alcohol we will have to leave it a whole day to dry properly. If we obtain the desired result, we can pull a few more proofs before starting the final printing. Among other things, the proofs will show whether the incisions are deep enough and

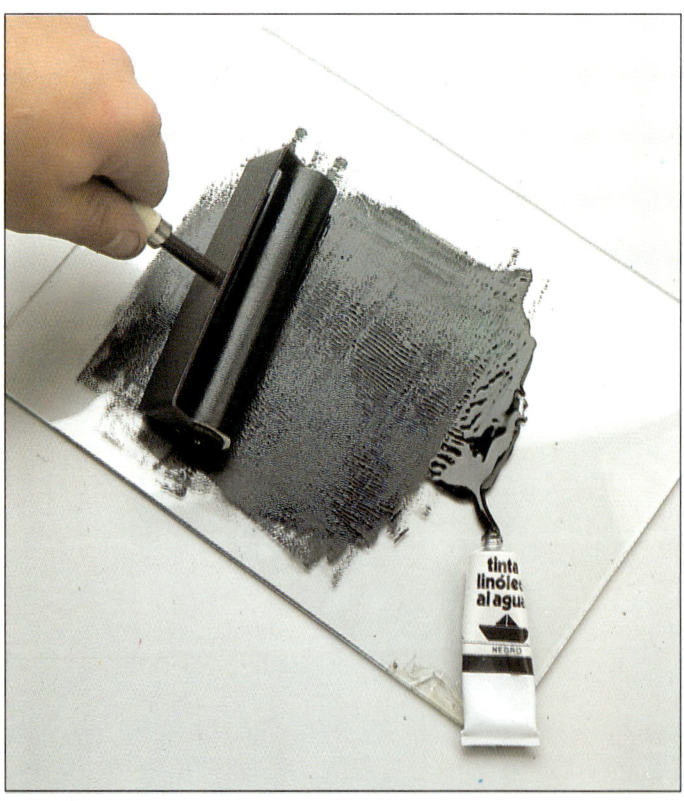

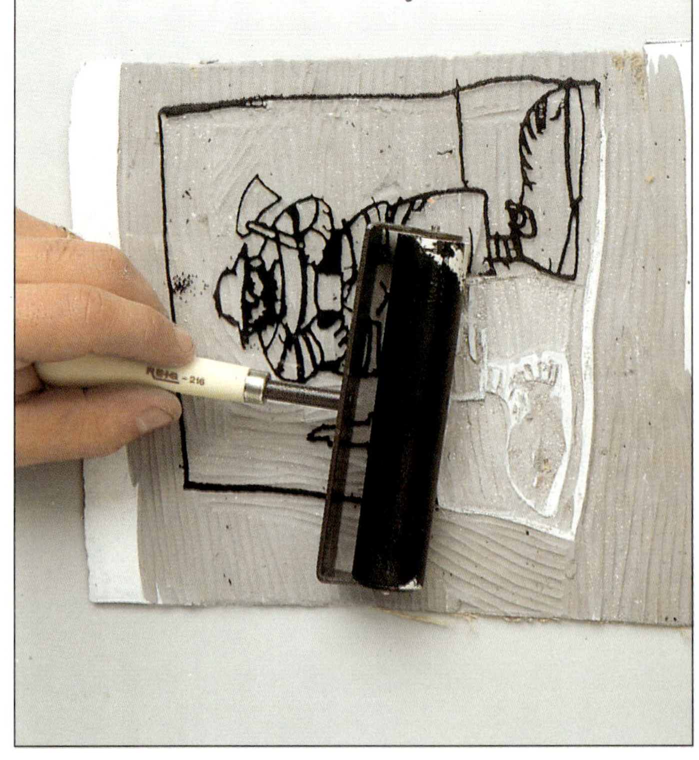

clean enough, whether the ink responds to the paper in the way we want, whether the paper is of the appropriate type, etc.

The number of prints produced from a linocut should not be too many for several obvious reasons, the most important being that, because linoleum is a soft flexible material, too much repeated pressure on the same point will make the plate lose its original form.

It should be noted that when an edition is printed there are a series of initials and numbers that identify each print from the rest:

The most usual initials are:

A.P. Artist's proof.

I.P. Inking proof.

1/50 means that this is print number 1 of an edition of 50; the second print would be numbered 2/50 and so on.

In general, for an edition of each engraving to be considered an original work, the number of prints should not exceed ninety. There are some prints on which a very high number can be seen; these refer to the order of lithographic prints, which, in that case, should not be considered an original work by the artist. For reasons having to do with marketing and personal ethics, plates are usually defaced or destroyed after the prints have been produced so that they cannot be used again.

As each print is made, it should be carefully laid out to dry in an airy place, well separated from the others in order to avoid any staining.

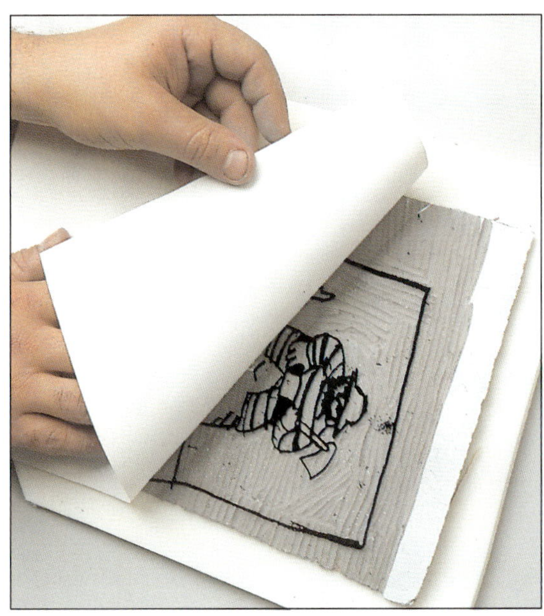

Place the inked plate beneath the paper, taking care not to mark it. Lay another sheet of paper against the plate to avoid any possible staining of the print.

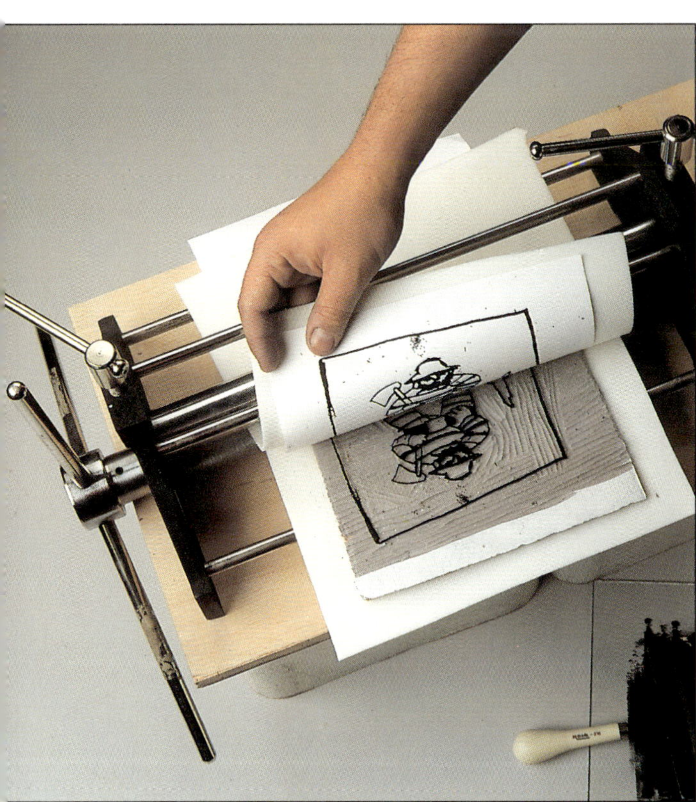

The pressure of the press on the plate should not be too strong, since, due to its softness, the linoleum might expand and crack the lines of the drawing.

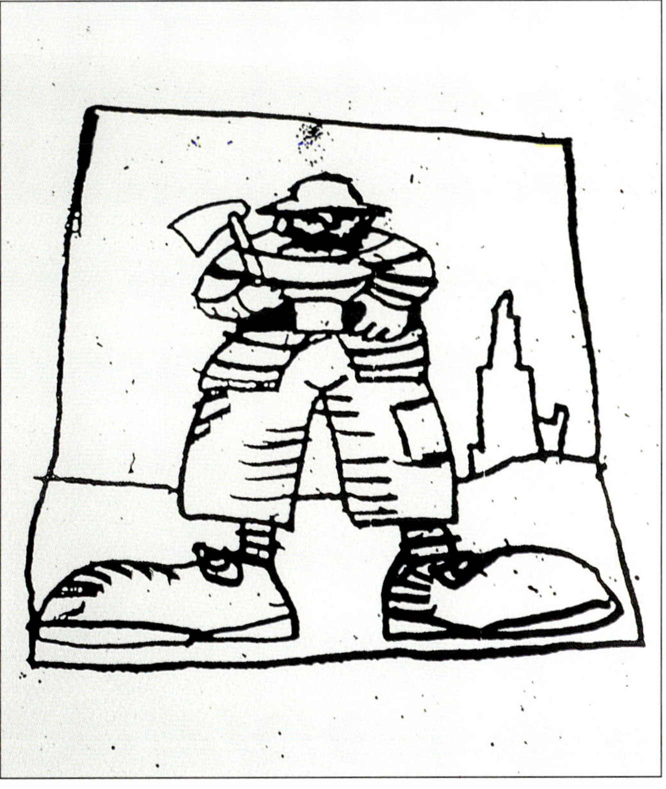

This is the result of the pressure exerted on the plate; as you can see, the print is the negative of the plate.

Drypoint engraving

1. Introduction

At the beginning of this chapter we referred to the drypoint technique as the most direct method of engraving a plate. (Although linoleum is easy to ink, the engraving process is slow and laborious.)

Drypoint is done by working straight on the plate. In fact, any tiny mark on the plate will later show up as a mark on the printed paper, so obviously the plate must be scrupulously clean for this technique.

2. The plates

When it comes to printing, the plate is the basic element. We can obtain plates of various metals but, as mentioned earlier, copper and zinc are the ones most commonly used. Generally speaking, we can buy ready-cut copper plates both in art supply stores and in large hardware stores. We will generally find that the plates we purchase have one side covered in a resistant material. These plates are already prepared for immersion in acid, but with drypoint the acid bath is not necessary, since we incise the plate with our own hand.

As we mentioned, zinc and copper plates are fairly easy to come by. You will find that zinc plates are the cheapest, but copper will endure a longer print run and will allow us to draw much finer lines. We can try both types of plate to compare results. If you like this engraving technique and decide to continue with it, you will end up preferring one type of plate to the other. We can also experiment with iron plates, but these are very hard to work and when printing they always leave a grayish trace.

Plates can be bought ready-cut in different sizes or we can cut them ourselves with shears or a paper cutter; however, it is advisable to have them cut at the store, since the staff is more experienced at cutting. Whether you purchase a ready-cut plate or not, we will need to check the edges. A newly cut plate will naturally have a sharp edge that must be filed off, as otherwise it would cut the paper during printing. The way to do this is to place the file and the plate at a 45° angle and smooth away the sharp edge.

Generally speaking, a new plate should not be scratched, but it may get scraped or marked during transportation or in some other way. We can remedy this with the burnisher, rubbing its rounded end over both sides of the scratch and pressing the edges into it, then polishing it with metal polish until it is perfectly smooth and clean.

Very often, drypoint and etching techniques can be combined in the same plate. In this chapter we will discuss both techniques, starting with drypoint.

These are the materials we will use for making a drypoint engraving: a copper or zinc plate, engraving needles, burnisher, pencil, household metal polish, cotton rags, tarlatan, and newspaper.

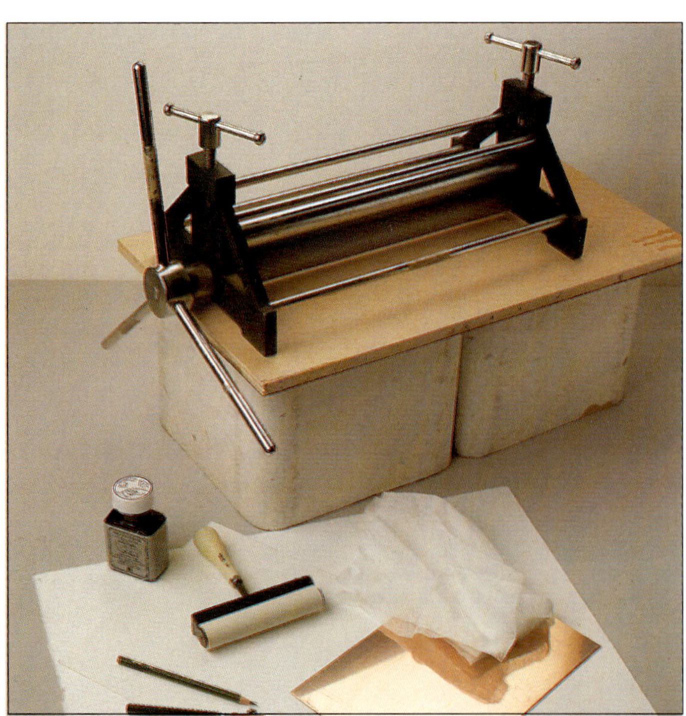

Clean the zinc plate with metal polish in order to remove any grease or rust. Take the original drawing and trace it onto the plate; the tracing may be done in a number of different ways.

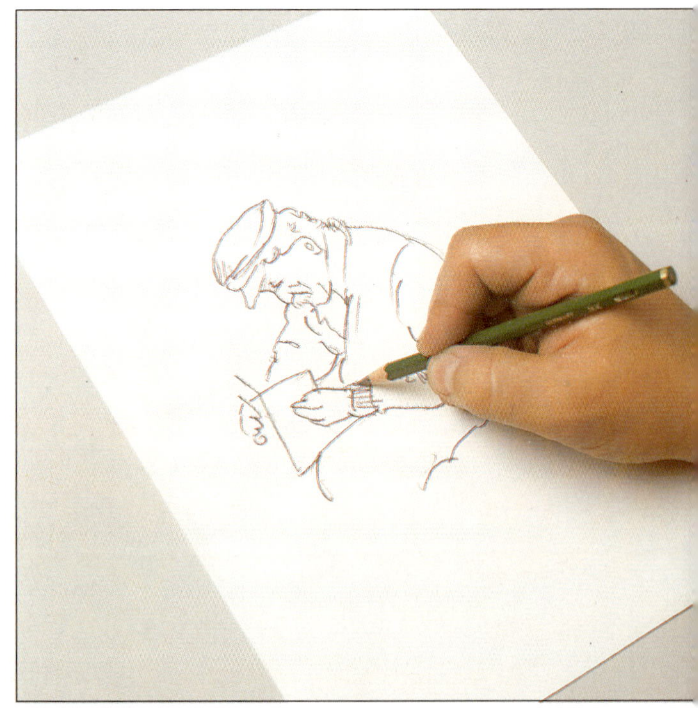

3. Differences between drypoint and etching

Drypoint is a direct engraving method, whereas etching is a method that requires an acid to incise the plate.

When employing the drypoint method, we work in a linear fashion, using hatching if we want to cover large areas or to indicate shading. Etching, on the other hand, is used for covering large surfaces rather than for drawing fine lines. Very often we can employ a combination of both techniques, using the direct biting method first and then touching up or adding lines by the drypoint method. Another procedure would be to prepare an etching and then scratch the unexposed area with a drypoint needle that would allow the acid to penetrate into the furrows in this area, thus creating a line that is not as fine as a drypoint line but has something of the nature of a graphic mark.

4. The drawing

The drawing will be the starting point of our work. We will have to adapt it to a very specific technique. This factor will condition our work much more than when we draw in preparation for a painting. Before we produce any kind of engraving, we must have a very clear idea of what we want to do, while keeping in mind that we will have to wait until the paper is printed before we can see the final result of our design.

We will start off with a drawing done on paper. (It should be noted that we can also work directly on plate, drawing on it first in pencil and then going over the lines with the drypoint needle.)

We could have drawn directly on the metal, without any preliminary work, but in this case we are going over the drawing on paper with a soft pencil.

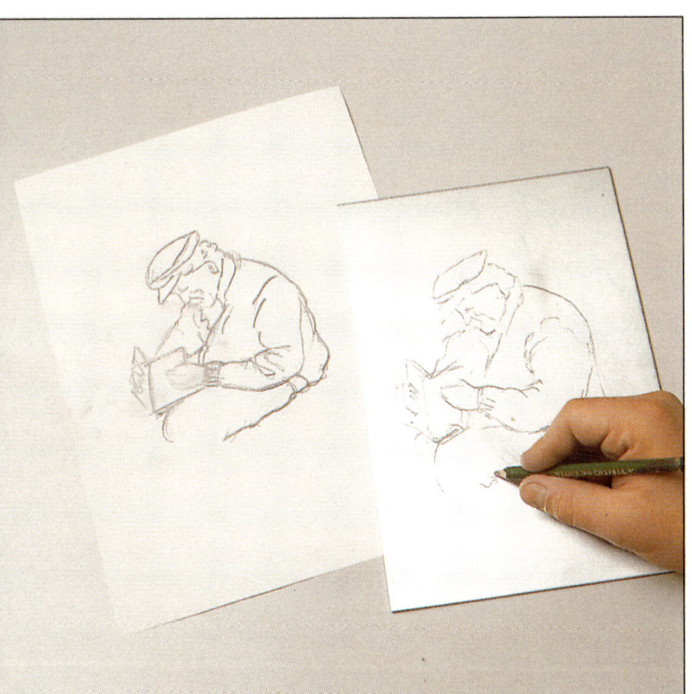

Here you can see how we begin engraving the plate. A characteristic feature of drypoint is the formation of a burr on both sides of the line, which will hold a greater or lesser amount of ink. Any possible errors can be rectified with the use of a burnisher, although the results will never be entirely perfect.

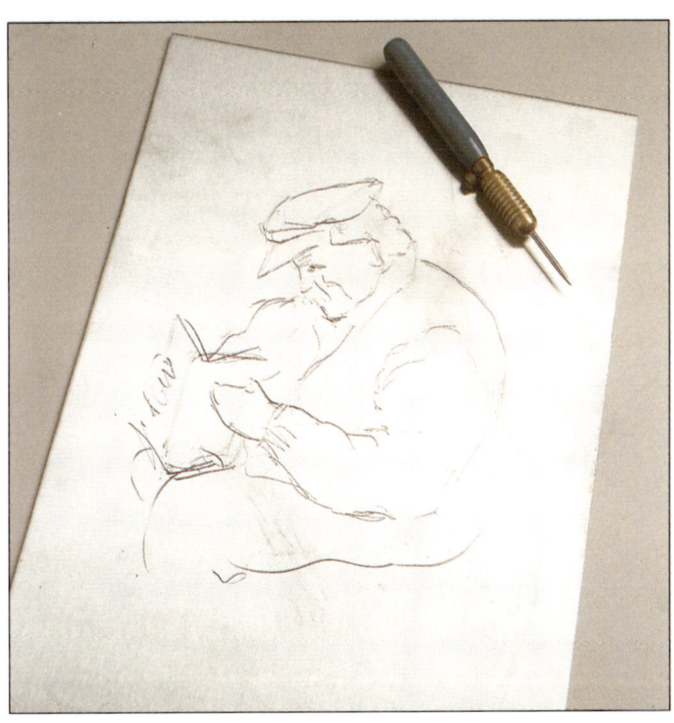

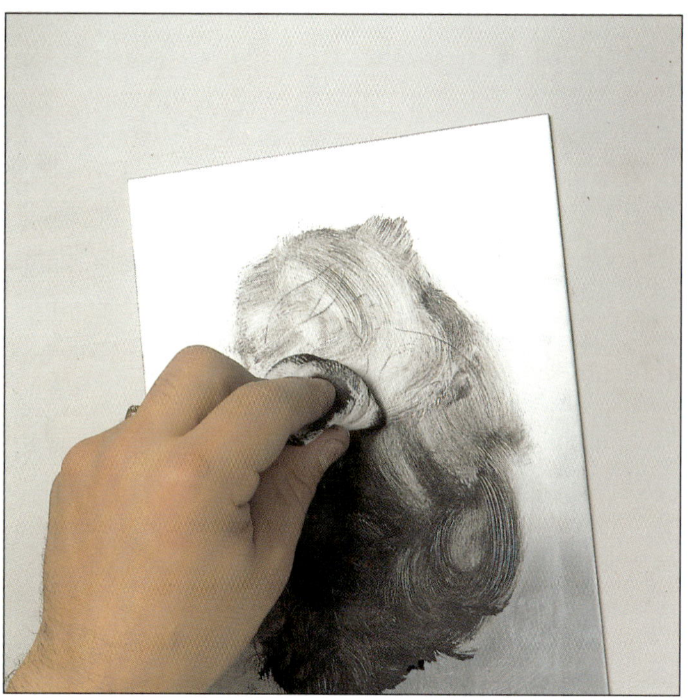

Taking a piece of inked tarlatan, we dab it over the entire surface of the plate. If the plate has previously been warmed, the ink will flow more freely over the surface.

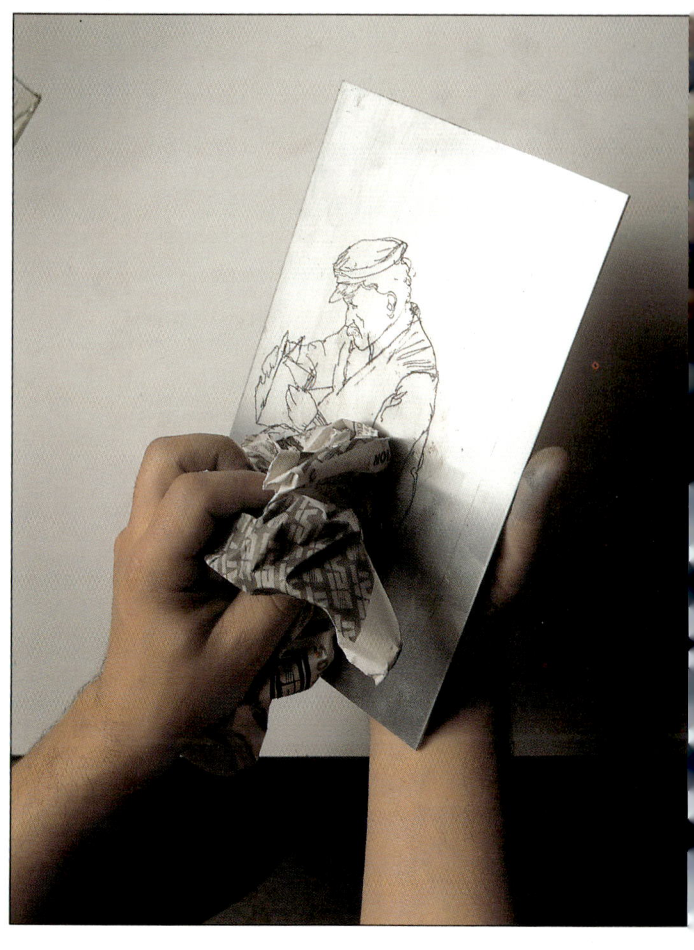

Newspaper is ideal for cleaning the plate. This task should be done gently and quickly, removing all the excess ink and taking care not to extract any ink from the furrows.

5. How to engrave the drawing

Once we have completed the preliminary drawing, we will place a sheet of carbon paper on the plate and on top of this the original drawing on thin paper, in order to be able go over it on the reverse side. This way, with the aid of a fine pencil, we can transfer the inverted drawing onto the plate. From time to time, while working on it, we should lift up the paper very carefully to check that the drawing is complete.

Once this operation is finished, the drawing will be transferred intact to the plate. Now, with the aid of the engraving needles, we can start to "fix it" on the plate. The needle point must be sharp but rounded, so as not to tear away the metal. A burr will form on both sides of the line; this is characteristic of drypoint engraving. This burr produces a less hard line than etching, since it retains a certain amount of ink.

The position of the needle will influence the type of line produced. If we hold the needle in a vertical position, a burr will appear on both sides of the line and the printed result will be clean. If, on the other hand, we slant the needle, the burr will appear on one side only, producing a fuzzy or blurred effect on that side of the line when printed.

Another effect that can be obtained with this technique is to increase the darkness of the line by pressing harder on the plate to make a deeper furrow; this way, it will hold more ink and, therefore, the density of the color will be greater.

6. How to correct mistakes

The next step is to go over the entire drawing on the plate, playing around with the variety of lines and strokes, just as we would if it were a pencil drawing on paper. This allows us to work with a certain freedom. We should remember, though, that contrary to a pencil drawing, a drypoint error cannot be corrected simply with an eraser. If we make a mistake and want to rectify it, we will have to resort to the burnisher.

Using the rounded end of the burnisher and working in the direction of the line, we can press back the burr into the furrow and seal it. We then polish the repair with metal polish, leaving the surface as smooth as possible. Bear in mind that it is very difficult for a damaged plate to recover its smoothness altogether, so there will be a faint line that need not offend us; on the contrary, we should take advantage of our own mistakes to improve the final result and be

After laying the paper on the plate, taking care not to mark it, we place both items between two sheets of clean felt. The pressure must be strong enough to force the paper into the furrows, where it will pick up the ink.

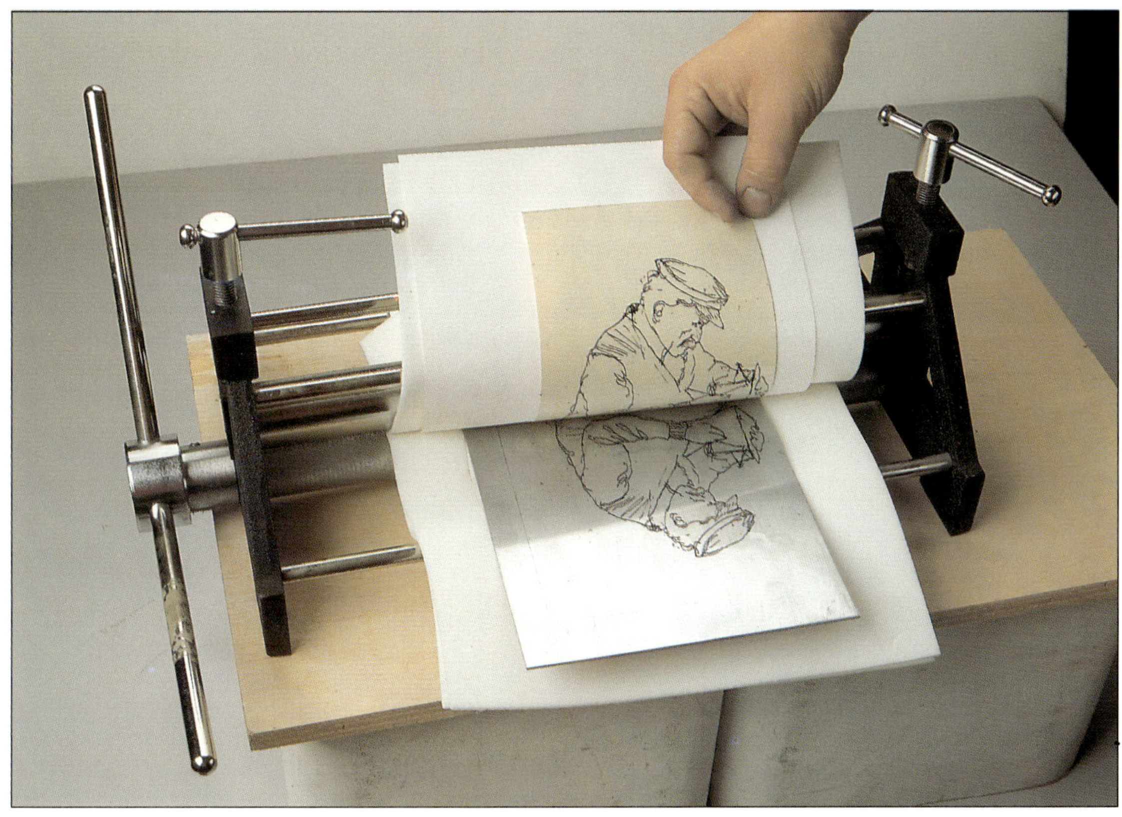

prepared to improvise as we go. This was a customary practice of Pablo Picasso, who, although very skilled at this technique, was, like any mortal, not infallible. Picasso's corrections were so clear and interesting that it scarcely mattered that they were the result of his own mistakes.

If, when drawing a line, our hand runs away with itself and prolongs the line unnecessarily, we can either try to correct it or turn it into something else—either a new line or perhaps a shading that will give more body to a figure.

As can be seen, we are not giving a step-by-step guide to the drypoint engraving shown in the illustrations since it is unlikely that your drawing will be identical to ours. Drypoint engraving is an interesting challenge, and is worth trying.

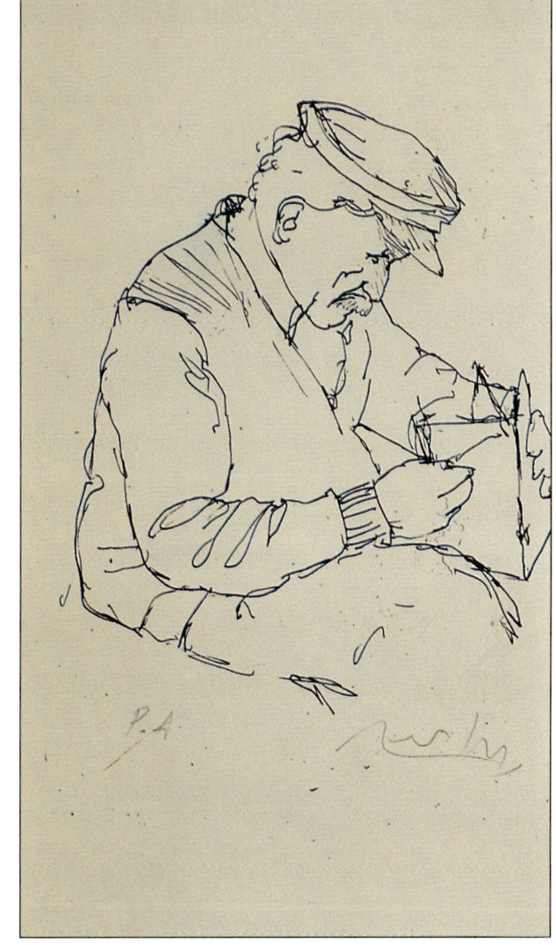

This is the result of a good impression. As you can see, hardly any burr has remained on the lines, due to the fact that we made gentle incisions that have not raised the metal.

1. Inking and the press

As explained at the beginning of this chapter, engraving in any form is a method of technical reproduction, situated somewhere between publishing and an artist's original work. If we stick to this definition, therefore, we must obviously include the reproduction of the plate we have just produced. In general, it is extremely difficult to have an etching press at home, since they are particularly expensive and heavy. But there are workshops where, for a modest charge, we can print our plate. Another option would be to join one of the many fine arts societies, which generally have their own printing workshops that we would be able to use without any problem. The latter option is more attractive than the former because of the greater freedom that these societies allow.

With our clean, prepared plate, we are now ready to pull the first proofs; for this we will need printing ink, printing paper, blotting paper, tarlatan or linen rags that don't leave any fluff, solvent, newspaper, inking spatula, and felt to act as a cushion for the paper and the plate.

The inking of the plate is carried out as follows: With the aid of a spatula, we deposit a certain amount of ink on a sheet of glass or other perfectly smooth surface. At the same time, we take a small wad of tarlatan and dab it over the inked surface so as to impregnate it with ink. Holding the ball of tarlatan in our fingers, we take it over to the plate and rub the plate firmly enough for the ink to penetrate into each and every one of the lines we have incised.

The illustration shows the materials we will need for producing an etching. With this method, the use of acid is essential and, as in every engraving technique, a press is also necessary.

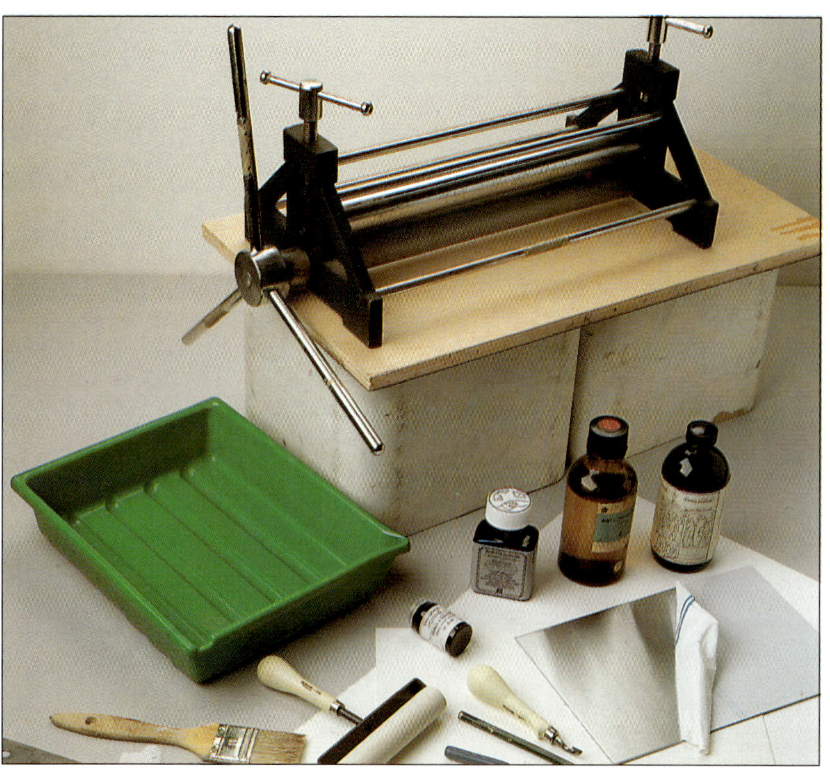

On completing this inking operation, we must scrupulously remove any trace of ink from the surface. For this we use newspaper, rubbing it horizontally over the surface and repeating the operation as often as necessary. When the plate has been cleaned, we wipe it with a white cotton rag; this will certainly show us whether or not the plate is perfectly clean, for the only ink remaining will be in the furrows we have drawn with the needles. As you can see, the process is exactly the opposite to the one used for linocuts. In the linocut, as you will remember, the ink remained on the uncut surface; with drypoint, it penetrates the incised furrows.

2. Printing

The printing process is as follows: After dampening the paper to be printed, as we did at the beginning of this chapter, we place it on a few sheets of blotting paper to draw off the excess water. We must make sure that the paper is damp, since the moistened fibers become slightly spongy and, when pressure is applied, they penetrate the ink-filled lines and absorb the ink.

After placing the plate on the bed of the press on top of a piece of clean newspaper, we pick up the sheet of printing paper—using two strips of paper to avoid accidentally marking it—and place it on the backing sheet, leaving the plate between the two sheets. We then carefully lower the felt blanket, smoothing it out to prevent any possible creases. Finally, regulating the pressure of the press, we pass it over the plate. Then we lift the blankets and, again using two strips of paper, carefully remove the printed proof and check the result. This operation is repeated for each print we want to make.

We have now made the first proofs and corrected a few details with the aid of the drypoint needle. Each time we have had to ink and clean the plate, to ensure that the whole edition is of similar quality from the first to the last print. Each of the prints pulled should be laid out to dry naturally. When they have all dried, we lay them one on top of the other with a sheet of sulphurized paper between each and place them all under uniform pressure to flatten them. Needless to say, they should be placed in order so that we can number them correctly.

One word of advice: When inking the plate it is advisable to warm it slightly first so that the ink runs more easily over the surface.

3. The printing ink

If we like, we can make our own printing ink. It is an easy process and will notably reduce the costs of the engraving. All we need is black pigment and raw linseed oil.

We mix them together, grinding the pigment on a smooth, hard surface until we get a soft, creamy consistency. Transfer the ink with a flat, wide spatula to metal or plastic jars with an airtight seal or screw top.

4. Etching

As we have mentioned earlier, this method involves biting away the metal with a corrosive acid. The plate is covered with a resistant material, or ground, so that not all of it is bitten. The parts that are not to be touched by the acid must be covered completely. This can be done in many ways, either by painting on the ground or—and this is easier—simply by covering the area with plastic adhesive tape.

The items we will need for making an etching are as follows: a gas lighter to warm the plate, metal polish, etching varnish or beeswax, asphalt, powdered wax (for making the hard ground), and etching acids.

The etching acids must be handled with great care as they can cause serious burns. Various types of acid may be used. For copper or zinc we will use either ferric chloride or nitric acid. If we use nitric acid, we mix ten parts of water with one part of nitric acid; if we want a weaker solution, it will be twenty parts of water to one of acid.

If we want to etch on copper, the proportion would be ten parts of water and five of acid.

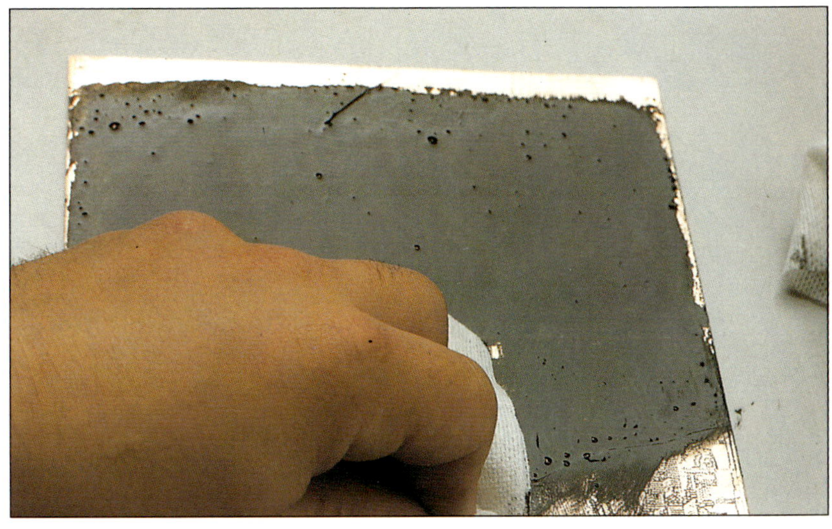

First, we must apply the resist, also known as the "ground," to the plate. After cleaning the plate properly to remove any traces of grease, we give it one or two coats of etching varnish.

Copper, zinc, iron—which to use?

We spoke earlier of the different characteristics of the metals and said that each produces different results, copper being the finest and the one that produces the purest blacks and whites. We should add that a great many different effects can be obtained with a copper plate. Zinc is perhaps the intermediate material as far as hardness is concerned; fully malleable and much appreciated for etching, it does not perhaps allow the same degree of subtlety as copper. We can also etch on iron plates. These do not give perfect whites for the surface of an iron plate is slightly rough and therefore difficult to clean. The effect produced by an iron-plate etching will be that of a large grayish surface with whatever designs we have made on it.

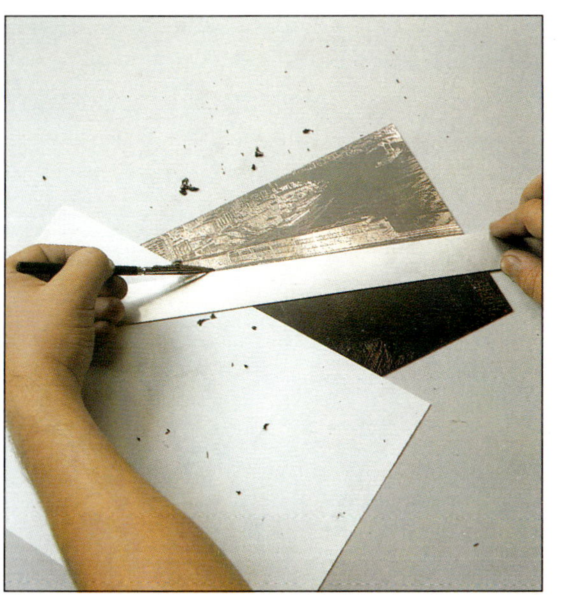

We place our model on the plate and with the aid of tools for removing the varnish, such as a ruling pen, punch, burin, etc., we work on the surface of the plate, removing part of the resist. Where there is no resist, the acid will bite into the metal, producing the lines in which the ink will be deposited.

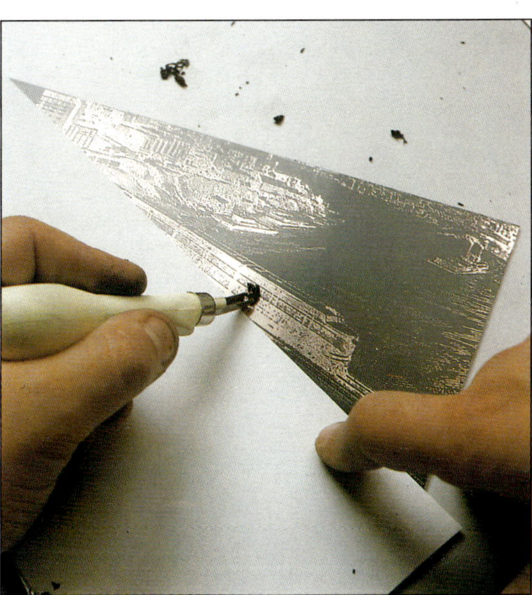

We remove areas of varnish where we want the acid to bite. The areas that are to contain the blacks must be perfectly clean.

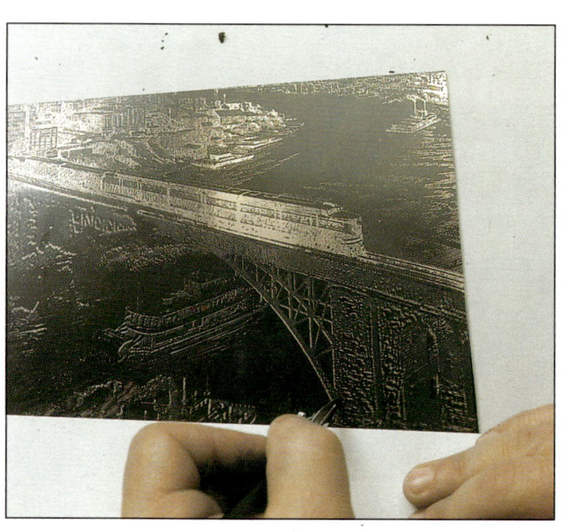

We continue in the same way until the drawing is complete. If we make a mistake, we can simply cover the line again with varnish.

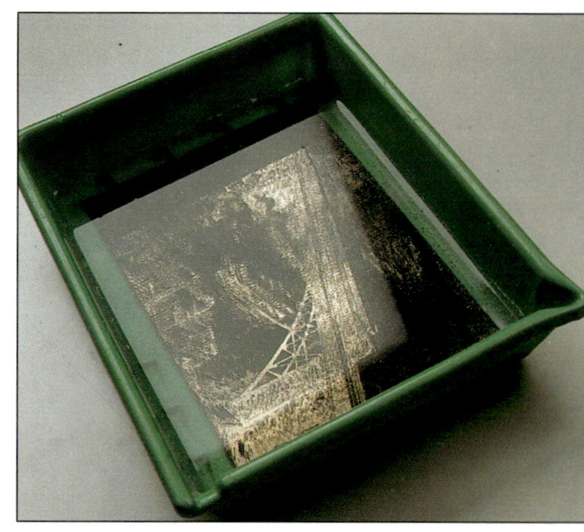

We place the plate in the acid bath. The degree to which the plate is bitten by the acid will depend on the strength of the solution, the length of time it is immersed, and the temperature.

5. Cleaning the plate

Before starting to prepare the plate, we must thoroughly clean it in order to remove any traces of grease. For this we will use plaster of Paris and ammonia, rinsing it off with water and drying it with a soft cotton cloth.

We will generally find that etching plates have one side covered with a sheet of transparent or colored plastic film; this is to stop it from being bitten when we place it in the acid bath. If the plate has no such isolating film, it doesn't matter, because we can cover this side with plastic adhesive tape. One small but important point: Since we have to warm the plate in order to apply the hard or soft ground (depending on our preferences as etchers), we should remove the plastic film and replace it when the plate has cooled down.

After taking the plate from the bath, we wash it with water and remove the varnish with solvent, eliminating any remains with a clean dry cloth.

6. Etching varnish, hard ground and soft ground

The plate we are going to use for our etching must above all have every part that is not to be bitten by the acid completely covered. There are plenty of methods of protection available; one is etching varnish, a type of varnish marketed by most manufacturers of artists' materials that is easy to apply. It is spread directly onto the cold plate with a paintbrush so as to cover it completely. This varnish is fairly quick-drying and is an effective ground, making it very popular.

Another type of ground or resist that is made by hand is what is known as hard ground. It acts in a similar way to varnish since it covers the plate, but it is applied with a leather roller and the plate must first be warmed. It is produced as follows: Take two parts of pure beeswax, two parts of asphalt, and one part of powdered resin. (All these materials can be found in hardware stores.) Melt the wax in a metal receptacle and gradually add the other ingredients, stirring slowly until a homogenous mixture is obtained. As soon as it has cooled, we form small balls with our hands, the size of Ping-Pong balls, and store them in a can or similar container. This mixture is applied to a plate that has been warmed sufficiently to melt it, but without burning it. We dab the ball over the surface of the plate and spread it with the leather roller; if we were to use a cork roller, we would risk it being spoiled by the heat.

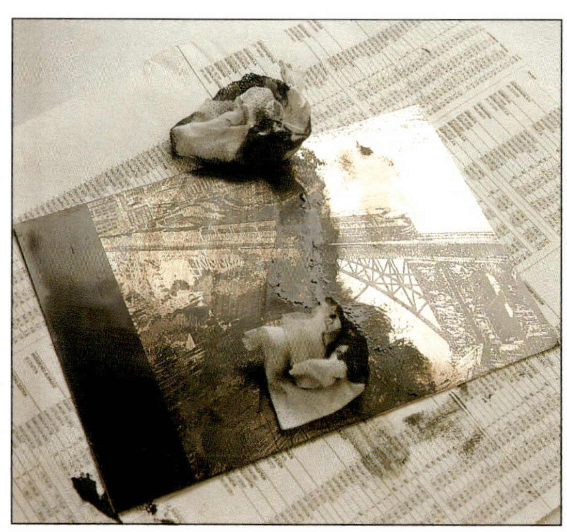

The inking and printing is done in the same way as with drypoint. With the aid of a piece of tarlatan, we cover the entire surface of the plate with ink and then clean it off so that the ink remains solely in the furrows produced by the acid.

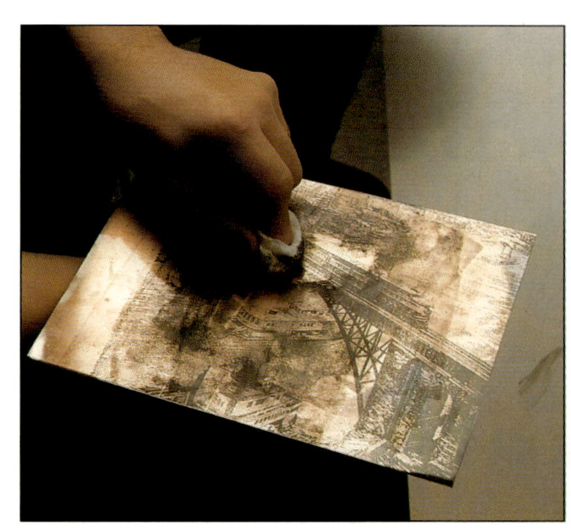

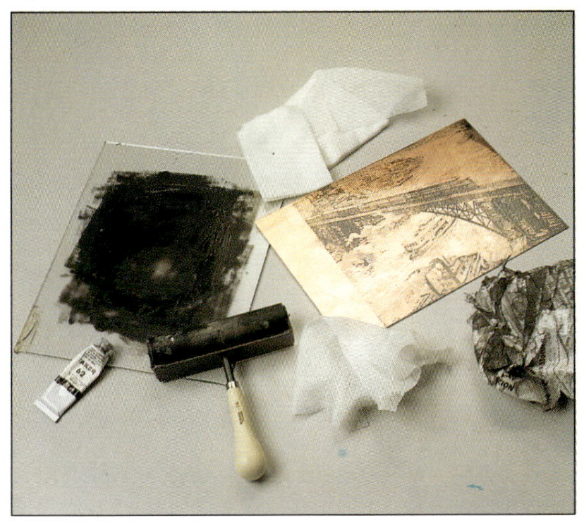

The fully inked plate together with the materials we have used. The result is the negative of our model, since the ink contained in the incised lines will be deposited on the paper as a mirror image.

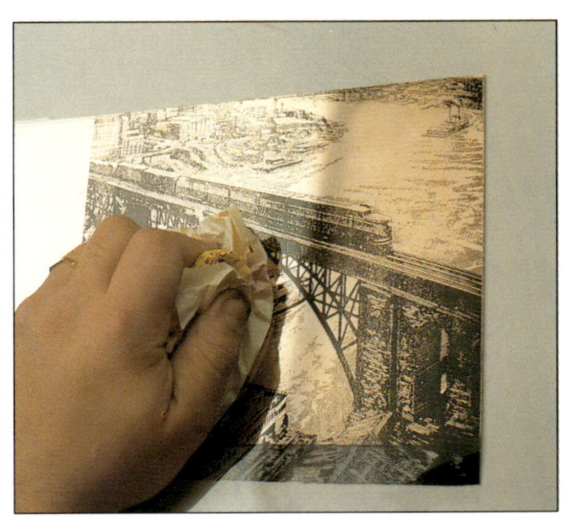

Cleaning the plate properly is essential for the correct printing of the final result. Any marks on the plate will be reproduced exactly on the paper.

When the plate cools, the surface will be hard and acid-resistant, and we can therefore work on it with punches and needles of varying sizes, uncovering those parts of the metal that are to be bitten by the acid.

The other method we have mentioned is to make a soft ground, which is easily worked on by laying a sheet of paper on it and pressing on the paper to lift off the ground adhering to it. Work produced with this type of soft ground generally gives very pleasing, spontaneous results.

The soft ground can be made by hand, like the hard ground, but this time the method is as follows: We will need to add two further parts of animal fat to the hard ground mixture, which will make it much less stable and more delicate. It is applied in the same way as the hard ground, but we must take particular care in doing so because any friction would be enough to mark the ground. We can work in several ways on the soft ground, one of which is to add different items to give it a particular texture, such as threads, fabrics, wire mesh, etc.—anything with a texture that can be reproduced. We then place a sheet of waxed paper, or paper coated with some other grease-resistant material, on top of the plate, and we put this in the press. The pressure will impress the items on the plate. Upon removing these very carefully, we will also remove the part of the ground adhering to them, thus leaving their imprint on the plate. We then carefully immerse the plate in the acid, as explained below, and obtain the negative of the objects we placed on it; the acid will have bitten into the unprotected areas.

Another way of working with soft ground would be to place a sheet of paper on the plate and draw directly on it with a pencil. The pressure will make the ground stick to the surface pressed or marked with the pencil, and on

The printing process will be the same as for etching. The pressure exerted between the plate and the paper will determine the cleanness of the line or the saturation of the ink.

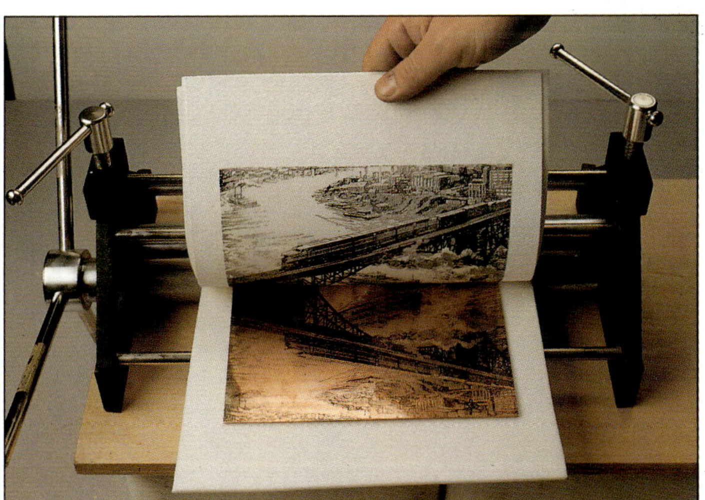

On completion of the process, we can consider the impression to be correct if the lines are sharp and the intensity of the black is good.

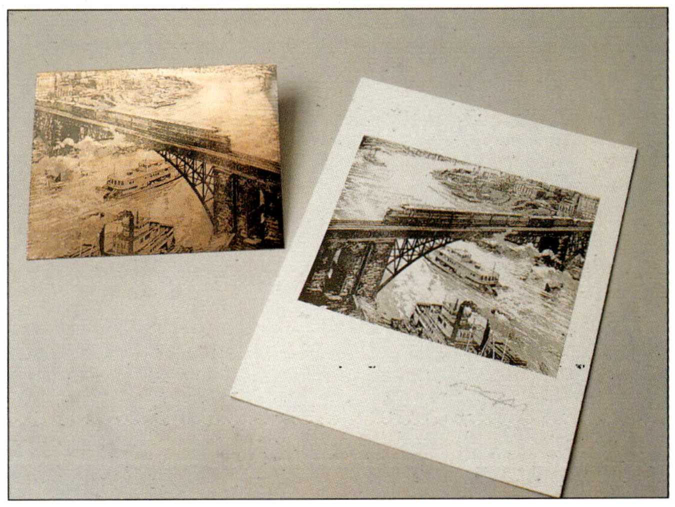

removing the paper only the drawn lines will lift off.

7. Drawing on the plate: The acid solution

Contrary to working with drypoint, when using an etching plate we do not need to cut into the plate ourselves since this is done by the nitric acid in the proportion indicated above. Our drawing can be made simply with a blunt spike, a sewing needle, or any other article that can scratch the hard surface without cutting into the metal. As with drypoint, we can do fine hatching and also thick lines covering large inked areas. Remember that we have to place the plate in the acid, and therefore any exposed area of the metal will be unavoidably bitten and marked. For this reason it is advisable to continually check the ground before putting the plate in the nitric acid solution. Note that the edges of the plate must also be protected with varnish or hard ground.

The acid should be kept in properly labelled containers, and when handling the solution in water we should do so wearing gloves and in a well-ventilated area to avoid toxic fumes. We can use plastic trays such as those used for photography and, for measuring, a small plastic tumbler is more than sufficient although a measuring receptacle is always more practical and accurate.

The time required for the acid to etch the plate is never precise. It can vary according to the temperature and to the acid itself, but we can more or less calculate that a strong nitric acid solution will take around five or six minutes to etch the plate, whereas a weak solution will be much slower-acting and will probably take around ten minutes.

Shortly after the plate is immersed in the acid, bubbles will form that delay the biting. These can be easily removed with a paintbrush. After the necessary time has elapsed, we extract the etched plate—wearing rubber gloves—and wash it under running water to remove all possible traces of acid. Finally, we dry the plate and, using a rag soaked with solvent (turpentine or alcohol), clean it thoroughly. All that remains then is to take a clean cloth to remove any traces of solvent.

Having completed all these preliminary operations, we can now ink the plate and take the first proofs, following the same process as that described earlier for drypoint engraving.

The final result can be seen below: We have achieved a clean line and intense blacks. This is a long, laborious process that requires meticulous care in timing the biting of the plate by the acid. Reproduction of the plate involves cleaning and re-inking it for each print. Although the entire process requires immense patience, it gives excellent results when carried out correctly.

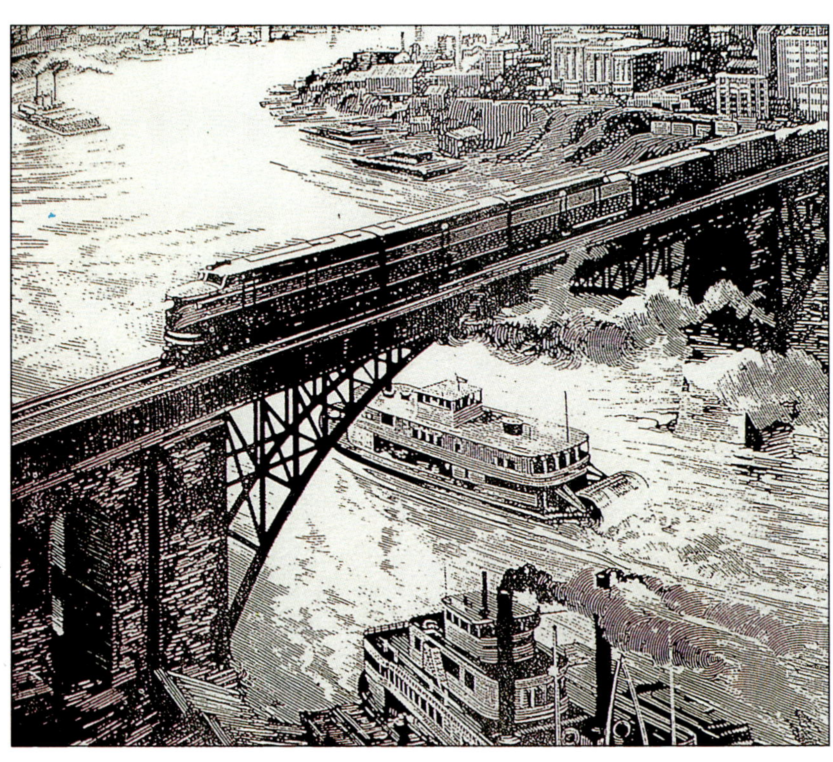

Airbrush painting

lever
air control
paint control

External atomization airbrushes and mouth atomizers are based on the same principle: When a vertical tube is submerged in a paint pot, the air pressure sucks up the liquid, which is pulverized and pushed forward.

needle-setting screw
lever
button
nozzle
valve
nozzle with needle
tank

The airbrush is a tool that allows painting by means of a flow of pulverized, or atomized, colored liquid. The control of this flow largely depends on the pressure of the air, the consistency of the paint, and the distance between the airbrush and the surface that is being painted. There are external atomization airbrushes, in which the air-paint mix takes place outside the device, and internal atomization airbrushes in which the mix takes place within the airbrush itself.

These are the sort most airbrush artists work with. This chapter deals with airbrush painting: materials, colors, supports, and tricks of the trade, as well as a series of exercises that we hope will provide you with the basics to get started in the popular world of airbrush art.

There are three basic types of internal atomization airbrushes:

• *Single action airbrushes.* These have a lever that only controls air entry and provides no direct control over color, so the amount of atomized paint is entirely dependent on the airflow that sucks it in. Since this is the cheapest type, we recommend it for beginning airbrush artists.

• *Double action airbrushes.* These models have more functions. The lever controls both the incoming air and the position of the needle that controls the flow of liquid, so that the amount of paint leaving the nozzle is always directly proportional to the airflow that atomizes it. These high-precision instruments are very practical. They are recommended for experienced beginners or professionals.

• *Independent double action airbrushes.* These are the most versatile and sophisticated types. The lever has two movements that control both the airflow and paint flow, together or separately. You can, for instance, project only air and use the lever to add a gradual flow of paint. This sort of airbrush is more difficult to master than the others; it is generally used only by experienced professionals.

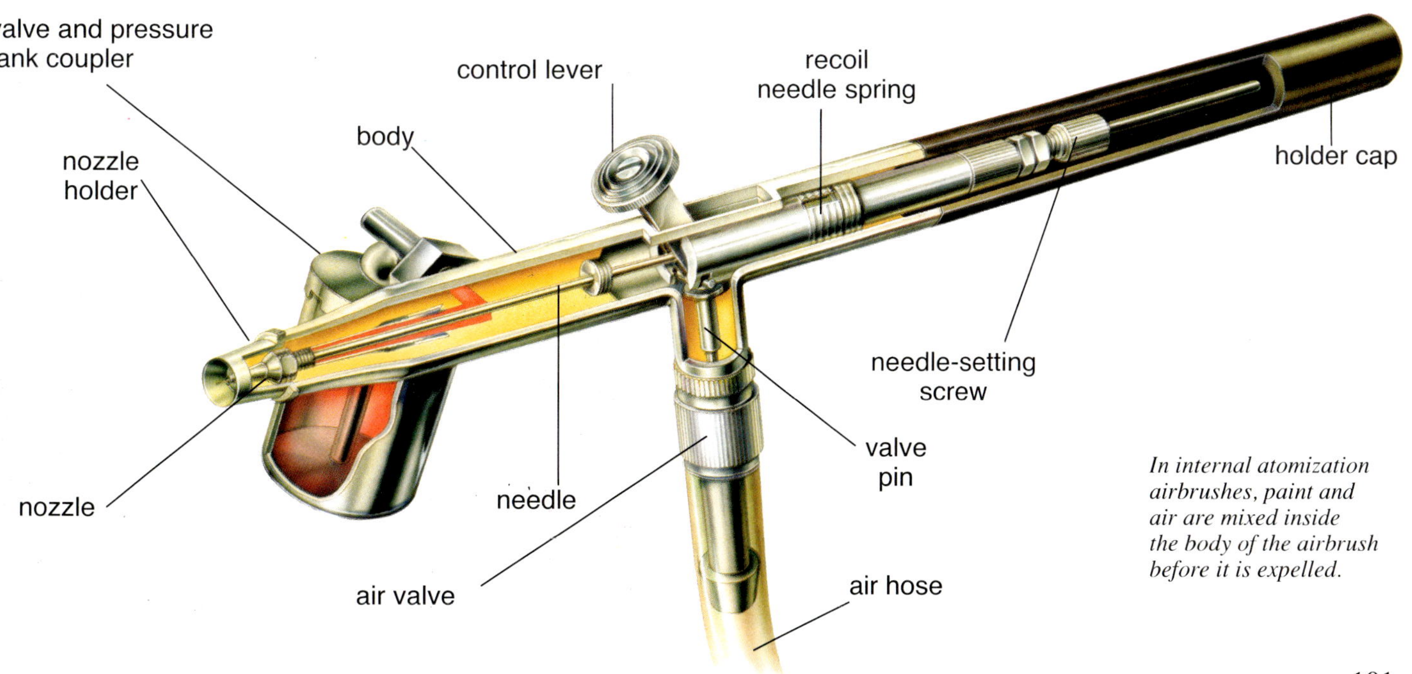

In internal atomization airbrushes, paint and air are mixed inside the body of the airbrush before it is expelled.

Air supply

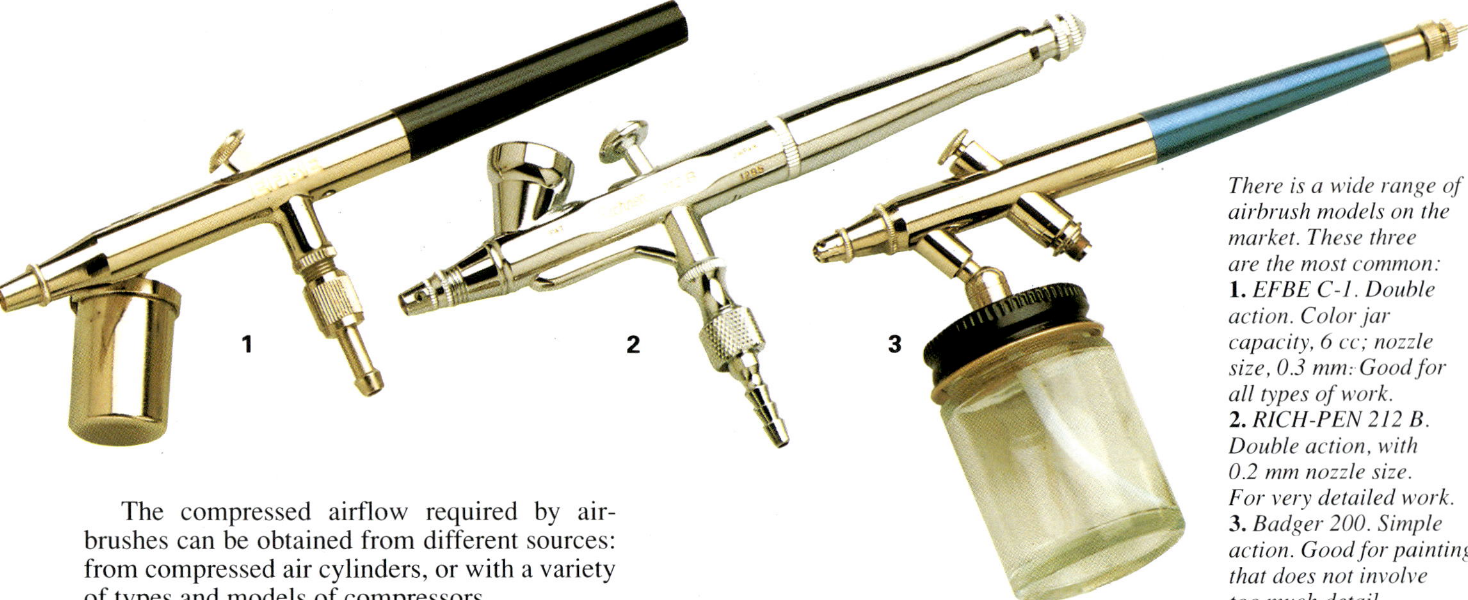

There is a wide range of airbrush models on the market. These three are the most common:
1. *EFBE C-1. Double action. Color jar capacity, 6 cc; nozzle size, 0.3 mm: Good for all types of work.*
2. *RICH-PEN 212 B. Double action, with 0.2 mm nozzle size. For very detailed work.*
3. *Badger 200. Simple action. Good for painting that does not involve too much detail.*

The compressed airflow required by airbrushes can be obtained from different sources: from compressed air cylinders, or with a variety of types and models of compressors.

Compressed air cylinders

Air cylinders are the traditional source of compressed air for airbrush painting and are still used in industrial airbrush workshops. They provide a continuous airflow, controlled by a pressure gauge. They are quiet and do not require an energy source.

There are disadvantages to air cylinders, however; they tend to run out suddenly and, once empty, you'll need to get a full one from your supplier.

Air cans

These small cylinders resemble common aerosol spray cans. They are very handy for beginners and for artists who use the airbrush only occasionally. Their main disadvantage is that they tend to gradually lose pressure.

Compressors

These devices take in atmospheric air, compress it to the appropriate pressure, and release it. Depending on their characteristics, compressors fall into two main groups:

- *Compressors with diaphragms.* These units take in air though an inlet conduit and compress it in an interior chamber, expelling it immediately through another conduit.
- *Compressors with reservoirs.* These units come with a tank in which compressed air is stored.

4. *20 Plus. Tubular 0.4 gallon (1.5 L) capacity reservoir; produces an air flow of 5.3 gallons (20 L) per minute.*
5. *AS 30. A 2.6 gallon (10 L) reservoir with a 30/1 min. airflow.*

6. *Air can containing 500 cc of propellant.*
7. *Compressed air cylinder with a gauge, 1.3 gallons (5 L) capacity.*

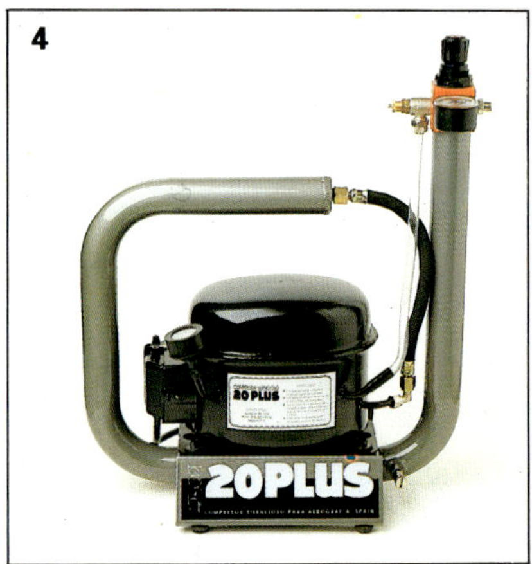

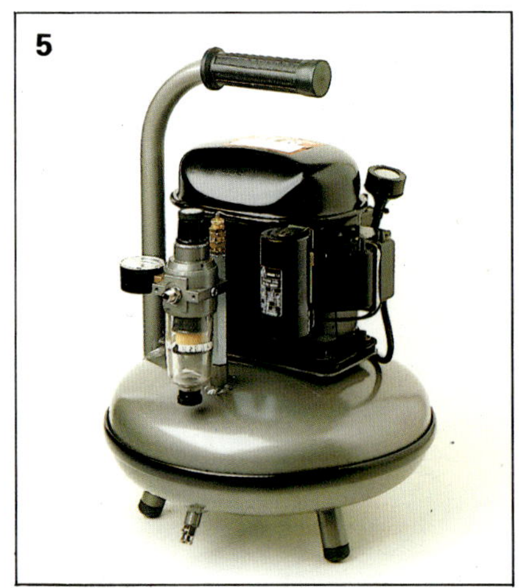

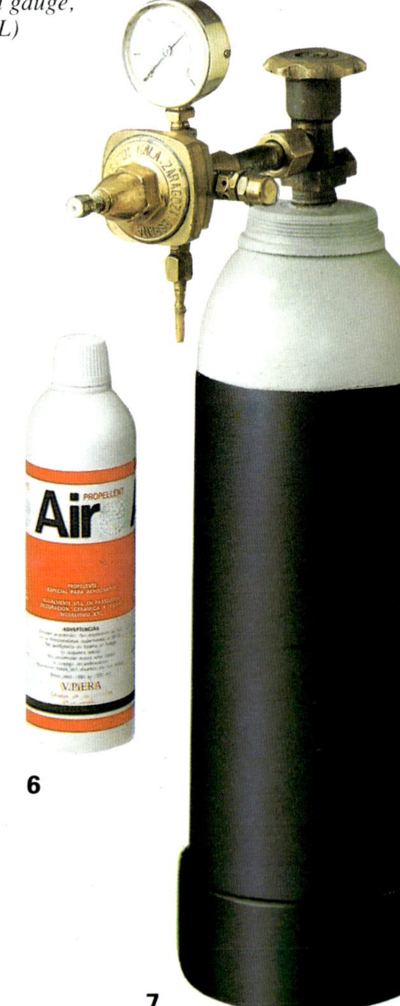

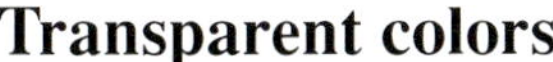

Transparent colors

As with any other pictorial medium that makes use of transparent colors, artists must keep two main principles in mind:

• First, they must paint from "lesser to greater," beginning with the lighter tonalities and taking into account that both light versus shadow and color saturation will be obtained by applying successive coats.

• Second, they must avoid white pigments, although to get certain lights they can, now and then, take advantage of the opacity of gouache. Artists should use white paper to take advantage of its color.

Because of these demands, it is best to work on a very accurate drawing, one that offers a detailed layout of the placement of colors and whites.

The transparent colors available to the airbrush artist are:

• Traditional watercolor paints in tubes.

• Liquid watercolors.

• Liquid inks and special colors for airbrush painting.

Watercolor paints in tubes

These are still the best paints for airbrushing and the most convenient for beginners, since they are relatively inexpensive and rarely cause maintenance problems with the airbrush. Watercolor in tubes must be diluted in at least 50:50 water.

Liquid watercolors

These are ideal for airbrushing. They offer high luminosity and concentration and can be used directly from the pot or diluted in distilled water, especially if the tap water has a high concentration of lime. They come in a wide variety of color ranges and produce perfect mixes, without any apparent reduction in transparency.

Liquid inks

These are solutions pigmented with synthetic colors (anilines). Most are water soluble though one or two are alcohol-based. They come in matte colors or in bright, glossy shades. They are often used in design and illustration.

Special airbrush colors

Nontoxic acrylic solutions with a high concentration of pigment offer intense colors for the airbrush painter. These colors produce a notable transparent effect, and, on drying, are very resistant to water and light. These paints have a fine or ultrafine grain, so they won't clog the airbrush.

They come in either small pots of concentrated colors that have to be diluted or in larger containers that need no dilution. Although the standard solvent is distilled water, some brands provide special liquids for cleaning and diluting.

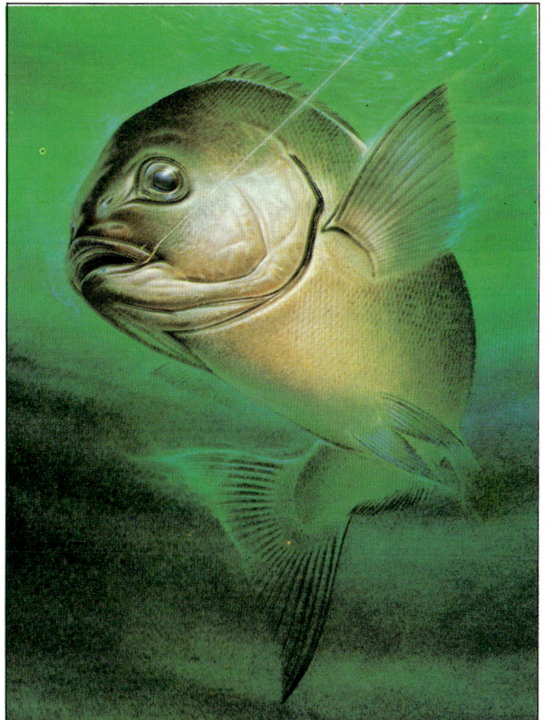

Left: An example of an airbrush painting with transparent colors. This work is by the Japanese artist Shiro Nishiguchi.

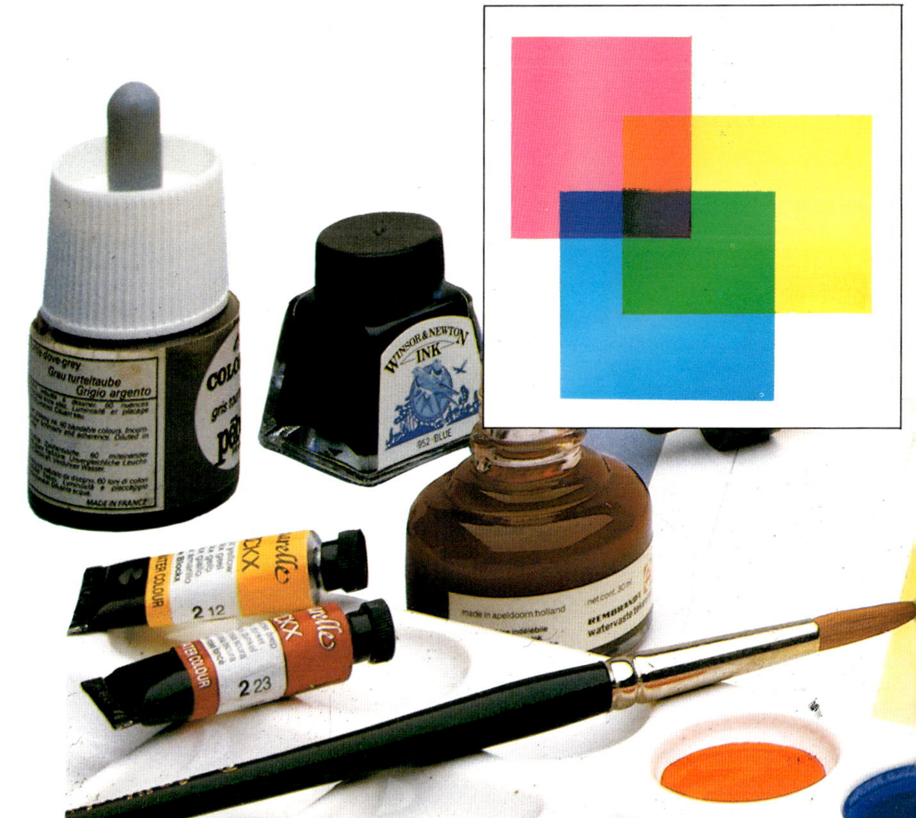

Below: A small collection of transparent airbrush materials: watercolor tubes, an ink pot, and special transparent colors with dropper.

These three primary colors obtained with inks demonstrate the optic possibilities of superimposing transparent colors.

Colors and supports

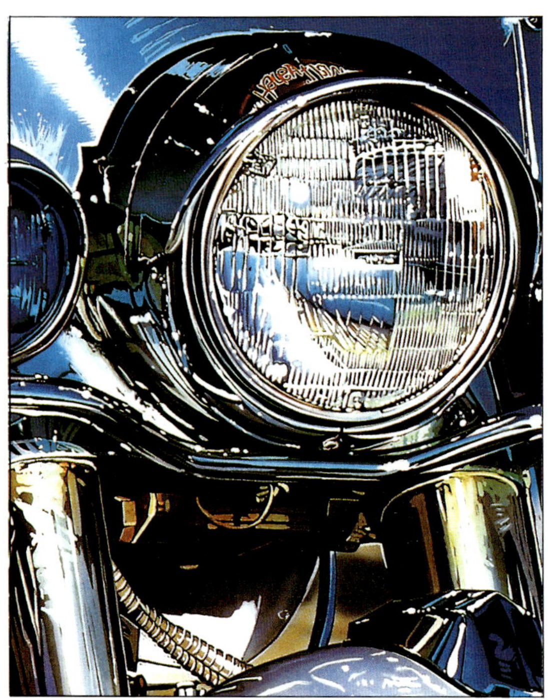

This illustration by Hideaki Kodama (detail of a Harley-Davidson motocycle) is a magnificent example of how to obtain shiny, bright, smooth color shading by the clever use of opaque and light colors on dark surfaces.

Opaque colors

All special colors made for airbrushing can be turned into opaque colors by simply using white in the mix.

There are, however, two very common types of opaque paint available: gouache and acrylic.

Gouache

Also called tempera, gouache is excellent for covering broad areas and touching up photographs. It comes in tubes or jars, and, because its consistency is pasty or creamy, it must be diluted with water to achieve the proper fluidity. A too-fluid gouache covers irregularly, but one that is thick will block the nozzle of the airbrush. Thus, it is essential to know when the gouache has just the right fluidity.

The coverage potential of each color must be taken into account; cadmium pigments, as well as emerald green and rose madder, create a certain transparency; when they overlap a dark background, it's advisable to add a bit of white.

Acrylic colors

These are classified into two groups: low-viscosity colors that can be diluted only in water, and high-viscosity paints to which a special solvent must be added.

Acrylic colors dry very quickly, leaving a hard, plastic film that is nonsoluble. It is necessary, therefore, to use a special liquid to clean the airbrush with every color change. Furthermore, when working on one picture for an extended time, the artist must add a special dry-retardant solution to the colors. The artist should also be aware that some of the components of acrylic colors are toxic, making it advisable to wear a protective mask when painting.

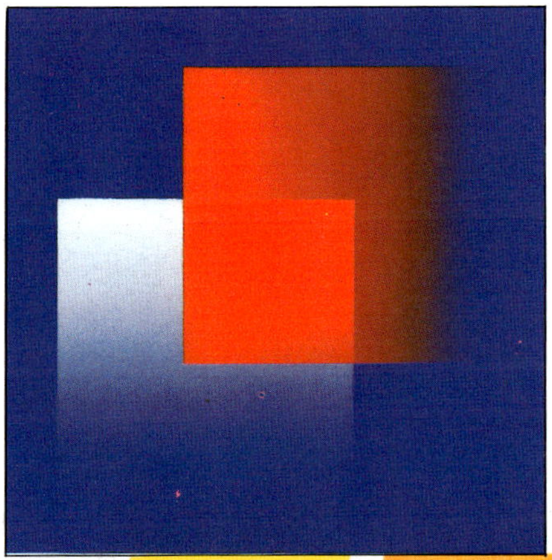

Surfaces obtained with consecutive sprays of an opaque paint, with light colors overlapping dark ones.

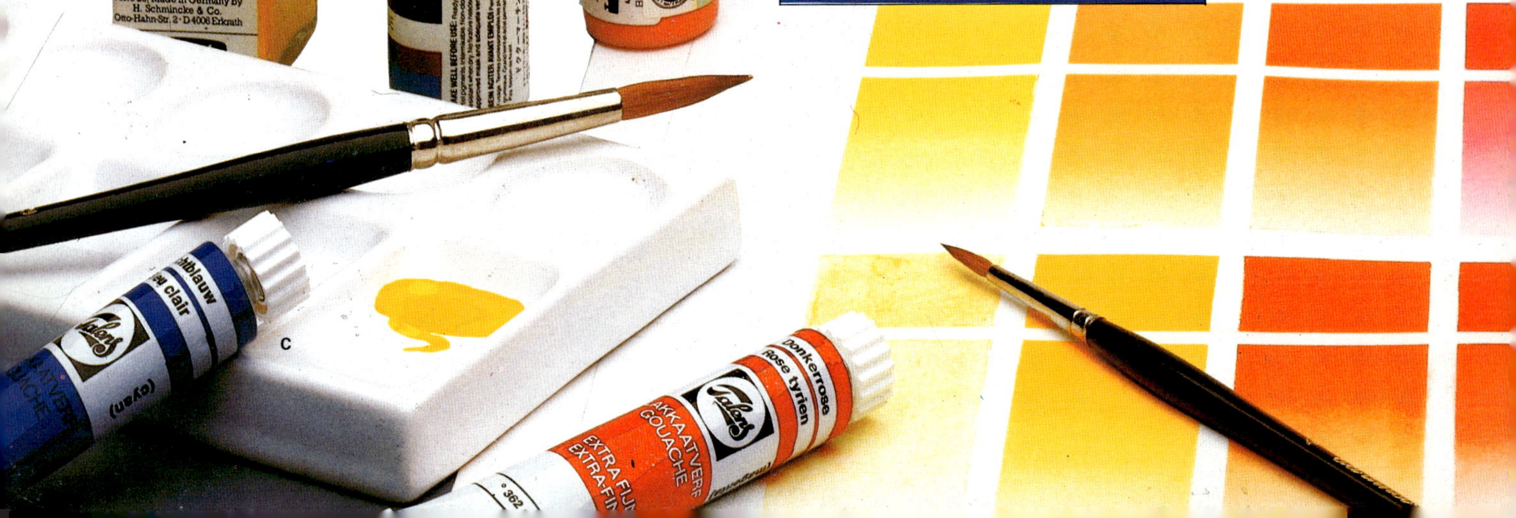

Below: A small sample of opaque colors for the airbrush, including two drop-bottles (a); a drop-bottle of fine-pigmentation paint designed for use with airbrush (b); and two tubes of gouache (c).

b

a

c

Supports

Airbrush painting can be executed on a wide variety of supports. In fact, any surface, provided it is properly prepared, can be airbrushed. On the other hand, when the work is of an artistic nature, the choice is somewhat more restricted.

Paper

Without a doubt, paper—or, more accurately, certain types of paper—is by far the most commonly used support for airbrush painting.

Particularly suitable are smooth-surfaced and coated papers, as well as paper manufactured especially for airbrushing.

Heavy stock—heavier than 300 g/m^2—is preferred since it tends not to warp. When the format is larger than DIN A4, it is best to set the sheet on a wooden board.

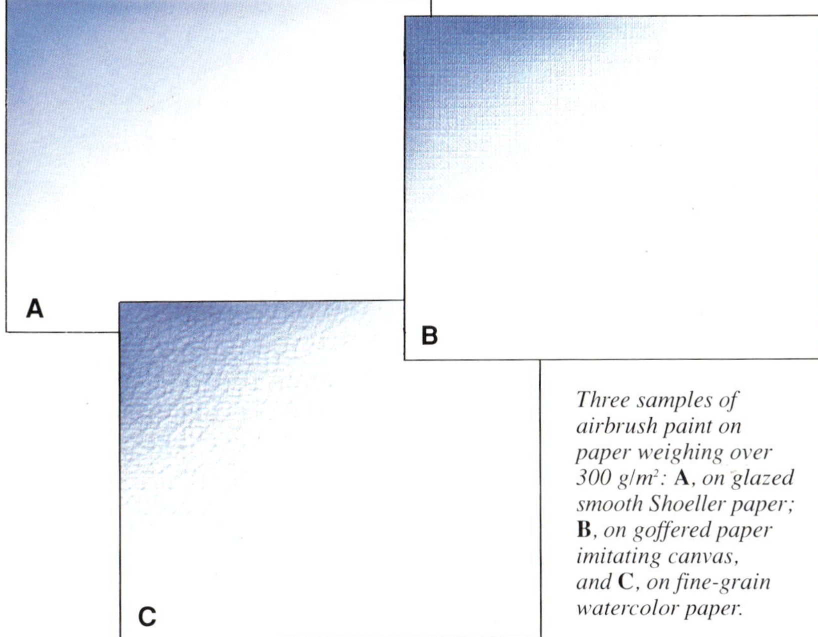

Three samples of airbrush paint on paper weighing over 300 g/m^2: **A**, *on glazed smooth Shoeller paper;* **B**, *on goffered paper imitating canvas, and* **C**, *on fine-grain watercolor paper.*

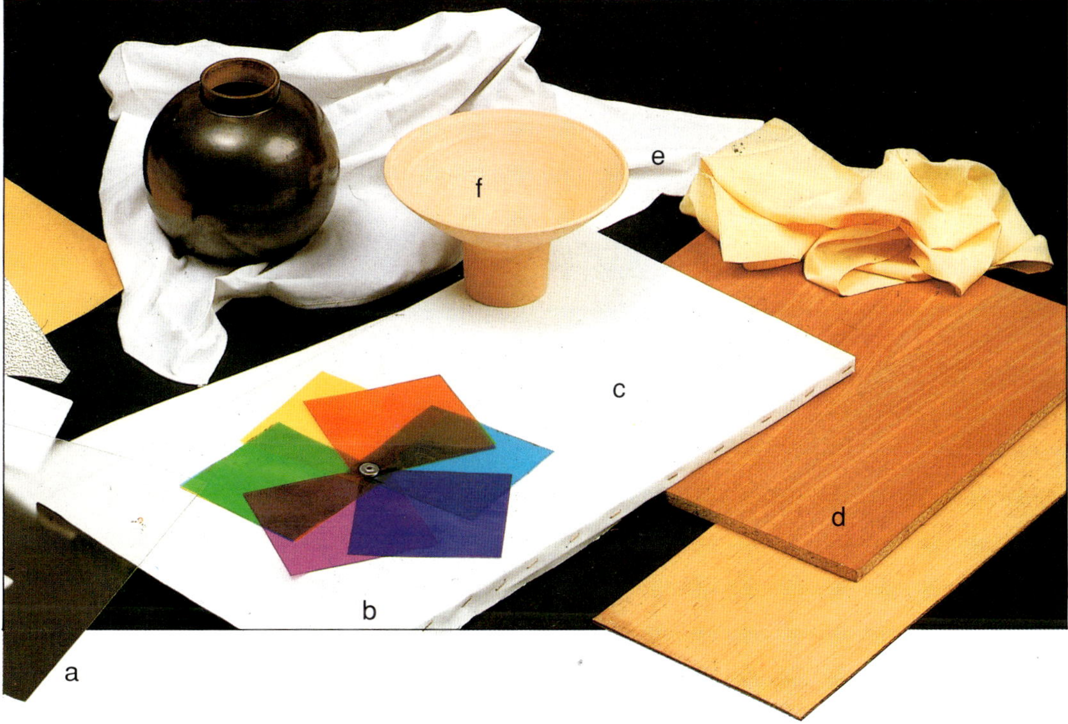

There is a wide variety of airbrushing supports. The choice of support depends on the type of work you want to do. Sometimes it is necessary to use special media, generally cellulosic paints and enamels: a, b, metals and plastics for making models; c, canvas mounted on a stretcher; d, wood for models and furniture; e, cloth used in the fashion field; ceramics, one fired in a kiln and the other enameled with a spray gun.

Photographic paper

In advertising, work is sometimes done directly on a photograph with either a matte or glossy finish. Since matte papers are generally thicker, they are more suitable for large-size works, because they maintain their rigidity and can be easily mounted.

Other supports

These include adequately primed and polished wooden boards and canvases on stretchers or mounted on cardboard. Acetate and glass make fine supports for airbrush works, provided you use the appropriate medium in each case.

Ceramic material and textiles are possible supports for the airbrush artist.

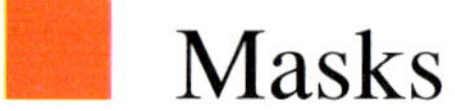

Masks

Types of masks

When we refer to *masks* in airbrush painting, we mean any element placed between the airbrush and the support in order to prevent paint from reaching certain parts of the work. Masks can either be mobile or fixed.

Fixed masks

Fixed masks are those that are attached to the paper or canvas. They are generally made of transparent adhesive film that covers the area to be protected, preventing color from seeping under it. Despite its high adhesiveness, the film comes loose easily when it's time to remove the mask without damaging the work. What's more, it is possible to draw on the film, making it the best mask for working on satin paper.

Polyester paper is another type of fixed mask. It can be cut to fit any shape and is applied with rubber cement, which can be removed without damaging the image. This type of mask is ideal for working on rough paper.

Mobile masks

Mobile masks are not attached to the support. They can be made of any material (paper, cardboard, absorbant cotton, dried leaves, etc.), or objects (rulers, technical drawing masks, even the artist's own hand, etc.) depending on your requirements.

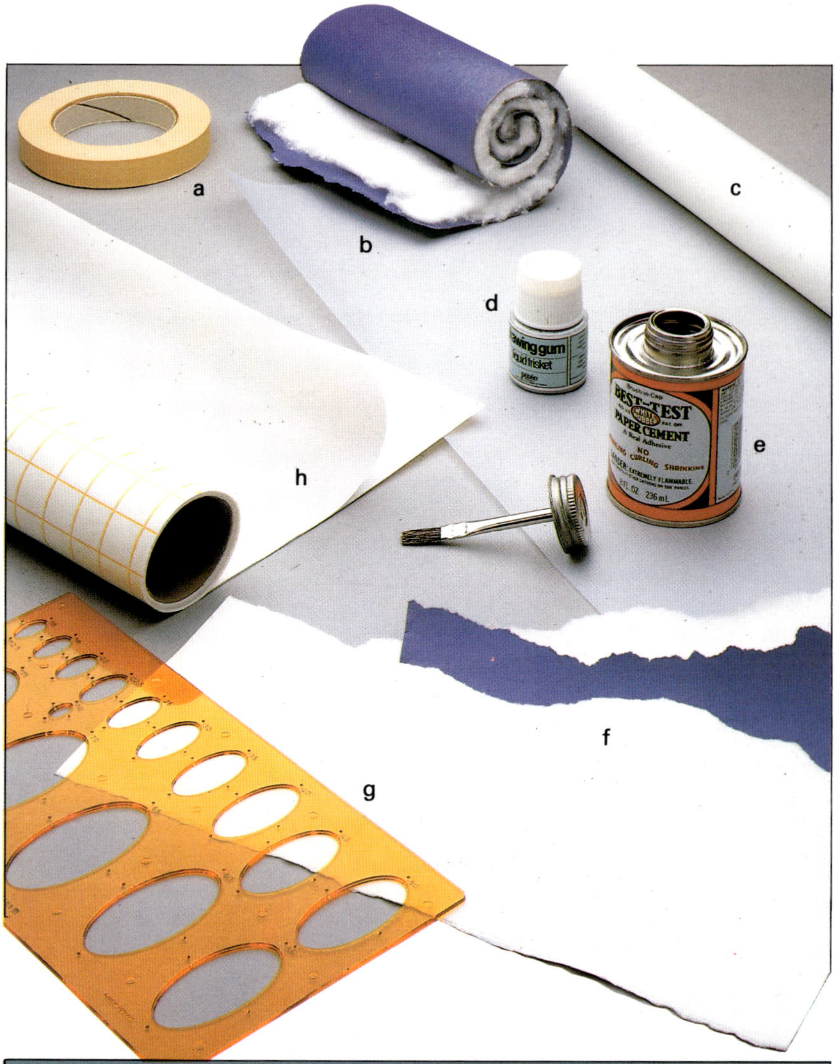

Top right: This illustration shows the most frequently used masking materials in airbrushing: adhesive tape for attaching masks to the support and creating margins (a), raw cotton, useful for masking clouds (b), polyester paper, used for fixed masks glued with liquid gum (c), masking fluid (d), a small tin of rubber cement (e), torn papers for use as mobile masks (f), templates for use as mobile masks (g), adhesive film for fixed masks (h).

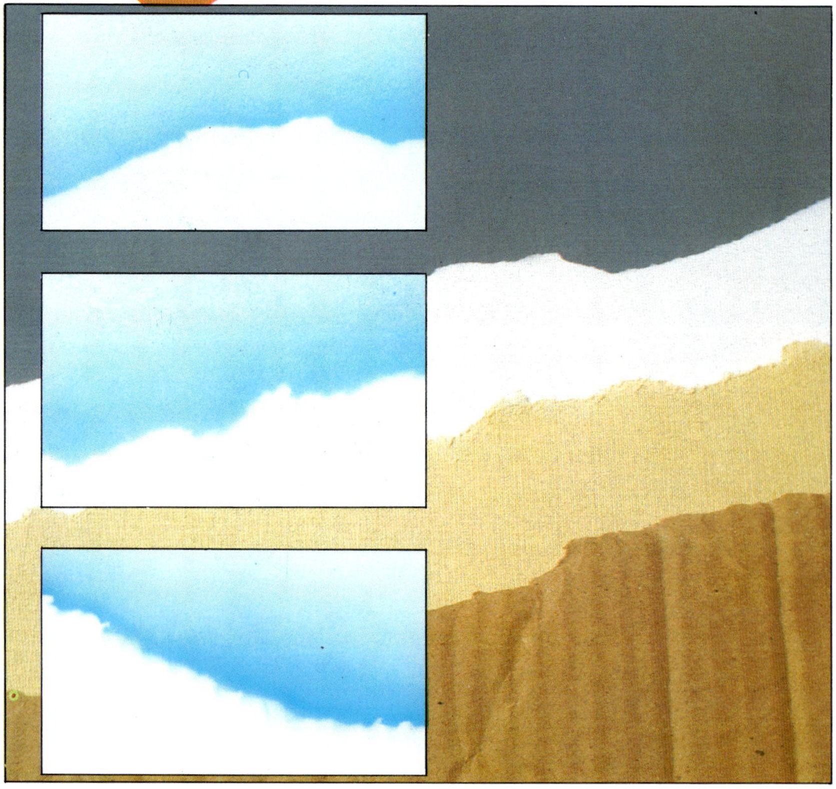

Right: Corrugated cardboard and similar types can be used to obtain effects like those shown here. The result depends on several factors; including the distance of the mask from the support, the movements of the airbrush and the angle at which it is applied, and the amount of spray used.

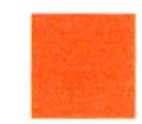

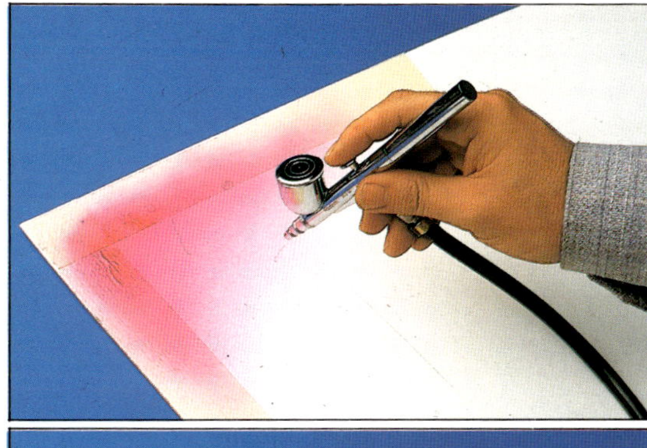

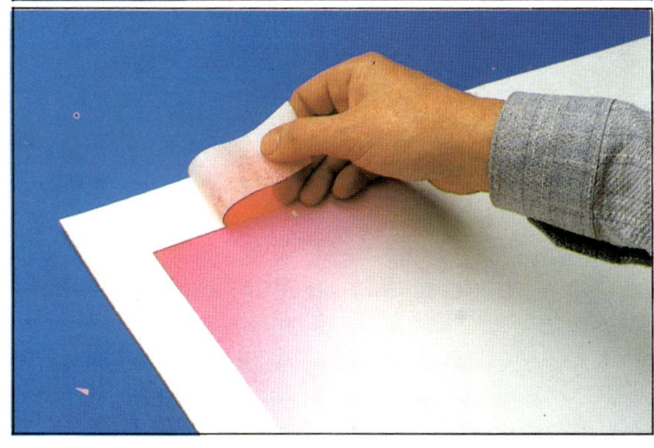

1. *Adhesive tape is first placed around the edges of the support to protect the white areas. When the tape is removed, the margins will be as white as they were at the start.*

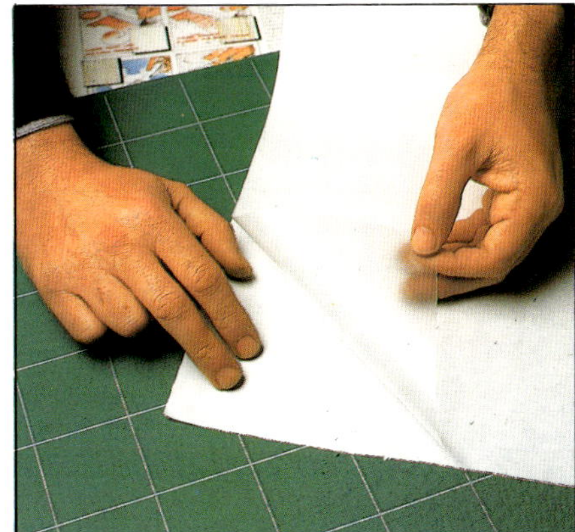

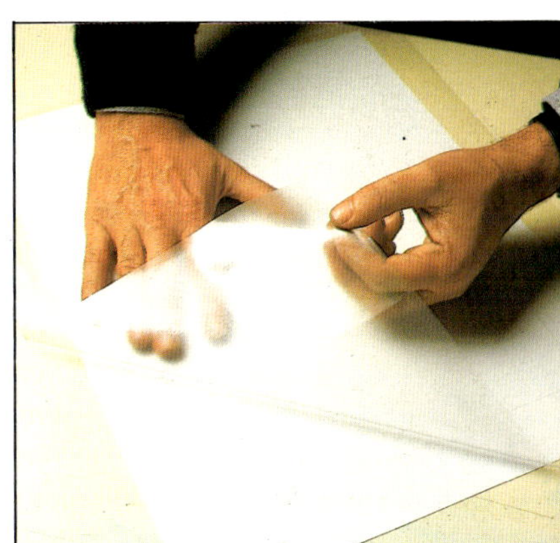

2. *The adhesive mask is a transparent film whose sticky side is protected by a strip of special paper that must be removed before it is applied to the support. In the second photograph, the adhesive paper is smoothed down by running your hand over it. This works well when the tape covers only a small area. When the masked areas are larger, it is best to use a ruler to smooth down the tape while it's being laid.*

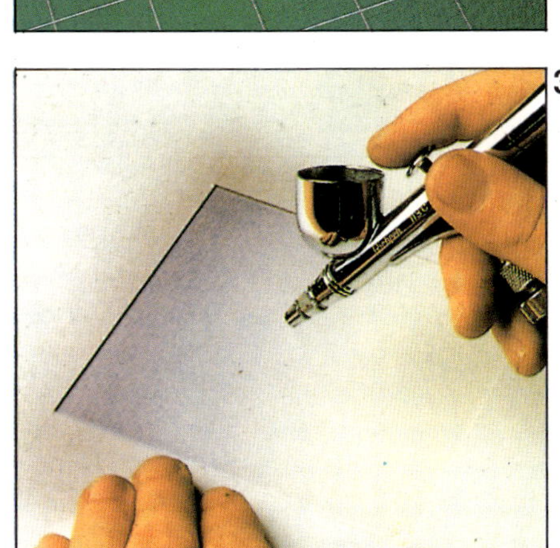

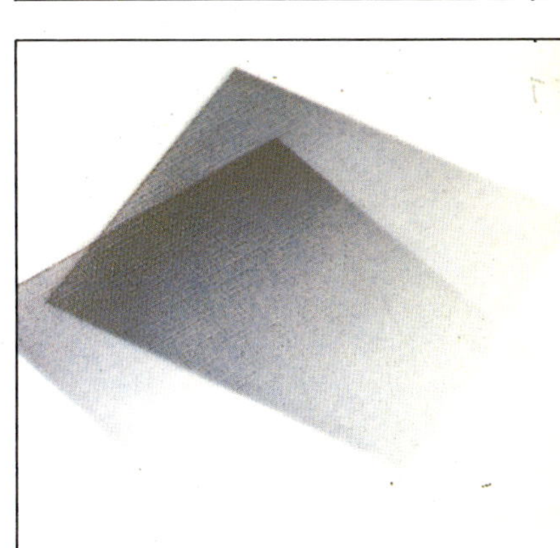

3. *As you can see in these two photographs, a rectangular-shaped paper mask is placed and superimposed over a previously airbrushed area to create different intensities of color.*

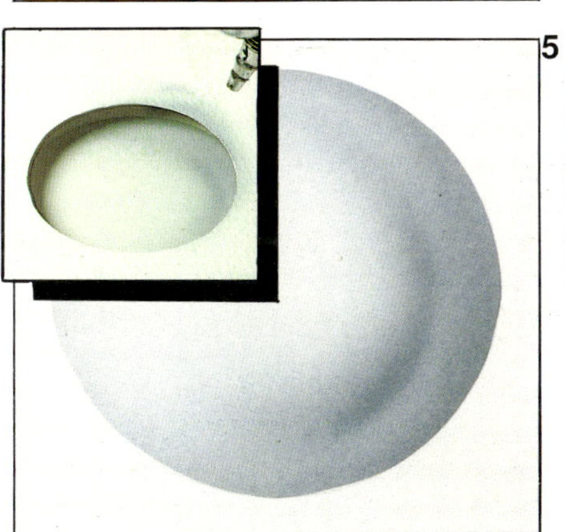

4. *The circle in this photo has been airbrushed using a circular mask. To paint the shadows, the mask is held slightly off the surface of the paper; it is moved closer to create darker shadows.*

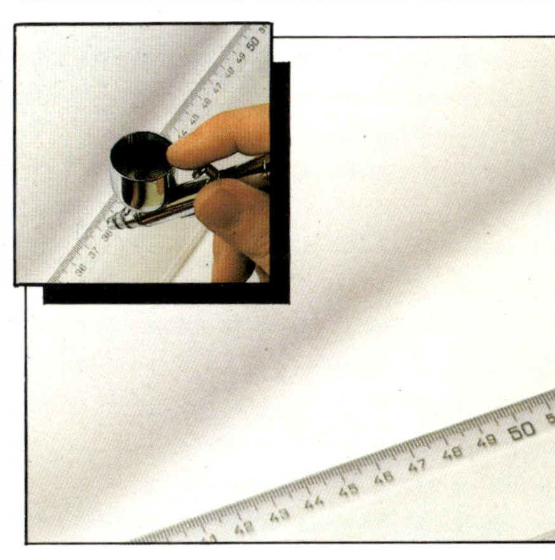

5. *A ruler is used to obtain gradations with a more or less straight edge. The farther away the ruler is placed from the paper, the less defined it will be, and vice versa.*

You can get many different results according to how you use the mobile mask. The nearer or farther away the mask is from the support (aerial masking), as well as the movement employed while spraying, allows you to obtain a wide, sometimes very surprising, range of gradation effects.

The liquid mask

This is a special solution that is applied with a brush in order to isolate small areas of the drawing. The liquid dries quickly and the resulting rubber coating it leaves can be easily removed.

Basic exercises

If the mastery of any pictorial medium requires a good previous apprenticeship, this is especially true in airbrush painting since the instrument employed is totally unrelated to any of the classic tools of drawing and painting.

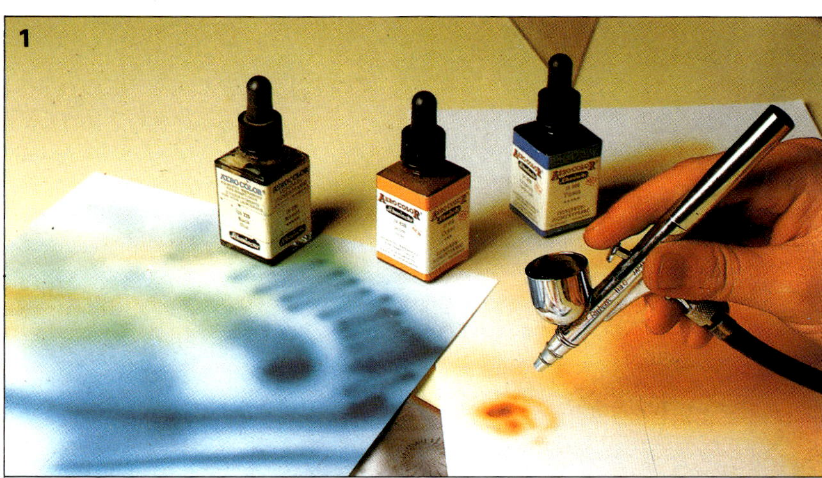

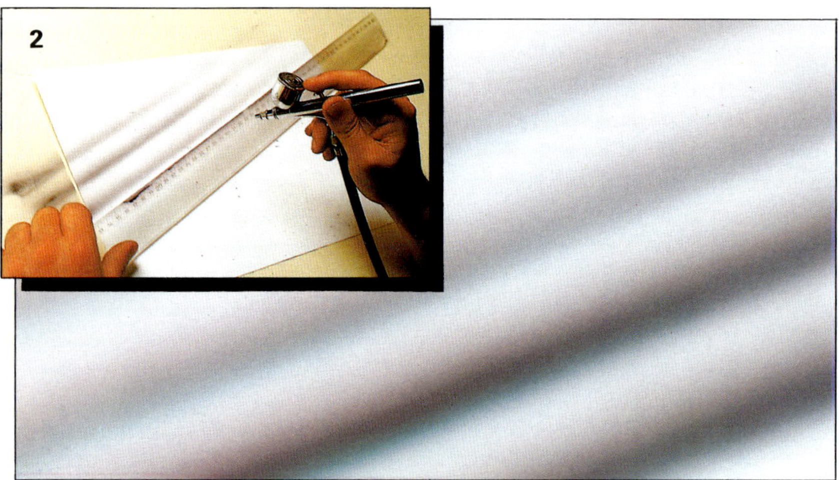

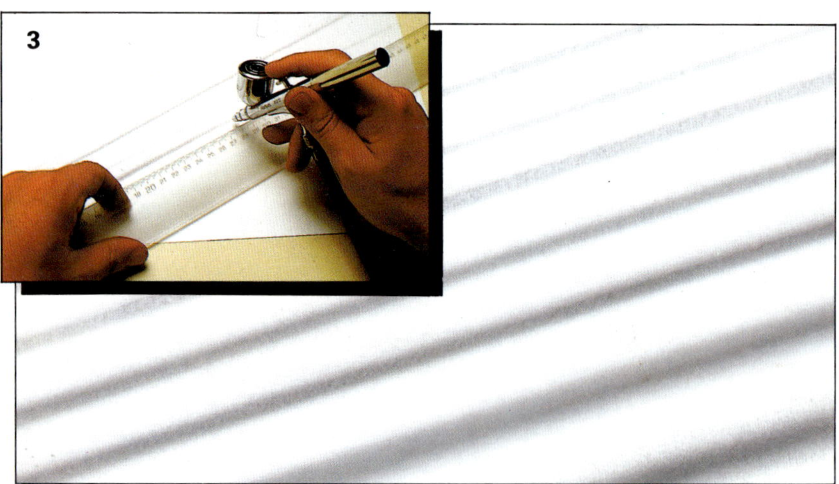

It is essential to acquire a command of the basic techniques. We must start by learning how to hold the airbrush as comfortably as we would hold a pencil or a brush. Before we begin thinking of ambitious compositions, it is necessary to learn to draw straight, curved, and wavy lines (fine, thick, and gradated), with the aid of a ruler, with a mobile mask, or simply with our hand.

Using an airbrush is similar to using a good brush, especially when painting straight or curved lines and uniform backgrounds. As a rule, the airbrush should be held between the thumb and index finger, which controls the spray-adjusting lever.

The following practical exercises using one color will give you an insight into the possibilities of this instrument for obtaining different types of lines and gradations.

1. As a rule, the airbrush should be held within the curve of the hand, supported by the thumb and with the index finger placed on the spray-adjusting lever. You should have the feeling that all the fingers, except the index finger, are used to sustain the instrument.

Practice holding the airbrush before you begin doing these exercises. See to what extent it obeys your orders. Make many tests with a medium blue color, for instance, that allows you to obtain pale tones when holding the airbrush away from the surface of the paper, and darker tones by overlaying different sprays.

2. Practice drawing with the airbrush using a ruler, painting along the ruler's length to obtain parallel and gradated rippled lines. Draw from left to right and from dark to light. Check the intensity of the color shade, bearing in mind that the closer the airbrush is held to the ruler, the greater the amount of color is applied, and, the farther away the airbrush is from the ruler, the greater the color dispersion and the lighter the tonal result. Paint with lengthwise sweeps.

3. With the aid of a ruler, as in the previous exercise, draw several ungradated straight lines. The nozzle must rest on the edge of the ruler while you draw it along the ruler's length. Paint from left to right, operating the spray-adjusting lever when your hand begins moving, not before. The thickness of the line increases as the airbrush moves away from the paper (or as the ruler is raised) or with each successive spray.

4. Cut a wavy edge along a piece of cardboard. Place it carefully on the surface of the paper and work along the wave with the airbrush. The number of strokes and the distance will determine the hue and width of the gradation you achieve. Painting with the airbrush close to the support produces a finer line; the hue will depend on the speed with which you paint. If you wish to obtain a diffused edge, work with the wavy edge slightly raised off the surface of the paper.

The sharp-edged undulations in the lower part of the illustration were achieved with the mask sitting on the paper.

5. To obtain a gradated background, begin spraying in broad bands at about 4 to 6 inches (10 to 15 cm) away from the surface of the paper, increasing the distance as you reach the areas you want gradated. The direction of your sweeps will determine the direction in which the gradation is produced—vertically, when produced from left to right or from right to left; horizontally, when produced from top to bottom and vice versa.

6. Here we achieve a double gradation by repeating the previous exercise, but in both directions, starting from a darker central band. Color should fade toward the left and right, or upward and downward if you are doing gradations lengthwise on the paper.

7. Although this may look like the easiest of the exercises shown here, it certainly is not. Achieving colored surfaces and even tones is more difficult than it might appear. Practice first on small surfaces and with highly diluted paint. Always spray in the same direction, 6 to 11 inches (15–29 cm) from the surface. Make successive passes until you obtain the desired color shade.

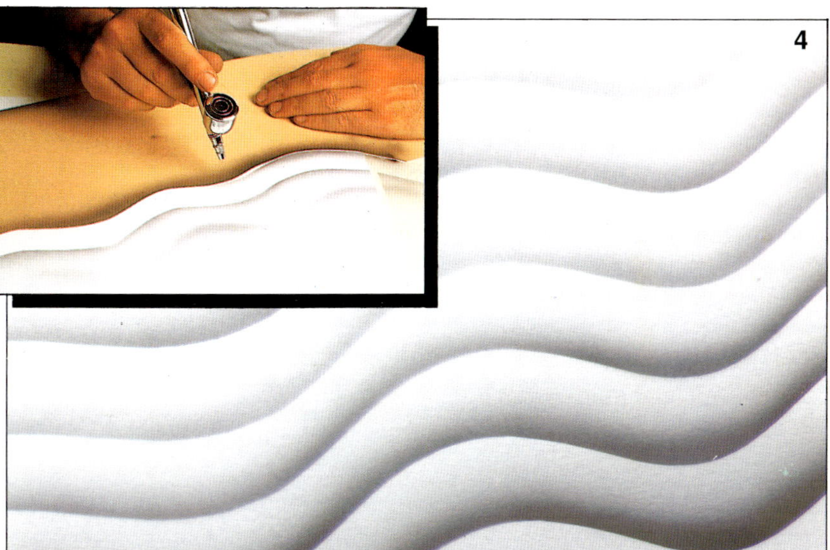
4

5

6

7

Painting geometric figures with the airbrush

Painting a cube with the airbrush

This is a highly effective exercise for learning how to create contrasts, gradations, and gray tones with the airbrush. Here you must use basic airbrush techniques in order to achieve, with a single color, the perfect relationship between the different hues on each side of the cube, the effect of light and shadow, and, consequently, a sense of volume.

We will use a very simple fixed mask made of special airbrush adhesive tape. We will airbrush three squares in perspective, unmasking only the one we're working on, of course. We will begin with the darkest of the three sides of the cube and work our way to the lightest.

We recommend you use medium intensity colors diluted in water, which can be lightened and darkened with superimposed sprays.

1
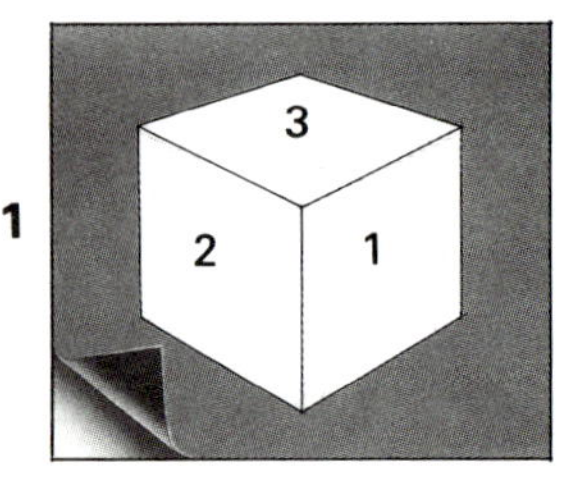

1. *We draw the cube in oblique perspective and apply a mask over the entire work surface.*

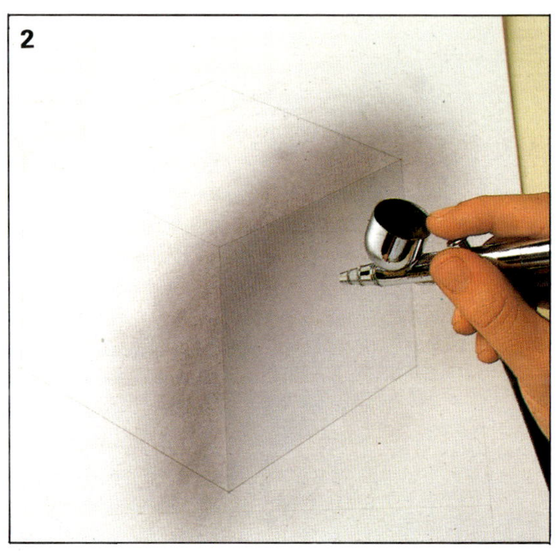

2. *Now we unmask side 1 and paint it. The gradation is carried out from left to right, somewhat darker in the upper part.*

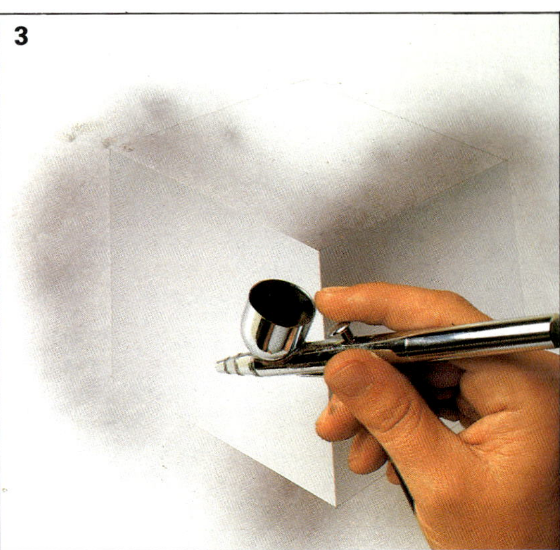

3. *Once again we mask side 1 and uncover side 2. Here we apply a left to right gradation that is somewhat lighter than that used on side 1.*

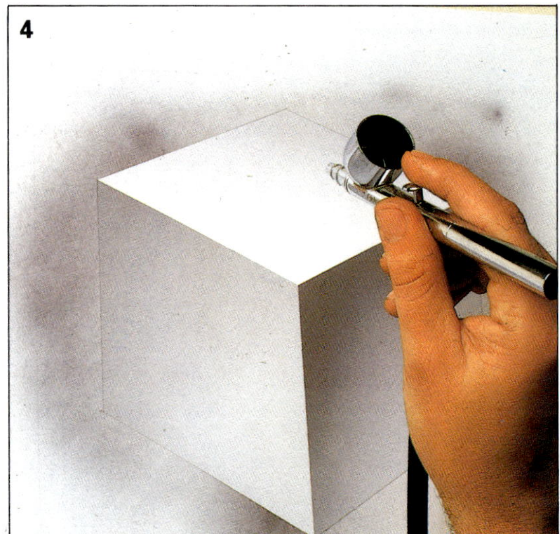

4. *Last, we uncover side 3 and apply an even lighter gradation than on side 2. We start with a gentle spray on the upper part and leave the bottom almost white.*

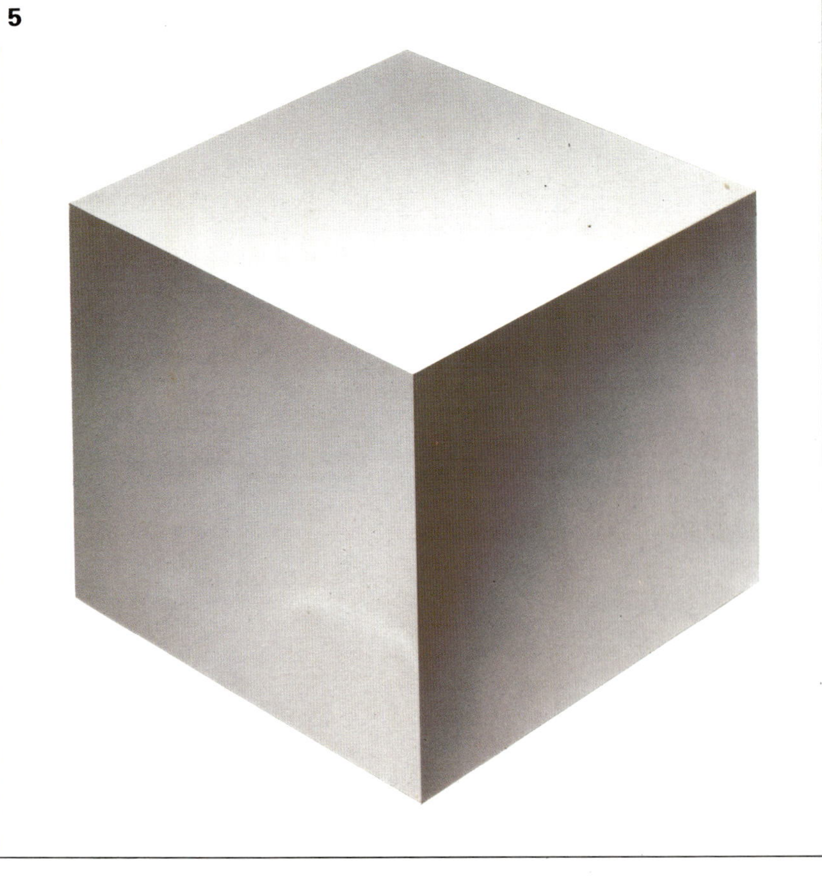

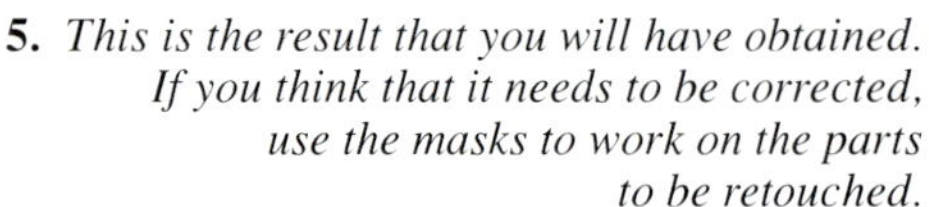

5. *This is the result that you will have obtained. If you think that it needs to be corrected, use the masks to work on the parts to be retouched.*

Painted and stained glass

Glass can be painted in various ways thanks to the development of transparent colors that dry relatively fast on glass and acquire considerable hardness. Professional stained glass artists, however, use just one technique: they color glass by smelting mineral colorants in special kilns at approximately the same temperature at which solid glass becomes liquid.

Stained glass art consists of joining separate pieces of colored glass together using lead strips. This technique allows the artist to make linear pictures and create chiaroscuros by applying with a brush patinas and glazes that are then fired.

This ancient method was first used toward the end of the eleventh century, at a time when new construction techniques allowed larger windows in cathedrals. The development and perfection of stained glass art was closely tied to the advent of Gothic art, which began in France in the middle of the twelfth century.

The emergence of techniques like the flying buttress and the ribbed vault enabled builders to make thinner walls and create larger windows that had to be sealed off from the elements, while keeping the monumental interiors filled with light. The solution was stained glass. This technique allowed the enormous windows to be covered with small fragments of glass, which, to a certain extent, replaced the frescoes that until then had been used in naves. Indeed, stained glass is one of the most remarkable features of Gothic cathedrals. It was the transparent support on which stained glass artists depicted biblical scenes and the feats performed by saints and kings, the place where they could unleash all their creative imagination by means of strictly decorative and geometric motifs.

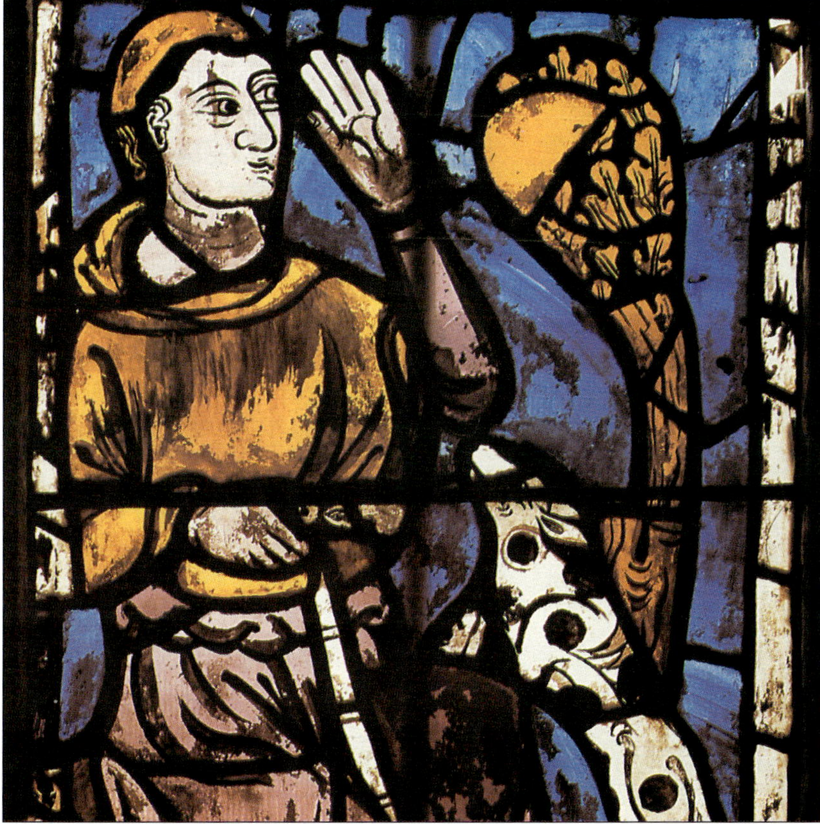

Fragment of a stained glass window in the church of Seo de Girona (fourteenth century) that forms part of Annunciation to the Shepherds.

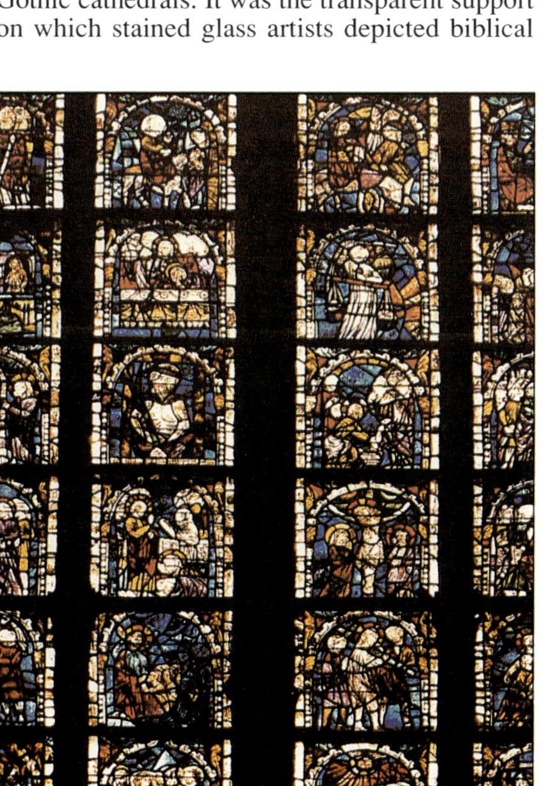

Scenes of the life of Christ *(c.1300) in the Church of Santes Creus, in Catalina, Spain.*

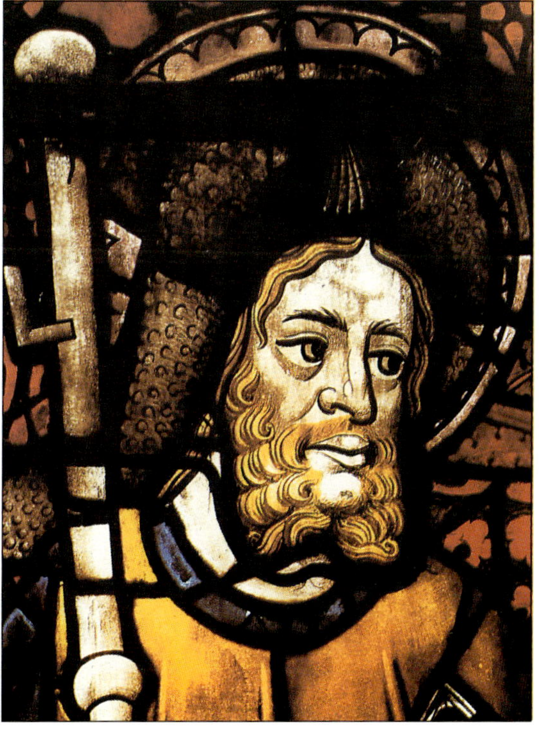

Fragment of an historical window in the Girona Cathedral, showing a characteristic Saint James. If you observe closely you can make out the grisaille applied on top of the glass to create lines and chiaroscuro.

Artistic stained glass

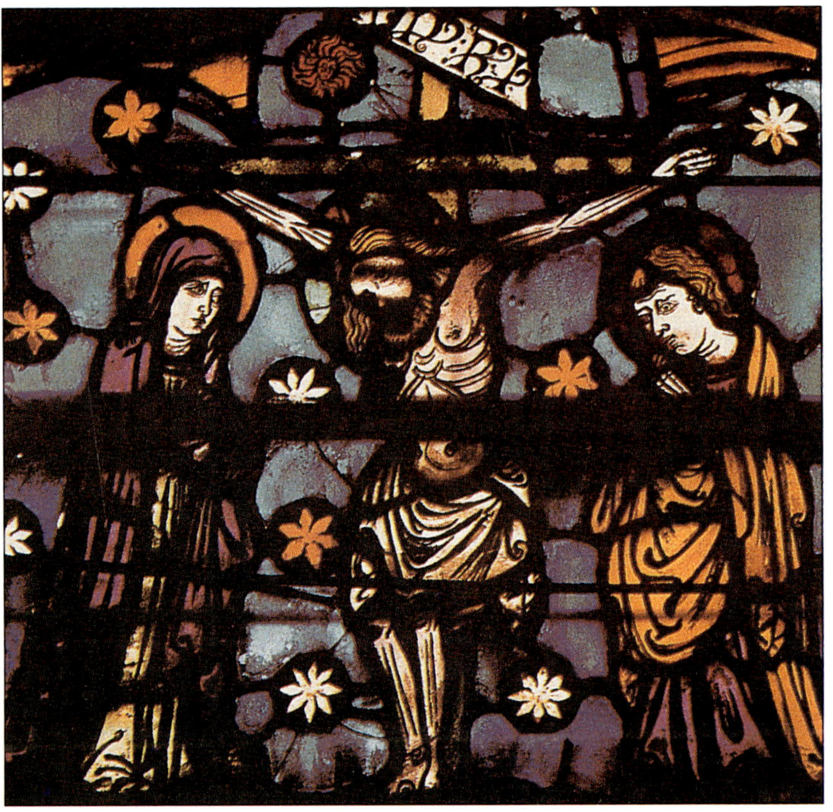

Gothic stained glass works not only lent light and color to cathedrals but also became prominent features of palaces and public buildings, as signs of wealth and magnificence.

The stylistic development of stained glass art later followed the demands of the new artistic movements of the Renaissance and the Baroque period when excessive use of grisaille and glazes turned stained glass paintings into almost opaque works.

The new artistic trends (neoclassicism and romanticism) marked the decline of stained glass art, which was not revived again until the advent of French art nouveau and of modernism.

This aesthetic movement exalted artistic craftsmanship, since it saw all objects as potential works of art. In Paris and Barcelona, the Modernist movement triggered a reemergence of the decorative arts, which were integrated into architecture to lend conceptual unity to all types of buildings. Both cities enthusiastically supported the work of William Morris (1834–1896), the great English artist who renewed stained glass art, and later, of American artist Louis Comfort Tiffany, its greatest technical innovator.

After modernism, stained glass art has undergone a conceptual and technical evolution in order to adapt to new tastes and requirements. Despite everything, its fundamentals remain largely unchanged.

This stained glass window in the chapter house of the Pedralbes monastery, in Barcelona, represents the crucifixion of Christ. It is executed in a style usually associated with enamels, and is highly influenced by Italian Gothic.

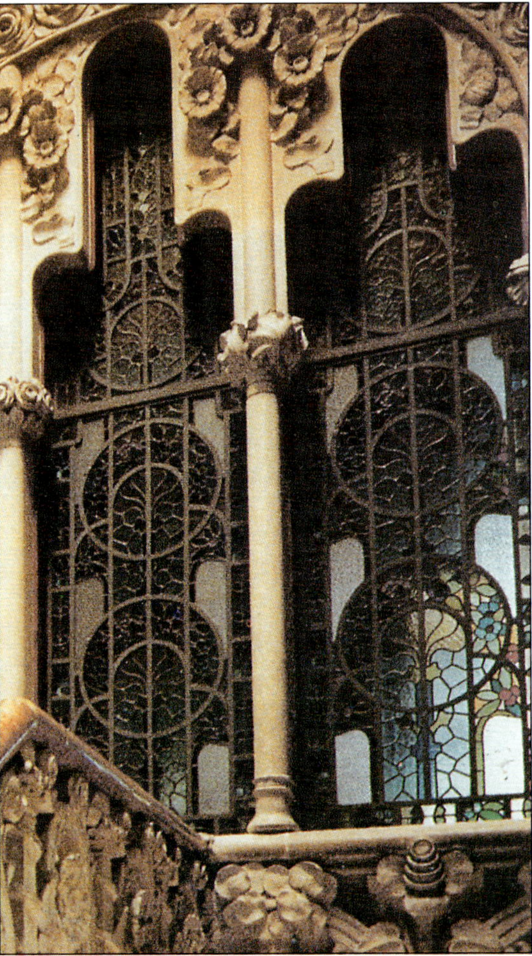

When modernism introduced the decorative arts into architecture, stained glass played a major role in a number of major works. These stained glass windows in the Casa de Navas, in Reus, Spain, were designed in 1901 by Lluís Domenèch i Montaner.

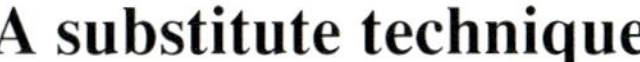

A substitute technique

Before we show you how to make *true* stained glass, this simple technique will allow you to get immediate and highly decorative results without a large studio and sophisticated equipment. All you will need is enough room to work on the glass while it is in a horizontal position, and a way to light the glass from below so you can see the colors as transparencies.

Materials

You will need the following materials and tools in order to follow this step-by-step exercise:

1. A sheet of acetate (this item is not indispensable).
2. Transparent colors specially manufactured for use on glass (more about this later).
3. One or two jars for preparing the color solvent.
4. Cellulose nitrate solvent.
5. Transparent lacquer to tone down the colors and obtain paler tones.
6. Two markers, one with a regular tip (0.8 mm), and a thicker one with a bevelled tip.
7. A 2B pencil.
8. A strip of self-adhesive lead, about 0.31 inches (6 mm) wide. This can be bought in art and crafts stores and is sold in standard rolls of up to 50 yards (46 m).
9. A small plastic applicator (it often comes with the roll of lead).
10. Several round-tipped fine hair brushes of various thicknesses. A small brush comes in handy for painting in tight corners.
11. A sculpting spatula (either homemade or purchased) to apply the lead on the glass. (Whether you use the plastic applicator or the spatula is entirely up to you; we believe that the spatula is much more practical).
12. Cups or similar containers, to prepare the colors. It is better to use inexpensive, disposable ones.
13. A sturdy pair of scissors to cut the lead.
14. A large strong knife or cutter.

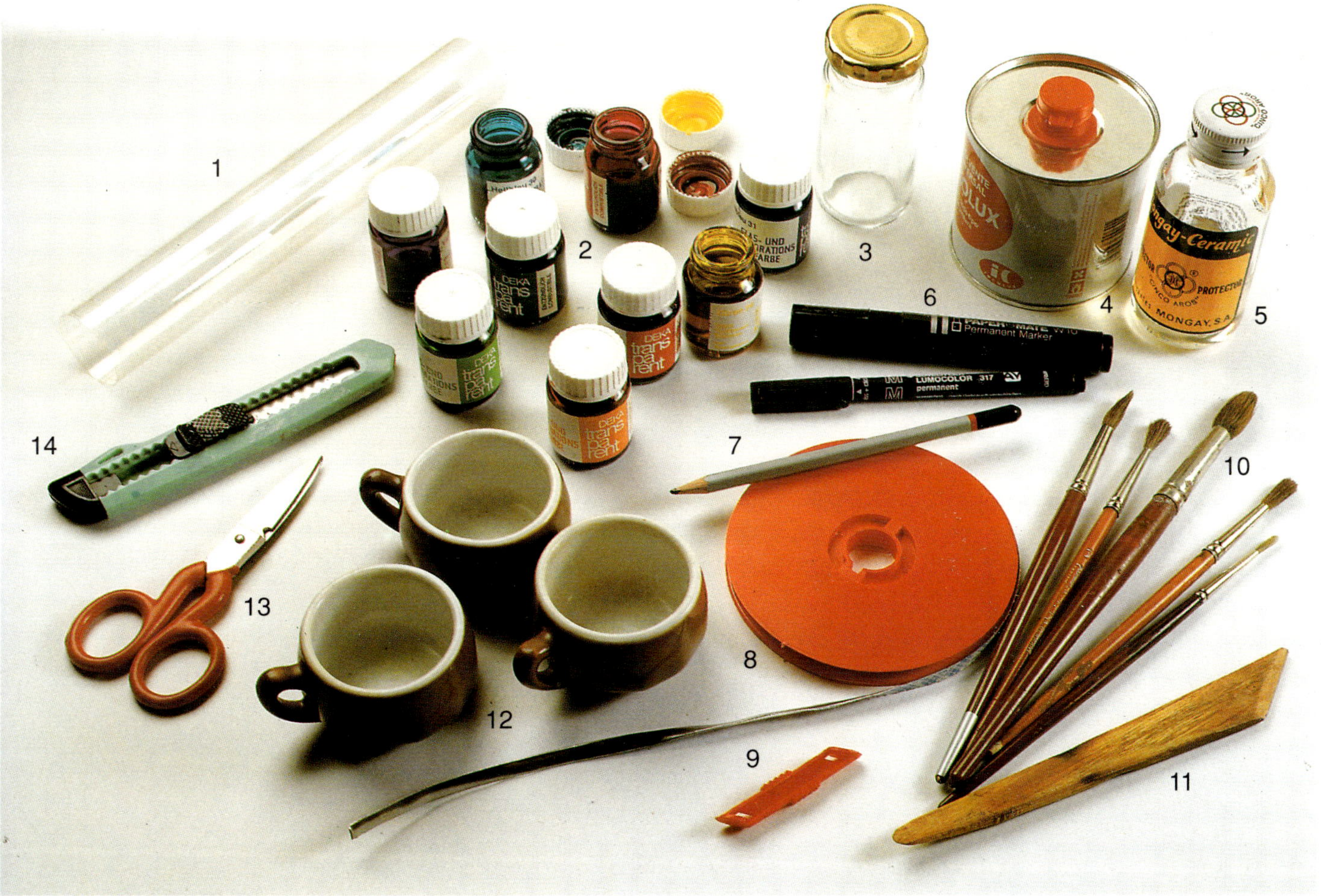

Materials and accessories needed for the imitation stained glass exercise that we are about to begin. You do not have to buy the brands shown here in order to obtain good results.

Imitation stained glass: The colors

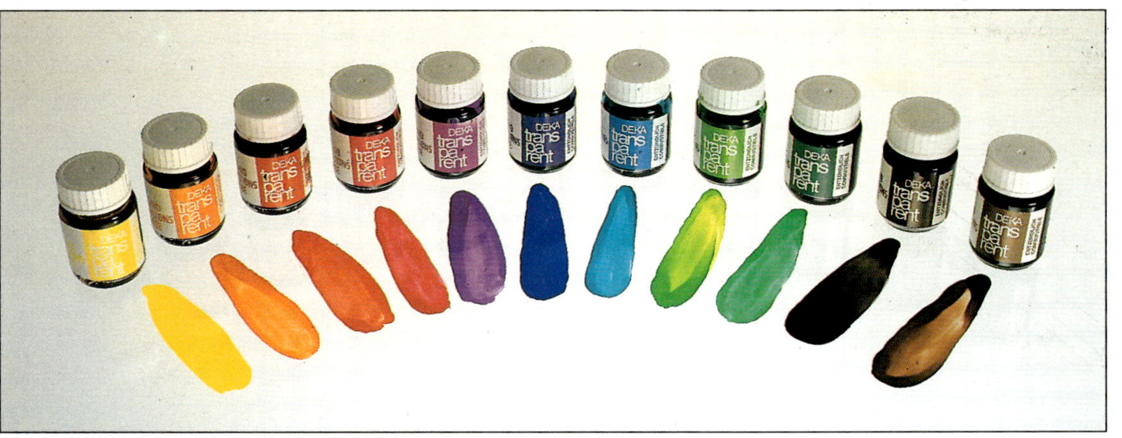

Transparent Deka colors. The range is not broad, but it is sufficient. The color of each jar can only be appreciated when viewed under a light, taking into consideration that the tone varies depending on the light's intensity.

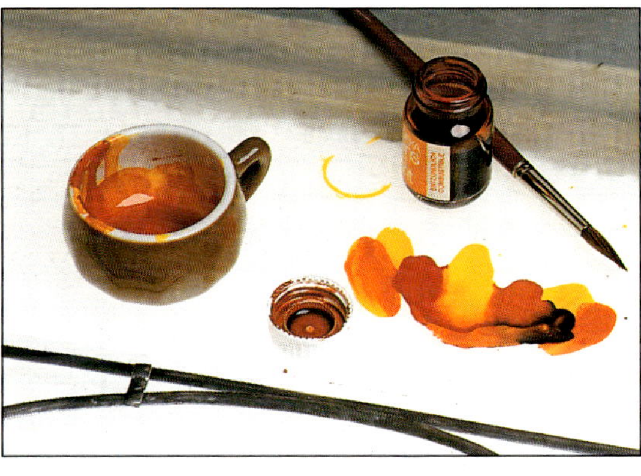

It is useful to work on a light-table in order to check the effect of each color (whether pure or mixed), before applying it to the pane of glass chosen for the design.

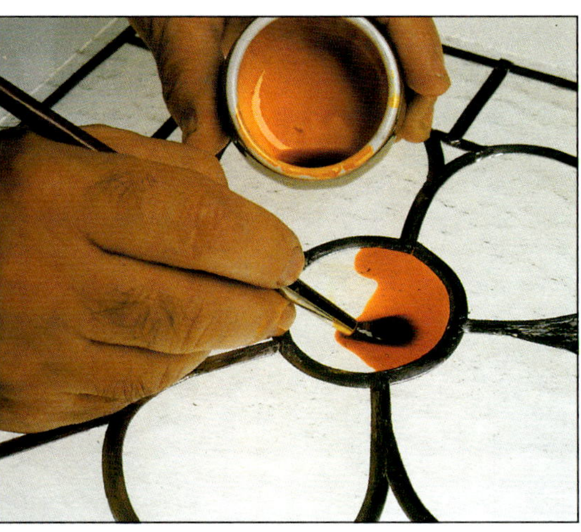

The color must form a thick and uniform layer. The paint should be applied thickly, using a soft brush. The brush should be used to spread the color in order to apply it uniformly, but without applying excessive pressure. The fluidity of the color as well as the abundance with which it is applied, forces the artist to work on a perfectly flat surface in order to prevent the color from running.

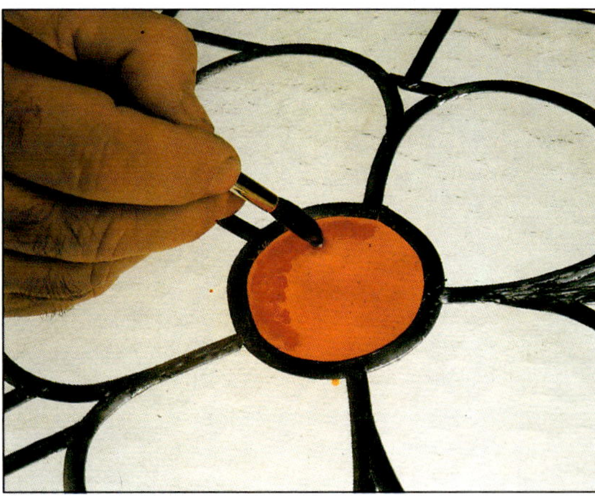

While color is watery, it is easy to obtain different tones and hues simply by adding more to the brush and dripping it on the glass, where it will blend easily with the background.

Characteristics of colors for glass

Colors for glass—cellulose transparent lacquers—come under different brand names. We have used Deka Farben lacquers, although this in no way implies that other brands are inferior. Due to the special nature of these colors, it is important to follow these guidelines:

1. Shake the colors before using them.
2. Before you apply a color, make sure that the glass is absolutely clean and dry, and free of dust, grease, and fingerprints.
3. Paint with soft brushes, applying thick layers in order to obtain a uniform film.
4. The best tonal uniformity and resistance to light is obtained by applying the paint undiluted; however, since the colors are extremely intense in their pure state, this is not always possible.
5. To obtain paler tones, the colors must be mixed with a transparent ceramic lacquer.
6. The colors dry and thicken relatively quickly. You can obtain a more fluid application by thinning the paint with a nitrodilutant.
7. While a flat painted surface takes about two hours to dry, thicker layers need about 24 hours.
8. Colors can be mixed together to make up new tones.
9. Remember that since these are transparent colors, they can only be truly appreciated when lit from below.
10. Color intensity will decrease when light increases and vice versa. In other words, more light equals lighter colors; less light equals darker colors.
11. As with any other transparent medium (watercolor, for instance), the tone of a color darkens with each successive layer.
12. Colors are more easily blended when they are watery.

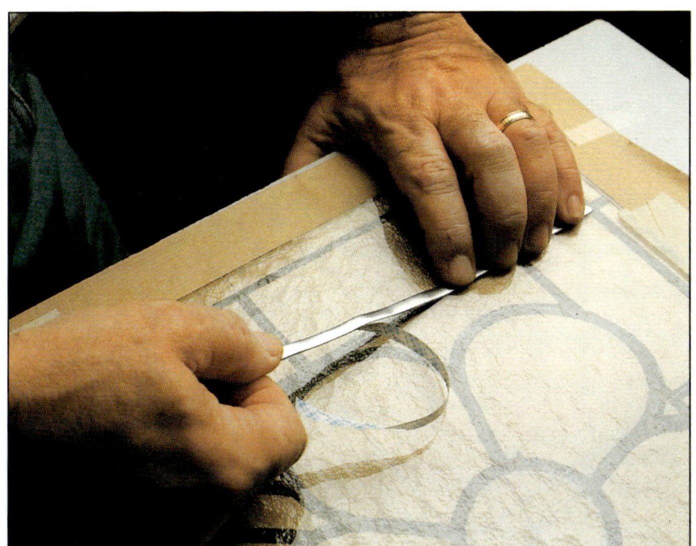

Apply the lead strip to the glass with your hands. Once it has been laid, do not attempt to remove it, since the sticky side will lose its adhesiveness. Work carefully in order to avoid having to rectify, even if it is possible to do so.

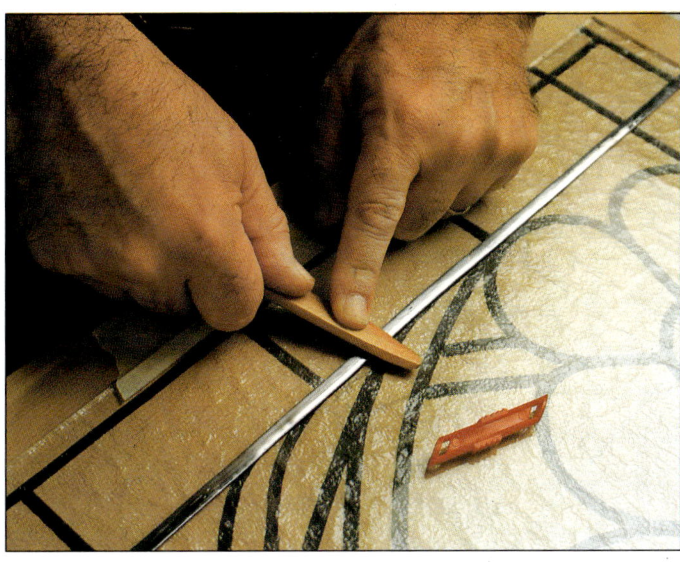

Once it is in place, the lead strip should be fastened permanently by pressing it down against the glass and running the applicator over it several times. Make sure the edges of the strip are firmly secured to the glass.

Lead strips: How to apply them

The strips of lead employed in imitation stained glass art are sold in handicraft stores. They can be bought in standard measures of up to 50 yards (46 m). There are two thicknesses: 0.23 inch (6 mm), the most commonly used for this type of work, and 0.15 inch (4 mm), for very small formats. Of course, strips of both widths can be combined in the same work.

These lead strips are self-adhesive and pliable, and easy to bend and shape before they are attached to the glass. While the lead is on the roll, it is covered by a protective wrapping that peels off on its own as the strip is applied, just as you can see in the photograph in the top left corner of this page.

The lead is first applied with the hands, and is fed along the line of the drawing. Pressing down slightly secures the lead to the support.

The next step consists of applying more pressure with the applicator. Although you may use the one supplied with the lead strip, we recommend that you make your own from a sculpting spatula, similar to the one illustrated, which is much easier to handle. Run the applicator over the entire length of the strip while pressing down on the glass. You should apply as much pressure as needed until it has completely adhered, but remember that too much pressure may break the glass.

Once the length is in place (see bottom right photo), separate it from the roll by carefully cutting off the end. Make sure you don't cut the strip too short, or you'll have to rip it off and start all over.

When laying down short and straight lead strips, you can measure and cut them before applying them on the glass. With longer strips, especially curved ones, it is best to play it safe and attach the strip to the glass before cutting it. Always remember to measure the lead strip, to avoid miscalculating the length. Lead is not cheap; it should not be wasted.

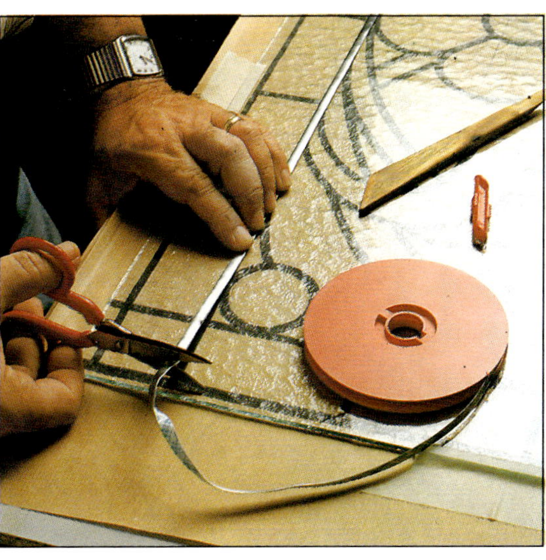

Lead strips can be cut with scissors. It is best to cut them after they have been stuck to the glass, in order to avoid mistakes, especially when you are working with curved strips that are not easy to measure.

Imitation stained glass: An example

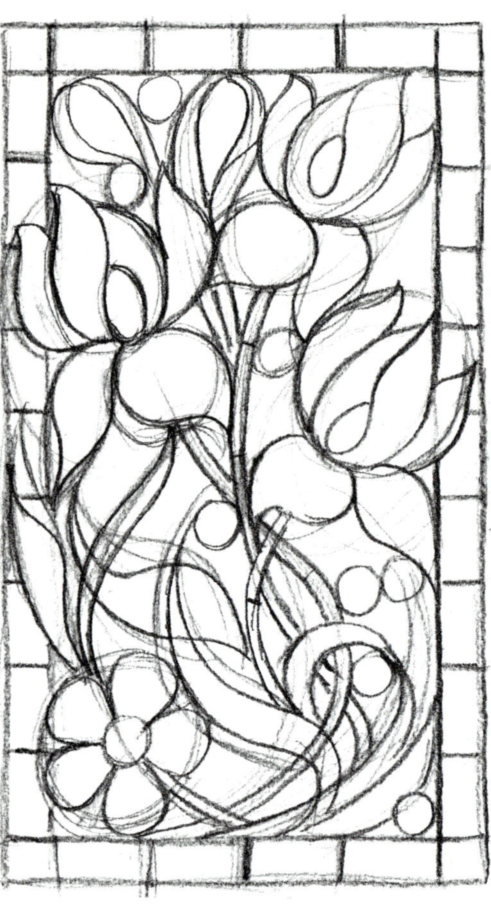

This is the final drawing that we will use for this exercise. We have softly sketched our idea on a sheet of fine-grain Canson paper using a 2B pencil. Then we have gone over certain parts of the drawing until we reach the stage you can see here on the left. This is the most common way of going about the initial sketch. Don't think that the first attempt will always produce the desired result. Improvise until something positive begins to emerge. Then carry out the necessary alterations, corrections, and details until you get the definitive design.

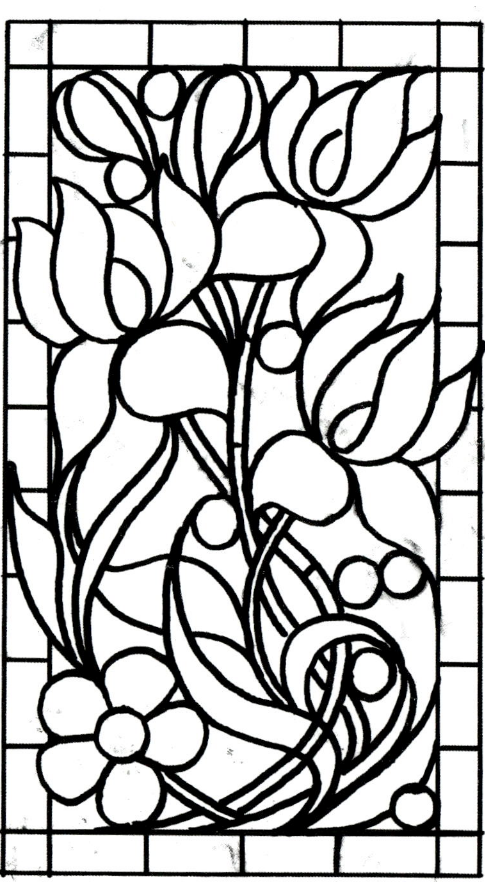

Using a 0.03 inch (1 mm) cone-shaped tip marker, we have outlined each one of the flowers and petals. The result is an array of perfectly designed flat figures, each of which will be given a particular color. In real stained glass, each would be created by different pieces of colored glass.

The project

All artistic works start out with a simple idea that is fleshed out through a number of sketches to obtain a definitive design.

Since the measurements of our future stained glass work are dictated by the window opening, its design must be drawn to scale. For large glass panes, a 1:10 scale is generally used; for smaller formats, a 1:5 scale is employed.

Sources of inspiration

From the outset, you should bear in mind that imitation stained glass will never be the same as the genuine article. In imitation stained glass we work with a single pane of glass, whereas in real stained glass work, we use different pieces of glass.

Of course, you can still create highly decorative designs with imitation stained glass; it all comes down to imagination rather than technique.

It is advisable to look at photographs of stained glass works; the vegetable motifs of art nouveau and modernism are, perhaps, the most suitable for beginners. Instead of copying designs, you should select and combine motifs, adapting them to your format.

Other good sources of inspiration are works by contemporary artists such as Braque, Kandinsky, Klee, and Picasso, who executed their drawings and paintings in a purely two-dimensional form.

Stage one: The sketch

We will begin this step-by-step exercise with a design inspired by Modernist vegetable motifs. Instead of merely copying the floral and vegetable stained glass designs of the Modernist period, we will use them to create our own original and personal drawings.

We are going to work on a glass pane for the front door of a house. The glass pane will be exposed to intense daylight. This is an important fact that we must take into account when we prepare the colors, which must be applied in thick layers in order to prevent the light from fading them too much.

The design has now been drawn on a 1:5 scale using a 2B pencil on a sheet of fine-grain Canson paper.

Once the drawing is final, we outline it using a 0.03 inch (1 mm), round-tipped black marker. We erase the pencil lines and add some color with water-soluble pencils to get an idea of what they will look like. You don't have to use pencils; watercolors or ink are equally good. Bear in mind that these colors serve only as a point of reference. They are not necessarily the definitive colors that you will get on the glass pane, which will depend on the quality and intensity of the light, the greater or lesser degree of transparency of each color, and the type of glass used.

If you want to avoid making mistakes, it is absolutely essential that your scaled-down drawing be exactly the same as you want the definitive pane to look like.

The next step entails drawing a life-size sketch of the pane. Since it won't be possible to correct, this sketch must be precise.

Stage two: The life-size drawing

Now that we are entirely satisfied that the drawing is a true representation of what we want to see on the glass pane, we begin the life-size drawing.

When dealing with large surfaces, professionals generally use an opaque projector, but since our model is not very big, we can make do with a simple grid.

In order to not damage the sketch, we have drawn the grid on a sheet of acetate, and, to help us focus on it, we have placed a black cardboard frame around it.

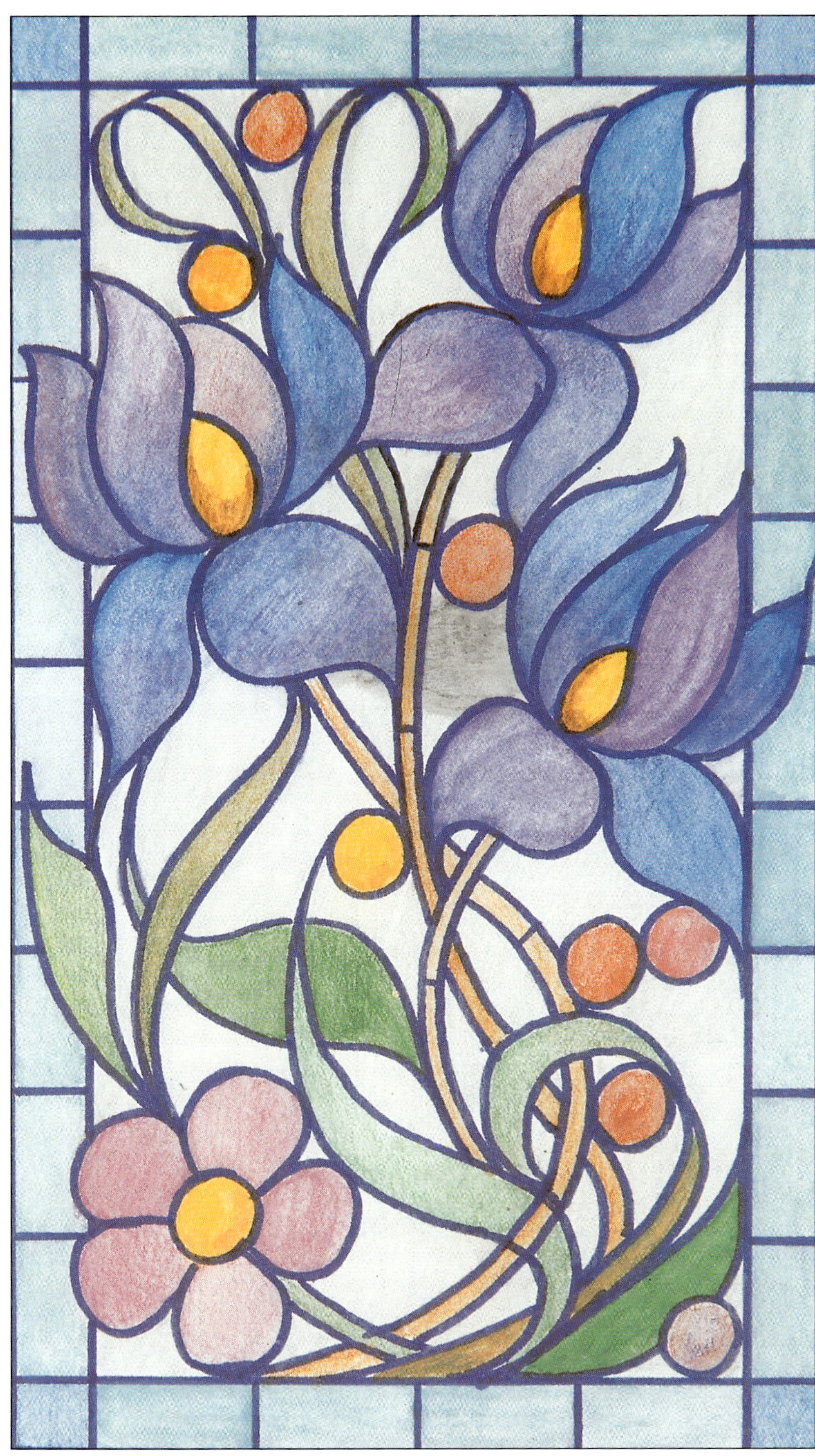

This is the definitive sketch, drawn in a 1:5 scale, of the glass pane we are going to paint as an imitation stained glass window. The colors here are mere approximations, since in all probability they will be somewhat different when applied transparently on glass.

Imitation stained glass: An example

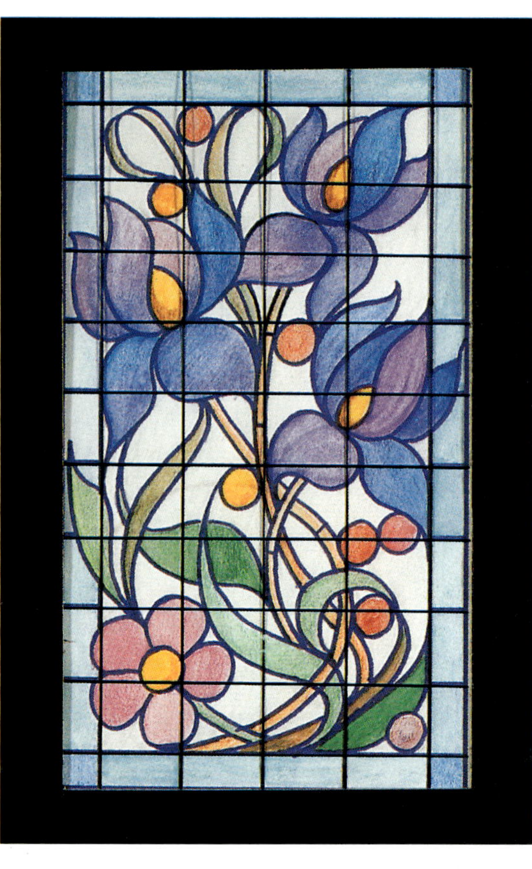

This is what the sketch looks like covered with an acetate grid and a black cardboard frame. Although rudimentary, this technique makes it easier to work on large formats. The acetate grid allows us to transfer the lines of the drawing to a larger format without damaging the original drawing. The black cardboard frame focuses the artist's attention.

We have drawn the life-size version on brown wrapping paper attached to a wooden board that we have placed on our studio easel.

The drawing has been amplified using the grid system. Then, as you can see in the photograph below, we have gone over the pencil lines using a 0.23 inch (6 mm), thick tip marker (the same width as the lead strip we are about to use).

Stage three: Preparing to work with lead

One thing we should do before beginning to work with the lead strip is to put the glass pane over the drawing. It is always advisable to work on a flat surface like a large table. We make sure the edges of the glass coincide exactly with those of the paper before attaching both with transparent adhesive.

The glass

Up to this point, little has been said about the glass.

Leaving aside the question of the color of the glass (a question that does not arise in this exercise), there are many types of glass we can use, depending on their texture.

Going over the lines with a wide, bevelled marker, we draw the life-size drawing on wrapping paper. The width of the line is the same as that of the strips of self-adhesive lead we are going to use on the glass.

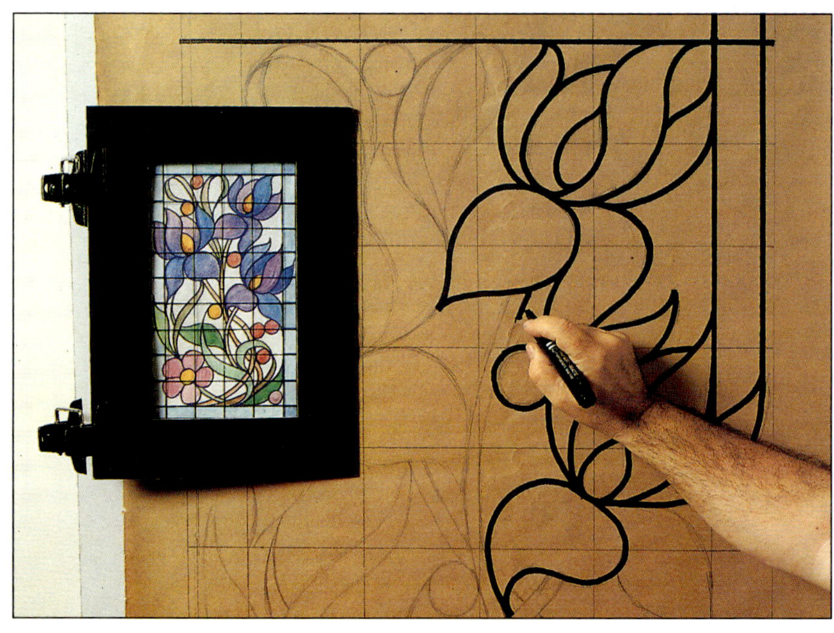

This is the final drawing. The black lines will eventually be covered over with strips of lead.

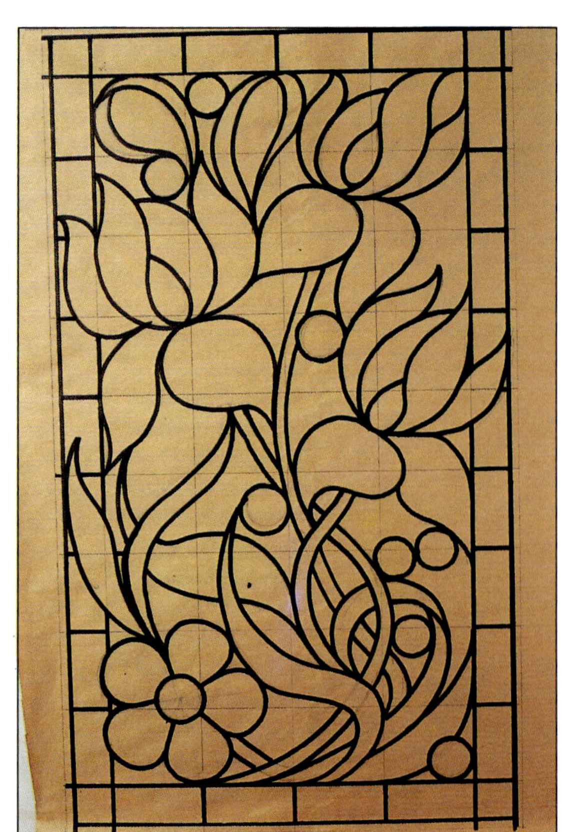

When making imitation stained glass, we recommend you use cathedral glass, so called because it is an industrial type of glass commonly used in church windows. Its textured sides produces a diffuse light that homogenizes the tone of the color applied on its smooth side.

If you try to paint on a regular smooth, transparent glass pane, you will see how difficult it is to obtain a uniform color over the surface, unless the surface is tiny.

Cleanliness

Make sure that the smooth side of the glass, where you will lay the lead strips, is completely clean. This is essential for the lead to successfully adhere to the surface.

Any household product for cleaning glass will do.

Make sure that you do not leave any fingerprints on the surface, since they will show up under the paint.

Remember that on cathedral glass the lead strips and the color should be applied on the smooth side; therefore, when you place the pane over the drawing, make sure the smooth side is lying face up.

Stage four: Laying down the lead

In the next pages, we will quickly review how the lead strip is applied; when you do it yourself, you will see how easy it really is. All you need is a little common sense and patience, without forgetting the basic guidelines we have given you up to now.

We suggest that you begin with the straight lines, if there are any. Then move on, for instance, to the smaller, curved, or circular ones.

How to close off a circle with a lead strip

The easiest way of doing this is to cut out a cardboard mask of the circle's interior, in order to use it as a guide for the lead strip.

• Use the fingers of one hand to hold down the cardboard mask and feed the lead around it with your other hand.

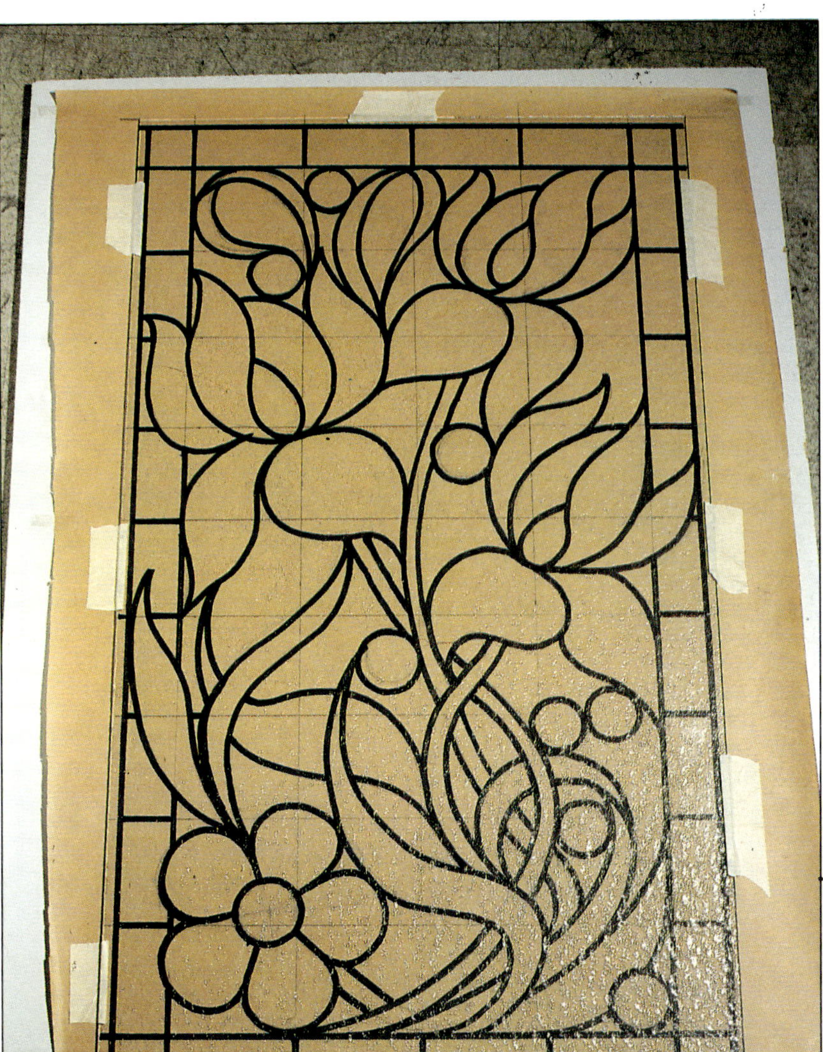

The glass pane has been placed over the life-size drawing. The lines can be clearly made out through the glass. A few strips of transparent adhesive tape will prevent the pane from sliding over the drawing while we are laying the lead strips.

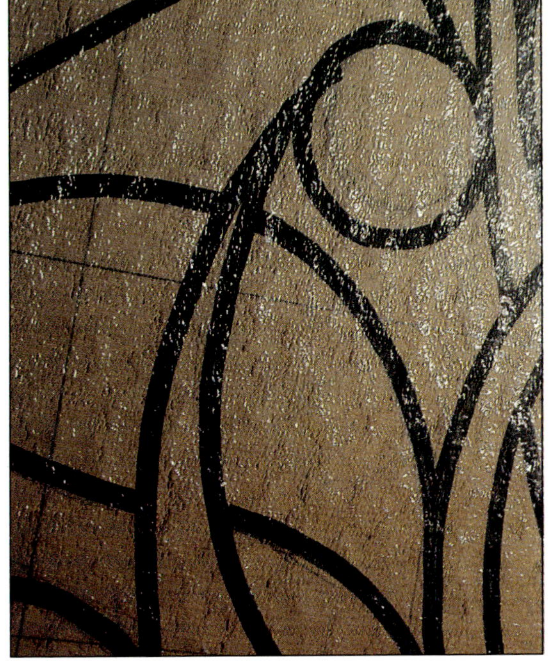

In this detail of the photograph above, you can see the characteristic texture of cathedral glass.

Imitation stained glass: An example

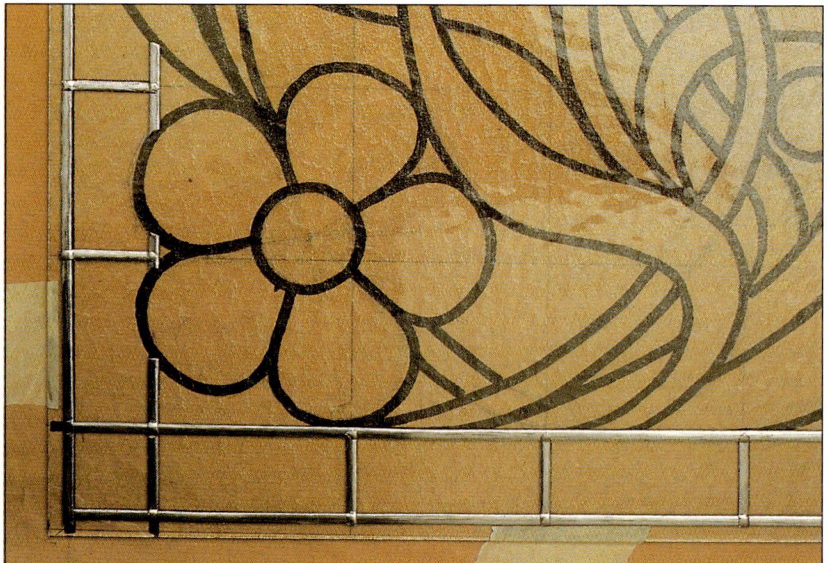

A corner of the glass pane, showing the lead strips over the straight lines. Some extra length is left at the end of the strips so that they may overlap.

In these two illustrations, we can see how a circle is made using a cardboard mask. The blade of the cutter is used to remove any uneven parts.

- Make sure one end overlaps slightly.
- Run the applicator over the lead circle.
- Note in the bottom left photograph how we use the screwdriver. The tip of the screwdriver is much harder than the plastic or wooden applicator, so it is useful for flattening the overlapping strips.

Joining the strips: Overlaps

There are no precise rules on the best way to join two strips of lead together. The most important thing to bear in mind is always to allow the end of the strip to overlap slightly. In other words, it is not enough for the two ends of the strip to meet; one end must overlap the other. It is important to avoid cracks through which paint can seep and ultimately penetrate the sealed off areas within the strips.

- In tangential joints, where the two parts form the curve, the overlapping part of the strip must be cut so that it perfectly follows the direction of the curve.
- Using a large blade, remove the excess lead and, at the same time, shape the overlapping part so that it follows the direction of the end it is connected to.

As you can see, this is not a difficult task.

If you want a more perfect version of imitation stained glass, you should turn the glass pane upside down and lay lead strips on the flip side. Before you do this, think how the glass pane will be used, since it may not be worth the trouble.

Stage five: Removing imperfections

Now it is time to remove the drawing from below the glass and examine the results of the previous stage of work. We were lucky enough to work on a large light-table, something that you are not likely to have. Don't worry, because, as the saying goes "half a loaf is better than none." All you need is a couple of easels or trestles on which to place the glass pane, and an ordinary lamp placed below the glass.

By checking the work in this way, without the drawing underneath, we can make out any imperfections, such as stains produced by the adhesive side of the lead or unevenness in the

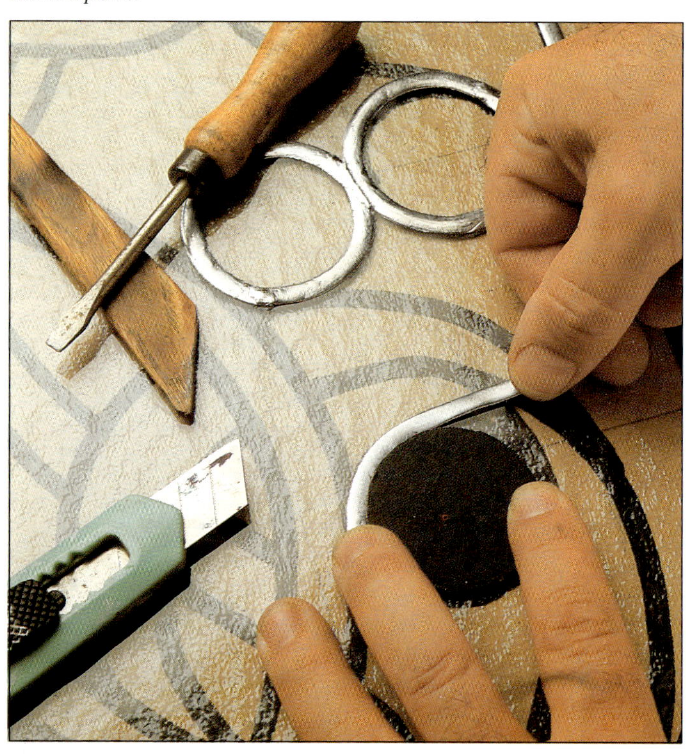

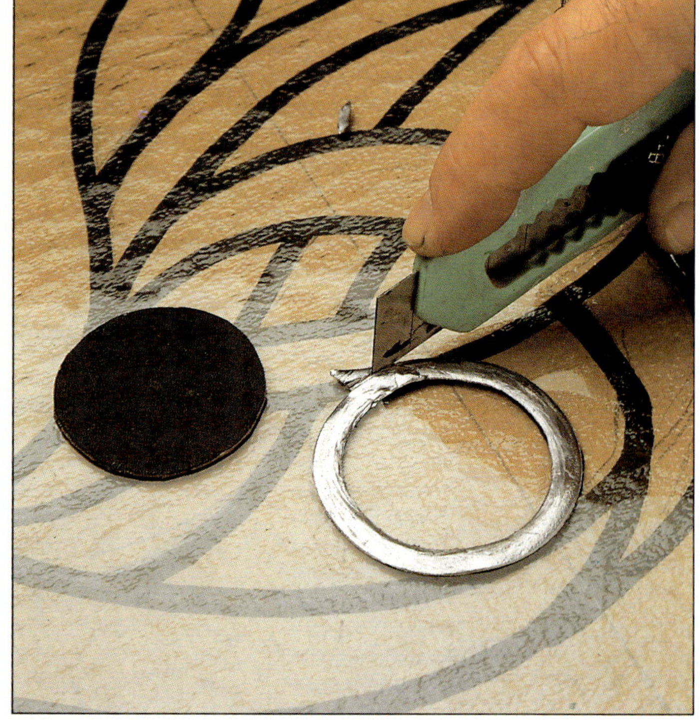

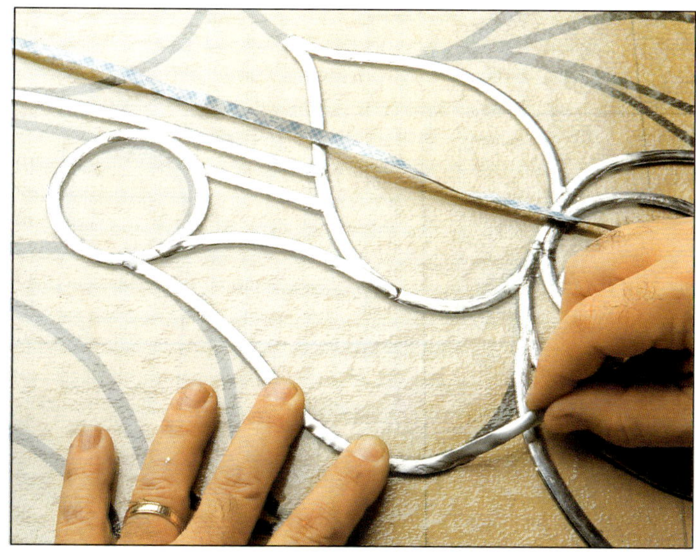

Applying a strip of lead on an irregular curve. This is done little by little, using one hand to feed the lead in the right direction and the other to hold it in place.

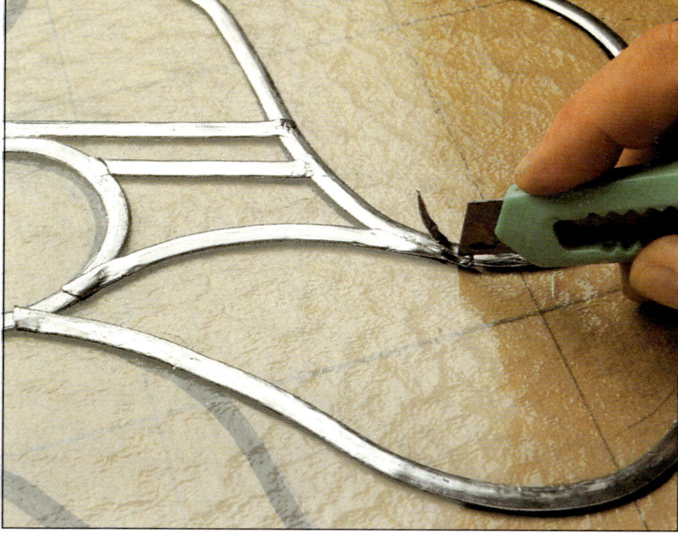

A cutter is used to tidy up the overlapping part of the strip. Then the joint is sealed by pressing down on the applicator or screwdriver.

joints of the strips. These must be removed before color is applied.

Adhesive stains are easily wiped out with a clean cloth and a drop of solvent; irregularities in the joints can be rectified by scraping or cutting with the tip of a sharp knife.

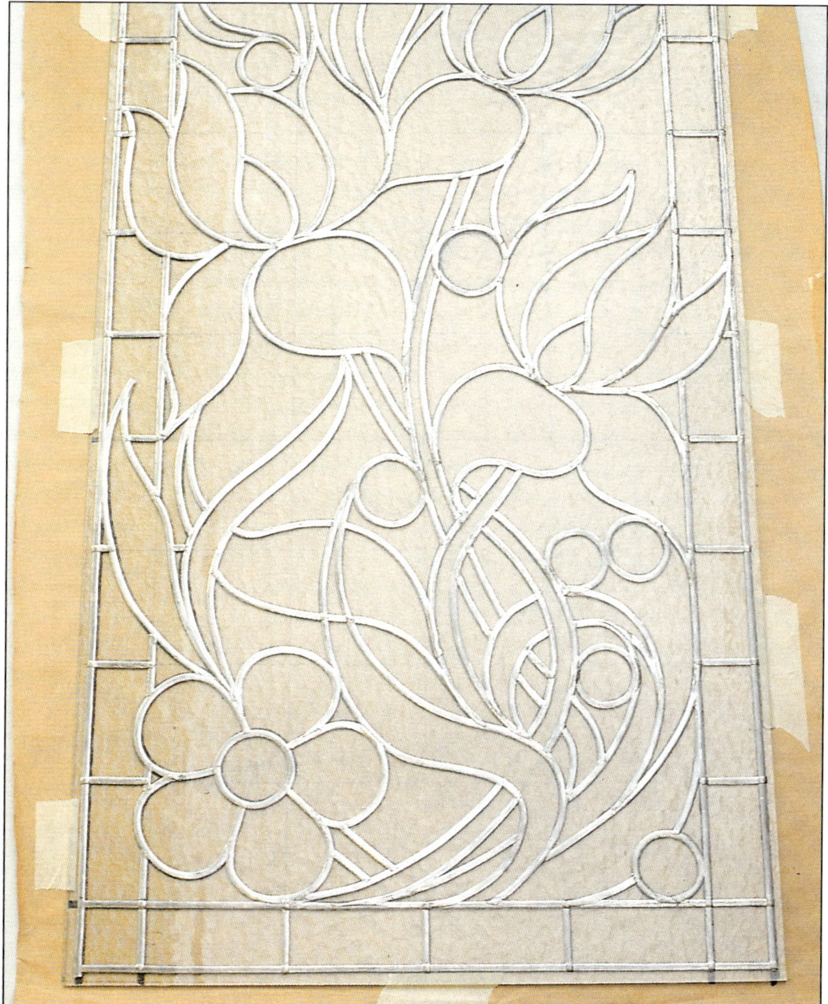

This is what the glass looks like now that it has been entirely covered with lead strips. The lead follows perfectly the lines of the original drawing. Now the enclosed surfaces will be filled with transparent color.

Imitation stained glass: An example

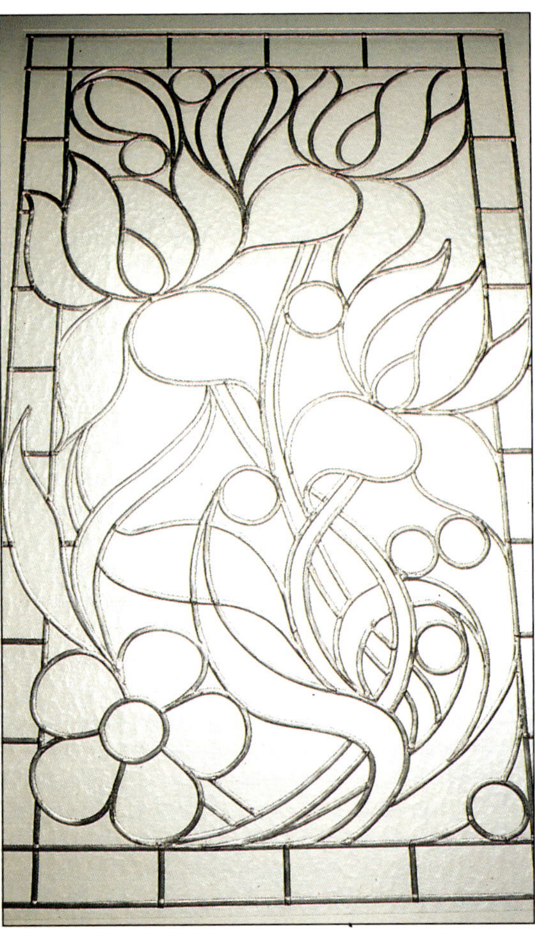

This is how the glass pane looks after the lead strips have been attached. Notice how they perfectly reproduce the original drawing.

Stage six: The color application

With the glass placed in a horizontal position and lit from below, we begin to apply color, bearing in mind that the color of the paint you see in the pot will appear different once applied on the glass. Now is a good time to renew what we have said earlier on the subject of transparent colors.

Begin with the smallest surfaces

No matter how well you master the craft, always be careful. Begin with the smallest surfaces, in this case the circles and the centers of the flowers, which we will paint in hues ranging from dark yellow to amberish orange. They are obtained by adding different amounts of orange or vermilion to the yellow, as well as enough transparent lacquer for the palest tones.

We paint with a fine-hair brush (No 14). We touch up some freshly painted circles with a few drops of pure color taken directly from the jar.

When you embark on your own projects, remember that color should be applied generously but with great care, making sure that it reaches the inner edges of the lead without going over them. If, despite everything, the color does stain the lead strip, wait for it to dry before attempting to remove it with a cutter or a rag soaked in solvent.

Glue stains are removed by wrapping a cloth soaked in solvent around your finger and rubbing it over the affected area. Make sure that the solvent does not drip; otherwise, it might affect the lead strips near the stain we are trying to remove.

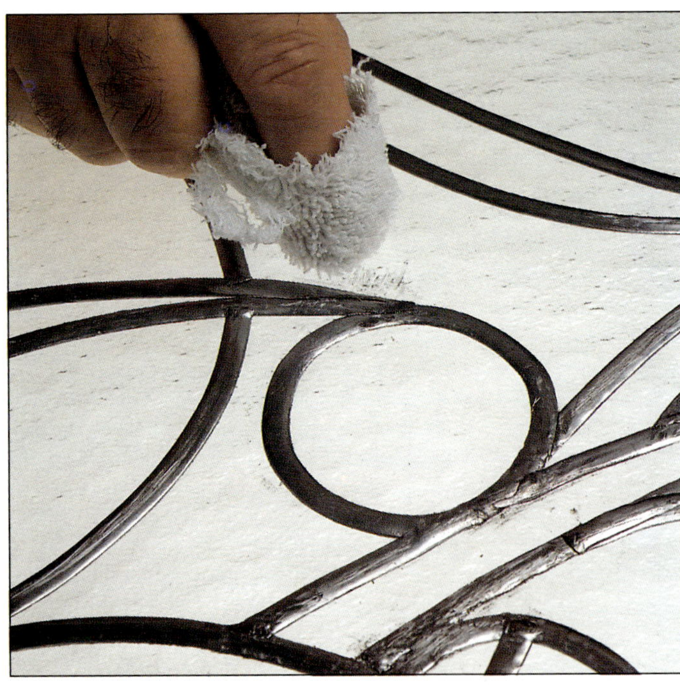

The cutter is used here to retouch the joints between the two lead strip lines and a circle.

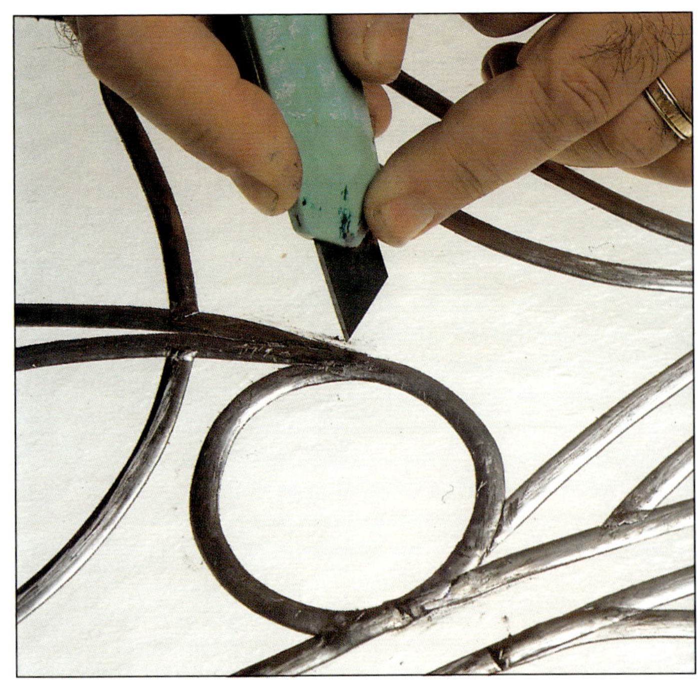

Stage seven: Filling the larger spaces with color

We have to fill in with color each and every one of the enclosed areas. The largest areas are the most difficult, especially in terms of obtaining a uniform tone. If you are painting with brushes, even thick ones, the speed at which the paint dries makes it extremely difficult to obtain a uniform color.

We can recommend a technique that, although somewhat unorthodox, works incredibly well: filling the area with a paint-filled dropper.

- First, prepare enough color, adding solvent if it appears too thick.
- Fill the dropper.
- Now, while moving the dropper over the area to be painted, release the color, always squeezing with the same amount of pressure in order to obtain a uniform layer.

On the next page, you will see how we have used this technique in the green areas. First we prepared three different shades of green, with which we painted the large petals of the flower in the lower left side of the composition. Then we prepared three shades of violet for the petals, based on the color chart provided by Deka.

Note in the photographs how some of the blue surfaces have gradations, obtained by applying a more intense shade in those areas we want to darken. If the paint maintains its fluidity, the darkest tone will show a gradation, from dark to light, within the blue of the background.

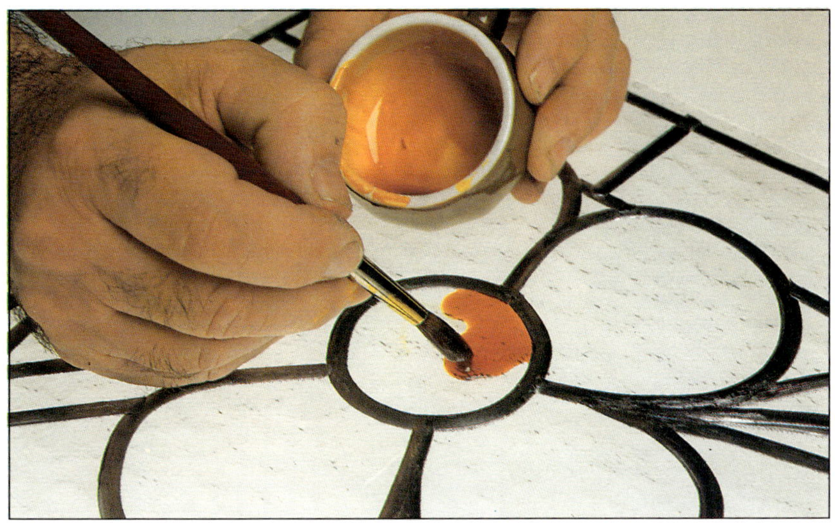

Applying color within a circle. The brush is used to spread color over the surface rather than to apply brushstrokes.

Applying pure red in the center of a circle previously painted with orange.

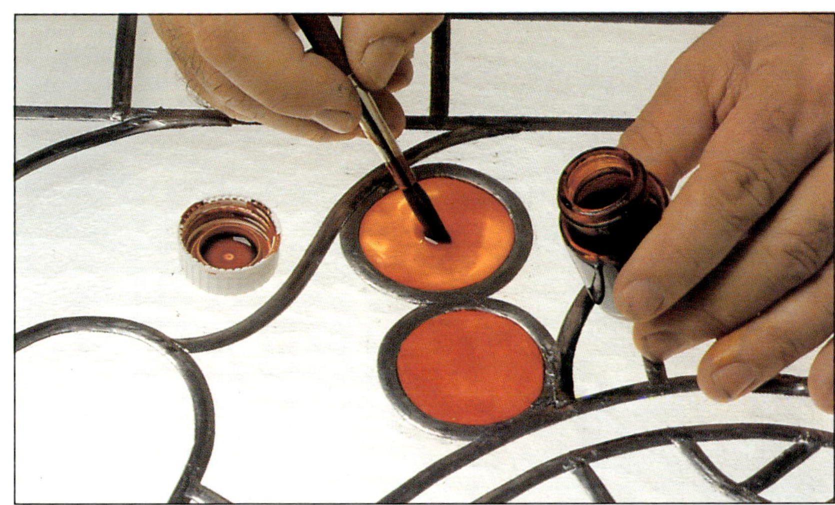

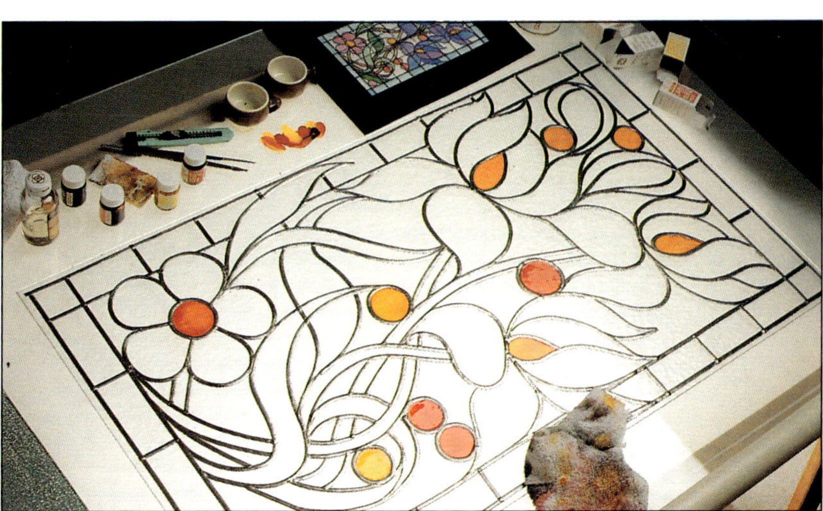

This is what our work looks like after the circles and the centers of the flowers have been painted. Note how the colors have been tested at the edge of the light-table before they are applied.

Imitation stained glass: An example

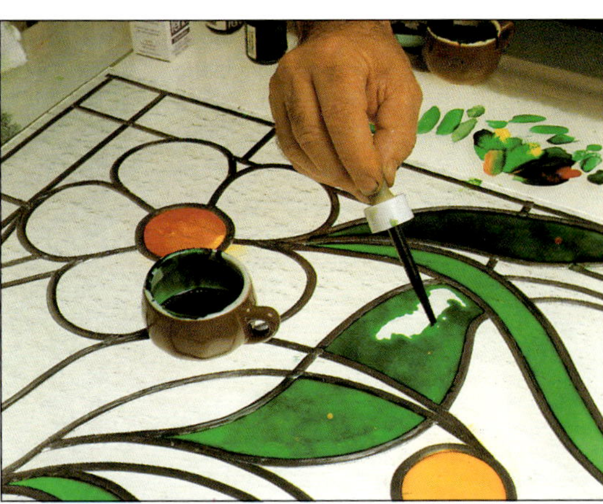

Colors are now added to larger surfaces.

An ordinary dropper is excellent for coloring open surfaces.

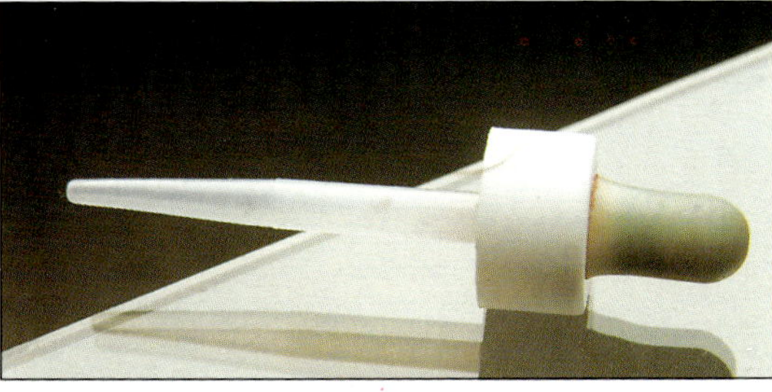

This is the result of the work at this stage. As you can see, we have used a dropper to apply much of the color.

Because the flower stems are extremely narrow surfaces, they should be painted by "depositing" color on the surface with an appropriately sized brush.

As is the case with many other pictorial techniques, what needs to be done can be explained with few words. Theory is simple, but to master it is another story. There is no other alternative than practice. Now, start thinking about a windowpane in your home that might look good with a decoration.

Before painting each area, rub it with a cloth dampened with solvent to remove any color stains. If color stains the lead strip, don't try to clean it right away; first, let it dry completely.

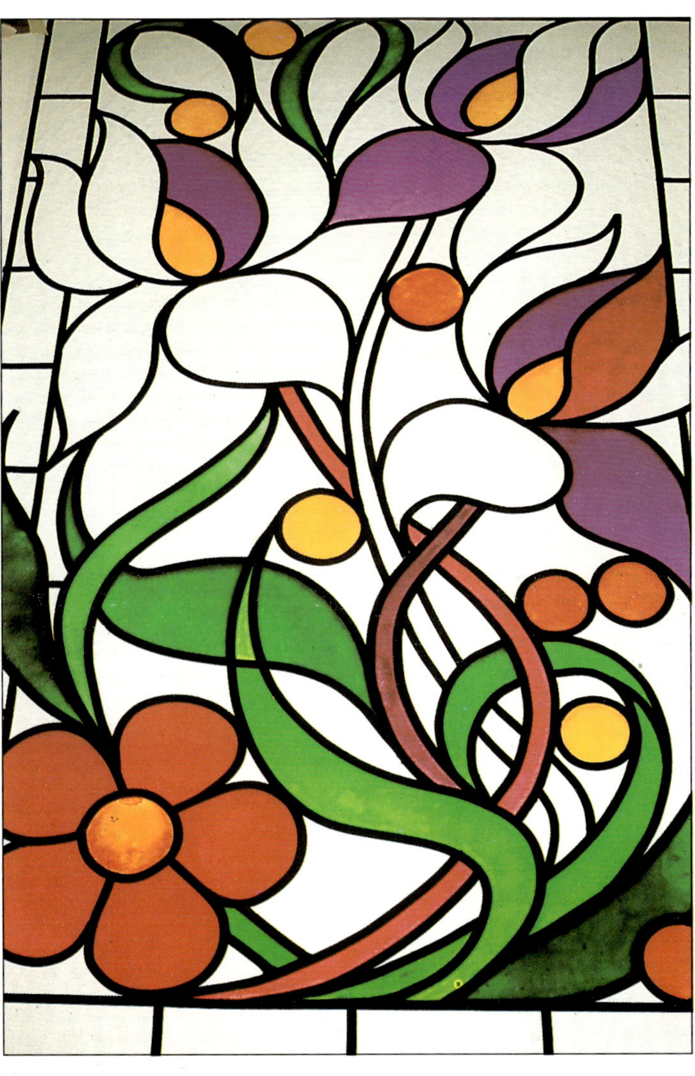

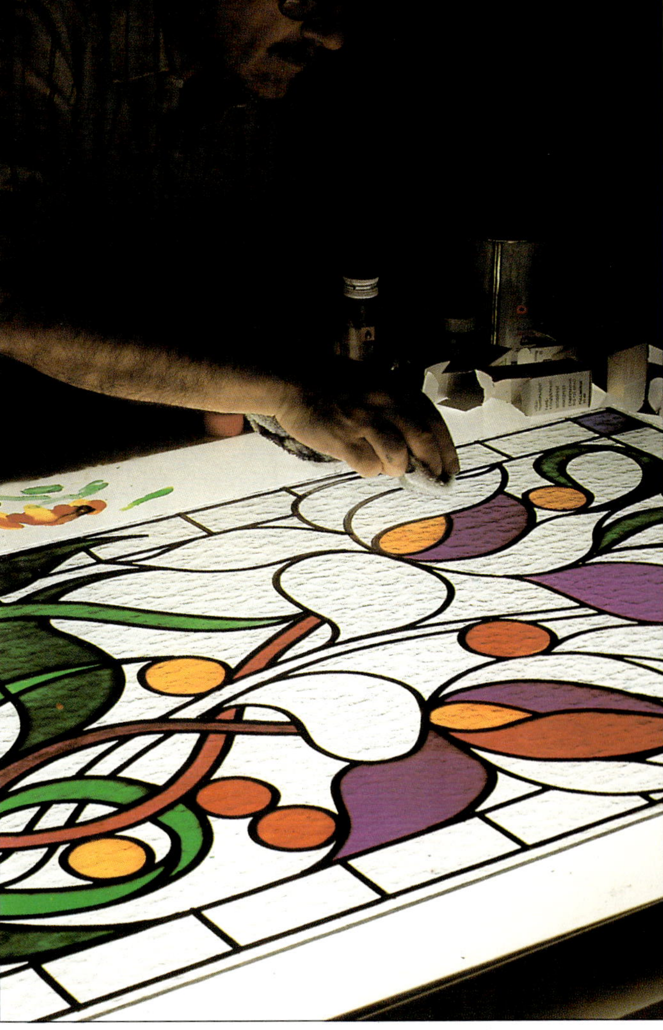

Below and right: Notice the luminosity and transparency of the blues and violets, as well as the gradations obtained in the blue petals. The darkest blue at the top of each petal is gradated downward until it blends with the palest blue.

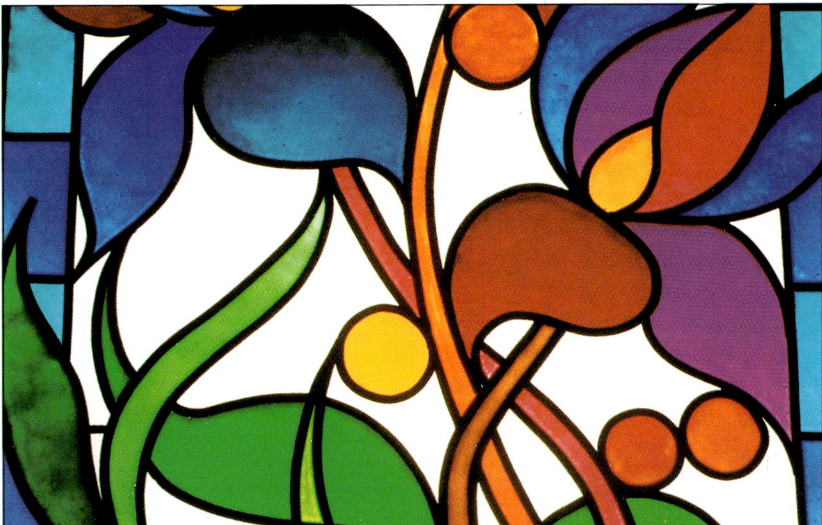

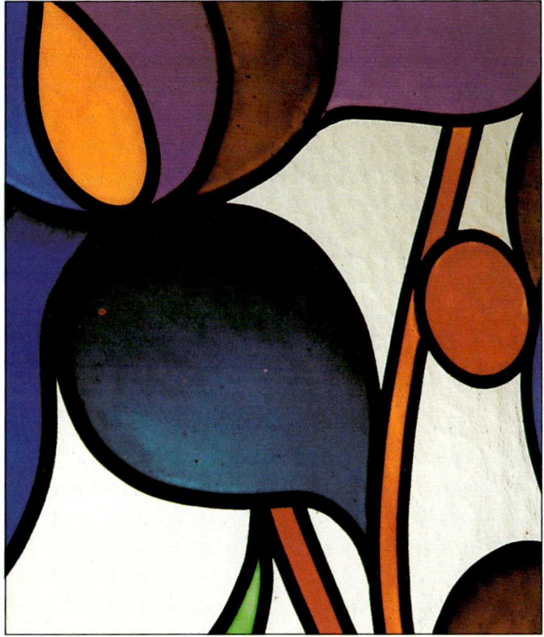

The stained glass in place

When you have finished your first imitation stained glass pane, you will see that the real finish cannot be appreciated until you set it in the window. There is no doubt that the glass, seen in its frame and definitively lit, will look completely different from what you viewed on the light-table. The transparency of color allows a changing luminosity, according to the time of day. This means that our creation gives off different and interesting shades of color throughout the day, which is why, when you work with stained glass, you should try to roughly guess the amount of light that it will receive when installed so you can regulate colors to obtain the desired effect. We end this exercise with the hope that in the future, you will be able to share in this ancient art.

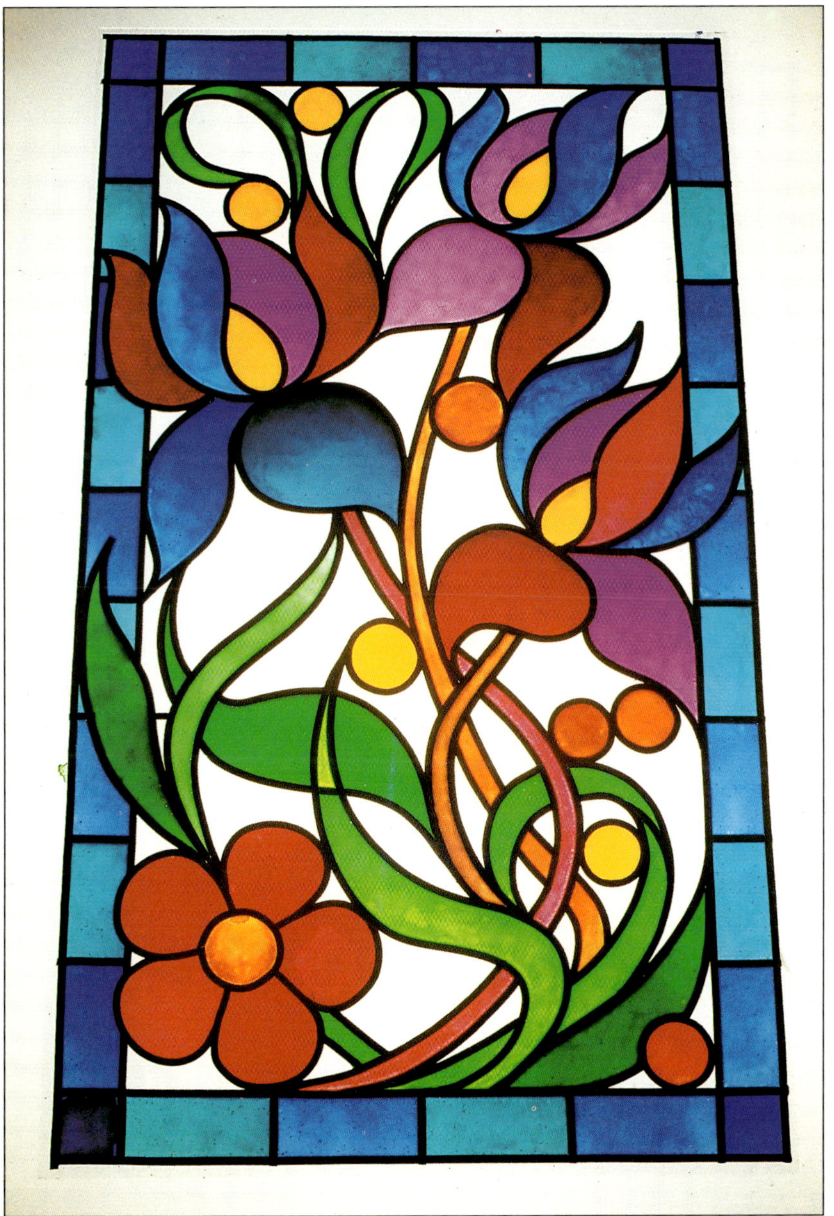

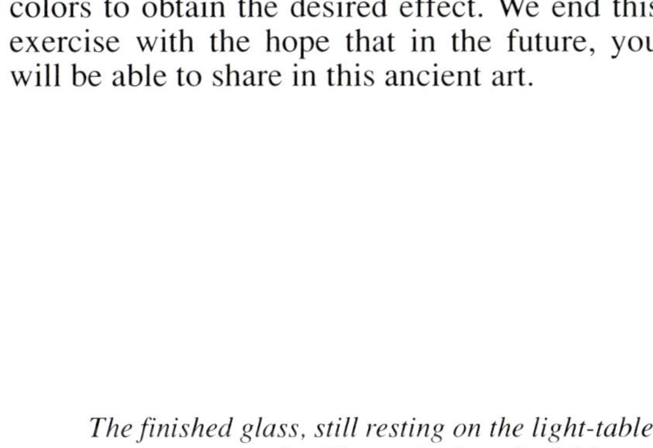

The finished glass, still resting on the light-table. It will remain there for 24 hours, the time it needs to dry thoroughly.